The Art of
Islamic Banking
and Finance

Founded in 1807, John Wiley & Sons is the oldest independent publishing company in the United States. With offices in North America, Europe, Australia, and Asia, Wiley is globally committed to developing and marketing print and electronic products and services for our customers' professional and personal knowledge and understanding.

The Wiley Finance series contains books written specifically for finance and investment professionals as well as sophisticated individual investors and their financial advisors. Book topics range from portfolio management to e-commerce, risk management, financial engineering, valuation, and financial instrument analysis, as well as much more.

For a list of available titles, please visit our Web site at www.Wiley Finance.com.

The Art of Islamic Banking and Finance

Tools and Techniques for Community-Based Banking

YAHIA ABDUL-RAHMAN

WILEY

John Wiley & Sons, Inc.

Published by John Wiley & Sons, Inc., Hoboken, New Jersey.

Published simultaneously in Canada.

For general information on our other products and services or for technical support, please contact our Customer Care Department within the United States at (800) 762-2974, outside the United States at (317) 572-3993, or via fax (317) 572-4002.

Wiley also publishes its books in a variety of electronic formats. Some content that appears in print may not be available in electronic books. For more information about Wiley products, visit our Web site at www.wiley.com.

Library of Congress Cataloging-in-Publication Data:

Abdul-Rahman, Yahia, 1944-
   The art of Islamic finance and banking : tools and techniques for community-based banking / Yahia Abdul-Rahman.
      p. cm. – (Wiley finance; 504)
   Includes index.
      ISBN 978-0-470-44993-6 (hardback)
   1. Banks and banking–Islamic countries. 2. Banks and banking–Religious aspects–Islam. 3. Finance–Islamic countries. 4. Finance–Religious aspects–Islam. I. Title.
   HG3368.A6A244 2010
   332.10917'67–dc22   2009028344

Printed in the United States of America

10 9 8 7 6 5 4 3 2

Contents

PREFACE

My Story With Islamic Banking and Finance in America

I came to the United States on my own from Egypt to study for my MS and PhD degrees at the University of Wisconsin, Madison in 1968. I had essentially nothing except my BS degree in Chemical Engineering from Cairo University and a letter from the University of Wisconsin, Madison accepting me as an International Special Student on a trial basis. I did not have the funds to pay for tuition nor for accommodations, books, and other expenses. It was a big challenge for me, but I made it, through hard work, to where I am today managing a pioneering effort in America to establish what I consider a revival of the banking system that built America. Using a platform we call the LARIBA system (www.LARIBA.com), we offer socially responsible, faith-based, and *riba*-free banking. Throughout this book, I will abbreviate it as RF banking.

In 1987, a group of dedicated friends invested $10,000 each to start a small company we called American Finance House LARIBA. We gathered $200,000 as the startup capital. To my knowledge, this was the first time ever a group of Muslims had bonded together to start a joint project that would eventually become an important force in the American Muslim community and in many non-Muslim communities. Our goal was to start a finance company that would operate without the charging of interest and according to the foundations of Islamic law (*Shari'aa*). Today, in 2009, and after 22 years the LARIBA shareholders own LARIBA (www.LARIBA.com), the oldest Islamic RF finance company in the United States, and the Bank of Whittier (www.BankOfWhittier.com), a national bank. The LARIBA System (the finance company LARIBA and the Bank of Whittier, NA) serves all 50 states in America and services a portfolio of riba-free shari'aa-compliant financing that is worth approximately $400 million. The portfolio includes home mortgages, automobiles, fast food franchises, medical doctors' clinics, dialysis centers, commercial buildings, schools, churches, and Islamic centers. It was, and continues to be, a wonderful journey.

This book is a strong effort to introduce this new brand of banking, which is based on the Judeo-Christian-Islamic value system while upholding the laws of America.

I must acknowledge that, after traveling the world over and doing business in many nations, I concluded that *only in the United States* can a new immigrant realize his/her dreams, even with a new idea that might have looked unbelievably outrageous at the time. I am deeply indebted to Almighty God, who created the reasons for me to come to America, start a family, and live here. I am thankful to my fellow Americans of all faiths and backgrounds for making our country, the United States of America, what it is. It is unfortunate that America is viewed internationally through the lens of Hollywood movies and the sometimes controversial aspects of our foreign policy. It is unfortunate that the wonderful average American neighbor, colleague, farmer, worker, professional, student, and volunteer do not get a chance to be fully and fairly represented and exposed to the United States and the rest of the world.

My feeling as a Muslim moving to live in the United States was one of curiosity. Moving to America changed my social standing and grouping; I went from a majority Muslim country to being a member of the Muslim minority in the United States, which was an unknown minority belonging to an unknown religion at that time. Reflecting on it, I concluded that God in His infinite wisdom wanted us Muslims in the United States to experience living as a minority. If we were wise, we, the Muslims, would learn from this golden opportunity and better understand how to deal with non-Muslim minorities in the Muslim majority countries. At the same time, we might be able to further enrich a country that was—after all—built by successive waves of immigrants, each bringing something new to the broader culture of the nation. Being a member of the small Muslim minority created an interesting basic feeling, an instinct and need to discover ones' roots and to define whom one really is. That was the beginning of our journey, my wife and I, in the service of Islam in America in the form of serving the Muslim community and the integration of Islam and the American Muslim community to make them part of the unique American mosaic through interfaith and civic activities.

My story with Islamic finance began in Dallas, Texas in 1971. I had completed my PhD in chemical engineering, and my wife had completed her MS degree in chemical engineering. I got a job at the Production Research Center of Atlantic Richfield Co. (ARCO, which is now owned by British Petroleum). At the time, ARCO had just discovered oil in Alaska and was expanding its research on how to produce that oil and transport it south to the mainland under the most severe operating conditions. We moved from Madison, Wisconsin to Dallas, Texas in November 1971. We looked for a *masjid* (mosque) where we could perform our weekly congregational prayers (*jum'aa*). We started by looking for people with a Muslim last name. The most prevalent and easy to find in the phone book was Khan. We called and we got in touch, but we learned sad news: There were no Friday prayers yet in the Dallas/Fort Worth area. We started the first-ever Friday prayers in Dallas, Texas on Friday, November 26, 1971. Only two persons attended the prayer which was held at a park behind the Southern Methodist University (SMU) campus.

The community grew, and we started collecting donations to build an Islamic Center of our own, The Islamic Association of North Texas (IANT). We eventually raised approximately $17,000 in donations, and we found a home on a nice sized piece of land in the city of Grand Prairie, Texas (between the cities of Dallas and Fort Worth), which was selling for approximately $34,000. A medical doctor friend and a board member, who was more sophisticated because he knew how to borrow from banks (as he had financed his clinic and his convertible Mercedes), suggested that we borrow money from the bank. Members of the community were up in arms because we were entertaining the thought of dealing with interest, which is prohibited in Islam. When I was asked to give an opinion about the issue, I indicated that I was an engineer and a practicing Muslim who takes interest in studying the Qur'aan and Islam, but I knew nothing about money, banking, and finance.

That was the beginning of a journey that gradually took me away from engineering to banking and finance. It was also an amazing coincidence that God created another reason for that transformation. In 1972, the Strategic Planning Group at ARCO was convinced that oil prices would increase drastically because of an impending supply/demand imbalance. ARCO had huge reserves of oil shale in Colorado and "wet" coal in Wyoming. It was decided that the Research Center would start developing new processes for the production of synthetic oil and gas from shale and coal. I was one of those assigned to the task. I developed a number of processes that were patented by ARCO. The next step was to study the economic feasibility of these new processes. To do that, ARCO, in 1974, agreed to help finance my studies towards an MA degree in International Management and Finance at the University of Texas, Dallas. There, I chose to study monetary theory, to understand what money is and how money is created, international monetary theory, financial accounting, credit analysis, and international economics.

It was also amazing that God created another reason for me to get a once-in-a-lifetime opportunity to obtain hands-on banking experience. One day in 1974, during the month of Ramadan, while working in my ARCO office in Plano, Texas, I received a phone call from a stranger who said that he was from Kuwait, that he was one of the Executive Directors of the World Bank representing Kuwait and that he was given a mandate from his government to start the Industrial Bank of Kuwait, IBK. When I asked him how he found me, he said that he was looking for an engineer in the petroleum field, preferably one who understood finance and could speak Arabic. It happened that two different persons recommended my name. I went to Washington, DC to interview him and was offered a job on the team that would start the Industrial Bank of Kuwait. My responsibility was to take care of financing small- and medium-sized oil-related development projects and other chemical and petrochemical projects. ARCO management was elated and encouraged me to go. They granted me a leave of absence, with a guarantee that my job would be waiting when I was done with the assignment. It was a wonderful experience that introduced me to the process— and the associated challenges—of starting up a bank. The bank developed an industrial development plan for Kuwait. We financed projects ranging from mega-sized petrochemical plants to offshore drilling rigs to projects that were as small as juice packaging facilities and cookie manufacturing plants. In 1975, I returned to Dallas, became a United States citizen in 1976, and completed my MA degree, while my wife completed her MS degree in Physics and a PhD in Environmental Engineering.

At the end of 1976, I was invited to join the ARCO Strategic Planning Group, which took us to ARCO's Los Angeles headquarters. There, I eventually became the Senior Planning Consultant in charge of projecting oil prices based on studies of energy sources, supply, and demand from oil, gas, shale, coal, nuclear, and hydro power, both in the United States and overseas. The group made recommendations to ARCO's management for investing in oil, natural gas, and coal in the United States. This was a wonderful experience that taught me strategic thinking, integrating the thoughts of many experts and executives in their own fields, and translating the conclusions to reach specific, well-defined strategic recommendations and decisions. The experience also gave me a chance to deal with many company executives, leading politicians, and government employees in the field of energy. In 1979, the Islamic Revolution erupted in Iran, and ARCO lost its oil production and supply from Lavon Island (which is off Iran's coast). In 1978, during the peak of the oil crisis, ARCO management assigned me the responsibility of managing the effort to find more than 250,000 barrels of oil per day to supply the shortfall due to the loss of production from the Lavon oil fields. This gave me a chance to see the world. I went to Africa, Asia, and Latin America looking to sign oil supply deals with almost every country that produces oil. I received an attractive offer to be an Executive Vice President of an independent refining company in Houston, Texas.

Later on, I started my first company as an entrepreneur trading in oil and petroleum products.

In Houston, I was invited to become a founding member of a new bank, Woodway National Bank (it was acquired by a larger bank later). In 1983, and during our bank board meetings, we were briefed on delinquencies and non-performing loans that were given to some of the biggest entrepreneurs, companies, and executives in Houston. I also noticed a lot of tension in one of the briefings given by the then-mayor of Houston, Kathy Whitmeyer, and the city's financial manager. Business in Houston had slowed drastically due to the decline in oil prices. Houston was hit as the oil, economic, and real estate bubble burst. (I saw the scars of this crash every time I visited Houston until the early 2000s, 20 years later.)

I went home to discuss this alarming situation with my wife. We decided to sell our house in the expensive Memorial area of Houston. We wanted to sell it fast. We asked a well-educated real estate broker (a former mathematics and statistics high school teacher from Canada) to give us a good estimate for a price that would help us sell it as soon as possible. He invited over 100 real estate agents to our house and polled them. Based on his statistical analysis of the poll, he recommended $595,000, but he hesitated because the house next door was listed for sale at approximately $895,000. We told him to go ahead. We sold the house within weeks for $575,000 and moved to a nice apartment close by until our two daughters finished the school year, at which time we prepared to move back to our house in the city of Altadena near Los Angeles, California (which we hadn't been able to sell because interest rates had risen to nearly 19%). We considered ourselves very lucky, because we were able to sell our house before the Houston real estate crash, and not being able to sell the California house meant we had a home waiting for us in California. (The next-door neighbor was not able to sell his house until he lowered the price from $895,000 to $300,000.)

Returning home one day in 1984, while still in Houston, I found a telegram from the Industrial Bank of Kuwait; the bank I had helped start 10 years before. In 1983, Kuwait was hit by a devastating stock market crash because of a nationally practiced pyramid scheme. I went to interview with the new chairman and received an offer to return to the Industrial Bank of Kuwait. I took my family back to California, fixed the house, and settled our children in school. My wife went back to work for CF Braun designing fertilizer plants and oil refineries before she moved later on to work for Northrop, the defense contractor. In September 1984, I started working at the Industrial Bank of Kuwait. As the projects manager, my team responsibilities included

1. taking care of non-performing assets and recommending a course of action to work out the loan portfolio,
2. identifying new projects that were needed in the economy to help growth and to finance them, and
3. training a new generation of young Kuwaitis to take over as the new industrial bankers in Kuwait.

Because my daughters were in school, my family did not join me this time; they stayed in the United States. I lived in a half-suite at the Sheraton in Kuwait. During this time, between 1984 and 1986, I had a chance to see how a bank loan portfolio can grow in a fictitious boom and how many took advantage of "easy" credit terms and loose credit standards. I experienced how corruption can change the fiber of a society and how money matters can cause deep feuds between leading families and create irreparable fractures in a society. I also was close to the raging Iran-Iraq war, and I saw daily convoys of hundreds of trucks carrying tanks, military supplies, wheat, and food supplies traveling to Iraq from a Kuwaiti port dedicated to support the Iraqi war efforts. Before I left Kuwait to go back home in 1986, I told my Kuwaiti friends, "Those tanks you are sending to Iraq may come back to threaten your safety and security." Indeed, in 1990, the late President Saddam Hussein invaded Kuwait, and the U.S. Marines came to the Kuwait Sheraton! The rest is history.

In 1986, I returned to California and found a job as a financial consultant with Shearson Lehman (later to merge with American Express and subsequently in many other mergers to become Smith Barney/Citigroup). As I began to work in the financial industry, a dream started forming in my head. My dream was to start a bank or a financial institution for our community.

During all these years, I had remained in close and continuous touch with the community by serving with my wife in the Islamic Center of each city we lived in. My wife and I helped start Sunday schools for the children; I delivered the Friday sermon (*khutbah*) and led the congregational prayers. I also performed and officiated at wedding ceremonies, presided over marriage conflict resolution and family matters, prepared the dead for burial, and taught in the Sunday program to the youths and adults. I was called upon to travel around the United States and Canada to help motivate local Muslim communities to donate generously for the building and financing of masajid (mosques) and full-time Islamic schools designed along the same models of Catholic and Jewish schools in the United States, Europe, and the rest of the world.

When we moved from Dallas to Los Angeles in 1977, I was elected to the board of directors of the Islamic Center of Southern California. I left the board when we moved to Houston in 1981. In Houston, my wife and I started activating, formalizing, structuring, and institutionalizing the Islamic Sunday school and helped in the organization and operation of the Islamic Center there. After moving back from Houston to Los Angeles, I was again elected to the Board and was given the responsibility of chairman of the finance committee. There, I applied what I had been learning all these years. Our team restructured the Center's finances, started a program for automatic donations from members' checking accounts to ensure that the Center employees' salaries could be provided on a regular basis, and developed operating policies for the Center. Most important of these policies was to rely only on donations from the American Muslim community. Our policy allowed the acceptance of donations from non-community sources and others from outside the United States, but not from governments. It was difficult in the beginning. However, it has been my experience that when you put people to the challenge and articulate your goals to them, you will capture their imagination to join you. Then what seems impossible can become possible. Doing this for all those years gave me the opportunity to understand the community, share its joys and dreams, and feel its pains. It also gave me a chance to meet the youth and children—the new breed of Americans who are Muslim. I saw the future in them, and I had no doubt that it was going to be a very bright and promising future.

During my many fundraising trips, and on my way back home, I started thinking about the future of our community. I asked myself: When were we going to stop "begging" and start building the financial muscles of our community? How could we develop an Islamic finance solution to help solve the problem of many Muslim "puritans," who preferred living in small, crowded, and shabby apartments rather than commit the grave sin of borrowing money with interest to finance the purchase of a home? How could we bring these families out of the apartments and into suburban America, where they could meet new neighbors, live a more comfortable life, and send their children to wonderful neighborhood schools, integrating them in America to live a full American life, but without interest? How could we create a financial institution that would be capable and qualified to gather the community's savings and be qualified to invest these savings prudently back in the community, with qualified, dedicated, and honorable community members who have experience, good ideas, and good projects? If we could realize this dream, I knew, we could empower the community, help its growth, and create wealth and economic prosperity and job opportunities for many. The answer to this question was to start a bank or a finance company. The biggest problem was the challenge of operating that institution without interest.

In 1987, I met a visionary who was busy developing Islamic finance companies and banks around the world. He was in Los Angeles on vacation, and he heard me deliver a Friday sermon (jum'aa khutbah) at the masjid. We became close friends, and I shared with him my dream of starting Islamic banking services for the community in America. He was another gift from God, because he encouraged me to proceed. He was also instrumental in introducing me to his contacts: significant lawyers, bankers, and religious scholars who specialized in the field of Islamic finance. He also wanted to start a stock portfolio under my management. He further asked our team to develop parameters that would qualify a company stock on world stock markets to meet Islamic finance investment criteria. In cooperation with a few dedicated and highly qualified Islamic bankers and scholars, we developed these parameters, started the portfolio, and diversified it among different portfolio managers around the world. We reviewed the different screens used to identify Shari'aa-compliant stocks and the performance of this $250 million portfolio on a quarterly basis. To my knowledge, that was the first time in history an Islamic stock portfolio was developed and brought to life. It would be years before the Dow Jones Islamic Index was developed, made public, and marketed throughout the world.

We started American Finance House LARIBA in 1987. In the beginning we were not sure if our efforts would be accepted or if they would be misunderstood. We used the name American Finance House: *American* to acknowledge that our company is American, and *Finance House* to imply its nature as an Islamic treasury; in the early history of Islam, the Treasury was called the House of Assets (*Bayt ul Maal*). We also added the word LARIBA. In the beginning, we explained to those who did not know about riba-free financing that LARIBA stood for Los Angeles Reliable Investment Bankers Associates. Those who knew about riba-free Islamic financing also understood that in the language of the Qur'aan (Arabic), *la* means *no* and *riba* means the act of renting money at a price called interest rate (the Old Testament uses the sister word *ribit* for the same concept). We made it very clear that we were not out to change, dismantle, or demolish the conventional banking and finance system in the United States. We simply offered a humble alternative that would serve those "puritan" Muslim Americans who wanted to live according to their religious beliefs while obeying the laws of the United States. We articulated this at the outset when we made it clear that changing U.S. laws was not one of our objectives.

As we developed LARIBA, we wanted to make sure that it would be a grassroots organization for our community. That meant that we should rely on our own resources, not go hat-in-hand soliciting capital from the oil-rich communities in the Gulf. We believed that if we were really serious, we could entice many of our community members, starting with each one of us putting our own money where our mouths were. We also wanted to train members from our community on Islamic banking and finance. We made sure that we did not use the American Muslim as a marketing front for the same conventional finance operations to take advantage of a market niche. The strict guidelines were severe and challenging. They meant that we would have a steep uphill battle to develop and achieve what we wanted. However, we believed that the turtle approach would be much more effective than the jumping frog approach. A turtle goes slowly to its target; and if a hurdle stands in its way and prevents it from progressing, it takes a side step and proceeds. Compare this to the frog, which jumps up and down and back and forth and often ends up where it started. Yes, it took us a long time, but that time helped us develop a system, learn from our mistakes, sharpen our models, train a new generation of Americans who believe in our LARIBA concepts, and prove ourselves to the community at large.

We started LARIBA in 1987 (in the month of Ramadan) out of a box. We slowly grew it out of the box and moved it to the apartment above the garage in my house. Then we moved to its current location in Pasadena, where we expanded three times, ending with almost four times the initial square footage. We started with one part-time employee and grew to 22 employees. One thing that helped us grow was the Internet. In 1997, LARIBA was contacted by a young man who was doing his masters degree at USC (University of Southern California) in computers and Web development. He needed a $3,000 loan to buy a computer to help him in his studies, but no one would finance him. We financed him at LARIBA. We asked him to develop the first LARIBA portal, www.AmericanFinance.com, which later became www.LARIBA.com. The LARIBA site became very popular. From the time we started keeping track of the number of unique visitors in the year 2000 through July 2009, the LARIBA site has attracted more than 1 million unique visitors. It became the most information-rich site available on the subject of riba-free Islamic banking.

In 1994, I authored and self-published my first book: *LARIBA Bank— A Foundation for a United and Prosperous Community*. It was a simple book that summarized what I had learned and read over the years about Islamic banking, and in it, I also articulated our community dreams. The demand for the book was great. We printed it twice and distributed more than 6,500 copies in the United States. A publisher in Malaysia acquired the printing rights and continues to distribute it on a large scale in Malaysia and Indonesia. LARIBA became an important household name in the United States and Asia, as well as the Middle East. The brand name LARIBA is now considered to be like "Coca-Cola"—recognized throughout the world as the brand of Islamic finance. We were invited to speak at universities such as Harvard University, the University of Illinois, the University of California at Los Angeles (UCLA), Claremont Graduate College and many others, in addition to Islamic centers, churches, and synagogues all over the United

States and Canada. In addition, we were invited to present at international conferences in Malaysia, Bahrain, Brunei, Saudi Arabia, Kuwait, Singapore, Canada, England, Turkey, South Africa, and Egypt. The media began taking notice. ABC Nightly News (with Peter Jennings) had a segment on LAR-IBA, as did the Voice of America, Malaysian television, National Public Radio (NPR), and American Public Media's *Marketplace. The Los Angeles Times* had a front-page article on LARIBA, with a full-page inside report. Since that time, we have been reported about in *USA Today, The Dallas Morning News, The Wall Street Journal, The Washington Post, The Houston Chronicle, The Chicago Tribune,* and *The Detroit Free Press,* to mention a few.

One day, we received a phone call from the U.S. State Department to thank us at LARIBA. They explained that when they had published an article about LARIBA in their newsletter to the Middle East, many media outlets in the Middle East had picked up the story and republished it. The caller remarked that this was one of the few times they had been able to forward a positive story from the United States that appealed to the press in the Middle East.

In our effort to popularize the concepts we used, we started a new tradition. The tradition was to have an annual recognition award for significant distinguished contributors to the field of riba-free Islamic banking in the world. We awarded every "who's who" leader in the field, and we tied the award dinner to an annual seminar on Islamic Banking. This effort ran for 12 years. The event was designed to be graceful, but full of subliminal notions that underlined our American affiliation and our respect for the United States political system and its laws. For example, we invited color guards to start our events. We were the first Islamic organization in the history of American Muslims to start its events not only with an invocation and recitation from the Holy Qur'aan but also with the national anthem, sung by a professional singer and later by a wonderful young lady from the community. We invited our congressmen, state representatives, mayors, and many other public figures to the dinner. The awards that were handed out were not only awards from LARIBA but also included Certificates of Commendation from the Congress of the United States, the California State Assembly, the Los Angeles Board of Supervisors, and the Mayor of Pasadena, California (a city 20 miles northeast of Los Angeles, where our LARIBA offices are located).

We also did something very bold in the year 2000. After the currency crisis of Southeast Asia, Malaysia, under the leadership of Dr. Mahathir Muhammad, was the only country in the region that weathered the storm and was able to contain the problem without sacrificing its foreign currency reserves or resorting to heavy borrowing from the IMF. The Board of

LARIBA decided to create a new award called the Life Time Achievement Award, and we gave it to then-Prime Minister of Malaysia Dr. Mahathir Muhammad. Dr. Mahathir came to Chicago to receive his award. We at LARIBA also did something unique for the ceremony. Instead of holding the function at a local hotel, we held it in a Chicago suburb, in the auditorium of a prominent and well-appointed Islamic Center built by American Muslims who emigrated from Bosnia. This move gave LARIBA wide coverage in the community and in the world press, as well as good political and operating credibility.

LARIBA had very humble means and it lacked enough capital. We used to finance a home once every two to three months (the terms of financing were onerous: 40 percent down and a seven-year term) and a car every month, because we had a tough time convincing our friends to invest in the company. The U.S. regulations regarding solicitation of funds are strict and in general do not allow solicitation unless an offering is registered with the government. The process of registering for a public offering with the United States Securities and Exchange Commission (SEC) is lengthy and very expensive. However, we persevered, and our patience paid off. The community learned more about us, and the volume of calls started to increase. However, we could not meet all that growing demand.

In the year 2000, we received an e-mail from a banker who used to work for Freddie Mac to obtain information about LARIBA. We explained to him what we do. In response, he introduced us to an executive at Freddie Mac who was interested in growing its mortgage finance activities among minorities in America. We talked, and he loved what we were doing. A delegation from Freddie Mac came to evaluate the company and its operations. We explained to them that for every home we finance, we and the customer each have to come up with three rent estimates for a similar home in the same neighborhood to evaluate the rate of return on investing in the house as if it were a commercial venture by using the market measured rental rate to ascertain the economic prudence of the investment. We explained that we do this because our faith prohibits us from renting money at a price called an interest rate, but allows us to rent a tangible and rentable asset like a car, a home, or a business. If the investment (not the lending) makes economic sense, we finance the house mortgage; if not, we do not finance. The analyst in the team was apprehensive; he asked if they could review some of the financing files. They were all impressed when they audited the files.

Freddie Mac gave us approval in less than six weeks (they put out a press release about it on March 26, 2001). This was a record for approval time by Freddie Mac, which usually took an average six months under normal circumstances. We then were confronted with the issue of the format of the operating relationship and how to do business with them without charging or paying interest. We at LARIBA agreed with Freddie Mac that we would look at them as an investor in each deal, and that we would *not* borrow money from them. We felt that it would be hypocritical to borrow money from Freddie with interest and turn around and claim that we were financing mortgages riba-free! This *first time ever* event in the history of the United States and the American Muslim community helped make LARIBA an important factor in mortgage financing in general and in Islamic riba-free financing in particular.

In 2002, we were contacted by the larger Fannie Mae, and they also approved us. LARIBA, a year later, became the *only* riba-free company in the history of the United States that issued riba-free mortgage-backed securities (RF MBS *sukuk*—*sukuk* means *Riba Free asset-based bonds*) with Fannie Mae. We are all grateful to God and to the many dedicated men and women fellow associates at LARIBA for their dedication and quality work, which made LARIBA among the top one percent quality producers for Freddie and Fannie.

It had always been difficult to raise capital for LARIBA. Many of the community members indicated that they would be willing to support us if we were an FDIC-insured bank. We, the shareholders of LARIBA, were very interested in buying a bank. We wanted to find a small bank that we could afford and that we could manage and grow slowly. After investing seven years in the search for a bank, we found the Bank of Whittier, National Association (NA). The project of acquiring and working on the change of control of the Bank of Whittier plunged me into another valuable and educational experience. The process was enhanced by the support and encouragement of an expert attorney in the field, Gary Steven Findley, Esq. The Bank of Whittier, being chartered as a National Bank, is regulated and supervised by the U.S. Department of Treasury. We learned many lessons in dealing with the United States government for the first time. We learned why the United States is what it is, and we all learned why the American banking system has no equal in the world.

We are aware of the unfortunate financial meltdown of 2008. It is known that many politicians claimed that it resulted from the lack of sufficient regulations. That may be partially true in particular and specific situations, but not in general. It is historically known that one of the most important results of the Great Depression was the ratification of the Glass-Steagall Act, which prohibited commercial banks and investment banks from combining their businesses. This act was repealed by the Congress during the Clinton administration. At Smith Barney I was one of those who witnessed the attempts made to combine the two cultures without much success. It is also important to stress here that all the regulations that man can exert in the system will not be able to stop fraud, dishonesty, greed, and the irresponsible behavior of people who are supposed to be the trusted custodians of our assets and savings. Ethics and morality are not instilled in people by regulations but by parents, the school system, and the society at large, starting at an early age.

In 1998, we at LARIBA received approval for change of control and were elated to own a bank affiliate. We initially selected managers to run the bank who had a strong background in traditional banking but little familiarity with the community served by the bank and no knowledge of the riba-free business model.

In July 2003, I attained vesting with Smith Barney, talked to my wife about taking early retirement, and went to reorganize the Bank of Whittier. Today, the Bank of Whittier operates as an RF bank, but in a seamless way. We chose a slogan that described the riba-free system we used: *We Do Not Rent Money—We Invest in Our Customers*. We also told people what RF banking and finance is all about. It is a faith-based and socially responsible community effort. We shared with our customers our approach to finance, to banking, and to client service and they experienced our services. Their consistent feedback was "We have not heard bankers talk like that before!" We shared with our clients what I sincerely believe is the first LARIBA banker in America: George Bailey, the banker played by Jimmy Stewart in the movie *It's A Wonderful Life*.

The heinous crime of September 11, 2001, shocked us all. I was in the kitchen preparing breakfast and saw it live on TV. I went to the office and I received a call from the Mayor of Pasadena, California. He asked me what to do. I told him that I have disciplined myself so that when I am in a situation like this, I resort to praying. He and I led an effort to organize, for the first time in Pasadena, the first prayer response to the catastrophe. We invited the leaders of 35 religions and communities in southern California for a prayer at the footsteps of the Pasadena City Hall. It was heavily attended, and it helped us develop wonderful friendships with many religious leaders of all faiths in southern California.

Reflecting on my personal experience as a naturalized U.S. citizen who has lived in America since 1968, I concluded that I need to pay respect to the rest of America by understanding the majority faith of America, Christianity. I, as well as many other American Muslims, was also deeply hurt by the vehement attacks and unfortunate remarks some significant church leaders made about Islam, the God of Islam, and the Prophet of Islam. In response, I decided to work on building bridges of friendship and goodwill with the Christian seminary closest to my home; Fuller Theological Seminary in Pasadena. There we made good friends and participated in a pioneering conflict resolution effort to soothe relations between our two communities. The most important outcome of that effort was an historic announcement that concluded that the Christian God and the Muslim God (Allah) are indeed the same. This announcement was published in *The Los Angeles Times* on December 3, 2006. We all also discovered in this process of pondering and soul-searching that we at LARIBA had a way to promote better understanding and lasting bridges between the communities of faith: riba/ribit-free faith-based financing.

LARIBA devoted its Annual Awards and Symposium series of 2002 to the subject. We asked professors from the University of Judaism in Los Angeles and a prominent Rabbi in North Hollywood (who has a keen interest in the field of riba/ribit-free financing) to present the Jewish view. For two Christian points of view, we invited professors in the fields of lending with interest charging at Loyola Marymount University to present the Roman Catholic view, and professors from Fuller Seminary to present the Evangelical view. It was a wonderful and enriching experience that made us understand more fully and clearly the problem of charging for the use (rent) of money. We also learned the source of the word *usury*, which is now defined as excessive interest—but nobody could answer the question: "Excessive in reference to what?" In fact, usury was defined long ago as the price one pays for renting the right to use money. It was wonderful to hear the metaphor of trying to rent the right of use of an apple, which is impossible because an apple can only be owned when its ownership right is transferred. That is exactly the case with money, which is nothing but a measuring tool. It is not like an automobile, which one can own but can also assign the right of its usage by renting it. Money is a thing; it cannot be rented. We also learned that in the early days, if a person of the Jewish faith charged interest, he/she could not stand as a witness in a Jewish court; similarly, a Roman Catholic who dealt in interest was denied the right to a Catholic burial.

Faith-based riba/ribit-free (Islamic) banking and finance—RF banking and finance—is much simpler than it is perceived by the public. It is a concept that makes perfect sense. RF banking is based on the belief that credit is a basic human right. It is socially responsible, environmentally compliant, and ethical. RF bankers are trained to make sure that the financing facility makes prudent economic sense to the family because the decision to finance (invest) is based on the prevailing actual market prices. Its bankers are trained *not* to help a community member dig a deeper hole of debt, but rather to help that person get out of debt as soon as possible. RF banking is a system that commits itself to being involved in real activities, not simply "renting" money in order to make money on money. Its financing activities involve asset-based or service-based financing—that is, a commodity, a tangible asset, and/or a service must change hands. The primary passion of true RF banking is community service and development. It is interesting to note that this is not much different from the foundation of the well-known U.S.

bank regulation titled the Community Reinvestment Act. Our vision is to have an RF banking and finance unit started next to every place of social assembly: trade organizations, clubs, and places of worship (e.g., temples, synagogues, churches, and masajid).

Based on our experience since 1987, the outcome has been and will continue to be superior service and a solid credit (loan) portfolio. This is so because the evaluation of the economic viability of each credit facility is based on comparing each asset and/or service with the market to ensure that it is a prudent investment. Because of the low risk and solid products offered by the RF system, the overhead expenses are lower. Because the system is based on the knowledge of each member of a smaller community, the "cardinal" rule of banking (i.e., *know your customer*) is practiced to the fullest. The net result is much higher returns than conventional banks, mainly due to the low levels of non-performing loans and the deep spirit and culture of voluntarism and service instilled in the RF banker.

This preface has covered a lot of history, experiences, and topics. The book will attempt to introduce the spirit of RF banking as I understand it, as we practice it, and as we have lived it since 1987. I have invested at least 27 years of my life reading, researching, developing finance models, authoring papers, giving lectures all over the world, writing books (including this one), arbitrating between Islamic banks and businesses holding credits with these Islamic banks worldwide, and training Islamic bankers in Malaysia, the United States, Canada, and Turkey. I have the honor of sharing all these experiences with you, the reader of this book.

I have a deep interest in the spirit of Judeo-Christian-Islamic law (Shari'aa) and the reason this law was put into effect, as revealed to mankind by God of all prophets, including Prophets Noah, Abraham, Ishmael, Isaac, Jacob, David, Solomon, and all subsequent prophets (may the peace and prayers of God be showered on all of them),[3] and by the founders of the three monotheistic faiths, Moses (pp), Jesus (pp) and Muhammad (pp). I have tried the best I can to be educated in my own faith, Islam, as well as Christianity and Judaism. I consider myself as a servant of God and hence a servant of the people who live the life of loving God—God of all people of all backgrounds and walks of life—and this must be translated in disseminating love to all people. It is not enough to lecture people and try to capture their imagination, touch their hearts, and influence their minds. What is important is to touch their pocket and to make a difference in the quality of life they and their families live.

I want to conclude by quoting a *hadeeth* (pronouncement) of Prophet Muhammad (pp), which has been my motto over the years: "The Best of people are those who benefit others the most."

NOTES

1. Freddie Mac is a government-sponsored corporation that provides a secondary market for home mortgages and hence helps provide liquidity to mortgage companies.
2. Fannie Mae is a sister company of Freddie Mac, but much larger and older. It provides liquidity for home mortgages in the secondary market.
3. Throughout the book I shall use the abbreviation (pp) to stand for the prayer every Muslim is taught to utter every time he/she hears the name of a prophet mentioned: "May God's peace and prayers be showered onto him."

ACKNOWLEDGMENTS

As I sat down to reflect on whom to acknowledge, I found it to be a very difficult task. Many people in many parts of the world contributed in making me the person I am. Mentioning a few names as is usually done in the front of a typical book would be unfair to the lands I grew in and the people who contributed to my life and character. That is why I decided to play back my life since I was born in Cairo, Egypt in a religious district named after the granddaughter of Prophet Muhammad (pp). It is called Al Sayedah Zeinab district, where the masjid (mosque) of the granddaughter of the Prophet—Zeinab—figures prominently. I am deeply indebted to the teachers at this masjid who instilled the foundations of believing in God in me and the many millions who worshipped there. I am also grateful for the main reason of my being: God. He has given me a wonderful full life complete with wonderful parents, family, wife, children, grandchildren, teachers, friends, and colleagues.

The Qur'aan teaches that God has ordained never to worship other than Him and to excel in dealing and caring for one's parents and family. The physical reason for my being here goes back to my dear parents.

First, I want to acknowledge my dear, late mother whose name is also Zeinab. The Qur'aan enumerates to us the hard work a mother goes through from the time of conceiving and bearing a child to the time of delivering that child, weaning him/her, and raising that child. She was educated and ambitious. She was the household financial planner who saved a bit on the side in order to meet the family's extra needs such as buying a refrigerator for the family or paying for a summer vacation in Alexandria. She was widowed at the prime age of 39 and sacrificed dearly to raise a family of five children. I know how difficult it was for her to be standing alone to meet the challenges of a lower income without the support of a husband in these very difficult years, especially when I left Cairo to further my education in America two years after the sudden death of my father. Words cannot express my gratitude and love for her.

My father was a wonderful self-made man. He started his career in the ministry of education as a humble laboratory technician. His ambition prompted him to advance his education and training to become the under secretary of education in the field of finance and administration when he died. His last post was in an education district which has a high content of non-Muslim—Coptic—Egyptians. I saw him treat all people equally with unconditional love regardless of their faith. During the religious celebrations of our fellow Egyptian Copts, he took the family to their homes to celebrate with them Christmas and other Coptic traditions. He invited them to our house and celebrated together the Muslim festivities. He disciplined us to have a transparent eye, heart, and soul for all people regardless of their faith or stature. His biggest prayer and dream was to die at his desk while serving people. He was a workaholic. He did die of a heart attack at his desk while working late in the evening. His funeral was attended by thousands of people—both Muslims and Christians—many of whom I had never met. Many told me how my father helped them and served them without expecting even a word of thanks. He authored a book on finance and administration which was a useful reference for young finance and administration employees. I remember that we had boxes of the unsold copies stored on our balcony at our house in Cairo, Egypt. As a young man I did not know why these books were not sold. Now that I am older, I've learned that the average Middle Easterner does not read. I was told by a major Arab publisher in Cairo that a bestselling book in the Middle East prints 7,000 to 10,000 copies! This may be one of the major sources of problems and one of the major reasons of the miseries of the Middle East.

I also was deeply influenced by the character and coaching of my mother's father—Syed Effendi Hegazy. He started as a simple farmer. He learned math and accounting on his own and climbed the ladder to become the Chief Cashier of the vast agricultural land and real-estate properties and Estates of Prince Muhammad Ali. He used to take me with him to the office at the Manial palace, which was a block away from our home, and show me how to count the cash and balance the accounts. I shall never forget the scenes of my grandfather wearing his temporary black sleeves to protect his white shirt and the look of the money and vault as well as the sprawling flower gardens and fruit orchards of that palace, which was located in a Cairo suburb called "Manial El Rodah."

I still remember my primary school teacher, Mrs. Fowziyah. She was a kind and astute teacher. I will never forget how one day I went out with my parents and did not do my homework until I came back. My grandfather helped me with the homework since I was so sleepy from being out, and my teacher learned of what happened. She told me privately that a "bird" told her that I did not rely on myself in doing the homework and that she wanted me to promise to not do it again. I gave my promise. As far as I can remember, this was an important lesson and milestone in my life at the tender age of 7. I am indebted to her for her coaching and the promise she took from me. Since that time, I have done my homework and fulfilled my promise to the best of my abilities.

In middle school my character was shaped by two important figures. The first was my English school teacher, Mr. Abdel Ghani. He was a big man who carried a small stick with a small rubber hose on its end. He would kid with my best friend at school, but he would also instruct us to respect each other and to not call our friends sarcastic names. One day I did. My friend told him and I had to endure three hits on my palm from that small but hurtful stick. Since that day at the age of 9, I held full respect for everyone I met. To this day, I insist that my associates be called by the name his or her parents chose for each of them. I allow no nicknaming in any of the operations I am involved in. I am also indebted to the gymnastics teacher whose name I unfortunately do not remember. He trained me to work hard within our team and to help us become the number one gymnastics team in Egypt. We won the most distinguished trophy and recognition in the country that year.

In high school, I remember the principal, Mr. Abdul Samee Bayoumy, who was a very strict school head who wanted his students to be the best in the country. He believed in me and encouraged me to be in charge of the school's radio station. Here, I had fun practicing my preferred hobby of producing radio programs, managing others on the team, leading the morning assembly, planning with others on the team what radio programs would be shared, and of course resolving political issues among the team members. I also remember the Arabic language teacher. He was a towering man who was a true reflection of a dedicated Egyptian from the farm lands, was educated at the oldest University in the world—Al Azhar. He was serious, hardworking, and dedicated.

At the University, I met the man who took me as a low-key and shy young man and made all the difference in my character. He knew how to bring out what was concealed inside me. He believed in me and gave me the chance to become the President of the Society of Chemical Engineering at Cairo University. His name was Professor Muhammad Aly Saleh. If there is a person who taught me what life is all about, it was him. He was a wonderful man. He taught us not only Chemical Engineering but also how to be a citizen in Egypt and of the world. He became a friend and a coach until he died. I also remember a humble man who was an important factor in my life. His name was Professor Yahia Mostafa Al Agamawy. He was a humble servant of the people and he helped everyone. I learned from him to always stay away from the limelight, especially when you serve your people and those who need help. He worked hard for Egypt and I was honored to work with him.

As I concluded my life in Egypt and before I left for America at the age of 24 in the year 1968, I wanted to find my partner in the journey of life. In Egypt, at that time, the only place a man could find his potential wife was at the university. After graduating at the top of my class I was drafted to teach and do research at the Chemical Engineering Department at Cairo University in July of 1965. Because of the death of my father, I decided to rely on myself in saving as much money as I could to help my mother and to save for the airplane ticket and other expenses associated with the impending travel to America. This prompted me to work very hard in order to earn overtime pay. I worked from 7:00 am to almost 9:00 pm every day of the six-day week. As a side benefit this allowed me to see and interact with at least 3,000 students at Cairo University school of Engineering. I was able to know them and their characters. In my pursuit for a wife I looked for a young lady who was serious, hard-working, sincere, God-loving, reliable, and conservative. I considered many and I settled for the partner of my life, Dr. Magda Muhammad Tantawi Mobasher. I owe Magda many talents that she brought to our family. She worked hard with me in Madison, Wisconsin with very humble means; she taught me how to plan with the least available resources, how to keep smiling and stay cool under the most severe challenges, how to have fun and plan trips to enjoy time as well as make time to "smell the flowers," how to raise two very accomplished daughters, how to be loving and helpful to the community, and most respected by everyone in the community. She always said that a busy family is a happy family and she kept us busy with study programs, travel programs, school programs, and many programs that kept us happy and challenged. I am indebted to God who gave me Magda, the mother of our two daughters, Dr. Maie and Marwa and their wonderful children Amin, Nadim, Zane, and Jude. The best description of Magda was given by a very dear couple who are one of our best friends, Dr. Ahmad Khalifah and his wife Dr. Aida Gumei. They used to repeat the Egyptian folkloric proverb, "Madgda can dig a huge well by only using a simple needle." And she did. She always divided her work into small steps over many days and months until she achieved her ultimate goals. She and I used to dream together of our ultimate home. Sure enough, when we moved to Southern California we found exactly that house. It was a gift from God. She practiced her green thumb hobby and applied her stepwise approach to raise a wonderful garden. I am indebted to God and Magda for the wonderful life I've lived. She is a wonderful mother, a good wife, a great community servant, a great scholar and employee, a wonderful friend, and a great host. All these talents were acquired from her parents, Dr. Muhammad Tantawi Mobasher, and her wonderful mother, Mrs. Fatima Abdel Rahman—the world's best mother-in-law one can ever have. I also want to acknowledge my two sons-in-law

Richard St. John and Muhammad Elbeleidy. Richard St. John for introducing me to a new way of looking at Islam as the umbrella and the wings that cover and hug all faiths and as an extension of Judaism and Christianity in what I call the Judeo-Christian-Islamic world. I am honored to have him and his family, Judge Richard and Mrs. Judy St. John, in our family. I also honor Muhammad Elbeleidy for his love, respect, dedication, and graceful statesmanship. I am thankful to God for having met him, his father the late Mustafa Elbeleidy, and his mother Mrs. Nadia.

I want to conclude this part of my life in Egypt by thanking the people of Egypt for their generosity and their sacrifice. In Egypt, I was educated free of charge and the government paid me a generous monthly stipend to help me as a reward for a superior performance as a university student. My wife and I owe the Egyptian people a lot, and we hope that we shall be able to pay it back before we return to God, our creator.

On February 25, 1968, I arrived in America with very little means in order to try to prove myself at the University of Wisconsin in Madison. The family that sponsored me was Mr. Gordon and Mrs. Emilda Bubolz. They took it upon themselves to support my application, to guarantee my financial needs, and to be my family in America. Mr. Bubolz was a senator in the Wisconsin assembly and an insurance company executive. His wife, Mrs. Emilda, was a Norwegian immigrant who worked as a registered nurse. Magda and I owe this wonderful couple our success story in America. Words will never be sufficient to express our gratitude to God who made them a part of our life. At the University of Wisconsin, I met this professor who believed in me and in my wife. He supported us and gave us the wonderful example of a humble scholar who lived below his means. Professor E. J. Crosby used his bicycle year round in the cold, 30-below winters and in the hot, 90-degree summers to bike the 30 minutes to and from his office at the university. We are grateful for all he did for us.

In November of 1971, my wife and our little one-year-old daughter Maie packed up and moved to Dallas to work for an oil company—Atlantic Richfield Co. My bosses were two distinguished engineers. The first was Don Wunderlich, who believed in my abilities and gave me a chance to work on the projects I was hired for and on many other projects that I pioneered after his support and encouragement. He loved innovation and we produced wonderful research results. I also want to acknowledge my immediate boss who was a skipper in the U.S. Navy when he was in service. He was sharp, straightforward, sincere, truthful, and to the point. Sometimes his comments could be hurtful but I looked at him as my coach. I never forgot the day he handed me back my first report with many red lines, comments, and questions. He taught me how to write a memo, how to be specific and to the point. I thank him for his coaching. In Dallas I met many friends and developed a wonderful community. I shall always remember our friends Mr. Ghulam Hussein Siddiqi and Mr. Mohammed Solaiman. Mr. Solaiman helped build the first masjid in Richardson, Texas—literally—brick by brick.

In September 1974, my wife, my daughters Maie and the newly-born Marwa, and I moved to Kuwait to participate in the start of the Industrial Bank of Kuwait. I want to acknowledge a dear friend who was kind to give me the opportunity to know the people of Kuwait on the inside—something that many of the non-Kuwaitis who work in Kuwait did not even consider doing. He also happened to belong to the Muslim Shi'aa school of thought. He introduced me to local scholars who helped me study and broaden my knowledge of Islam to complement what I know based on the Sunni school of thought. I acknowledge Mr. Muhammad Abdul Hady Jamal's friendship.

In 1977 we moved to Los Angeles to join the prestigious Corporate Planning Division at Atlantic Richfield Company. There I met a man who had a profound effect on my character. He was Mr. Ron Arnault, who was the Chief Financial Officer in charge of Strategic Planning. His words still ring in my head, "when you go to a meeting, do more than your homework before the meeting and keep the answers in your 'hip pocket'; do not talk until you are asked, and when you are asked only give 20% of what you know." What a wonderful and wise way of living!

Between the fall of 1984 and the spring of 1986, I returned to Kuwait to participate in restructuring the Industrial Bank of Kuwait after a major stock market crash there. In 1986, I came back from Kuwait looking for a job. I want to acknowledge the man who saw my potential and gave me the chance to venture to a completely new field. That was the field of investment banking. Mr. Joseph Moure told me after a very long interview that he had decided that I join the team because I had proven to be successful many times before and that meant I'd be successful in this business as well. I learned from Mr. Moure to focus at will and to read using my finger. This habit has become an important part of the training of any who works on our team.

Perhaps the man who changed the course of my banking career from conventional banking to Riba-Free banking is my dear friend Sheikh Saleh Abdullah Kamel. Sheikh Saleh Kamel has given me wonderful opportunities to learn from and meet many of the distinguished scholars, attorneys, and practitioners of Islamic banking in the world. He believed in my potential and I thank him for his support and his visionary ideas.

We started LARIBA in 1987 in a humble way. I want to thank all those who believed in the experiment and who invested the very dear $10,000 to start the company. I want to acknowledge Dr. Misbah El Dereiny and

Mr. Sabry Abdel Azeez who worked with me to register the company and get it started. I also want to acknowledge some of the partners who helped in making LARIBA the success it is today. These are Mr. Hany El Messiry, Mr. Abdullah Tug, Mr. Mike Maguid Abdelaaty, Mrs. Maria Abdullahi, and the founding shareholders and directors of the company including my dear friends Zubair and Khatija Kazi, Salim and Françoise Shah, Mahmoud and Amal Abdellateef, Mahmoud and Hoda Hassan, Muhammad and Nabila Fahmy, Morsy and Rawya Badawy, Samir and Effat El Kobaitry, Sulaiman El Khereiji, and Ahmad and Magda Hassan.

In 1998, we were successful in acquiring the Bank of Whittier, California and in July of 2003, my wife and I agreed that I take early retirement to run the bank. My life was enriched by the many wonderful people that God has put into my path at the Bank of Whittier. I want to acknowledge the hard work and dedication of the wonderful staff, Board of Directors at the bank, and the bank holding company. I want to thank in particular Ms. Alexandra Dang and Mr. Wilson Yang for their contributions to the charts and the wonderful research work they conducted on commodity pricing and charting that are included in the book. I also want to acknowledge the trust that was invested in me personally by my dear close friends Mr. Zubair and Mrs. Khatija Kazi, who have chosen to be an important part of the Bank of Whittier project. I also want to thank our attorney Mr. Gary Findley for all his support and belief in us.

I want to thank all my friends who helped in making this book possible. In particular, I want to acknowledge Mr. Shahzad Malik, Esq., Professor Metwally Amer, and Mr. Salim Shah, who spent tireless hours to edit and proofread the manuscript. I sincerely appreciate your time and effort.

Finally, I want to thank a dear friend of mine who lives in London, and who recommended my name to John Wiley & Sons to invite me to write this book. He is Mr. Tarke Rifai, who is a wonderful researcher in monetary issues pertaining to Islamic banking.

Finally, I want to thank all of our customers, depositors, and investors of all faiths for their trust. I also want to thank my wonderful fellow Americans who are making Islam and the American Muslims part of this wonderful emerging new Judeo-Christian-Islamic America.

CHAPTER 1

Introduction

This book is for all people of all faiths. Many may think that Islamic banking is for the Muslims only and that Islamic banking is a gateway to the significant wealth amassed by the oil-producing countries in the Gulf.

That is not true! And that is why I am writing this book.

This book is about *riba/ribit-free banking*, or *RF banking*, a new brand of banking and finance service. It can be identified as a faith-based, socially responsible approach to banking. It is a service that aspires to serve all people of all faiths and backgrounds. It is believed that there is great demand for RF banking in the United States and the West, as well as in many developing nations worldwide. RF banking is a system that is not built on renting money at a price called the interest rate, but on renting a tangible asset, such as homes, tools and equipment, and businesses.

In the year 2001, we at LARIBA (www.lariba.com), and later (since July 2003) at the Bank of Whittier, NA (www.BankOfWhittier.com) started a dedicated effort to brand Islamic banking with a new name: *riba-free*, or *RF*, banking to describe what this new brand of banking and finance really is. The effort we invested has paid off, and the riba-free description is now used globally. It is slowly replacing the name "Islamic" banking. After living for more than 40 years in the United States, we came to understand the sensitivities of many in the country toward mixing state and church matters. In the United States, there is a deep-seated belief that the state and church must be separated. The U.S. system of separating church and state implies that a church is not permitted to run the state and, by the same token, the state cannot interfere in and run the affairs of a church. This way, churches (and other places of worship) can keep their independence and focus on producing spiritually, ethically, and morally qualified men and women to send to the state in order to run it.

The name we have advocated and are promoting is *riba-free*. It starts with the word *riba*, a sister-word to the term *ribit* used in the Old Testament. *Riba* means the act of taking advantage of those who need money to meet their basic necessities through the act of renting them money at a price called "interest." RF banking is a brand of banking that is socially responsible and is community-based in both spirit and intent. This brand of banking is the manifestation of Judeo-Christian-Islamic values, which are deepening in America. RF banking and finance is a new way of living without having to carry the burden of an ever-accumulating debt through the unnecessary overuse of loans (such as, for example, the use of credit cards to borrow, home equity lines of credit, and loans of all other types; secured and unsecured).

RF banking pays close attention as to whom and what to finance. RF banks do not, for example, finance alcohol- and gambling-related businesses, such as liquor stores or gambling casinos. It also does not finance environmentally irresponsible companies and businesses that are not fair to their employees. It is believed that RF banking will bring back to the United States and the world the characteristics of the banking movement that built America, as dramatized by the famous Hollywood actor Jimmy Stewart in the movie *It's a Wonderful Life*. I believe that Jimmy Stewart was the first American to present, in this movie, the real character of an RF banker. Based on actual operating experience, our customers of all sorts of religious beliefs including people of Hindu, Buddhist, Judaic, Christian, and Muslim faiths, appreciate and love to use the concepts of RF banking. Their consistent feedback is " . . . we have not heard other bankers operate like this before. . . . we feel that you care about us as members of your family." Escrow company officers love the way we serve people and our approach to financing. It is interesting to note that a few escrow company employees, after reviewing our closing documents for their customers, voluntarily called us to finance their homes with us. It is important to note that RF banking is cost-competitive with conventional riba-based banks.

The modern Islamic banking movement started in a humble way as a small community finance effort in Egypt (1963) and grew gradually to become a small emerging finance industry in the Middle East (1973). Today, with the increase in demand for oil and gas and the increase in energy prices, many of the Gulf's oil-producing countries have accumulated large amounts of cash. Some of the owners of this cash have decided to use Islamic banks to manage it. This has helped the RF banking industry become better established and a high-growth industry. Islamic banking came to Europe in the early 1980s. Britain has an Islamic bank (Islamic Bank of Britain, IBB). Many European municipalities and governments are dealing in *Islamic banking* products, mainly bonds (*sukuk*). In Asia, many countries have Islamic banks and/or finance companies. Malaysia has one of the pioneering and most sophisticated Islamic banking industries in the world.

At the time of writing this book, the United States and the rest of the world were experiencing a major financial and economic meltdown, the likes of which had not been experienced since the Great Depression. The crisis moved the world from the financial and monetary norms of the 20th century to a new era for the 21st century. It is believed that this shift may bring most banks—of all brands—closer to the values, methods, and philosophy of the RF (Islamic) banking brand. In addition, an increasing number of Americans will eventually choose to live a life that is riba-free, which reflects the real manifestation of the Judeo-Christian-Islamic value system.

In 2007 and 2008, we in the United States suffered the worst housing crisis in our history. This crisis dwarfed the economic meltdown of the Great Depression. This time around, the meltdown involved the major economies of the world. Subprime lending and manufactured securities made by packaging mortgage promissory notes called mortgage-backed securities (MBS) were sold to commercial and investment banks around the world as high-quality (AAA) securities. This was not the case. With the decline of the real estate market and the nonperformance of many of the mortgages, investors discovered that these were not high-quality AAA securities after all. This massive discrepancy created huge historic losses for the largest banks in America and the world, resulting in the failure of major banks and severe declines in the stock markets of the whole world. These events caused the financial system to suffer a deep lack of trust between banks' managers and chiefs of investment units. Many banks in America and around the world ended up holding financial papers that suddenly became illiquid. The result was a liquidity crunch of major proportions, leading to a worldwide credit crunch. This situation has led many banks to refuse to support each others' overnight borrowing needs to provide short-term liquidity. Many banks all over the world woke up to see their capital wiped out or drastically reduced. Some U.S. banking icons, such as Lehman Brothers, were pronounced bankrupt. Others, such as Washington Mutual, Wachovia, Citibank, and Merrill Lynch, to name a few, announced hundreds of billions of dollars in writeoffs. The U.S. and European governments announced financial rescue packages of more than $2 trillion to help inject fresh capital into the banks, insurance companies, and finance companies. The U.S. government took over the giant mortgage finance institutions Fannie Mae and Freddie Mac, and is devising ways and means to rescue other industries like the automobile industry.

On the other hand, Americans, especially the hard-working middle class families who wanted to realize the American dream of owning a home, to save for a comfortable retirement, or to save in order to be able to send their children and grandchildren to better schools, lost their savings. Their savings were in the form of retirement and pension plans, the assets of which were invested in the failed company's stock or in mutual funds. Some also lost their homes after losing their jobs. The main reason was the fraudulent mortgage lending practices of many of the unregulated so-called mortgage "bankers," and the new mortgage loan products they manufactured and marketed throughout the United States under glitzy acronyms like:

- *ARMs*, or adjustable rate mortgages, start at a very low interest rate (and hence a low monthly payment). They are sold to gullible consumers by convincing them that interest rates will not go up! Because families intended to move within two years to a new house (before the interest rates change), ARMs were considered a great financing idea by many, including Alan Greenspan (former United States Federal Reserve Board Chairman). People acted as though they could predict the future of the financial markets with precision. As has been usually the case, the market has proven them wrong. Interest rates jumped higher and the monthly payments doubled, making it difficult for the consumer to service the mortgage loan.

- *Interest-Only Loans* misled the public by promising them low monthly payments on their home mortgages by paying only the interest on the loan and no principal, while enjoying the promise of home price appreciation. The underlying assumption was based on the premise that home prices would rise to no end. This, theoretically, would benefit the consumer by building a "huge" equity at a very small monthly payment! The rest of the terms were not made clear—for example, one such loan's "fine print" might state that the loan would balloon and would be due in full, in three to five years. This meant, although it was not explained or forewarned by the mortgage sales person, that the customer would have to either sell the house (and hopefully make a "lot of money" to pay off the loan and keep a handsome profit) or refinance the home. As has been the case, home prices declined and most of those who used this finance method lost their homes.

- *Negative Amo (Amortization) Loans* were engineered so that the buyer would agree to a monthly payment that would suit his/her budget needs; if rates were low, then the small monthly payment of the loan would cover the interest and principle. Conversely, if interest rates rose higher, the loan value would increase, because the constant small monthly payments would not cover the needed payment of interest and principal. The shortfall was added to the existing loan, making it bigger. The hope was that home prices would appreciate eternally. Unfortunately, these loans were most often sold to retired senior citizens, who ended up losing their homes.

■ *Stated Income/No Docs Loans*[1] required no documentation to get approval! The only disclosure needed from the applicant was to state his/her income, and the mortgage broker or banker would not even have to verify it. This accommodation was created by commercial banks in very special cases. It was meant to be used only by sophisticated and highly experienced bankers for the services and needs of very high net worth individuals and entities, which represent a small portion of the population, to reduce the time and the huge efforts necessary to gather and document their vast and diversified assets in full. Instead, this approach was used by the commission-motivated mortgage "bankers" and brokers to lure those with undocumented income—such as those who run cash businesses—regardless of their ability to make the payments and service the loan.

■ *Subprime Loans* were used when a loan application based on stated income did not qualify for approval because the applicant's credit rating was very low. The idea was to still finance them, but at a premium because of the high risk involved. With the collaboration of investment bankers, a huge *subprime lending* mortgage business started to bloom. In this supposedly win-win business, the mortgage banker won because he or she made a hefty commission that could be as high as 6–8 percent of the value of the loan, and the investment banking firm won because it could "package" these loans inside a mortgage-backed security (MBS) that combined some of these subprime promissory notes with a certain higher proportion of the low-risk, high-quality mortgage notes. Rating agencies in the United States rated these packaged MBSs AAA. This blending of the good-quality mortgage notes with the lower-quality subprime notes helped enhance the yield of the resulting MBSs. Investment bankers sold this higher-yield—supposedly AAA—class of securities to banks, pension plans, and finance and investment companies around the world. In the process, the investment banks realized a huge commission. To squeeze more profits, they used additional derivative speculative techniques that turned against them, leading to the crisis. A significant mortgage investment company invited me to a "Top Executive" industry conference designed to entice participants to participate in the "booming" and very rewarding subprime market. I simply refused, because our values—Judeo-Christian-Islamic values—require us never to dig a deeper pit of debt for those who we know cannot service that debt.

We have experienced interesting situations in the course of conducting our mortgage banking business. For example, a typical mortgage "banker" in America during the mortgage boom years from 2000 to 2007 was typically a young person, just graduated from—in most cases—high school, with no experience. They introduced themselves as the owner, president, or senior vice president of a loan brokerage or mortgage banking firm. These mortgage bankers were primarily motivated by the commission they make on each loan, which can be up to 8 percent of the loan (e.g., for a $200,000 loan, they would make $16,000). Many of them closed at least 10 loans a month, for an income of more than $160,000 a month! Some of these brokers prospected very low-income families to get them to buy homes and take loans they could not afford. One of these low-income hard-working families was that of our own gardener and his wife. The only thing the mortgage broker asked them for was their Social Security numbers, dates of birth, and signatures on the bottom line of a loan application. Bingo! They got the loan and the young mortgage banker kid got a fat commission. When our gardener (a U.S. citizen of Latino origins) told us that he had signed up with a mortgage broker to finance a home for $345,000 with no down payment, we suggested that we finance his mortgage at LARIBA to make sure that the process was made easy and inexpensive. In fact, we could not compete. For example, LARIBA required detailed documentation, while his loan broker did not. In addition, the loan pricing offered by Washington Mutual in a special program for minorities was much lower than the market.

It is believed that two fundamental reasons caused this crisis and all previous crises, and may cause many more future crises if not fixed. The first reason is the monetary regime the world is following. This regime was devised by the Bretton Woods Agreements after World War II. It was broken in August 1971 by President Nixon when he closed the "Gold Window" and allowed the gold price to adjust to the market forces of supply and demand, instead of fixing it at $35 per ounce as stipulated by the Bretton Woods Agreements. The Bretton Woods system has not been thoroughly overhauled since. The world ended up working with an incomplete and broken system since 1971. The second major reason is our dangerous culture of greed and selfish consumerism. The values of responsible citizenry and civilized behavior can only begin at home, with parents (and especially a mother) who set the tone, the ambience, and conscience of the household by insisting that everyone does what is good and what is right. Every Christmas season, the American public watches on television and is deeply touched by Frank Capra's movie *It's A Wonderful Life*, in which Jimmy Stewart played the small-town manager of the Building & Loan Society. He had humble means at his disposal, but he and his staff and family made memorable inroads in improving his community and the lifestyle of its families. The movie also dramatizes the way this community banker and his supportive wife were appreciated by their community.

In contrast, today's bankers have been lost—lost from the community—in the maze of trying to manufacture new products and schemes to make money through fees and speculation, aggressive lending practices to meet their sales goals, and the excessive use of hedging. One example is hedge funds with mammoth assets, which are active speculators in stock shorting,[2] options,[3] futures,[4] and derivatives.[5] These techniques have prompted the bankers to devise games to corner and outmaneuver competitors, making more money on money without a measured productive contribution to the community or the country. It is true that all these activities have been done with the objective of realizing more profits. We have no problem with earning money and realizing great returns on shareholders' equity while benefiting the shareholders. However, we must ask how these earnings were realized and whether they added value and productivity to the community.

Today's lingo is amazingly descriptive of what is happening. Some financiers and bankers tell us that they represent the capitalistic system's promise of *making money*. We respectfully submit that this is not true! *Making money* (i.e., manufacturing money) is done at the printing presses by order of the Federal Reserve or the Central Bank. The words we should use and we should train our bankers, our financial officers, and our children to use are: *earning money*. The word *earn* implies that the person has gained an income as a reward for a responsible service or an activity they offered. We all remember when parents taught their children to ask themselves before they went to sleep " . . . how much I earned today and what good I have done to earn it."

The culture of making, spending, and wasting money has now become prevalent worldwide. It is based on the false premise of making money on money, which is done by renting money at a rental price called interest rate. Applying this process of reasoning, one can lend money at a rental rate of 8 percent to another person. The borrower is happy, because he/she can pay the money back later, after satisfying his or her instinct to acquire things so as to be perceived as a respectable member of society and a successful businessperson! Credit card companies have made it even easier to overindulge.

But the ultimate excess of all excesses has been to encourage people, through the culture of money rental, to use their home equity as a credit card by taking out *home equity loans*. It is understood that a family would use a home equity line of credit to improve and upgrade their house, for example, to add a new room for their new baby or growing child. But the home equity line of credit should *not* be used to generate cash through another buzzword (cash out); to speculate by buying another home to take advantage of low interest rates and capture the potential of a rising real estate market; or to buy an expensive car, take an expensive cruise or European tour, or simply gamble with it in the stock market. For these reasons, bankers should be trained to ask "Why do you need the money?" and decide whether the line of credit is justified and necessary. Of course, we live in a free society, and every citizen is free to do what he/she wishes; we all must respect that freedom dearly. On the other hand, each banker is also free to set the rules and policies of investing the bank depositors' money and shareholders' capital that will be applied to finance peoples' needs. Any banker can decide whether he/she is really out to invest in—and, conceptually, with—people in the community, or if he/she is simply renting them money at a rental rate called the interest rate.

The concept of the interest rate and the resulting culture of renting money is the subject of this book.

It is sincerely hoped that this book will make a humble contribution to a better future for the United States and the world by bringing the American banking system—the most fair, most sophisticated, and most regulated and governed banking system in the world—back to the forefront.

Islamic banking has become an important factor in the world. A few years ago, we conducted a nonscientific survey among our friends. We asked them what came to mind when we said the words "Islamic banking." The answer was: "vast amounts of oil money from the Gulf countries which are waiting to find investment opportunities!" Unfortunately, what you'll read about in this book is more than just getting hold of these vast resources. This book *will* help you understand the basic concepts of Islamic banking, which will help your creative mind communicate with the fund managers in these oil-rich Gulf countries and hopefully develop mutually rewarding business relationships. It is hoped that this book will help in achieving better understanding among all people of all backgrounds and of all faiths.

The Jewish Bible, the Christian Bible, and the Qur'aan all prohibit the act of charging rent for the use of money. In the Old Testament, it is called *ribit*; in the Qur'aan, it is called *riba*. So *riba/ribit-free banking* is involved in investing in and conceptually with people in the community, rather than with renting them money and charging them for the use of that money. In earlier days, the act of charging for the use of money was called *usury*. Unfortunately, today *usury* is defined as *excessive interest*. Sadly, no one offers to complete the definition of *excessive* by telling us the reference point above which it becomes excessive!

As outlined earlier, the preferred way to refer to Islamic banking is to call it what it really is. The preferred term must be descriptive and inclusive of all faiths, especially the Abrahamic Judeo-Christian-Islamic cultures, value systems, and faiths. We advocate for calling this system *RF banking and finance* (R for riba/ribit, and F for free).

In 1987, when we started the operations of American Finance House LARIBA in Pasadena, California to deliver RF banking and finance services, we met and interacted with many wealthy individuals, learned scholars, and experienced practitioners, as well as accomplished international business and corporate attorneys. Some of us, including myself, were fortunate to attend many meetings with distinguished religious scholars, during which various financial, investment, and monetary aspects of modern banking and finance were discussed and explained by practitioners in the presence of expert attorneys. We also were fortunate to attend meetings with international corporate attorneys to explain to them the religious scholars' opinions and suggestions regarding making the banking service and/or products riba-free (Islamic). This fascinating and educational experience was combined with our dream of establishing an RF financial institution for the community in America, and made us think of what is ahead.

The major challenge was determining how to build an RF finance company or bank that delivers RF banking and finance services to the community, especially in a world that is run using riba. It was a daunting and difficult task to devise an RF banking system that satisfies the requirements of the Judeo-Christian-Islamic Law (Shari'aa) while simultaneously abiding by and following the laws and standards of the Western system, which has been at least 600 years ahead of RF banking in the sophistication of its standards, systems, and products.

The book has been organized in two parts. Part One, which consists of eight chapters, focuses on the building blocks of the RF banking system:

- The faith-based aspects of the Judeo-Christian-Islamic value system, which prohibits ribit/riba, will be discussed in Chapter 2.
- The unique principle of *marking to the market*, which disciplines RF bankers to evaluate every financing and "lending" operation as an investment, will be discussed in Chapter 3. In this methodology, the real market rent of a car, a home, or a business is used to evaluate the viability and the monthly payment for a financing deal instead of the straight rental of money at a cost called interest rate.
- The wisdom and processes used to arrive at the faith-based rules, regulations, and laws by applying the Judeo-Christian-Islamic foundations and the methodology of the law (Shari'aa) will be detailed in Chapter 4.
- The definition of money and how money developed from being real as defined by Shari'aa (gold or silver) to becoming paper—*fiat*—money to suit the diversified large needs of the world (Chapter 5). The creation and management of money and the monetary system, the role of the central banks and the Federal Reserve System, and the definition of interest designed and implemented by the government to manage the amount of money in the system will be discussed. The foundations of riba in commercial transactions will be reviewed. The new and unique

rules put forward by the Prophet Muhammad (pp)[6] to normalize market prices, in which he required the use of *commodity indexation* process in measuring market prices, and his rule of pricing every item on the basis of its market value using real currency (*noquood*, defined to be in silver or gold or a commodity that represents a staple and needed commodity, like rice or wheat). Chapter 5 presents very useful and interesting correlations that have been tested thoroughly during the past 26 years for a bubble pricing environment for specific commodities using the commodity indexation rule pioneered by the Prophet Muhammad (pp). This chapter will take the reader on a wonderful journey that will provide insight on pricing things in the market using reference basic commodities, and the implications learned from these correlations will be discussed.

- The social responsibility of citizens entrusted with the keeping of people's money and assets—that is, the RF bankers—will be discussed in Chapter 6. The concepts of civility and social responsibility based on the Judeo-Christian-Islamic value system will be presented as a means to establish the most important spirit, substance, and foundation for the RF banking brand.
- The American banking system's tremendous achievements (and its associated banking regulations and acts developed over the years) have been an important force in the world. Chapter 7 details the system and the ways in which it is based on a huge body of human experience rooted in the Judeo-Christian-Islamic value system that cannot be ignored. Chapter 7 also recommends that RF banking religious scholars, regulators, and practitioners understand U.S. banking regulations and systems and build on them. Many of the regulations, as is shown in this chapter, are rooted deeply in the values of the Judeo-Christian-Islamic system.
- Many ask about the difference between RF banking and conventional riba-based banking. Chapter 8 is an attempt to explain the history of RF banking and how it has developed since the early 1950s. In addition, the chapter discusses and attempts to articulate the differences.

Part Two, which consists of six chapters, attempts to integrate the pieces discussed in Part One to develop a reliable, well-designed, and beneficial RF banking system that is true to Judeo-Christian-Islamic Law in both spirit and substance.

Part Two begins by summarizing the goals defined by two groups of Islamic bankers. The first group started in good faith and with good intentions from the existing contracts and systems and tried to sometimes force an "Islamic" solution and terminology on the system. This approach has been followed since the early 1960s, and is called *Shari'aa compliant*. The second group, pioneered by the author, developed a *Shari'aa-based* approach that uses the spirit and substance of the real intent and methodology of "Islamic" banking, stressing the fact that it is rooted in the Judeo-Christian-Islamic value system and that it is designed for all people of all faiths. This Shari'aa-based approach is the basis for the RF banking system.

Following are the issues that will be discussed:

- Chapter 9 focuses on the the Shari'aa-compliant techniques and methods used in Islamic financing in the 20th century, detailing the most important aspect of the use of form (as in the case of Shari'aa-compliant banking) versus the use of substance (as in the case of Shari'aa-based RF banking). The contract and the way it is structured in the Shari'aa-compliant approach will be contrasted with the Shari'aa-based approach.

- The art of Islamic banking is developed and analyzed in Chapter 10. This chapter introduces what is believed to be the new wave of Islamic banking in the 21st century, Shari'aa-based RF banking. This chapter will detail the many currents involved in the application and implementation of RF banking and the way these currents have been integrated in a way strictly based on Shari'aa, while being operated according to the laws of the land. Perhaps the most important aspect of this 21st-century Shari'aa-based RF banking and finance model is that it saves its clients from participating in an economic and speculative bubble by testing the prudence of the investment based on the renting of a tangible asset and not the renting of money. RF bankers help the clients make sure that the investment is prudent and will make a real difference in peoples' lives and in the business itself. Eventually, this approach will have a wonderful impact on stabilizing the markets.

- The unique and historic experience of restructuring an American bank to operate riba-free will be detailed in Chapter 11. This chapter will give thorough details on the steps that were taken to change fortunes, restructuring an American bank in a RF format and turning it around to profitability and compliance.

- In Chapter 12, the operation of an RF bank in the United States will be detailed, including the training and preparation of the RF bankers and descriptions of the different RF products offered at the bank. The challenge in the United States is to abide by the laws of the land and the banking regulations while not violating the tenets of Shari'aa. The other challenge is competing with the products, services, and huge experience and capital available to conventional riba-based banks in America. We will discuss these challenges as well as strategies for RF banking growth in the United States.

- Chapter 13 includes examples drawn from real life to illustrate the development and application RF banking investment products.
- Chapter 14 gives a peek into the future regarding the author's vision of the RF banking brand in the current economic climate, and offers advice to those who are considering a riba-free lifestyle.
- In Chapter 15, the author addresses challenges and strategies for popularizing RF banking in the United States and the world.

It is sincerely hoped that this book will open many eyes and hearts in all fields to realize a better world that will share prosperity fairly and become more peaceful and prosperous.

NOTES

1. Also known as *NINJA Loans* (No Income, No Job Application) and *Liar Loans* because many applicants gave incorrect information while completing the application.
2. *Stock shorting* is a method of profiting from a decline in a stock's price. It is the opposite of investing (or *going long*), in which the investor profits from a rise in the stock's price. *Shorting against the box* means shorting of a stock that one owns to protect against a loss in the value. However, *naked shorts*, or shorting of stocks that are not owned, may create market instability and dislocation that may have a negative impact on the company involved.
3. Trading an *option* on the stock exchange means giving someone the right to buy or sell a certain stock at a certain price by a specific time. If you buy an option to purchase securities, it is called a *call option*. If the option you buy is to sell securities, then it is referred to as a *put option*. Some traders even go so far as to purchase both calls and puts on the same stock, with agreed prices and by an agreed date; then it is called a *double option* or sometimes a *put and call option*.
4. *Futures trading* is unlike many other forms of speculating in the markets, because one is not required to own or even buy the commodity. All that is necessary is to speculate on where the price of a particular commodity is going and make a decision based on that. If a person was speculating on crude oil, for instance, and he or she expected the price to go up in the future, that investor would buy a *crude oil futures contract*. And if he or she expected that the price would go down, the investor would sell *crude oil futures*.
5. A *financial derivative instrument* is a financial contract whose value is based on, or derived from, another financial instrument (such as a bond or share) or a market index (such as the Share Price Index).
6. (*pp*) stands for "May God's Prayers and Peace be showered onto them" (in Arabic, "Sallaa Allahu Alayhi Wa Sallam"), a standard idiom that is uttered by all Muslims after mentioning (or writing) any of God's prophets' names or hearing any these names mentioned.

CHAPTER 2

The Faith-Based Judeo-Christian-Islamic Foundation of the Prohibition of Interest and the RF (Riba-Free) Banking System

The basic foundation of faith in Islam is belief in God; in all of God's prophets, including Prophet Abraham (pp[1]) and his children Ishmael (pp) and Isaac (pp) and their descendants; and in subsequent appointed prophets, including Joseph (pp), Moses (pp), Jesus (pp), and Muhammad (pp). A Muslim is a person who submits his/her will to that of God. A Muslim believes that the "people of the book" (as the Qur'aan refers to them) are those brothers and sisters in Judaism and Christianity who received a book of guidance from God: the Torah in the Jewish Bible, and the Gospel in the Christian Bible. It is part of the creed of a Muslim that he/she believes in Moses (pp) and Jesus (pp). Moses (pp) liberated the Hebrews from the slavery practiced against them by the ancient Egyptian Pharaohs and spoke with God to receive the Ten Commandments, which were further developed into the Jewish Bible. The Qur'aan[2] reveals:

> 4:164 Of some apostles We have already told thee the story; of others We have not; and to Moses God spoke direct;

Jesus (pp) was later commissioned to revitalize and expand on the teachings of Moses (pp). He taught the words of God and set the ultimate example of offering himself in sacrifice in order to stay the course and leave behind a shining example for all generations to come.

> 3:45 Behold! The angels said: "O Mary! God gives thee glad tidings of a Word from Him: his name will be Christ Jesus, the son of

Mary, held in honor in this world and the Hereafter and of (the company of) those nearest to God.

As the world grew, its resources diversified, and its people started traveling to chart new local and international trading routes (resulting in growth in trade and commerce), the Prophet Muhammad (pp) was commissioned by God to expand further on the teachings of Moses (pp) and Jesus (pp) and to offer the people of the world at large a universal working model on how to live, raise a family, build a community, govern, and conduct business with each other.

He was a revolutionary, like Moses (pp), leading a movement to free the slaves and remove slavery of the body and the soul from Arabia and the world. He worked hard to educate and liberate the pagans in Arabia and the rest of the world, to set them free by worshiping only one God. He also followed and built on the example of Jesus (pp) by intensifying people's commitment to God; by softening peoples' hearts toward those who are poor, deprived, underprivileged and in need; and by standing up in righteousness to those who abused their riches and powers in the name of religion. In doing so, he made it easier for people to live in peace, with justice and fairness for all.

With the emergence of the Roman/Byzantine Empire and the Persian Empire as the two leading superpowers during the time of Prophet Muhammad's (pp) mission, he was commissioned to offer the world, through the revelations of God's words in the Qur'aan and his living model (the *Sunnah*[3]) a detailed example of a living prophet who was a spiritual leader, the head of a state, and a businessman.

His actions and model of living were all fully documented because he was commissioned in the light of history brought on by the invention of paper and the printing press. He acted as a prophet and as a shepherd (like Jesus (pp) and Moses (pp)) and as a political leader and as head of the state defense forces. He expanded his responsibilities to offer a role model for being a successful merchant, an accomplished money manager, and an admired and trusted investor. Michael Hart, who was born in a Christian family,[4] states: "He [Prophet Muhammad (pp)] was the only man in history who was supremely successful on both religious and secular levels." While studying the Qur'aan and the style of living (the *Sunnah*) of the Prophet Muhammad (pp) depicted in the vastly researched, meticulously authenticated and documented body of his sayings (the *Hadeeth*[5]) and his traditions and story of his life (the *Seerah*[6]), we learn about similar models of living offered by Moses (pp) and Jesus (pp). Prophet Muhammad's life expanded on the examples of Moses (pp) and Jesus (pp) to demonstrate how to live in the more complex world of the sixth century. This new world included more sophisticated communication systems, transportation methods, and trading routes, as well as new businesses, more integrated markets, and expanded villages and cities—and a more sophisticated monetary and economic system. We read in the Qur'aan:

> *2:136 Say: We believe in God, and in that which has been bestowed from on high upon us, and that which has been bestowed upon Abraham and Ishmael and Isaac and Jacob and their descendants, and that which has been sent to Moses and Jesus; and that which has been sent to all the [other] prophets by their Sustainer: we make no distinction between any of them and it is unto Him that we surrender ourselves.*[7]
>
> *42:13 The same religion has He established for you as that which He enjoined on Noah—that which We have sent by inspiration to thee—and that which We enjoined on Abraham, Moses, and Jesus.*

The religion of Islam as understood from the Qur'aan and the tradition of Prophet Muhammad (pp) reinvigorated the basic concepts brought by Abraham, Moses, and Jesus. Being a Muslim means to submit our will to the will of God by worshiping only Him and by abiding by His injunctions, which He revealed to all His prophets. Conceptually, Islam can indeed be looked upon as part of a Judeo-Christian-Islamic tradition that extends back to the father and patriarch of all prophets, Abraham (pp). One well-read American Muslim stated that he researched all religions and philosophies to find a faith to which he could adhere. He concluded that Islam was it for him, because it did not take away from him Moses (pp) and his Jewish beliefs of the Old Testament or his Christian beliefs in Jesus (pp) and in the Bible. He said that Islam, to him, was the umbrella that covered all. He added that Islam was to him like a tent that brought under it in one house the teachings of Moses (pp) in Judaism and Jesus (pp) in Christianity; it did not discredit these teachings, but rather intensified and deepened them.[8] This concept is exactly what is meant in this book by the Judeo-Christian-Islamic lifestyle.

The original teachings of Judaism, Christianity, and Islam prohibit lending money and charging interest/usury (the original word *usury* was used to mean paying a rent for the use of money; the meaning was changed to mean, in today's language, lending at an excessive interest rate), ribit (which means an increase over the original amount of debt, in the language of the Old Testament), and riba (which also means an increase, in the language of the Qur'aan). It is also interesting to note that charging interest is prohibited in Buddhism, Hinduism, and many other faiths and philosophies.[9] Muslims are taught that participating in the culture and practice of interest (charging interest on lending money, borrowing with interest, and witnessing contracts that involve interest) is divinely prohibited (*haram*) and is one of the worst sins by the Islamic— that is, the Judeo-Christian-Islamic—laws (the term that will be used throughout this book for Judeo-Christian-Islamic law is Shari'aa, "the Law"). The act of borrowing money with interest (riba) is not a socially and religiously acceptable behavior. In a typical Muslim society, borrowing money and paying interest is only reserved for meeting a dire need, and it is socially considered a shameful act.

Charging interest is also divinely prohibited in Judaism and Christianity. It is important to study, learn, and reflect upon the history of the prohibition of interest from the original teachings of Moses (pp) in the Torah (Jewish Bible) and the teachings of Jesus (pp) in the Christian Bible with an eye toward how these attitudes developed into the more relaxed practices of today. A more appropriate and credible approach to studying the charging of interest in Judaism and Christianity is to ask an adherent to each faith who is an expert in the financial field to summarize the position and the original teachings of his/her faith on the charging of interest, and then to discuss how these clear Judeo-Christian-Islamic injunctions that prohibited the charging of interest were modified and reconstructed to become the current acceptable practice of charging interest. In March 2002, the Board of Directors of LARIBA in Pasadena, California invited a Jewish rabbi, a Catholic professor, and a Protestant professor to author and present papers on the subject.

AN INTRODUCTION TO THE JUDEO-CHRISTIAN-ISLAMIC FOUNDATIONS OF FAITH

The following is a brief summary of the building blocks needed to develop a unified understanding of our approach and to study various religions and their position on charging interest:

The Book

> *Jews*: People of the Jewish faith abide by the Jewish Bible, which is called the Torah and is referred to in the Qur'aan. The people of the Jewish faith believe that it is the book revealed by God to Prophet Moses (pp). It is considered to be the main source of the Jewish law.

Christians: Adherents to the Christian faiths abide by the Christian Bible. The Christian Bible comprises the Jewish scriptures, which Christians traditionally refer to as the Old Testament, as well as documented writings from the period of Jesus (pp) and just afterward, which are referred to as the New Testament. The New Testament includes four versions of the life of Jesus (pp); each one was written by one of the saints of the Christian faith (St. John, St. Mark, St. Matthew, and St. Luke). The Bible also contains letters from Jesus's (pp) early disciples to various communities and groups; these letters elaborate on the teachings of Jesus (pp).

Muslims: Muslims abide by the Qur'aan. Muslims believe that it is God's last and final revelation to mankind. The Qur'aan affirms the revelation of the book to Prophet Moses (pp) which is referred to in the Qur'aan as the Torah. It also affirms the revelations to Jesus (pp), who came to confirm Moses' (pp) teachings and to expand on such teachings in the Gospel, which is called in the Qur'aan the *Injeel* (a word that is used by Christian Arabs to refer to the Bible). Muslims are taught that Islam came to affirm the teachings of all the Prophets of God, including the patriarch and father of all prophets, Prophet Abraham (pp), and all of his children and grandchildren, including Prophets Ishmael (pp), Isaac (pp), Jacob (also known as Israel [pp]), David (pp), Solomon (pp), and the many prophets who preceded the last three (i.e., Moses [pp], Jesus [pp], and Muhammad [pp]). The Qur'aan and the religion of Islam are believed to affirm the messages of Moses (pp) and Jesus (pp) and to expand upon them through the teachings of Prophet Muhammad (pp) in his dual role as the spiritual Prophet and the head of the state. Conceptually, Islam popularizes a Judeo-Christian-Islamic culture and law that are rooted in the teachings of all prior prophets from Abraham (pp) to Moses (pp) and Jesus (pp). A Muslim is required to believe in all of God's prophets, who are all looked upon as equal. The Qur'aan reveals:

2:136 Say: "We believe in God, and in that which has been bestowed from on high upon us, and that which has been bestowed upon Abraham and Ishmael and Isaac and Jacob and their descendants, and that which has been vouchsafed to Moses and Jesus; and that which has been vouchsafed to all the [other] prophets by their Sustainer: we make no distinction between any of them. and it is unto Him that we surrender ourselves."

The People of the Faith

Jews: *Ami* in the Hebrew language means "my people" (i.e., the people of Moses or the people of the Jewish faith). The Jewish people are also known as the family of Israel, as Israel is another name for Prophet Jacob (pp). The word *Israel* means in Hebrew a person who strives and struggles (just as in the Muslim concept of doing *jihad*). In other words, Prophet Jacob's (pp) name—Israel—means "the struggler" or *mujahid* in Arabic. The word *ami* may be interpreted to mean all God's people, or all followers of the Jewish faith.

Muslims: *Ummah* in the Qur'aanic language (Arabic) is defined as the people (nation) of the faith who have chosen to submit their will to the will of God. Notice the similarity between the words ami and ummah. The foundation of the teachings of Islam is an affirmation of Judeo-Christian-Islamic values and law. The teachings of Islam state that there is no superiority of a people or a nation over other nations, except through the level of revering God, following His scriptures, and living by the model of all God's prophets, as manifested by the lifestyle and example of all of God's prophets. Muslims are taught that discrimination of any kind is a sin.

Loans

Jews: In the language of the Torah (*Hebrew*), the words *neshek* and *neshah* mean[10] "interest." The word *neshek* literally means a bite. Some other passages also use the words *ribit*, *tarbit*, or *marbit*, which literally mean "increase" and are similar in meaning to the word *riba* used in the Qur'aan. The word *noshem* means lenders. *Noshem* is the term used when speaking of lending to the general public. The word *lawah* is used when speaking of lending to friends and family members, but not for commercial transactions.

Muslims: In the language of the Qur'aan, the word *loan* is *qard*, and it too is derived from the verb "to bite" (taking a bite from one's assets). To prevent any circumvention of the Judeo-Christian-Islamic law, Shari'aa, only one type of qard is allowed—the *qard hassan*, an interest-free (good) loan that is extended for a good cause to the poor, the needy, or the distressed.

Usury/Interest

Paying a rent for the right to use something was called *usury* from the early days of the Catholic Church until the 15th century. The Roman Catholic church's original prohibition against usury was slowly relaxed by using the word *interest* instead of the word *usury*. The original meaning of *usury* was to charge a price for using (or renting) money. Today, however, *usury* is defined as excessive interest.

In the case of fungibles (such as wheat, which will be consumed), it would be unjust to pay a price for renting them. This means that fungibles can be sold through a process of title transfer, but not rented. Applying this concept to money, one cannot charge a rent (interest) for the right to use money, because money is a thing.

In the case of nonfungibles, like an owned real estate property, title can be transferred for a price in a buy/sell agreement. In Shari'aa, it is called *Milk ul Raqabah* (which means ownership). There is also another right that a nonfungible property offers, which is the right of the owner to rent (or lease) the use of that item (such as renting a car or a house) to a lessee. In Shari'aa, it is called *Haq Ul Manfa'aa* (which means the right of usufruct). One can charge for the right to use a nonfungible.

The original teachings of the Old and New Testaments agree with the rules that taking usury on money lent (rent for the use of money) is unjust, because this implies selling what does not exist; this evidently leads to inequality, which is contrary to justice. This is not much different from Islam's position on riba.

Riba charging and its divine prohibition (*haram*) in Shari'aa become clearer after learning about the history of the prohibition of interest charging (usury) in the Jewish and Christian Bibles. It also brings to mind an exciting thought: If all faiths of the children of Abraham (pp) agreed on the issue of prohibiting the charging of interest on loans, perhaps we can develop a Judeo-Christian-Islamic window that could lead to cultural unity in the United States and the world. This unity eventually would bring better understanding and cooperation between the people and the leaders of the three Abrahamic faiths, which would eventually lead to a different mindset and a new style of living that could ultimately lead to peace, prosperity, and social harmony in the local communities of the United States and the world at large.

All divine revelations in Judaism, Christianity, and Islam started from prohibiting the grievous act of taking advantage of the poor and the needy by charging them interest on the loans that they needed to help them survive and meet their basic needs. Cutting out a bite (*qard*) of one's own money and giving it as an interest-free loan to those who are in need is a difficult decision to make, because there is no return on it. The Judeo-Christian-Islamic revelations consider this qard as a loan to God, who promises abundant return on it in this life and the hereafter.

Some of the rich and affluent may lend to the poor and the needy reluctantly, with the intention of showing off in front of others or of using the loan as a tool to control the needy by exploiting their labor or eventually confiscating their lands, houses, and crops. Historically, some of the rich gave their lower quality assets and foods to the needy. They also used harsh language and actions to remind the poor and needy of the favors that had been bestowed on them. All original teachings in Judaism, Christianity, and Islam prohibit such behavior.

Islam advanced and expanded Shari'aa one step further by divinely institutionalizing the rules of lending to the poor, pronouncing that the only loan that is recognized is known as *qard hassan* (a good bite/loan). It is divinely considered the only loan allowed in Islam. The qard hassan can be a term loan, with a time limit for the money to be paid back—in a flexible and merciful way, depending on the specific situation and needs of the borrowing poor and needy—or, in most cases, without a time limit. In fact, in Shari'aa the qard hassan is looked upon as a donation to be paid back by the heavily indebted (for good reasons) whenever they can afford to. The qard (or the bite) out of the owner's assets is considered a loan to God. In Islam, as in the original teachings of Judaism and Christianity, no additional direct or indirect benefit (such as labor, free use of the indebted person's residence, or receipt of gifts from the person who took the loan) can be drawn out of such a loan, because these are considered services that command a value and, hence, are considered payments of implied interest. Shari'aa even encourages that the payback be made at the place of residence of the poor borrower, to relieve them from paying the cost of travel (which itself can be considered an implied interest payment). Judeo-Christian-Islamic rules stress that the dignity of the borrowers should be preserved by never telling others about the loan given to them, never trying to take advantage of the borrowers, never trying to pressure them to expedite the payback of the loan, nor even frowning in their face. The Shari'aa goes further, encouraging the Muslim to forgive the loan in case the borrower is heavily indebted and in no position to pay the loan off. The Department of Treasury of the State (*Bayt ul Maal*) is also made responsible by Shari'aa to collect alms (*zakah*) from the citizens and use part of this money to relieve those who are heavily indebted and cannot pay the loans back (giving alms in Islam is called *the ritual of zakah*, which means the ritual of purifying one's assets by paying back the right of God in these assets). Shari'aa requires that if the indebted person dies, the lender forgive the loan as a gesture of good will if the family cannot meet the demand. If the family is able to pay back, the heirs are required to pay the loan off.

By the advent of Islam, the world economic systems had changed from the slavery system of the ancient Egyptians during the time of Moses (pp), and the agrarian systems that were prevalent when Jesus (pp) was commissioned. The world had progressed with the development of sprawling villages, towns, and cities. Larger commercial trading caravans managed by money managers traded commodities and merchandise products and manufactured goods. They needed money, not because they were poor and needy, but because they wanted capital to help them grow their business, finance the goods, and expand their commercial activities. To resolve this demand for capital and to develop divine rules for financing without riba, Shari'aa, as prescribed in the Qur'aan and the tradition of Prophet Muhammad (pp), expanded on the original teachings of the Jewish and Christian Bibles. Prophet Muhammad (pp) was also a businessman and a money manager. He understood the need to finance trading and business activities. Islam presented an expanded Judeo-Christian-Islamic set of rules concerning the financing of trade and business in the seventh century. This expanded on the original teachings of Moses (pp) and Jesus (pp) to develop a unique and complete Judeo-Christian-Islamic law (Shari'aa) concerning finance. This law brought about a pioneering new riba-free (RF) finance system that can be used for just, fair, and equitable RF banking and finance. The RF finance system makes credit available to all people without discrimination (to meet personal credit needs, to finance commercial activities, and/or to finance business) and considers the ability to obtain credit to be a basic human right. This RF Judeo-Christian-Islamic approach comes with an important goal in mind: to bring about peace, justice, fairness, harmony, prosperity, peace of mind, job opportunities, and mutual respect among all people of all faiths and backgrounds, leading to a wonderful future of peace and happiness in the whole world.

THE JUDAIC POSITION ON THE CHARGING OF RIBIT (INTEREST): MONEY, LENDING, AND INTEREST IN THE TORAH AND THE JEWISH TRADITION[11]

Rabbi Yosef Kanefsky leads a Jewish congregation in one of the suburbs of Los Angeles, California. The Board of Directors of LARIBA contracted him in March 2002 to author a paper that summarizes the prohibition of charging interest on loans in the Jewish tradition. The following is an abbreviated summary of his work.[12]

Loans to the Poor

Judaism's teachings regarding lending money are all based upon the biblical passage in Exodus, chapter 22, verses 24–26. The verses read as follows:

24. When you lend money to any of my people, to the poor among you, you shall not be to him as a creditor, nor shall you impose upon him any interest.

25. If you take your neighbor's [night] garment as a pledge (collateral), you shall return it to him by nightfall

26. for that is his only covering; it is his garment for his skin. In what shall he sleep? And it shall come to pass, that if he cries unto Me, I will hear it, for I am compassionate.

The word that sets the tone for the entire legal discussion is the word *ami*—my people—which is found in verse 24. God specifically regards those in need of loans as being His special people, to whom He is very close. The phrase "you shall not be to him as a creditor" is interpreted to mean that the lender is prohibited from reminding the borrower of his dependent status in any way. The borrower is beloved of God, and the lender must bear this in mind. Even a facial expression on the lender's part can constitute a violation of this prohibition.

But the most concrete expression of God's love for the debtor is, of course, the prohibition against the taking of interest. By rabbinical interpretation, not only is the lender prohibited from charging interest, the borrower is prohibited from offering to pay interest. The Torah rejects the entire notion of a loan as a transaction that brings benefit to the lender. According to the *Halacha* (rabbinical law), a person who either lends or voluntarily borrows with interest is disqualified from being a witness in court.

By rabbinical definition, interest can include considerations aside from cash (Bava Metzia, Chapter 5, Mishna 2). For example, it is prohibited to allow one's creditor to live in and use one's home or workplace rent-free. It is even prohibited for the debtor to offer space to his creditor at a discounted rent. These are understood to be gestures through which the creditor realizes benefit from the loan he extended, and therefore are defined as "interest" by rabbinical definition.

It is important to note that all Jewish communities have "*Free Loan Societies*" that preserve both the spirit and the letter of the laws of interest. Often the local Jewish federations or other community-wide organizations administer these interest-free loan societies.

Lending to Non-Jews with Interest

The question as to the permissibility of lending with interest to people who are not part of the Jewish community is debated in the Talmud (Bava Metzia 70b – 71a). The Talmud's discussion is inconclusive, and the post-Talmudic rabbis take up the question. Moses Maimonides,[13] in his great Jewish legal code (Laws of Loans, chapter 5, law 2), rules that it is permissible for a Jew to charge interest to a non-Jew only when there is a dire need and in the amount necessary to provide himself with a basic living. To charge a usurious (higher than normal) rate is prohibited. The great rabbis of medieval France and Germany were somewhat more permissive under circumstances in which Jews were barred from most professions, and Jewish communities were singled out for taxation above the ordinary rates (commentary of Tosafot to Bava Metzia 70b).

Business Financing

In the 16th century, as life became much less agrarian and much more commercial, loans were no longer primarily extended for personal reasons, but rather to provide commercial capital. As these kinds of loans were vital for commercial success and were not the kinds of loans first envisioned by the Torah, efforts were made to find a permissible vehicle for this kind of enterprise.

Rabbis in Poland and subsequently in other parts of Eastern Europe drafted and refined a document called *heter iska*. The essence of this document is to transform the lender-borrower relationship into an investment relationship. The provider of the capital becomes a partner in the venture in which the borrower will be engaging; the borrower will share a specified percentage of the realized profits with the lender/investor. This technical redefinition of the loan as an investment allowed Jewish commercial enterprises to succeed without violating the laws of prohibiting the charging of interest. The *heter iska* was refined several times to help ensure that the lender/investor would not be exposing himself to an unacceptable level of risk and that some measure of return would be contractually guaranteed. The *heter iska* is in common use to this day.

THE CHARGING OF RIBIT (INTEREST) IN THE ROMAN CATHOLIC TRADITION[14]: THEN AND NOW[15]

Professor Christopher Kaczor teaches at Loyola Marymount University in Los Angeles, California. The Board of Directors of LARIBA contracted him in March 2002 to author a paper that summarizes the prohibition of charging interest on loans in the Roman Catholic tradition, with an eye toward the history of the relaxation of the original prohibition. The following is an abbreviated summary of his work.[16]

Lending to the Poor

Jesus (pp) said:

> When the Son of man comes in his glory, and all the angels with
> him, then he will sit on his glorious throne. Before him will be gath-
> ered all the nations, and he will separate them one from another as
> a shepherd separates the sheep from the goats, and he will place the
> sheep at his right hand, but the goats at the left. Then the King will
> say to those at his right hand, "Come, O blessed of my Father,
> inherit the kingdom prepared for you from the foundation of the
> world; for I was hungry and you gave me food, I was thirsty and
> you gave me drink, I was a stranger and you welcomed me, I was
> naked and you clothed me, I was sick and you visited me, I was in
> prison and you came to me."[17] Then the righteous will answer him,
> "Lord, when did we see thee hungry and feed thee, or thirsty and
> give thee drink? And when did we see thee a stranger and welcome
> thee, or naked and clothe thee? And when did we see thee sick or in
> prison and visit thee?" And the King will answer them, "Truly, I
> say to you, as you did it to one of the least of these my brethren,
> you did it to me." (Matthew 25: 30–42)

In his *Summa Theologica*, St. Thomas Aquinas writes:

> To take usury for money lent is unjust in itself, because this is to sell
> what does not exist, and this evidently leads to inequality which is
> contrary to justice. In order to make this evident, we must observe
> that there are certain things the use of which consists in their con-
> sumption: thus we consume wine [grape juice] when we use it for a
> drink, and we consume wheat when we use it for food. Wherefore
> in such like things the use of the thing must not be reckoned apart
> from the thing itself, and whoever is granted the use of the thing, is
> granted the thing itself and for this reason, to lend things of this
> kind is to transfer the ownership. Accordingly if a man wanted to
> sell wine [grape juice] separately from the use of the wine [grape
> juice], he would be selling the same thing twice,[18] or he would be
> selling what does not exist, wherefore he would evidently commit a
> sin of injustice. In like manner he commits an injustice that lends
> wine [grape juice] or wheat, and asks for double payment,[19] viz.
> one, the return of the thing in equal measure, the other, the price of
> the use, which is called usury.[20]

St. Thomas Aquinas draws a distinction between the use of a thing and
the thing in itself. Some items one can use without the item being destroyed

by its very use—for instance, a house can be rented out and returned in good condition. On the other hand, the use of other things, like an apple, destroys the very thing used. Thus, you could not rent the eating of an apple, but only sell the apple, and in selling it, the transaction would be complete. Since money, on this model, is a thing consumed in its use, to charge a person interest on a loan is to demand payment for selling the money (principal) and another payment for renting the money (interest).[21]

Usury is condemned by St. Ambrose (d. 397), St. Jerome (d. 420), St. Augustine (d. 430), and Pope St. Leo the Great (d. 461), characteristically in connection with taking advantage of the poor. Bishops condemned usury at the Council of Elvira (305 or 306), the Council of Arles (314), and the First Council of Nicea (325). Canon 13 of the Second Lateran Council (1139 A.D.) reads:

> *Furthermore, we [Catholics] condemn that practice. It is looked upon as despicable and blameworthy by divine and human laws, denounced by Scripture in the old and new Testaments. Namely; the ferocious greed of usurers; and we sever them from every comfort of the church, forbidding any archbishop or bishop, or an abbot of any order whatever or anyone in clerical orders, to dare to receive usurers, unless they do so with extreme caution; but let them be held infamous throughout their whole lives and, unless they repent, be deprived of a Christian burial.*[22]

Several popes also condemned usury, including Alexander III, Gregory IX, Urban III, Innocent III, and Clement V. Condemning usury is reflected in the first universal compendium of Catholic teaching in more than 400 years, the Catechism of the Catholic Church, written with the input of all the bishops of the Catholic Church and published by the authority of John Paul II. The Catechism mentions usury in a condemnatory way:

> *The acceptance by human society of murderous famines, without efforts to remedy them, is a scandalous injustice and a grave offense. Those whose usurious and avaricious dealings lead to the hunger and death of their brethren in the human family indirectly commit homicide, which is imputable to them.*[23]

Position of the Contemporary Roman Catholic Church on Allowing the Charging of Interest

Professor Kaczor states that the Catholic Church maintains that usury is wrong; but does not hold and never did hold that all charging whatsoever of amounts beyond the principal is wrong. Germain Grisez points out:

The Church never taught that all charging of interest is wrong, but only that it is wrong to charge interest on a loan in virtue of the very making of the loan, rather than in virtue of some factor related to the loan which provides a basis for fair compensation.[24]

John Noonan notes:

By 1750, then, the scholastic theory and the counter theory, approaching the same problem form different theoretical viewpoints, agree in approving the common practice "of demanding interest on loans."[25]

As time went on, the majority of theologians approved of taking interest on loans. The Holy Office did not condemn these opinions, and confessors were not obliged to disturb those involved in the practice. In 1917, Canon law actually required Catholic institutions, such as hospitals, schools, or universities, to invest their assets profitably.

According to St. Thomas Aquinas:

1. The lender may require, over and above the amount of the loan, indemnity protection or insurance against loss or damage.
2. The lender may be repaid not just for the principal but also for expenses incurred in making the transaction, including what was "lost" in the transaction. For instance, if the borrower pays back the principal late, the lender may ask for an additional return, since he was deprived of the use of the money during a time when he could have made use of it. As Finnis notes, what is "lost" could therefore include money that could have been generated had the loan not been made. Aquinas apparently considered this possibility and rejected it: "But the lender cannot enter an agreement for compensation, through the fact that he makes no profit out of his money: because he must not sell that which he has not yet *and may be prevented in many ways from having.*"[26]

Professor Kaczor argues that the truth of this last phrase would seem to depend greatly upon existing market conditions. In some markets, such as the ones existing in Aquinas's day, the growth of an investment would be highly speculative; in other markets, like the ones existing today, the growth of an investment would be virtually assured [or so it was thought, until the meltdown of 2008]. With the rise of such secure ways of investing money, the person who loans money loses what with reasonable assurance he could have made. In other words, Aquinas assumes that money is a sterile, nonfungible commodity; but in contemporary markets, money may be quite productive indeed. John Finnis concludes:

> *Aquinas's account of usury, taken with his general theory of compensation, thus identifies principles (not rules made up by moralists or ecclesiastics) which enable us to see why in his era it was unjust for lenders to make a charge (however described) in the nature of profit, but with the development of capital market for both equities and bonds it was to become fair and reasonable to make precisely such a charge, correlated with (which is not to say identical to) the general rate of return on equities.[27]*

Aquinas's conclusions about lending at interest were adequate given the financial assumptions and market conditions of his time, but must be adjusted to account for contemporary circumstances.

THE CHARGING OF RIBIT (INTEREST) IN THE TRADITION AND TEACHINGS OF THE EVANGELICAL CHRISTIAN CHURCH[28]

Professor John Goldingay teaches at Fuller Seminary in Pasadena, California. The Board of Directors of LARIBA asked him in March 2002 to author a paper that summarizes the prohibition of charging interest on loans in the Christian (evangelical) tradition, with an eye toward the history of the relaxation of the original prohibition. The following is an abbreviated summary of his work.[29] Please note, in contrast to the Catholic thesis, Goldingay's reliance on Moses's (pp) teachings in addition to the teachings of Jesus (pp).

Lending to the Poor

The exhortation in Exodus indicates that it is quite possible for creditors to keep the regulation forbidding lending with interest, yet still treat debtors oppressively. The Old Testament refers to this as a personal issue, a community issue, a national issue, and an international issue.

Individual lenders are not to take the necessities of life as pledges, such as an ox or ass, or a garment, or a millstone—or a baby (Deuteronomy 24:6, 17; Job 22:6; 24:3, 9). One oppressive lender is a man who insists on taking away a widow's children (so that they can work for him) because of the family's debt (2 Kings 4:1).

A story about community controversy in Nehemiah 5 concerns oppressive lending: It may refer to charging interest or to other tough actions, such as foreclosing on personal properties. It alludes to two reasons for debt: crop failure and imperial taxation. The two stories also make clear the results of default. One may forfeit fields, orchards, and houses, and/or one may end up in slavery.

The way imperial taxation burdens individuals and leads to debt was anticipated in the way national taxes burdened people. When Israel asked for stronger central government, the prophet Samuel warned them of the burden that such government would be on them (1 Samuel 8:10–17).

Internationally, Habakkuk 2:6–7 warns about the way a major power that has behaved like a creditor, accumulating pledges from weaker and poorer countries, will in due course become the victim of its debtors. The tables will be turned.

The passage in Exodus forbids Israelites to impose interest on poor members of "my people" when lending them "money"—literally silver, for coinage was a development of the Persian period. The reference to the poor indicates that the text does not refer to regular commercial loans.

In Moses's (pp) teaching, Leviticus 25:35–37 expands on the point in Exodus.

> *If any of your kin fall into difficulty and become dependent on you, you shall support them; they shall live with you as resident aliens. Do not take interest in advance or otherwise make a profit from them, but fear your God; let them live with you. You shall not lend them your money at interest taken in advance, or provide them food at a profit.*

The passage supports the ban on lending with interest by speaking of the poor person as "your kin," members of your family, and of the need to "revere God."

Professor Goldingay states that "people who are doing well are expected to lend freely to the needy and to accept payment in the form of labor, or of the eventual repayment of the debt in money that the person had earned through labor. So debtors would seek to work their way back to solvency by committing themselves to indentured labor for a set period or to paid employment in relation to someone who did have land—the equivalent to getting a job, rather than the norm of being self-employed."[30]

Another passage in Moses's (pp) teaching makes explicit that people must not impose interest on any form of loan, in money or in kind:

> *You shall not charge interest on loans to another Israelite, interest on money, interest on provisions, interest on anything that is lent. On loans to a foreigner you may charge interest, but on loans to*

another Israelite you may not charge interest" (Deuteronomy 23:19–20 [23:20–21 in Hebrew Bibles]).

Professor Goldingay states—in contrast to what Rabbi Kanefsky stated—that the passage quoted above explicitly states that Israelites are permitted to impose interest in lending to a foreigner, someone who is not a member of "the people." This is an example of a number of obligations that did not apply to foreigners.

Beyond Moses's (pp) teaching, Proverbs 28:8 promises that someone who makes a profit by lending with interest "gathers it for another who is kind to the poor" (i.e., they will not see the profit themselves). It is a personal experience of something that the prophet Habakkuk (pp) envisages for the leading world power of his day. Psalm 15 asks the question,

LORD, who may abide in your tent?—

(i.e., stay in your presence).

The answer includes the general requirement of a life of integrity and truthfulness, and also some concrete expectations, such as avoiding slander, keeping oaths, refusing bribes—and not lending money with interest. The prophet Ezekiel (pp) speaks in similar terms, listing obligations that people should fulfill if they wish God to treat them as righteous, such as not worshiping by means of images, not defiling their neighbors' wives, not robbing people—and not lending with interest (Ezekiel 18:8, 13, 17). Ezekiel implies that people were not fulfilling these obligations and later makes explicit that the well-to-do in Jerusalem have committed many of the wrongs he lists, including this one having to do with lending with interest (22:12).

Professor Goldingay goes further to say that Christians tend to understand Moses's (pp) teaching as "law," but the word *Torah* has broader meaning. While Moses's (pp) Torah or teaching includes regulations that look designed for quasilegal literal implementation, other material in the writings look more like illustrations of a particular lifestyle. We would miss the point if we took it legally—we might fulfill the law's letter, but not its inner demand [the spirit of the law]. Similar issues are raised by Jesus's (pp) Sermon on the Mount.

Exodus 22 begins "If you lend . . . ," but it presupposes that you will do so. To refuse to lend would contravene other exhortations regarding concern for the needy. The point is explicit in Deuteronomy 15, which urges people to lend generously to poor members of their "family." Righteous people do well in life and are therefore in a position to give and to lend and thus to be a blessing (Psalm 37:25–26). Things go well for the person who deals generously and lends (Psalm 112:5).

The New Testament confirms the stance of the Old without adding to it. The New Testament refers to lending with interest only in the context of a parable, about a man entrusting his assets to his servants (Matthew 25:27; Luke 19:23).

Lending to the Enemy

Jesus (pp) does urge his followers to lend to whomever asks for a loan (Matthew 5:42) and explicitly states that this applies even to enemies and even if you do not expect to gain in any way from the act (Luke 6:34–35). *Maccabaeus*, a Jewish work from about the same period which some Christians came to treat as near-canonical, claims that when people start conforming their lives to Moses's (pp) teaching, even if they are by nature greedy they start lending to the needy without charging interest (2:8).

Business Financing and Relaxation of the Rules of Prohibiting the Charge of Interest

Professor Goldingay states: "I imagine that the ban on charging interest would indeed have been intended for literal implementation, but that in asking about its implications for us in a different social context, we need to look at it in the light of the various aspects of its stated rationale (e.g., in its concern for the poor). In more commercial contexts and in a competitive situation people might charge interest on commercial loans without infringing the principle underlying this teaching." He further states that through the first millennium of the Common Era, the Christian Church simply affirmed the Old Testament principle that lending with interest was disapproved, on the continuing presupposition that lending was an aspect of care for the needy. But in practice, lending with interest was tolerated, as long as rates were not judged excessive. Where Christians refused to engage in commercial lending, Jewish moneylenders were able to fill the vacuum on the basis of the Deuteronomic permission to charge interest to foreigners. In the second millennium, commerce began to develop in new ways and the practice of lending with interest became prevalent, despite the church's opposition. In due course, however, in keeping with the usual pattern, the church conformed itself to the secular pattern and provided a theological rationale for it. In the fifteenth century, Italy's public pawnshops developed with Franciscan support to offer loans to the poor more cheaply than those offered by regular moneylenders, charging a very low interest designed simply to cover expenses. In 1516, the Fifth Lateran Council approved these. As years went by, these pawnshops also began to lend for commercial purposes at higher rates. Feeling unbound by the course of discussion within the medieval church, and perceiving that the Old Testament was concerned with caring for the poor and not with commercial loans, John Calvin[31] removed the ban on lending with interest, with safeguards that predictably were conveniently forgotten. In due course, the Roman Catholic Church also removed its ban on lending with interest.

As the capitalist world developed, it lost the idea that the point about lending is to be caring towards the needy. In Victorian Britain, the development of the co-operative movement and the building society movement attempted to recover it. In effect, the customers of the co-op were the shareholders, while building societies worked by attracting safe investments from people who hoped eventually to buy a house and lending the money to people who were already in a position to do so.[32]

THE PROHIBITION OF CHARGING OF RIBIT/ RIBA (INTEREST/USURY) IN ISLAM

Almost 800 years before St. Thomas Aquinas and John Calvin were researching ways to resolve the prohibition of charging interest as taught by Moses (pp) and Jesus (pp) to accommodate the needs for financing of the growing commercial business, Muslim traders were practicing RF financing to address the capital needs of Muslims and non-Muslims to finance their trading and commercial activities. The RF finance system and code for financing of commercial transactions by Muslim traders and merchants and the non-Muslims who dealt with them was conducted in India, China, Central Asian countries, the Middle East, and some European countries. The RF financing rules and codes were based on Shari'aa, which can be considered the Judeo-Christian-Islamic law and values. This law finalized and detailed RF financing rules, and it was popularized by the revelation of the Qur'aan, which inculcated all God's messages from the Torah and the Gospel when it was revealed between the years 611 and 634 (approximately).

The Development of the Universal Riba-Free System in Islam

There is an important fundamental red line in the teachings of Islam—the line that separates what is divinely permissible, or *halal*, and what is divinely not permissible, or *haram*. Every Muslim is trained by his/her parents—regardless of the level of their religiosity—to know these two most important words in the vocabulary of Islam from childhood. It suffices for a mother to tell her child that lying is *haram*, because the child is trained to know the divine consequences of committing that *haram* act. These divisions can be called the basis of the Judeo-Christian-Islamic law (Shari'aa). Using this concept, we can state that riba is haram. The Qur'aan reveals:

> *3:130 O ye who believe! Devour not usury, doubled and multi-plied; but fear God that ye may (really) prosper.*
> *4:161 that they took usury, though they were forbidden; and that they devoured men's substance wrongfully; we have prepared for those among them who reject faith a grievous punishment.*

Charging riba was described as one of the worst sins, as reported in the *Hadeeth* (pronouncement) of Prophet Muhammad (pp) that describes "the seven most despicable sins." The Prophet (pp) also was reported to have said that dealing in riba is like committing murder.[33]

The following discussion presents a stepwise development that will help in understanding the structure of the RF system.

The Concept of God Owning Everything

In Islam, it is believed that every asset in this world is owned by God. We read in the Qur'aan:

> *31:26 To God belong all things in heaven and earth: verily God is He (that is) free of all wants, worthy of all praise.*

In other words, we, as the servants of God, do not own anything in this world. We are chosen by God in His infinite wisdom to act as His responsible trustees on the assets with which He entrusts us. We are expected to be responsible before God and the public for protecting and preserving these assets. The custodian is also expected to invest these assets prudently and successfully back into the community. This type of investment will help to achieve economic prosperity, job opportunities, and peaceful coexistence within the community, in a fair, just, and equitable way. We act as the trustees of these assets on behalf of their real owner—God—and we will be accountable before Him for any and all breaches, abuse, or misuse of this trust.

Encourage the Rich to Spend in the Way of God

■ *Help the Poor*—The Qur'aan reinforces the original teachings of Moses (pp) in the Torah and Jesus (pp) in the Bible about caring for the poor and needy and not taking advantage of them. The Qur'aan reveals:

■ *God knows all things*

2:270 and if you spend or promise to spend in the way of God, He knows all and those who transgress and practice injustice by not fulfilling their promises have no one to support them.

■ *Charity to help the poor can be done in public, but it is better to be done in secret*

2:271 If you give charity and declare it in public, that is acceptable, but if you give it in secrecy and give it to the poor, it is better for you, and He almighty will forgive you your misdeeds in return, and He Almighty is the one who Knows what you do.
30: 38 and give your kin their rights, the poor and way-farer. This is a better way of living for those who seek God's accep-tance, and those are the real winners, and

■ *Riba cannot be charged when you lend to the poor*

30:39 that which you lay out for increase through the property of (other) people will have no increase with God. But that which ye lay out for charity, seeking the Countenance of God, [will in-crease]: it is these who will get a recompense multiplied.

■ *A Muslim should help the poor, regardless of whether they are Muslim or non-Muslim*

2:272 you are not expected to influence them to be guided to the righteous path [addressing the Prophet Muhammad], but indeed the Almighty guides whomsoever He will and chooses to, and whatever you spend in goodness will be for your own sake and ben-efit and will be rewarded back to you, and you will never be treated unjustly.

■ *The poor and needy must be treated with respect and dignity.* Those who give should not judge the needs by appearance. It is their duty to search for those who are poor and needy but do not show it. God knows all things, and God will reward those who help the poor and needy:

2:273 for the poor who were trapped by their poverty and those who know can recognize them by their sincere attitude. They are not able to work and contribute because they are poor, but they continue to keep their dignity. Those who do not know and the ignorant would expect them to be rich and capable, because they do not extend their hands and beg and ask people to help persistently in a repulsive way, and whatever you spend in goodness is well known by Almighty God.

2:274 Those who spend their money in public and in secrecy will bank their rewards with God, and no one should fear for their future well-being; and they will never grieve or be saddened.

■ *God's judgment is on those who charge riba on loans to the poor and the needy*

2:276 Almighty God obliterates and destroys Riba and He grows the charities paid in the way of God; and God does not like those who disobey His orders and who transgress.

2:278 Oh ye who believe, heed Almighty God and stop all what is left in the practice of riba if you are really believers.

2:279 and if you disobey and continue to charge riba, then expect the permission by God to the believers to stand to fight you by all means representing God and His Prophet; but if you repent, then you can get your original capital with you being treated unjustly or you treating others without justice.

■ *Debt forgiveness for those who cannot pay back*

2:280 And if the debtor who owes the money cannot pay back the principal capital because of his financial condition, then be considerate and work with them with mercy, ease, and compassion; and if you treat those who owe you money with kindness, charitable posture and ease is in fact better for you if you only know.

2:281 And be heedful of the day when you return back to the Creator and each soul will be given what it has earned while on earth and each will be treated with justice and equity.

Developing the Institution of Giving (*Zakah*) as a Required Islamic Ritual (Like Prayers)

To change the act of giving from being voluntary to being compulsory, and to underline the value of giving to the poor and needy and helping them, alms were included as one of the required five pillars of Islam. In other words, giving alms has the same weight as the pronouncement and witness of the faith, the prayers, the fasting during the month of Ramadan, and the *Hajj* (pilgrimage). It was also given a descriptive name, *zakah*, that implies that paying out alms in fact purifies and cleanses the rest of the assets.

The zakah is the annual obligatory ritual of purifying one's assets and income. The purposes of paying the zakah are to foster mutual caring and support between members of the community—both the rich and the poor; to purify the self, the soul, and the assets of each household; and to elevate the spiritual soul of purity and excellence. The Qur'aan reveals:

> *Those who pay out the zakah will be paid back by God and should not fear and consider zakah payment as a loss:*
> *2:277 Those believers who heed almighty God and do good deeds and pay their obligated zakah (alms) will be paid for their work by God, and there is no fear about their affairs and destiny, and they will not grieve or be sad.*

> *If you pay the zakah by helping to give the poor and needy without charging riba will multiply their returns on that investment with God:*
> *30:39 whatever you earned from riba sources to grow in peoples' assets will never grow in the sight of God, and whatever you pay in zakah, seeking the acceptance of God, indeed these are the ones who will multiply their returns and rewards.*

Zakah represents the backbone of the Islamic economic system and law (Shari'aa). Abu-Bakr, the first Caliph who assumed the responsibility of running the emerging Muslim State after Prophet Muhammad (pp), waged a campaign to capture those who refused to pay zakah after the death of Prophet Muhammad (pp) and put them on trial.

Prophet Muhammad (pp) also taught that one's assets never go down because of paying *zakah*. Prophet Muhammad (pp) pronounces (in the Hadeeth) that whenever the right of God in one's assets (that is, *zakah*) is not paid and stays mixed with one's assets, it destroys all assets. The *zakah* system and methods of collecting it are designed to gather and preserve assets in the House of Treasury of the community (*Bayt Ul Maal*) and to reinvest such assets in the community. The amount of *zakah* required to be paid depends on the way the assets of each household are saved and/or invested. The *zakah* system encourages community members to reinvest their assets and savings in the community (hence paying less *zakah*) and not to accumulate their savings as liquid (cash) assets (which requires higher *zakah*).

The rich who are expected to pay *zakah* may hesitate to pay it, because they may think that it will reduce their wealth. The Qur'aan teaches that it is one of the best investments one can make, because its return is 700 times the original investment:

> 2:261 *the parable of those who spend their substance in the way of God is that of a grain of corn: it grows seven ears, and each ear Hath a hundred grains. God gives manifold increase to whom He [God] pleases: And God cares for all and He knows all things.*

That is, a $1,000 investment with God in the form of spending to the poor and needy, as described above, is promised to yield 700 times the investment, or $700,000 in this life and more in the hereafter.

This money is used to primarily fulfill the needs of the poor and the needy. The Qur'aan reveals:

> 2:273 *[Charity is] for those in need, who, in God's cause are restricted [from travel], and cannot move about in the land, seeking [For trade or work]: the ignorant man thinks, because of their modesty, that they are free from want. You shall know them by their [Unfailing] mark: They beg not importunately from the entire sundry. And whatever of good ye give, be assured God knows it well.*

To further institutionalize the ritual of giving, the Qur'aan has defined eight categories that should benefit from the collected *zakah*. The Qur'aan defines these categories, as revealed in Chapter 9 (*Surah Taubah*—Repentance), verse 60.

1. *The poor:*

   They are defined as those who cannot afford to feed or clothe themselves and their families. The purpose of paying the zakah is twofold. First is the short-term goal of feeding and clothing the poor. The other purpose, which is a long-term goal, is to teach the poor professions that can help them become employed. An example is to teach a poor person how to drive a taxi so that he or she can qualify as a taxi driver. Working as a driver will allow him or her to earn a halal income, and move him/her from being poor and at the bottom of the social ladder to a step higher up: becoming a needy.

2. *The needy:*

   They are defined as those who have a job and receive income, but that income is not sufficient to meet all their needs. An example is a low-income taxi driver, who does not own the taxi but leases it from another owner because he/she, the needy, cannot get credit. In the system of zakah distribution, the needy would be given RF credit that would help him/her own a taxi, drive it, and eventually grow to own other taxis that would hire the poor (see category 1). This improvement in employment would eventually raise his/her status from being needy to the next step up the social ladder: becoming a small business owner.

3. *The administrators*:

They are those who collect and administer the process of zakah collection, distribution, accounting, and investment.

4. *Those who need to be helped, to integrate them and to bring them and their hearts closer to the community*:

A portion of the zakah funds is paid to this category to build bridges between these people and the community, in an effort to create a dignified, united, prosperous, and peaceful community regardless of faith, color, national origin, political orientation, gender, and/or language,

5. *Freeing the slaves*:

This category of spending is used to pay for the freeing and liberation of the slaves. This category also applies to many communities that are forced to live under the rule of dictators and who are longing for freedom and liberty.

6. *Relieving the heavily indebted*:

These members of the community are defined as those who accumulated a lot of debt due to unfortunate circumstances that are out of their hands.

7. *Spending in the way of God*:

A portion of the collected zakah can be donated to support any charitable effort to please God. Examples include building a school or a place of worship, or helping a student, a refugee, or a new immigrant.

8. *Helping travelers/wayfarers*:

These are newcomers and travelers who move to new locations or travel to establish a new life, to search for new opportunities, to develop new contacts, relationships and businesses, and/or to open new markets, but do not have the resources to do it. This money can be used to build hostels, community hotels, and facilities that would make it easier for people to travel and achieve their goals.

It is interesting to note that each outlet represents 12.5% of the total *zakah* collected. If an outlet does not need money, then the money is redistributed as needed to the other categories. Shari'aa allows the head of the state to levy an additional alms payment in case the treasury cannot meet its obligation.

Other sources of voluntary contributions to the poor and the needy come from voluntary donations to excel over and above the obligatory *zakah*. This voluntary giving, called *sadaqah*, can be paid through the system of zakah to the treasury of the community or can be managed and paid directly by the givers to the needy. Yet another source of funds for giving to the poor and the needy is *nazr*, a promissory donation that is the result of a personal promise between the believer involved and God. It is due and payable once the believer realizes his/her particular goal, dream, and/or wish. Nazr is paid directly by the giver to the specific entity identified while making the promise.

Behavioral Guidelines and the Discipline of Giving

Shari'aa places the following rules for giving. Some of these rules coincide with what was outlined earlier in the Jewish and Christian tradition. These rules are expanded further by Shari'aa to make them more standardized, fair, and universal:

1. Giving should never be associated with or followed by a grudge, a bad feeling (even in a concealed way), or even a frown. The teachings of Judaism, Christianity, and Islam are essentially similar on this front. The Qur'aan teaches:

   2:264 *O ye who believe! Cancel not your charity by reminders of your generosity or by injury—like those who spend their substance to be seen of men, but believe neither in Allah nor in the Last Day. They are in parable like a hard, barren rock, on which is a little soil: on it falls heavy rain, which leaves it [just] a bare stone. They will be able to do nothing with aught they have earned. And Allah guides not those who reject faith.*

2. The motivation behind giving is only to please God. This will result in self-content, peace at heart, and peace of mind, leading those who practice it to further successes. Giving should not be intended to show off. Giving can be done in public, but it is preferred to be done in secret in order to receive the highest reward from God:

2:271 If ye disclose (acts of) charity, even so it is well, but if ye conceal them, and make them reach those [really] in need, that is best for you: It will remove from you some of your [stains of] evil. And God is well acquainted with what ye do.

2:274 Those who [in charity] spend of their goods by night and by day, in secret and in public, have their reward with their Lord: on them shall be no fear, nor shall they grieve.

3. Giving should be from the same stocks that are available to us, and not from the lowest quality of products or assets in order to "dump" them on the poor and needy.

2:267 O ye who believe! Give of the good things which ye have [honorably] earned, and of the fruits of the earth which We have produced for you, and do not even aim at getting anything which is bad, in order that out of it ye may give away something, when ye yourselves would not receive it except with closed eyes. And know that God is Free of all wants, and worthy of all praise.

4. Those who can afford to give but they do not, the Qur'aan compares to those who follow Satan. And those who follow Satan are promised deep poverty and failure:

2:268 The Devil and Evil one leads you to poverty and bid you to conduct unseemly. God promises you His forgiveness and bounties. And God/Allah cares for all and He knows all things.

Business Finance

In the early days of Arabia, people were in need of capital to finance their growing trading and business activities. Lenders would stipulate the time at which the loan had to be paid back. The borrower would pay a monthly interest (the cost of using the money or usury), and the loan would balloon to the original amount at maturity. If the borrower could not pay it back for any reason—including reasons that were out of the borrower's control, such as crop failure due to a drought, or a severe downturn in the economy—the lender would agree to extend the term of the loan, but the extension would be conditional on increasing the amount of the original loan. In today's banking practices, this is known as an "interest-only term loan with a balloon payment" at the end of the term. If an arrangement is not reached, the lender would immediately foreclose on the collateral property. These loans have been used since the times of Moses (pp) and Jesus (pp) by the money lenders and money changers. When the loans could not be paid back, they would confiscate the farmers' land and properties, rendering them poorer and enslaving them by requiring them to pay the loans back with their labor.

The following is an outline of the RF business law (Shari'aa) as depicted from the Qur'aan and the tradition (Sunnah) of Prophet Muhammad (pp).

1. Shari'aa requires full documentation in writing and in the presence of witnesses when term credit is granted:

   2:282 O You who have attained to faith! Whenever you give or take credit for a stated term, set it down in writing. And let a scribe write it down equitably between you; and no scribe shall refuse to write as God has taught him: thus shall he write. And let him who contracts the debt dictate; and let him be conscious of God, his Sustainer, and not weaken anything of his undertaking. And if he who contracts the debt is weak of mind or body, or is not able to dictate himself, then let him who watches over his interests dictate equitably.

2. In "on-the-spot" trades of ready and available merchandise, there is no need for a full contract, but the transaction must be confirmed by witnesses:

   2:282 If, however, [the transaction] concerns ready merchandise which you transfer directly [on the spot] unto one another, you will incur no sin if you do not write it down. And have witnesses whenever you trade with one another, but neither scribe nor witness must suffer harm; for if you do [them harm], behold, it will be sinful conduct on your part. And remain conscious of God, since it is God who teaches you [herewith]—and God has full knowledge of everything.

   2:283 And if you are on a journey and cannot find a scribe, pledges [may be taken] in hand: but if you trust one another, then let him who is trusted fulfill his trust, and let him be conscious of God, his Sustainer. And do not conceal what you have witnessed for, verily, he who conceals it is sinful at heart; and God has full knowledge of all that you do.

3. Shari'aa strictly prohibits riba. The Qur'aan has ruled in a clear way that riba is strictly prohibited:

> *2:275 Those who eat riba stand as those who have been touched and electrified by Satan, because they claim that buying and selling is like charging riba . . . but be on notice that God has allowed buying and selling transactions and He has forbid riba. For those who receive God's admonition and stop the practice of charging riba, they will own what has happened before this admonition reaches them, and his case will be in the custody; and those who return to charging riba (interest) for the use of money (usury), they will be the acquirers and owners of hellfire and in there they will remain to eternity.*

Prophet Muhammad (pp) has further explained and elaborated on the prohibition of riba in the Qur'aan. In Islam, the offense of charging, taking, paying, or even acting as a witness in a riba-based transaction is considered one of the worst seven offenses in the faith.[34,35,36]

To establish a universal and standardized legal code for and to regulate business transactions, Shari'aa identifies the following two types of riba, based on the Hadeeth of Prophet Muhammad (pp).

Types of Riba

There are two types of riba: *riba al-jahiliyah* and *riba al-fadl*.

Riba Al-Jahiliyah Riba al-jahiliyah means "the riba of the age of ignorance and paganism." It is also called *riba al-nassee'aa* (the riba that is constrained by a time limit and is time dependent). This type of riba was widely practiced by the pagan Arabs at the advent of Islam. This practice was conducted by borrowing money to return it at a certain date. If the debt was not paid on time, the creditor would levy an additional sum to prolong the payment through debt restructuring. This type of lending is similar to what today are called interest-only loans with a balloon payment at maturity. In this type of loan, the borrower pays only the interest (the rent on the money he owes) and, at maturity, he/she pays the original debt. If he/she does not, then a new agreement is concluded that increases the principal amount and prolongs the maturity date.

This type of lending was prohibited in the original sources of Judaism and Christianity, as well as in Islam. As the world grew and became more sophisticated, these types of loans were also used by others for business and for other commercial needs. In Islam, there is no doubt that this type of lending is prohibited[37] as ordained in the original sources of the Qur'aan and the Sunnah (tradition and living example)[38] of Prophet Muhammad (pp), and in adherence to the original teachings of Judaism and Christianity.

This makes this type of lending prohibited in the Judeo-Christian-Islamic tradition.

Another interesting practice by the pagan Arabs was of *Nass'ee*, or transposing the months of the lunar calendar they used in order to suit their needs. Nass'ee could involve shifting the end of the calendar year to coincide with a special event; in many cases, the calendar could be accelerated or manipulated to render large riba-based contracts in default. Manipulating the calendar could generate a large amount of delinquency payment for the lender through the practice of riba al nassee'aa. The Qur'aan says about the prohibition of this type of riba:

> *9:37 Verily the transposing (of a prohibited month) is an addition to Unbelief: the Unbelievers are led to wrong thereby: for they make it lawful one year, and forbidden another year, in order to adjust the number of months forbidden by God and make such forbidden ones lawful. The evil of their course seems pleasing to them. But God guides not those who reject Faith.*

This variety of riba has been prohibited in the original teachings of Moses (pp) and Jesus (pp), but was relaxed later. Shari'aa still renders these transactions as haram (divinely prohibited).

Riba Al-Fadl   This type of riba is defined as taking a loan for payment at a later date for a higher value, or selling an item for a profit (the word *fadl* means an excess over the cost or a premium). An example of this type of riba in today's lingo would be taking a $100,000 personal consumer loan from a bank and promising to pay $120,000 back in two years, or borrowing ten pounds of rice and promising to pay it back in the form of twenty pounds of rice after one year. Another practice in the marketplace was the bartering of goods of different types, natures, and qualities. For instance, one would exchange ten pounds of small-sized and low-quality dates for two pounds of larger, high-quality dates. The critical question in these types of transactions is the level of the premium used, what makes it 20 to 50 percent higher at a later date, and what index should be used to determine that premium. Another factor in these transactions is how to regulate transactions to minimize deception, speculation, and hoarding activities in the marketplace, thus establishing a fair market price. Such practices were all prohibited by the Prophet Muhammad (pp) in order to ascertain healthy markets that reflect the true forces of supply and demand. This type of riba has been prohibited for two purposes:

1. To minimize, if not remove, deceptive practices from the process of business dealings and transactions, such as those involved in barter trading. This prohibition also helps stabilize the market forces of supply and demand, which will eventually help to stabilize market prices and to minimize, and eventually remove, deception or *gharar* (deceptive practices, including misrepresentation about quality, supply/demand factors, pricing, and product types and specifications). The big question and most challenging issue has been (and I believe still is) how to obtain the most fair and representative market value of an item in a free market system and how to price it, especially in a world that was at the time dealing with nonstandardized currencies made of different materials (as opposed to today's world, in which fiat (paper) money is used everywhere). This issue will be discussed in more detail in Chapter 5.

2. To prevent the application and charging of riba al-nassee'aa, in case the indebted person is not able to service his debt due to conditions that are out of his/her control.

Shari'aa Prohibits Deceptive and Speculative Activities in Business Transactions (*Gharar*)

Another strictly prohibited condition of sales transactions is *gharar*, or deception. In fact, calling a transaction riba-free implies that it is also gharar-free. The word is derived from the Arabic root word *ghoroor*, meaning arrogance and deception. Gharar results in dissatisfaction of one of the parties involved in the transaction when it is revealed; it includes defrauding people and improperly taking away peoples' money and properties[39] (which is haram). Another definition that is more attuned to modern economics was given by the late Professor Mustafa Al-Zarqaa. He defined the forbidden gharar sale as "the sale of probable items whose existence or characteristics are not certain, the risky nature of which makes the transaction akin to gambling."[40] The Qur'aan lays the foundations for fair business dealings, stipulating that contracts must fully disclose all aspects and specifications of the items involved in the transaction:

> 6:159 . . . *give measure and weight with (full) justice; —no burden do We place on any soul, but that which it can bear; —whenever ye speak, speak justly, even if a near relative is concerned; and fulfill the covenant of God. Thus doth He command you, that ye may remember.*

17:35 Give full measure when ye measure, and weigh with a balance that is straight: that is the most fitting and the most advantageous in the final determination.

83:1–6 Woe to those that deal in fraud —Those who, when they have to receive by measure from men, exact full measure —But when they have to give by measure or weight to men, give less than due. —Do they not think that they will be called to account? —On a Mighty Day, A Day when (all) mankind will stand before the Lord of the Worlds?

Professor Elgamal[41] concludes that the meaning of gharar is conceptually "trading in risk, which cannot be defined." Examples are naked options, financial futures, and derivatives that are not backed by a tangible and verifiable asset. Examples are the sale of the catch of a fisherman before he goes fishing, or of a calf before it is born. In conclusion, the Judeo-Christian-Islamic Law Shari'aa in business transactions prohibits both riba and gharar. The RF system advocated in this book should be in fact labeled a riba- and gharar-free system, but we use the term RF for short. The prohibition of riba in fact implies that the transaction must also be gharar-free.

NOTES

1. (pp) stands for "May God's Prayers and Peace be showered onto them." In Arabic: "Sallaa Allahu Alayhi Wa Sallam – usually abbreviated as 's.'" This is a standard idiom that is uttered by all Muslims after the mentioning or hearing any of God's prophets' names mentioned.
2. Translations of the Qur'aan were obtained from www.Islamicity.com and is from two sources: (1) The Meaning of the Holy Qur'aan by Abdullah Yusuf Ali, Amana Publication, Beltsville, MD, USA and (2) The Qur'an, a translation by Muhammad Asad, Andalus Press, Gibraltar 1980. Islamicity Web site: www.islamicity.com is acknowledged for its indexing and search engines of the Qur'aan in different forms, most important of which is the phonetic search engine.
3. *Sunnah* is an Arabic word for the style, way of life, and tradition of the Prophet (pp).
4. Michael Hart: *The 100*, New York, 1978.
5. *Hadeeth* is an Arabic word meaning the documented body of sayings of Prophet Muhammad (pp).
6. *Seerah* is an Arabic word that means the documented full life story and autobiography of Prophet Muhammad (pp).
7. The Qur'aan, 2:136.
8. Mr. R. St John, Esq: Private communication.

9. Wayne A.M. Visser and Alastair McIntosh, Centre for Human Ecology. First published in: *Accounting, Business & Financial History*, 8:2, Routledge, London, July 1998, pp. 175-189.
10. Professor John Goldingay, Fuller Seminary, Pasadena, California.
11. Rabbi Yosef Kanefsky, Los Angeles, California: private communication; an invited paper presented at the LARIBA 2002 Annual Symposium and Awards Symposium, Pasadena, California, March 2002.
12. Published by permission from Rabbi Kanefsky.
13. Moses Maimonides is a great Jewish scholar, philosopher, and medical doctor who lived in Egypt and was one of the most prominent in the court of Saladin.
14. Professor Christopher Kaczor (http://bellarmine.lmu.edu/~ckaczor/), Department of Philosophy, Loyola Marymount University; private communication: A paper presented at the LARIBA Annual Symposium and Awards, Pasadena, California, March 2002.
15. Professor Kaczor states: "I make no claim to original historical research in this article, but have drawn upon many sources in coming to a deeper understanding of the issues at hand. I have especially drawn upon:

    A. Vermeersche, "Usury," *The Catholic Encyclopedia*, Volume XV, 1912, which is available online at: www.newadvent.org/cathen/15235c.htm and was downloaded on March 5, 2002.

    A. Vermeersche, "Interest," *The Catholic Encyclopedia*, Volume VIII, 1912, which is available online at www.newadvent.org/cathen/08077a.htm and was downloaded on March 5, 2002.

    David J. Palm, "Usury," *Encyclopedia of Catholic Apologetics* (San Francisco: Ignatius Press, 2002).

    John Noonan, *The Scholastic Analysis of Usury* (Cambridge: Harvard University Press, 1957).
16. Published by permission from Professor Christopher Kaczor, Loyola Marymount University, Los Angeles, California.
17. In Islamic literature there is a *qudsi* Hadeeth, or the words of God spoken to Prophet Muhammad, that says exactly the same meanings of the words described here.
18. Two sales in one sale is also prohibited in Islamic law.
19. The Qur'aan has a verse about those who raise debts in many multiples:
    3:130 O ye who believe! Devour not usury, doubled and multiplied; but fear Allah. that ye may (really) prosper.
20. St. Thomas Aquinas, *Summa Theologica*, II–II, question 78, article one.
21. Riba in Islamic law can be defined as the act of renting money at a price called the interest rate; according to the law, money cannot be rented, but fungible and rentable assets and services can.
22. N. P. Tanner, S.J. ed., *Decrees of the Ecumenical Councils*, vol. 1, p. 200.
23. *Catechism of the Catholic Church*, 2nd edition, 1997, #2269.
24. German Grisez, *The Way of the Lord Jesus, Vol. II: Living a Christian Life* (Quincy, Illinois: Franciscan Press, 1993), p. 834.

25. John Noonan, *The Scholastic Analysis of Usury* (Cambridge: Harvard University Press, 1957), p. 377.
26. St. Thomas Aquinas, *Summa Theologica* II–II, 78, article two, ad 1, emphasis added.
27. John Finnis, *Aquinas* (Oxford: Oxford University Press, 1998), 210.
28. Professor John Goldingay, Fuller Seminary, Pasadena, CA.
29. Published by permission of Professor John Goldingay, Fuller Seminary.
30. Based on the Islamic (Judeo-Christian-Islamic) Law, it is preferred that the indebted work for a defined wage, then use the wage to pay the debt. This way the indebted person would be treated fairly and equitably by marking the wage to the market prevailing rates charged in similar situations.
31. French Protestant theologian who lived from July 10, 1509 to May 27, 1564.
32. The Ansar Group started a similar effort in Canada, the Islamic Housing Cooperative; however, its growth was limited because of the lack of liquidity.
33. This was reported by Bukhari, Muslim, and others.
34. In the saying of " . . . the seven most devastating Sins." the Prophet Muhammad (pp) counted: "believing in partnership with God, murder . . . and eating riba . . . " as reported by Bukhari, Muslim, and others, [al Targhib wa al Tarhib, V 3, p 1].
35. The Prophet Muhammad (pp) said: "Four [persons] very truly God will not make them enter Heaven . . . and the eater of riba . . . " as Al Hakim reported [Al Targhib wa al Tarhib, v 3, p 5].
36. The Prophet Muhammad (pp) said that God put wrath on (cursed) the eater of riba and its payer, and those who witness and transcribe the contract involving riba; this was reported by Bukhari and Muslim.
37. From the Farewell Speech Ceremony of Prophet Muhammad (pp) before he died: "Vo, everything of the affair of jahiliyyah (paganism and ignorance) is let fall under my feet, the riba of jahiliyyah is let fall, and the first riba I abolish is the riba of al Abbas son of Abd al Muttalib, it is discarded, all" (principal and increase); reported and authenticated by Muslim.
38. The Hadeeth (sayings of Prophet Muhammad pp.), narrated by Abu Dawood and Tirmidhzi, reads:

   . . . and every Riba of Jahiliyyah is abolished. Neither shall you make [the debtor] suffer injustice [loss], nor shall you be made to suffer injustice, But the Riba of al Abbas son of Abd al Muttalib [the uncle of Prophet Muhammad (pp), who was active in Riba transactions before he became Muslim], it is discarded, all.

39. Fiqh Al Sunnah, Al Sayed Sabiq in Arabic – Volume III Sections 12, 13, and 14, page 79; Daar Al Kitaab Al Araby, Beirut, Lebanon—November 1971.
40. Mahmoud Elgamal, *Islamic Finance: Law, Economics and Practice* (Cambridge University Press), p. 58. Professor Elgamal's book details the conditions of sale and the types of deceptive practices that are major and minor. This book is a wonderful and very useful reference for those who are interested in the legal Shari'aa aspects of the prohibition of riba and gharar.
41. Ibid.

CHAPTER 3

The Rule of Commodity Indexation and the Principle of Marking to the Market

It is well known that Prophet Muhammad (pp), in addition to being God's commissioned Prophet, had been through many life experiences. He was a shepherd, a trusted conflict resolution arbitrator, a community leader, and a trusted manager of peoples' assets in caravan trading and investments. Business enabled him to see the world and taught him how the world works and how business is transacted. At the time he was commissioned, two major currencies were prevalent. These were the *dirham*, used by the Persian Empire and made of silver (it was also used by the Greeks and called *drachma*), and the *denarius*, used by the Roman Empire and made of gold. An important aspect of trading in caravans was transacting business in different currencies depending on where the trade was conducted. The final step of the trader's transaction was to convert all proceeds into the local currencies of his/her clients, who entrusted him/her with the management of their money and assets.

Prophet Muhammad (pp) came with a simple but revolutionary idea to establish the principles of pricing at fair value and the free market system and to remove deceptive and fraudulent activities in such free markets. The major challenge for caravan trading was to establish standardized rules of exchange because of the variety of currencies used at the time of the Prophet. The other challenge was to determine how to exchange different products for different uses while being fair and ensuring that the principles of fair value pricing and fair free markets were preserved. Prophet Muhammad (pp) set the rules of a new and innovative system that would bring to bear the teachings of Moses (pp) and Jesus (pp) in one final system that is riba-free and would signify for the first time in history the foundation of a Judeo-Christian-Islamic system manifested by the Law (Shari'aa).

The system called for relating the price of every item to a standard commodity that was produced and/or is used in each community. The system called for pricing products and services either in terms of ounces of gold or silver (as metal commodities) or in terms of a food item that was a staple in the community, such as—at that time of the Prophet—wheat, barley, dates, or salt. He also went on to rule that if one borrowed an ounce of gold it should be returned to the owner in an equal amount (i.e., only an ounce of gold) even if the repayment was not done hand-to-hand and was made after one year. If the repayment was more than an ounce, the transaction was considered a riba transaction and was considered haram (divinely prohibited). However, one can exchange one ounce of gold into ten bushels of wheat on the spot (hand-to-hand) or fifteen bushels after one year. This transaction would be legitimate based on Shari'aa and would be considered halal (divinely allowed).

The Prophet Muhammad (pp) has ordained, according to his sayings (*Hadeeth*), the following rule regarding buying/selling, exchanges, trading, and bartering:

If a buy/sell agreement involves currency, then one can *only* exchange *without increase*:

- Gold for gold in same weight,
- Silver for silver in same weight

If the buy/sell agreement involved food items, then one could only use a set of staple food commodities reference/index commodity item without increase, regardless of the quality or the type of that food item. For example, exchanging ten small dates for two large dates is haram. The rule goes further to stipulate that the rule used for precious metals above is also extended to cover the following *Reference Index of Food Staples Commodities*:

- Wheat for wheat
- Barley for barley
- Dates with dates
- Salt for salt

To ensure and to be certain that there is no increase (riba), the exchange must be done on an on-the-spot basis (hand-to-hand).

Please also note that the items listed above were only for illustration purposes; the Prophet(s) used them because they were either the currencies used at that time (in case of the gold denarius or silver dirham) or staple foods used then. One can expand on the rule using the same concept, depending on the prevailing conditions in a certain country.

This concept is similar to using an index of reference commodities as a means of checking the stability of a certain local currency, especially in a world that is run by fiat or paper money. It is interesting to note that James Baker, III, former Secretary of Treasury of the United States, told world financial leaders in 1987 that the Reagan administration "is prepared to consider"[1] using the price of gold in trying to steer its own and the world economies. Gold, Mr. Baker explained, could be used in a specially designed index along with other commodities to help governments discern inflation and then adjust their policies by raising interest rates or taxes, for example.

Further research was conducted by many scholars to expand on the concept of using the six commodities above. Imam Abu Haneefah (the pioneer of a school of jurisprudence carrying his name, the *Hanafi* Law) and Imam Ahmad (another well placed scholar with his own school of jurisprudence) concluded that we could expand the list of reference commodities depending on the community in which we live, but with the condition that the commodity can be weighed or measured accurately without transformation over time (as in the case perishables or metals that are susceptible to being rusted out). Imam Shafi'ee (a scholar who has his own school of jurisprudence; the *Shafi'ee* Law) ruled that these indexation items can be eatables that can preserve value or legal tender such as gold and silver (and may be other precious elements). Imam Malik (a scholar with his own school of jurisprudence, the *Maliki* Law) suggested that these can be food commodities or items that can offer a lasting store of value.

The main rule goes like this[2]:

1. In barter exchanges, if the two items are the same in elemental form (e.g., gold for gold, silver for silver, etc.) or are used in the same way (e.g., food, in the case of wheat and barley), then for this exchange to be legal, the quantity (weight, volume, or numbers of units) should be the same, regardless of the quality of the item.
2. The exchange must be conducted on the spot (hand-to-hand).
3. If the two items differ in substance but not in use, then fadl (or increase in exchange ratio by adding a premium) can be practiced, but riba al nassee'aa (the charging of a delinquency penalty in case of not paying back in time as agreed, due to conditions that are out of control), cannot be applied. For example, if gold was sold in terms of silver (different substance, but same use as metals used as a value of tender or as an ornament) or wheat in terms of rice (wheat and rice are different substances but used for same purpose, i.e., as food), it is permissible to use a ratio that is not 1:1 as established by the free market forces of supply and demand as required when exchanging gold for gold.

4. If the two items differ in substance and in purpose of use, then it is halal (divinely permissible) to both practice fadl and defer payment over a certain period of time. For example, one can buy wheat for gold, and the payment can be deferred. There would be two prices: The on-the-spot price (hand-to-hand) can be set at 20 bushels of wheat for an ounce of gold, and the deferred price can be, say, 25 bushels of wheat for an ounce of gold after 1 year. However, it is very important to note that the rules of riba al al-nassee'aa should be implemented (i.e., there should be no late payment penalty if the lateness is justified, as in cases of job loss, crop failure due to weather conditions, an unexpected dire need, or a change in the prevailing economic situation).

Conceptually, to be fair to all people both inside a country and internationally, the price of an item—based on the Judeo-Christian-Islamic Law pioneered by the Prophet Muhammad (pp)—should always be related to the weight or volume of a commodity that either is mined from a natural resource, like precious metals, gold, copper, salt, oil, or silver, or is a food staple produced by the hard work of the farmer, using earth with its natural nutrients and water provided by rain, flowing rivers, and underground water tables, such as corn, wheat, dates, and barley. The Qur'aan reveals:

> 2:164 Behold! in the creation of the heavens and the earth; in the alternation of the night and the day; in the sailing of the ships through the ocean for the profit of mankind; in the rain which God Sends down from the skies, and the life which He gives therewith to an earth that is dead; in the beasts of all kinds that He scatters through the earth; in the change of the winds, and the clouds which they Trail like their slaves between the sky and the earth; —[Here] indeed are Signs for a people that are wise.
>
> 7:57 It is He Who sendeth the winds like heralds of glad tidings, going before His mercy: when they have carried the heavy-laden clouds, We drive them to a land that is dead, make rain to descend thereon, and produce every kind of harvest therewith: thus shall We raise up the dead: perchance ye may remember.
>
> 15:22 And We send the fecundating winds, then cause the rain to descend from the sky, therewith providing you with water [in abundance], though ye are not the guardians of its stores.

It is interesting to contrast the use of these basic tangible products as references to price other items in the market. It is well-known that commodities such as food, minerals, and metals are produced by the hard work of people. For minerals and metals, people explore for them and mine them out of the earth. For food, people plant and cultivate it on farms, producing staple foods like corn, wheat, barley, soybeans, or rice which require land preparation and special climates for each type of plant. Therefore, there are various products in various locations. Through free trade, people not only make business deals with each other, but also get to know each other and to respect each others' cultures as they trade together. Combining the hard work of the people with God's gifts to us, like the earth, its fertility, its water resources needed for irrigation, and the specific weather conditions in each of geographic locations, would produce basic staple food products that can be used as a reference commodity index.

These products were used by the Prophet Muhammad (pp) to set references or indexes for pricing and trading. Compare this concept with the printing press that produces paper banknotes with little effort, except for the analytical minds and political currents that decide how much money to print or withdraw from the monetary system, based on economic and monetary statistics. Printing too much of these banknotes (paper money) without paying attention to local economies of production can be a major contributor to inflation; the opposite can be true, as well. The system also depends on the great minds of economists, monetarists, statisticians, mathematicians, and computer-based modeling. Such talents, techniques, and expertise are important and they may not be available in every country. In fact, most countries—except for a few developed nations led by the United States, Germany, and the United Kingdom—are not endowed with a large pool of such talented experts.

In an attempt to apply the rules above, an effort was invested to study the price history of different commodities and to apply the commodity indexation rule, introduced earlier, to our regular investment transactions. For example, in 1974 we bought a house in Plano, a suburb of Dallas, Texas for $46,000 with a down payment of $3,500. In 1977, it sold for $65,000. We were very happy to have realized a return on the house value of $19,000. That translates to a price increase of 41 percent in two years on the house in terms of U.S. dollars. The dollar return on the original out-of-pocket investment of $3,500 was $19,000, or a 543 percent return on investment. It should be noted that all of these wonderful returns were in U.S. dollars. However, if we had measured the return on investment in terms of one of the six reference commodities listed above, the result would be revealing;

- ■ In terms of wheat, because bread is a staple food item in the United States: We bought the house for an equivalent of 9,957 bushels of wheat (wheat in 1974 was $4.62 a bushel). We sold it in 1977 for the equivalent of 29,630 bushels of wheat (wheat was $2.16 a bushel).

That is a return of 300 percent on the value of the house, in terms of wheat. As to the return on invested capital of $3,500, or the equivalent of 757 bushels of wheat, we realized a profit of $19,000, equivalent to 8,796 bushels of wheat—a return on equity in wheat terms of 11,620 percent.

- In terms of gold, the picture is different. The value of the house was equivalent to 421 ounces of gold (the gold price in 1974 was $103 per ounce). We sold it in 1977 for 428.6 ounces of gold (the gold price was $149.33 per ounce). This translates to an appreciation in the price of the house of 1.8 percent in terms of gold. The return on invested capital of $19,000, or 127.23 ounces of gold, on an original investment of $3,500, or 33.97 ounces of gold, yielded a return of 374.7 percent.

Naturally, life 1,400 plus years ago was far simpler than it is today. The matrix of an average citizen's production and demands in a country is more diversified now and is by far more complex and different between one country and another. For example, those who want to think in terms of wheat (in this case, wheat farmers) cannot live on wheat alone, because they will need to buy farm equipment, as well as fuel for heating and for operating the farm equipment. He or she will obtain credit to finance these agricultural activities. On the other hand, we cannot live on gold, because we cannot eat or drink it. It should be made clear here that in discussing the commodity indexation concept we do not imply a return to the gold standard. What is strongly recommended here is a pioneering new system that uses a reference commodity like gold or a basket of commodities peculiar to each country, depending on its production and demand matrix, similar to the concept for the basket used for measuring inflation and the concept proposed by James Baker III in 1987 to detect economic "bubbles" in a local economy. Fiat (paper) money can be used, and the U.S. dollar may continue to be the reserve currency of the world, but to complement it and to be fair, a basket of commodities based on the concept pioneered by Prophet Muhammad (pp), as described above, must be implemented to be fair to all people and all nations and to price things fairly in the market while detecting any "bubble" overpricing as is usually experienced in energy prices and as was experienced in the United States housing bubble that led to the 2008 economic meltdown. It also will help central bankers with their most important job of keeping inflation under control. It is interesting to note that this basket of commodities concept can change, not only from country to country, but also from time to time, with changes in the production mix in a certain country. This concept will prompt nations to produce and become efficient producers to improve the value of their currencies. It is hoped that economic and monetary research centers would research this concept to come up with useful ideas and propose policies that can be useful in the future.

DEVELOPMENT OF THE MARK-TO-THE-MARKET RULE

Another issue came up involving barter trading during the time this Law (Shari'aa) was being developed by the Prophet (pp). The challenge was how to deal with items that could be measured using more than one method—such as, for instance, palm tree dates, as experienced during the time of the Prophet Muhammad (pp). Palm dates can be dry or fresh; they can be measured in size (large, medium, and small) or in numbers of dates, or in terms of weight. Another example, in the case of food items, is that one can exchange rice for rice but the parties may disagree because one party's rice is inferior in quality to the other party's rice. For dates, it might be that one party had larger dates while the other's dates are smaller and of sweeter quality. In both these cases, using the commodity indexation rule required in RF banking and finance, one can only exchange the same weight of rice without increase regardless of size and quality. Another example is the case of dates or grapes. There are fresh dates or grapes and there are dried dates and raisins. The question was "Are they the same food items?" The answer was yes, and when they are exchanged they must be in equal amounts: that is 100 small dates for 100 large dates, because dates are dates. This issue came up when one of Prophet Muhammad's (pp) companions (Bilal, the Ethiopian) brought him a gift of large, very high-quality dates. The Prophet (pp) knew that Bilal did not have the means to afford buying these high-quality large dates. He inquired. Bilal told him that he saved his ration of low-quality dates for some time and that he went to the market and exchanged them for a smaller number of higher-quality, larger dates. The Prophet Muhammad (pp) told him that this transaction was classified as riba and was divinely prohibited (haram). When Bilal asked what he should have done, the Prophet (pp) said that the small-sized low-quality dates should have been marked to market by selling them in terms of another commodity, such as gold, silver, rice, wheat, or barley, and that he should have used the proceeds to buy the large, higher-quality dates. This way, deception (gharar), misrepresentation, and interference in the market forces would be minimized and hopefully eliminated. This process helps to standardize and stabilize markets, allowing the efficient working of the market forces of supply and demand.

This is what is called *marking to market*. This concept has been used by LARIBA since 1988 and is the main reason for its superior portfolio performance over the years.

The marking-to-market concept is believed to be one of the most important historic developments in this RF system. It lays the foundation of fair pricing for products and services, based on real market values within an open and free market operation. Marking to market is the foundation of the analytical system used by LARIBA[3] to operate in an RF finance mode that is unique. The RF banking brand is not based on renting money at a price (interest) but on the actual measured fair market rent of properties, businesses, and services. For example, consider buying a house. The buyer who wants to obtain RF financing and the RF finance institution should mark the house to market. The best way of doing that is to find out how much a similar house in the same neighborhood and with similar specifications would rent/lease for in terms of U.S. dollars per square foot. This mutually agreed-upon market lease rate is used to calculate the rate of return on investment of the purchase transaction, looking at it as an investment. If the rate of return on investment makes economic sense (i.e., it is equal to or higher than the expected return by our RF investors), the RF bank proceeds to finance (invest in) the property. In addition, the RF bank does its best to make the monthly payments in the RF mode of financing competitive with those offered by riba-based banks. A very low return implies that this investment would be inferior; the RF banker would advise the customer not to invest, and the RF bank would not finance (co-invest in) it.

RIBA-FREE BUSINESS TRANSACTION MODELS

The following is an abbreviated list of the RF finance models used to finance commercial transactions. This is not a comprehensive list. It is designed to familiarize the reader with the concepts used in the different models. It is important to note that it is preferred to call these models by the names that describe them; and the reader will notice that we have included the original Arabic name next to the English name of each model.

Cost-Plus (*Murabaha*)

The cost-plus (*murabaha*) model is mainly used for commodity and trade financing. In a cost-plus contract, the client would approach the RF finance institution to finance the purchase of a certain item, such as a cargo of soybeans, a car, a house, a commercial building, a business, or a franchise, because the client does not have the funds to purchase it in cash. Here is a brief summary of the steps taken:

1. The customer issues an order to the RF bank or finance company to buy the items on the customer's behalf.
2. The RF finance institution buys the item in its own name first. The title of that item transfers from the seller to the RF finance institution.
3. The RF finance institution sells the item to the customer at a mutually agreed-upon price over a period of time long enough to pay that price back on a monthly basis (for example). The sale price charged by the RF financial institution to the customer is equal to the original purchase price the RF bank paid, plus a profit element for the RF bank. As a result of this sales step, the title transfers from the RF finance company to the client. It is important to note that the profit element should be agreed upon in light of the marking-to-market principle discussed above, not to simply take the prevailing interest rate on money and call it profit!

It is important to note that the sale price agreed upon between the RF finance institution and the customer, as well as the period of time (term) to pay back, is final, as are the terms of payment. For example, if the term of payment was agreed upon to be five years and the customer had a legitimate excuse to extend it over a longer period of seven years, the agreed-upon sale price would stay the same and there would be no increase—otherwise, the transaction would be deemed riba al jahiliyah or riba al nassee'aa, which are divinely prohibited (*haram*).

On the other hand, if the customer wants to expedite payments so that he or she pays over a two-year period instead of a five-year period, the agreed-upon price would still be the same unless the RF finance company agrees out of its free will to reduce the price to accommodate a special request from the customer. This request can be denied, which is acceptable under Shari'aa and is deemed halal, or it can be accepted, as it is in most cases, and that is also halal.

There are a number of issues that are associated with the cost-plus (murabaha) transaction. These are:

1. The two buy/sell steps (from seller to RF finance company and then from the finance company to buyer) constitute, theoretically, two changes of title. This will trigger tax events that would call for the taxation of the transaction, making it more expensive to finance in many Western societies. The RF finance company selling to the customer at a higher price may be considered a capital gain, subject to capital gains taxes in the United States and many other countries. The tax burden in this case

may be onerous. That is why many of the cost-plus models used by "Islamic" institutions in the West include a *rider* or another contract that contains a condition that makes the ultimate buyer—not the RF bank—responsible for any capital gains taxes. This solution is unfair to those who want to abide by their faiths. It is also unfair that the RF Bank claims to be Islamic while throwing all the risk back to the customer.

2. Banking institutions are not allowed by the banking laws and regulations in the West to participate in direct transactions as principles or to take title of properties (unless the property is repossessed; however, such properties are handled in a special way, and banks are expected to dispose of them as soon as is practical). To get around this rule and appear to satisfy the legal aspect of Shari'aa while potentially sacrificing the spirit of Shari'aa, many attorneys resort to using structured financial tools involving a separate but expensive offshore (sometimes) Special Purpose Vehicle (SPV), which buys the property and sells it back to the customer. This approach helps the RF bank avoid the violation of the banking laws while appearing to fulfill the requirements of Shari'aa.

3. The well-known banking regulation called Regulation "Z" (Truth in Lending Act) in the United States requires disclosure of an (*implied*) interest rate of any operation that involves lending transactions.

4. Cost-plus transactions bear a striking similarity to regular interest-based banking transactions because of the way the profit element is figured out and calculated. This profit is usually tied to the prevailing interest rate in the market.

These issues will be further addressed in Chapters 9 and 10.

Leasing (*Ijara*)[4]

Rules   Shari'aa includes rules about renting (short-term) or leasing (long-term) of the right to use an item (usufruct). The rules that organize the act of leasing are as follows:

1. Renting or leasing is defined by Shari'aa as a contract to take advantage of renting the right to use an item. It is important to stress here that the item to be leased must have a usufruct. For example, one can rent the use of a car or a house while keeping title of ownership to the car or the house (because they are nonfungibles). However, one cannot rent the use of an apple (fungible), because once it is eaten, it will not exist and one would have infringed on its ownership.

2. The two categories of commodities indexation described in riba al-fadl, including gold or silver and food, cannot be leased or rented because they cannot be used without being consumed. For example, one cannot

rent a cow in order to collect its milk. That is because when one collects the milk, one acts as if one owns the milk. This is problematic, because the original contract was about leasing the origin (i.e., the cow), not about owning the product (i.e., the milk).
3. The usufruct—or the beneficiary use of the subject—can be the use of:
   a. An asset like a home
   b. The facility of an asset, such as the use of a car (for driving), a business like a franchise store, a medical clinic, or an X-ray machine
   c. The work or productive services of an individual, such as an engineer, a builder, a worker, or any person who can offer defined valuable work

The Riba-Free Legal Foundation on Leasing   Leasing is allowed according to the revelations in the Qur'aan, the Sunnah (way of life and the tradition) of Prophet Muhammad[5] (pp), and the unanimous opinion of the eminent scholars.

In the Qur'aan:

43:32 Is it they who would portion out the Mercy of thy Lord? It is We Who portion out between them their livelihood in the life of this world: and We raise some of them above others in ranks, so that some may command work from others [through renting their services]. But the Mercy of thy Lord is better than the [wealth] which they amass.

2:233 If ye decide on [renting the services of)] a foster-mother for your offspring, there is no blame on you, provided ye pay [the mother] what ye offered, on equitable terms. But fear God and know that He sees well what ye do.

28:26 Said one of the [damsels]: "O my [dear] father! engage him [rent the services of Prophet Moses] on wages: truly the best of men for thee to employ is the [man] who is strong and trusty."

28:27 He said: "I intend to wed one of these my daughters to thee, on condition that thou serve me for eight years; but if thou complete ten years, it will be [grace] from thee. But I intend not to place thee under a difficulty: thou wilt find me, indeed, if God wills, one of the righteous."

Process
1. At the request of the client, the RF finance company would purchase the item and lease it back to the client for a predefined term.
2. The RF financial institution, in its capacity as a lessor, would own title to the asset and in turn would lease the right for its use to the lessee, who

would proceed to use the item according to the term of the mutually agreed-upon leasing contract. The client pays a monthly or periodic lease payment at a market rate that is marked to market and has been agreed upon between the RF finance company (lessor) and the client (lessee).

The fundamental question here is the rate at which the asset is leased. In many cases, the "Islamic" banking officer would quote the interest rate of the day as an agreed-upon lease rate. This approach presents a serious problem with Shari'aa. The lease quote used must correspond to the actual market lease rate as researched by both parties. These and other issues will be discussed in greater detail in Chapter 10.

In this context there are two types of riba-based leasing available in the market. These are:

1. *Rental or Lease (ijarah):* This finance method offers pure leasing of assets. The asset is leased for a specific period of time and then returned to the title holder. These leases are similar to leasing an automobile for two or three years then returning it to the owner. However, it is interesting to note that in today's leasing practices, the monthly lease payment is based on a projected value of the item at the end of the lease term (like the projected value of a car, say, after three years). This practice is not acceptable in Judeo-Christian-Islamic Law, because no one can project the future market price of an item; only God knows the future. That is why the price at the end of the lease has to be marked to the active live market at that time.
2. *Lease-To-Own (ijarah-wa-imtilak* or *ijarah-wa-iqtinaa):* In this method of leasing, the user and title owner agree to a monthly payment that consists of two parts. One part has to do with the gradual purchase of the property by the lessee, and the other part has to do with the rental of either the money, as in the riba-based financial leases, or the rental of the actual asset at the prevailing market rate, as in RF leasing.

This model will be discussed in detail in Chapter 10, and a real case application will be presented in Chapter 14.

Joint Venture (*Musharaka*) Direct Investment/ Equity Ownership or Partnership

In this model, the RF financial institution or its investment subsidiary enters into a direct investment with the customer in the form of equity ownership. Profit or loss would be assigned to each joint venture according to a well-defined distribution formula.

Money Management (*Mudaraba*)

In this model, the RF financial institution itself can act as a money manager through its investment banking and finance company.

The RF financial institution can also delegate that function, as a trusted and appointed representative through a valid proxy, to other money managers.

The money management (*mudaraba*) contract would define the responsibility of the RF bank in its capacity as a money manager (*mudharib*) or as an agent of the client (*wakeel*, which means a representative with discretionary authority) to find money manager(s) who will meet the client's defined investment objective, investment time horizon, and the risk tolerance.

Financing Future Production (*Ba'i ul Salam*)

This model is used to finance the cost of future production of a manufactured product or an orchard. The customer would agree with the RF finance company to forward the cost of future production. The RF financial institution would come to an agreement to buy the production of an orchard, a farm, or a manufactured product (like equipment or automobiles) before it is produced, at an agreed-upon price. The money is paid in advance to the producer. The producer, in turn, would use the money as a working capital to purchase the basic services, pay wages, and buy raw materials necessary for the production. This way, the RF financial institution would help in the growth of the economy by providing the liquidity needed by the producing entity. An important guideline that should be guarded against is the possibility of hoarding or "cornering" of free markets by the financing entity.

The above RF financing techniques are presented to familiarize the reader with the models used. For a detailed outline and description of these techniques, please refer to an excellent book on the subject: *Understanding Islamic Finance*.[6]

NOTES

1. Peter Kilborn, "Baker Hints at Gold as Guide on Policy," *The New York Times*, October 1, 1987.
2. Syed Saabiq, *Fiqh Al Sunnah, Arabic*, Volume 3, p. 138, Daar Al Kitaab Al Araby for Publishing and Distribution, Beirut, Lebanon, November 1971.
3. Please visit www.LARIBA.com for more details.

4. Syed Saabiq, *Fiqh Al Sunnah*, *Arabic*, Volume 3. p. 177 Daar Al Kitaab Al Araby for Publishing and Distribution, Beirut, Lebanon, November 1971.
5. Prophet Muhammad (pp) was reported to have said, "Give the person you hire his/her wages before the sweat that they invested on the job dries up," meaning to pay them as soon as possible (related by Ibn Majah).
6. Muhammad Ayub, *Understanding Islamic Finance*, Wiley Finance, 2007.

CHAPTER 4

Shari'aa

Shari'aa Boards in Islamic Banks: An Overview and a Vision for the Future

Chapter 2 gave a historic overview of how interest was prohibited in the Judeo-Christian-Islamic faiths. During the early medieval period, the Islamic RF models were used by caravan traders conducting business between Arabia and the rest of the world, and in particular in trading through the Silk Road. As commercial and business activities increased, and with the growth of international trade and the creation of money, a sophisticated riba-based banking system emerged and developed in Europe. The prohibition of ribit/riba was relaxed by the rabbinical teachings, the Roman Catholic Church, and the Protestant churches, as detailed in Chapter 2. This chapter is designed to introduce the reader to the tedious, meticulous, and detailed processes used by qualified religious scholars in the faith to come up with legal religious rulings (edicts or *fatwa*) that would comply with the teaching of God and His prophets to offer solutions to everyday challenges experienced by the believer.

Muslims are required by Islamic Law (Shari'aa) not to deal in riba. Religious leaders and scholars at all levels of the Muslim Ummah, from the small village to the largest cities, are taught that dealing in riba is a major sin. With the growth of commerce, trading, and industrial development in Europe, more sophisticated riba-based banking operations and trade financing tools were developed to give credit and to help grow businesses. When Europeans began expanding their trade routes into the Turkish Ottoman Empire and colonizing many of their former member states, they brought this new riba-based banking system with them. The riba-based banking system was only used to serve the needs of most of the European business people and their local representatives. The local Muslim business community did not use it, because they believed that banking with interest was not accepted by the Muslims and their leaders. This produced, among the local Muslim population, a subculture of avoiding taking a loan altogether. Many may ask how the Muslims have managed their capital needs all these years. It was done as microlending between friends and family members on the local levels or between businessmen on the commercial level in an informal way; it is still being done now, in the 21st century. On the local community level, a group of, say, 10 friends might agree to start an informal small cooperative union, in which each of them places $10 with a trusted member of the group. They then agree, among themselves, as to the schedule of who gets paid in the first month, the second month, and so on. In this way, each member gets a sum of $100 in a certain month. There was no interest charged. The banking needs of the Muslim world, as in all developing countries, have been underserved, especially on the retail level. As these primitive societies began making contact with the world, they woke up to a big surprise. They found that they are at least 600 years behind. A sophisticated and far-reaching international banking system was installed, and banking with interest became part of normal business transactions in many of these countries. Dissent and concern were expressed constantly by the religious leaders, but no one responded, because the religious leaders in the early to middle part of the 20th century did not have enough stature and were ignored.

With the first oil price jump in 1973 came huge amounts of dollars to the oil-producing Gulf countries. The main concern at that time was the absorptive capacity of the local economies of the countries involved. Armies of commercial bankers and investment bankers landed in these oil-producing countries to expand the existing small riba-based banking operations and to link them efficiently with the international banking system. Many of the business and community leaders went along, but a few were very troubled at the sinful act of participating in riba.

One of them was the late King Faisal of Saudi Arabia. He pledged in 1974 to start a banking system that follows Islamic Law (Shari'aa). The major problem was the lack of a detailed code in Shari'aa that dealt with the existing and sophisticated needs of the customers of the banks and the varied products and services offered by these banks, which were all based on the prohibited riba. This marked the beginning of a brand-new field of scholarly research to develop codes of Shari'aa that pertain to modern RF business dealings and banking. Pioneering practitioners of Islamic banking in Egypt, Dubai, Saudi Arabia, and Kuwait began by contacting scholars in the highest placed Islamic theological seminary, Al Azhar Seminary in Cairo, Egypt. Because the idea was new, the task was very difficult; and because it involved bridging 600 years of a riba-based banking system in special banking-based English, which had not yet been mastered by the scholars, a solution was offered. The few leaders of the newly emerging Islamic banking industry formed a board of scholars that would start the difficult task of developing the RF banking and finance codes of shari'aa. That was the beginning of the creation of what is now known as Shari'aa Boards of Islamic Banks.

The religious scholars on the Shari'aa Board soon discovered that they did not know much about finance, banking, and monetary issues; they even did not know about the intricacies of bank operations and the riba-based aspects of it. All that was known then were two major rules: Interest cannot be charged; and the parties in a commercial transaction must share the profit and loss. In an effort to bridge the knowledge gap, the Islamic banking practitioners supplied the Shari'aa Boards with riba-based banking practitioners to teach and explain in a crash course format how modern riba-based banks operated and the features of each riba-based banking product and service. Because English was an international banking medium of communication, there was a new demand for scholars who understood and spoke English. Most of these English-speaking scholars did not come from the Arabic-speaking countries; they came from the Asian Muslim countries, such as Pakistan, Malaysia, India, and Bangladesh. Many of these Asian scholars who had mastered English had also mastered Arabic, because it is a prerequisite for Shari'aa scholarship.This cross-breeding of talents and diversified cultural and educational backgrounds created a rich body of qualified scholars at the Shari'aa Board level. However, because of the diversity in local cultural and educational backgrounds, there were a variety of opinions on what was considered compliant with Shari'aa and what was not. Two major directions were charted. In Egypt and Malaysia (most of the Malaysian scholars had been educated at Al Azhar seminary), Shari'aa opinions were more progressive and understanding. Scholars from India, Pakistan, and the Arab Gulf countries believed in a more strict approach toward interpreting what was halal (allowed) and what was haram (not allowed). As time went by, new leaders in the field of Islamic/Shari'aa-based finance law came from Pakistan, India, Egypt, Sudan, the Arab Gulf countries, Malaysia, Syria, Jordan, Lebanon, Europe, and the United States.

THE LAW: SHARI'AA

The word *Shari'aa* has been translated by most as *jurisprudence*. However, it is believed that the word *jurisprudence* does not fully describe what Shari'aa is. It is preferred to translate Shari'aa as "the Law." This approach follows the same tradition as the revelations to Moses (pp), which were translated as "the Law," and to Jesus (pp) as "the Gospel" (implying "the Law"). The use of the terminology "the Law," also confirms the Judeo-Christian-Islamic nature of the religion of Islam.

The word *Shari'aa* is derived from[1] the root Arabic word *Shara'aa'*, which means "to introduce." "to enact," and "to prescribe." It is comprised of and embodies spiritual beliefs and rules of the religion that includes ethics, morality, and behavioral admonitions. It is the divine, immutable Law. It details the set of rules a Muslim should live, judge, and govern by, and it includes the moral and legal rulings and mandates of Islam. In other words, it is the integration of all the laws sent by God through His prophets.

Sources of Shari'aa

The principles and sources of Shari'aa[2] are: the Qur'aan, which is the unchangeable and the proven inculcation of all God's messages to all His prophets, including the Torah and the Gospel; and the way of life and example of living (Sunnah) and sayings (Hadeeth) of Prophet Muhammad (pp).

The Qur'aan Being a Muslim is a description of the state of a person who has chosen to submit his/her will to that of God. Based on this foundation, the Qur'aan teaches that Noah (pp), Abraham (pp), Ishmael (pp), Isaac (pp), and their descendants, as well as Moses (pp), Jesus (pp), and Muhammad (pp) are all Muslims, as they all submitted their will, their way of life, and their style of living to the will of God. It is believed that to open up our hearts, our spirits, and our minds here in the United States and in the world, God's messages to His last three brothers in the faith—Moses (pp), Jesus (pp), and Muhammad (pp)—it is preferred and strongly recommended that we should popularize Islam, not as a standalone religion, but as a manifestation of the Judeo-Christian-Islamic integration of recorded human religious and spiritual experiences, as taught by God through His revelations to all His peoples and prophets (pp).

The Qur'aan[3] charts out the sequence of truths and its revelation throughout history:

> *3:84 Say: "We believe in God, and in that which has been bestowed from on high upon us, and that which has been bestowed upon Abraham and Ishmael and Isaac and Jacob and their descendants, and that which has been vouchsafed by their Sustainer unto Moses and Jesus and all the [other] prophets: we make no distinction between any of them. [68] And unto Him do we surrender ourselves.*

3:3 It is He Who sent down to thee [step by step], in truth, the Book [the Qur'aan], confirming what went before it; and He sent down the Law [of Moses] and the Gospel [of Jesus] before this, as a guide to mankind, and He sent down the [Qur'aan] criterion [of judgment between right and wrong].

The Qur'aan also confirms the sequence of revelation from the Torah (the Jewish Bible) to the Christian Bible. The Qur'aan uses the word *Injeel*, which means the Gospel or the teachings of Jesus Christ, based on the Old Testament and the New Testament. (Christian Arabs also use the word *Injeel* for the Bible).

5:46 And in their footsteps We sent Jesus the son of Mary, confirming the Law [of Moses] that had come before him: We sent him the Gospel: therein was guidance and light, and confirmation of the Law that had come before him: a guidance and an admonition to those who revere God.

46:12 And before this, was the Book of Moses as a guide and a mercy: And this Book [The Qur'aan] confirms [it] in the Arabic tongue; to admonish the unjust, and as Glad Tidings to those who do right.

Furthermore, the Qur'aan instructs the believers in an effort to tie together all of God's messages, messengers, and prophets in the chain of life and human development;

2:136 Say: "We believe in God, and in that which has been bestowed from on high upon us, and that which has been bestowed upon Abraham and Ishmael and Isaac and Jacob and their descendants, and that which has been vouchsafed to Moses and Jesus; and that which has been vouchsafed to all the [other] prophets by their Sustainer: we make no distinction between any of them. And it is unto Him that we surrender ourselves.

And referring to Prophet Abraham's offspring, the Qur'aan reveals;

6:84 And We bestowed upon him Isaac and Jacob; and We guided each of them as We had guided Noah aforetime. And out of his offspring, [We bestowed prophethood upon] David, and Solomon, and Job, and Joseph, and Moses, and Aaron: for thus do We reward the doers of good.

As to Prophet Moses (pp), the Qur'aan reveals clearly that he indeed spoke to God, and it details his history in a way very similar to what we read in the Old Testament:

> *2:53 And [remember the time] when We vouchsafed unto Moses the divine writ - and [thus] a standard by which to discern the true from the false - so that you might be guided aright.*

In our efforts as believers in Moses (pp), Jesus (pp), and Muhammad (pp), or the Judeo-Christian-Islamic foundation for building a decent and wonderful society, we are advised by God in the Qur'aan:

> *42:13 In matters of faith, He has ordained for you that which He had enjoined upon Noah—and into which We gave thee [O Muhammad] insight through revelation as well as that which We had enjoined upon Abraham, and Moses, and Jesus: Steadfastly uphold the [true] faith, and do not break up your unity therein. [And even though] that [unity of faith] to which thou callest them appears oppressive to those who are wont to ascribe to other beings or forces a share in His divinity, God draws unto Himself everyone who is willing, and guides unto Himself everyone who turns unto Him.*

That is, the application of the Law of God (the Torah and Prophet Moses [pp], the Gospel and Jesus [pp]) is confirmed, complimented, and expanded on by the Qur'aan; it is the responsibility of all people of all faiths, and especially Muslims. It is not the intent here to make this chapter a detailed study of the Judeo-Christian-Islamic promise of the future; however, it is hoped that this new approach will be researched and expanded upon in future books.

The Way of Life (*Sunnah*) of the Prophet   *Sunnah* means a system, a path, or an example, referring to the example as practiced by the Prophet Muhammad (pp). It is the detailed description of how Prophet Muhammad (pp) put life in the Qur'aan by living according to its teachings and God's inspiration. The details are included in the meticulously researched, documented, and recorded body of the Prophet's (pp) sayings, comments, and actions done with his approval, which is called the *Hadeeth*.[4] The Hadeeth provides information about the Sunnah (the examples provided by Prophet Muhammad of how to live by applying the rules of God revealed in the Qur'aan); it was recorded in the two centuries after Prophet Muhammad's (pp) death, in authenticated Hadeeth collections.

Application of Shari'aa

The Science and Foundation of Scholarly Research, or *Usul Ul Fiqh* Applications of the Shari'aa produce a whole body of scholarly research by a class of scholars called learned scholars (*fuquahaa*; the singular is *faqih*, scholar) in Islamic research circles and institutions all over the world, regardless of the local language. Shari'aa embodies the whole discipline of scholarly research and the detailed authentication of the codes, references, and rulings. It is called *The Science of Origins and Foundation of Scholarly Work* (known in Islamic circles as *Usul Ul Fiqh*). Scholarly research, or the science of Fiqh, is based on the best efforts of the scholars and the scholarly institutions involved in the research.

The opinions and edicts issued by the learned scholars may differ between countries, depending on local circumstances, roots, culture, and intellect. In the United States, one can experience an American federal law that covers the whole country; but at the same time, there are state laws that are specific to each state. That is why Fiqh opinions may vary or change with time and place of implementation, based on new scholarly research examining the applicability of what was ruled earlier in relation to the current needs of the specific situation at hand in a certain particular community or state.

Fiqh, for example, classifies human activities into the following five categories:

- *Divinely required duty or obligation* (fard *or* wajib): Every Muslim is required at a minimum to perform these specific rituals, obligations, and actions (such as prayers, fasting during the month of Ramadan, paying zakah, and performing the hajj, for those who can afford it). Failing to do so is classified as divinely disallowed and forbidden (haram); further, it is considered an offense against the faith, because it violates the established limits of what is acceptable (*hudood*).
- *Recommended and encouraged with pleasure, but not mandatory* (mandoob *or* musta'habb): A Muslim is only expected to perform these duties as an extra effort over and above the minimum required discussed above. Those who choose to do it are interested in excelling in the faith, the service of God, and in spirituality. The performance of these actions is rewarded, but there is not considered a violation if not done.
- *Allowed* (mubah): The origin of all Shari'aa rules is that all is allowed, except what has been clearly prohibited. The acceptability of these actions is analyzed by a process of deduction because there was no mention of these activities in the body of the scholarly Law (Fiqh), and the books of Law (Shari'aa and Fiqh) were silent about such actions.

- *Hated, disliked, disappointing, and frowned upon with disappointment, but not disallowed* (makruh): Although these actions are frowned upon, doing these activities is not punishable. It is an accepted fact that devout Muslims do not perform makruh.
- *Divinely unlawful* (haram): These actions are prohibited by Shari'aa and are punishable by penalties specified in the Qur'aan.

The branches of Fiqh (literally, Fiqh means "in-depth understanding") include but are not limited to worship rules, family law, inheritance law, commerce and trade transactions law, property law, civil law, criminal law, and laws and regulation covering administration, taxation, constitution, international relations, defense, peace and war ethics, and other categories.

Some of the scholarly scientific approaches used to arrive at a ruling and conclusions reached after comprehensive research, deliberation, and documentation are:

- *The consensus approach* (ijma): This includes rulings or edicts that have been agreed upon by the majority of the fuquahaa (scholars; plural of faqih) in Shari'aa. Consensus (*ijma*) applies to a situation where no clear conclusion can be made from the Qur'aan and the Sunnah. In this situation, the knowledgeable and well-versed and learned scholars (fuquahaa), in the form of a *Fatwa Board* (a board that specializes in, and is entrusted by the local government with the task of receiving inquiries and issuing edicts or fatwa), will confer and agree on a satisfactory solution to the particular problem,
- *The analogy approach* (qiyas): This approach uses reference or comparison of similar circumstances (*qiyas*), in which the fuquahaa use analogies and make comparisons that will allow them to interpolate and/or extrapolate the existing rules of Shari'aa and the body of scholarly research (Fiqh). The concept of qiyas, or analogy, is applied in circumstances where guidance from the Qur'aan and the Sunnah is not directly available. A problem is solved by a process of deduction, comparing the current situation to the ruling passed on a similar situation that occurred earlier.

A number of great Muslim scholars and leaders (*imams*)[5] devoted themselves to the collection, compilation, understanding, and application of the scholarly research (Fiqh) and the source and procedures of the Law (Shari'aa) and its practices.

Performing Scholarly Research to Develop and Pass Religious Edicts and Rulings: The Process of Issuing a Fatwa[6]   Shari'aa describes how Muslims should behave in every aspect of life, from private matters between the individual and God to relationships with others in the family and the wider community. Shari'aa is developed based on Fiqh, the detailed research work conducted by fuquahaa, the highly accomplished scholars who have a tested, proven, and recognized track record and body of accomplishments over many years. The body of detailed laws developed by these fuquahaa is called the Fiqh. Shari'aa is hence the referenced legal and canonical bar used by accomplished and recognized religious fuquahaa in developing detailed legal codes for different societies in different times, depending on local needs, problems, and circumstances, as well as on the time these needs arise.

It is also important to note that Shari'aa is only applicable to people who believe in the Islamic faith. Those who choose to not be believers are not required to abide by Shari'aa. That is why, for example, zakah, or alms-giving, an Islamic ritual ordained by Shari'aa, is replaced by the act of tax collection from non-Muslims who live in a Muslim country; this tax is called *jizyah*, which means taxes.

The Ultimate Intent and Goals of Shari'aa: *Maqasid* **Al Shari'aa**[7]   Accomplished and recognized fuquahaa have researched and developed over the years a set of goals that they use to guide believers on how to live comfortably while abiding by Shari'aa. They developed detailed sets of moral and legal rulings to guide those who are asked to issue an edict (*fatwa*) and those who are asking the religious legal opinion. These rulings are all assembled in the books of Fiqh, which are similar to books of legal codes.

To develop a legal canonical system of laws based on the Fiqh that leads to developing the Law (Shari'aa) about what is halal (divinely allowed) and what is haram (divinely prohibited), the following fundamental rules must be followed:

1. Whatever is not prohibited by the Qur'aan and Sunnah is usually acceptable and is considered halal.
2. The main objective of Shari'aa is to push away what is harmful to all aspects of life, family, assets, and the faith, and to bring what is good and beneficial to all (in Arabic, the rule is: *Dafu'l Dharar Wa Jalbul Manf'aa*[8]). Based on this important and basic rule, one cannot hurt himself, his family, his wealth, or his faith while attempting to apply Shari'aa.
3. If a person cannot live by Shari'aa in its entirety, he or she cannot be excused for not trying, in a step-by-step approach, until the goal is achieved. The rule states literally that if one cannot achieve the perfect goal of reaching perfect adherence to Shari'aa because of conditions that are difficult to meet, that would not give that person an excuse for not trying to achieve a part of that goal (in Arabic, the rule is: *Mala Yudraku Kulluhu La Yutraku Julluhu*).

As explained earlier, the legalistic expression of Shari'aa in a canonical fashion is called the Fiqh. Fiqh is changeable, depending on circumstances of places, people, specific experiences, and the accepted custom, which is known in the Islamic research and scholarly circles as *urf*. The science that organizes the process of generating edicts (fatwa) is called Usul Al Fiqh, or foundations of Fiqh. In general, Fiqh rulings that would lead to a set of canonical Laws (Shari'aa) are concerned with achieving five basic goals. These goals are, in order of priority, concerned with the maintenance of:

1. Religion, faith, and the Islamic way of life called *deen* (meaning religion or a way of life)
2. Life
3. Family and offspring, including children, grandchildren, and relations of kin
4. Intellect
5. Wealth

By applying these goals in sequence, one would conclude that:

1. Wealth should be spent and invested in gaining knowledge
2. Knowledge and advances in the field of intellectual accomplishment lead to better knowledge and intellect advancement
3. Knowledge and intellect are used to serve the family
4. The family is provided with a better, healthy, and honorable life
5. The ultimate achievement will be a faith-based capable community that upholds the faith and lives by Shari'aa. As a result, faith will be held in highest regard, will be made attractive to many, and will be accepted and followed by the community as a preferred religion, system, and a way of life.

For example, an edict or a question for an opinion of Shari'aa regarding wealth takes a second priority behind the benefits to the intellect, knowledge, and life. That is why the fuquahaa (learned scholars) permitted the use of alcohol-based antiseptics in surgical procedures to preserve and protect life, despite the fact that alcohol is haram. The reason it is allowed in surgical situations is that preserving life has a higher priority (priority 2) than preserving the capability of the mind and intellect (priority 4), which is needed by the faithful to know God and to exercise good judgment.

Scholars indicated that they must not only classify and prioritize the aim of Shari'aa based on the different levels of importance, but they must also consider another dimension of prioritization, and that is levels of urgency of the matter in the following three levels:

1. Basic requirements and needs (*dharuririyat*) of those who need a ruling on a certain matter
2. Complementary additions to further refine the basic requirements in priority (1) above, based on the need of the inquirer (*hajjiyat*)
3. Improvements, modifications, and further refinements of the complementary requirements (*tahsinaat*)

Working in this two-dimensional domain, and combining the five levels of goals with the three levels of urgencies, one gets at least 15 combinations of priorities. In other words, the faqih, in his or her pursuit of an edict (fatwa or opinion), should meticulously consider the fifteen possibilities and carefully analyze the situation at hand before reaching an edict. When competing rulings occur, the ruling that belongs to a higher block in the table in Exhibit 4.1 takes precedent over a ruling from the lower block. In other words any ruling that is classified as a refinement gives way to another which is classified as complimentary and so on. On the other hand, it would be very useful to think in other dimensions and to develop algorithms that can be beneficial to all people. This is where a new generation of sophisticated, computer-oriented, and analytical scholars will contribute in the future. It is important to ponder on this approach when making a ruling or developing a model for RF finance in a certain country or region of the world, especially where Muslims are minorities.

Dr. Adhami included in his article the table of priorities shown in Exhibit 4.1 that would be used by the qualified scholars (the issuer of the fatwa called *Mufti*) in making an edict (a religiously binding edict called *fatwa*). The table illustrates the concept of prioritization[9] discussed above.

For example, ablution (*wudu*, washing before prayers) is a prerequisite for prayers. However, if the person is ill and cannot use water on the body because it would hurt the health of his skin, the edict would call for allowing the person to do ablution (washing to prepare for the prayers) symbolically (in a dry way) by applying what is known as *atayammum* procedure (instead of using the hands to carry the water to wash with, wipe the hands on a dry clean object). In this case, ablution (wudu) is considered a refinement level in the category of maintaining the faith/religion (priority level B) while health and life are on the top row and are classified as required (priority level A). The same approach can be used when calling a stream of rent in an RF finance scheme by the name "implied interest" or using the word "interest" to satisfy the local laws in a non-Muslim land in order to uphold the laws of that land.

There has been a religious renaissance worldwide. Many people of all faiths are trying to discover the best way to live. They are searching deep within their faiths to find solutions to the many modern problems that they

EXHIBIT 4.1 Table of priorities

Priority	1 Faith/Religion	2 Life	3 Family	4 Intellect and Knowledge	5 Wealth
A Required	1. Required to Maintain the Faith/Religion	2. Required to Maintain Life	3. Required to Maintain Family	4. Required to Maintain Intellect and Knowledge	5. Required to Maintain Wealth
B Complementary	6. Complementary to Maintain the Faith/Religion	7. Complementary to Maintain Life	8. Complementary to Maintain Family	9. Complementary to Maintain Intellect and Knowledge	10. Complementary to Maintain Wealth
C Refined Further	11. Further Refinement in the Maintenance of Faith/Religion	12. Further Refinement in the Maintenance of Life	13. Further Refinement in the Maintenance of Family	14. Further Refinement in the Maintenance of Intellect and Knowledge	15. Further Refinement in the Maintenance of Wealth

face in the 21st century and to achieve spiritual fulfillment. The believers who are not well-educated in the faith and its rules or in Shari'aa want to live in a puritan way, conducting a true exemplary life as ordained by God in His books and according to Shari'aa. These puritans face many challenges that require a religious edict or ruling, but the resolution to challenges become a religious opinion first in the public domain. With the advent of efficient means of communication and mass media outlets in the form of hundreds of satellite TV channels, many programs have been devoted to answering questions about lifestyles, behavior, interpersonal relations, marital problems, financial and business dealings, and the like. This has generated a very high demand for religious leaders who are qualified to issue a religious opinion or edict, called a *fatwa*. The person who issues these *fatwa* is called a *mufti*.

The private *fatwa* issued by a local scholar or *imam* (religious leader) becomes, later on, a binding, legal fatwa once it has stood the test of scholarly, legal, and public scrutiny. Al-Azhar Seminary in Cairo, Egypt, the oldest university in the world, is the only Islamic seminary in the Sunni Muslim domain that teaches the Fiqh according to the five schools listed earlier, including the *Sunni* and *Shi'i* schools of thought (*madh'hab*). The seminary graduates students in different disciplines. One discipline is Shari'aa and Usul Ul Fiqh (the foundations of Fiqh). These graduates develop their skills as faqih through a continual process of supervised research and a long-term track record of interaction with leading and accomplished scholars.

In Egypt, at Al-Azhar Seminary, there is only one final and highest authority in authorizing a public religious edict, or *fatwa*. This highest authority has the title of the *Grand Mufti,* or the highest scholar in charge of legislation of fatwas. He presides over a committee of accomplished scholars who are classified as distinguished *fuquahaa*. This committee holds hearings, conducts and critiques research, and makes recommendations for fatwas, which are then submitted for the approval of the *Fatwa* Committee of Al Azhar Seminary and, eventually, of the Grand Mufti. Essentially the same process is followed in the Islamic republic of Iran (at the *Hawza* in Qum), in Iraq (at the *Hawza* in Najaf), and in Pakistan and India. In Pakistan and India, the elderly scholars, in an effort to train a new generation of Shari'aa legislators, started many colleges that graduate young scholars who carry the title of Mufti. It is important to warn the reader here to not being mislead by the title Mufti as used by many of these Indo-Pakistani graduates, because their achievements in their fields after graduation must be demonstrated. It is preferred to call them junior Mufti, or Mufti in residence training.

Obviously, people are free to choose whose opinions to follow, but it is important to share with the reader the parameters that should be used in recruiting and evaluating for assignment candidates to serve as advisors on

Shari'aa in their institutions. The following is an abbreviated list of the basic qualifications that must be met before a person is qualified to issue a fatwa and act as a scholar in Shari'aa:

- Mastery of the Qur'aanic language, Arabic, as demonstrated by a certificate of graduation from an accredited seminary or university
- Mastery in the knowledge, meanings, and historic reasons of revelation of the verses of the Qur'aan, as demonstrated by graduation from a recognized institute
- Formal education in the Law (Shari'aa) from a recognized theological seminary or a university that has a reputable department of religion
- Knowledge of the Jewish Bible and the Christian Bible; this is highly preferred but not necessarily required
- Proven analytical abilities, as witnessed by the guiding scholars, professors, and supervisors who were in charge of teaching; this includes the ability to methodically and scientifically analyze difficult issues and legal problems and to debate different opinions in recognized forums and in public
- Knowledge of computers, word processing, and the Microsoft Office suite (or the like) and of using the Internet
- Published research in respected media and trade magazines and other outlets, and documented research leading to the development of new legal codes
- Strong written, verbal, and communication skills, and the ability to speak in public
- Proven reputation in the community for public service, knowledge, caring, piety, and generosity
- Knowledge of family matters, which requires in most cases that the candidate is happily married and that his/her family presents a successful role model for the community
- Proven track record of issuing fatwa that have been recognized and agreed to by a learned body of scholars and seminary researchers, such as Al Azhar University (Egypt), specialized universities and seminaries in Al Madinah and Makkah (Saudi Arabia), Qum (Iran), Al Najaf (Iraq), and universities (such as the International Islamic University) in Pakistan, Malaysia, Kuwait, and the United States (like Princeton, Harvard, and Claremont) and Canada (like McGill).
- Proven expertise in one of the aspects of living (examples include advanced studies leading to a degree in business administration, economics, and/or finance, for a scholar who wants to practice in the field of RF banking and finance; or expertise in humanities, family law, and

psychology, for a scholar who wants to concentrate on matters pertaining to family law)

Obviously, the above list of stringent requirements is what can be called the ideal. It will take time to achieve all these requirements. All students who aspire to become scholars are strongly urged to work hard to achieve a high level of qualification as scholars. This approach is believed to produce a new generation of scholars for the 21st century who will be positioned to pave the way toward a happier lifestyle in all aspects of life for all people of all faiths, including the ribit/riba-free life style advocated in this book.

THE SHARI'AA BOARD IN AN ISLAMIC BANK OR FINANCE COMPANY

Despite the fact that the first formal Islamic bank was started in Dubai by Sheikh Saeed bin Lutah in the mid-1960s, there was no record of a formal effort to institutionalize the process of developing a formal body that would research and develop the RF banking and finance legal code according to Shari'aa. Later, after the sudden increase in oil revenues in 1973, three leading financial institutions were started in the mid-1970s, in a formal and dedicated effort to start Islamic finance and banking. These were: (1) *Dar Al-Maal Al Islami*, which was started in Geneva, Switzerland by the son of the late King Faisal, Prince Muhammad Al-Faisal; (2) *Bayt al Tamweel Al Kuwaiti—Kuwait Finance House* in Kuwait, which was organized as a shareholders' Islamic finance company headed by a Kuwaiti of Iraqi origin, Sheikh Bazee Al Yaseen; and (3) *Dallah Al Baraka Group*, in Jeddah, Saudi Arabia, started by Sheikh Saleh Kamel, a former auditor in the Department of Defense in Saudi Arabia and later an important force with vision and entrepreneurship who was, in many cases, at least 25 years ahead of his time.

They all were faced with the challenge of developing, for the first time in modern history, a financial legal code based on Shari'aa. At that time, they resorted to the highest religious authority in the Arabic-speaking part of the Muslim world which happened to be Al Azhar Seminary in Cairo, Egypt.

Prince Al Faisal appointed Sheikh Muhammad Khater, the *Grand Mufti* of Egypt (a position appointed by the President of the Republic of Egypt), to be the head of a board responsible for developing financial tools and methods that were compliant with Shari'aa. The aim was to help with investing—according to Shari'aa—some of the vast amounts of "petro-dollars" that resulted from the windfall created by the sudden increase in oil price in 1973.

Sheikh Bazee Al Yaseen chose Sheikh Muhammad Badr Abdel Basset to be his Chief Scholar in the Law. He was a scholar from the faculty of *Daar-Ul Uloom*, the House of Knowledge, at *Ain Shams* University in Egypt, a prestigious college that graduates many high-caliber and recognized leaders of thought and research in the Arab and Muslim world. Many of this college's graduates became effective imams and fuquahaa. Sheikh Basset helped develop the foundation of different models for RF financing for Kuwait Finance House.

Sheikh Saleh Kamel appointed a group of the highest religious authorities in many countries to develop an RF financing code based on Shari'aa. The group, which was later called—for the first time—the Shari'aa Board, was given the mandate to develop RF banking products and services that paralleled those available in the riba-based banking and financial services in the West. He appointed significant leaders from Egypt, Jordan, Syria, Sudan, and Saudi Arabia, and later from Malaysia, Pakistan, and India. He also organized annual seminars and symposia among these leaders and other financial and banking scholars to discuss and analyze different riba-based banking products and services available in the West and to develop ways and means to make them compliant with Shari'aa. He was very generous in his investments in the field of new scholarly research in this field. He started a pioneering library of Islamic banking and finance in Jordan, and departments of Islamic banking and finance at the University in Jeddah and at Al Azhar University in Cairo. In his efforts to develop Islamic banking and finance internationally, he opened a finance company in London and started Al Baraka Bank in London in the mid-1980s. He and his associates at Dallah Al Baraka laid the foundation for communications between some of the top bankers, financial experts, and business attorneys on one side and religious scholars on the other side for the first time in the modern history of Islam. Over the years, the group developed Islamic banking terminology, rules and regulations, operating standards, financing mechanisms, and products and services that comply with the Law and that offer an RF alternative to the conventional riba-based ones in the fields of trade financing, auto financing, home mortgages, and business financing, as well as investing in the stock markets.

The Role of the Shari'aa Board

The Shari'aa Board in a typical Islamic bank is responsible for overseeing the application of different aspects of the Law (Shari'aa) in the RF bank or the financial institution.[10] The Shari'aa Board (sometimes called Shar-i'aa Supervisory Committee), in general, certifies every product, finance model, and service provided by the RF financial institution. It also ensures that all the transactions are in strict compliance with the principles of Shari'aa.

The Shari'aa Board is comprised of experts in the research and development of religious rulings by applying Shari'aa to financial and banking products and operations. The Board also helps in devising, with the assistance of banking professionals, RF financing models that fit within and compete with modern-day riba-based banking. In some, but not all, Islamic banks, the Board is empowered with the right of issuing a contradicting religious edict—a fatwa—to the position of the bank's board of directors regarding any of the products, services, and/or procedures that violate Shar-i'aa, if such a violation were uncovered. Some banks' bylaws require that the board of directors be obligated to implement the fatwa(s) issued by the Shari'aa Board. In some banks, like the Dubai Islamic Bank, the fatwa is implemented irrespective of whether a unanimous or a majority of the Board of Directors consensus secures the decision (clause 78 of the Bank's Memorandum & Articles of Association).[11]

The Duties of the Shari'aa Board

The Shari'aa Board (or Council) is looked upon by bank management, board of directors, and shareholders as an expert source on the Law and its application in financial and banking transactions. The board of directors of the bank often appoints one of the Shari'aa Board members as a voting member of the board of directors of the bank in charge of overseeing the implementation of Shari'aa in the Board. The board of directors of the bank may also appoint one of its members to be a member of the Shari'aa Board, to serve as a liaison between the two boards. The following is an abbreviated list of duties for a typical bank's Shari'aa Board:

- Detailed documentation of the recorded religious bases and foundations as extracted from Shari'aa, with a complete record of the Shari'aa Board's deliberations and the reasons for and against a specific fatwa ruling. These proceedings, ideally, should be made transparent.
- Help in the process of innovating, manufacturing, and devising new Shari'aa-based products and services with the banking professionals.
- Help in devising a detailed set of operating manuals and transactional procedures that will be competitive with existing riba-based banking services and products.

- Review and analysis of any contracts and/or agreements related to the services, operations, or outside vendors of the bank, to make certain that such agreements comply with Shari'aa.
- Participation in the design of the bank's training programs, including education about the foundations of the faith, the rules on compassion and honesty, the importance of fair and equal rights without discrimination, and the character of an RF banker who shuns misrepresentation of facts and the culture of pure selling at any cost to meet a sales goal and make a high commission.
- Participation in a hands-on training program on Shari'aa compliance, including the models used for financing and how they differ from those offered by the conventional riba-based banks.
- Supervision of the bank's day-to-day operations, interaction with the staff, and pursuit of the highest quality of work in processing customers' applications and communicating with the outside world regarding truthful representation of the products and services offered by the sales force. This includes random checking of incoming and outgoing mail, telephone conversations on help lines, incoming and outgoing e-mails, and faxes.
- Attention to developments pertaining to Shari'aa issues and new products and services at other competing banks, as well as riba-based banks.

The Shari'aa Board is required to submit a complete annual report to the board of directors of the bank, summarizing all the issues referred to the Board, as well as the Board's opinion on the bank's transactional procedures.

Approaches Used to Appoint Shari'aa Boards

The role of the Shari'aa Board in a typical Islamic bank brings to mind the typical role played by a compliance committee within the board of directors of any conventional bank in the United States—but, of course, it is concerned only with issues that pertain to compliance with Shari'aa. It is important to note that two approaches have been used to implement Shari'aa in RF banking activities.

1. The first approach was implemented in Malaysia. In this approach, the Central Bank (Bank Negara Malaysia, BNM) has its own Central Bank Islamic Banking Division with its own books and regulations, as well as its own Shari'aa Board. The National Shari'aa Board of Islamic Banking in Malaysia issues edicts (fatwa) on different products, services, and operating standards. The opinions and rulings of the National Shari'aa

Board of Islamic Banking are binding to all RF banks in Malaysia. Then, at the individual bank level, each bank appoints its own Shari'aa Supervisory Committee to ascertain compliance of the bank operations with the rules set by the Central Bank's Shari'aa Board guidelines. This approach saves a lot of confusion and conflicts within different Shari'aa Boards. The involvement of the Central Bank adds credence and weight to the rulings. In addition, because the Shari'aa Board is operated and supervised by the Central Bank, there is no potential for conflict of interest, because the individual banks are not paying their own hand-picked scholars for their services.

2. The other approach is to allow each bank to appoint its own Shari'aa Board. The implementation of this approach has created a lot of confusion and conflicting opinions among the scholars in each of the Islamic banks. It also creates an implicit uneasy feeling of conflict of interest, because the bank pays the salaries of its Shari'aa Board members. This approach has also created a large demand for the limited supply of RF Shari'aa scholars available. The net result has been the appointment of some of the "superstar scholars" on the Shari'aa Boards of more than one bank. I know of scholars who serve on the Boards of more than 50 Islamic banks. This creates another conflict of interest situation, because these scholars are exposed to the inside information of many competing banks. This approach is used mostly by Islamic banks in the oil-rich Gulf countries and in some Asian countries (except Malaysia).

Concerns of Western Central Bankers and Bank Regulators Regarding Shari'aa Boards

This important issue is very sensitive, and it created some serious concern in the many efforts invested in trying to implement RF banking and finance in the West. There are three reasons for the concerns:

1. In most Western societies, especially in the United States, the government and its departments operate with a firm belief in the separation of church and state. Operating a bank with a formal Board that has the mission of implementing the laws of a certain religion may be a bit sensitive, especially with consumers who subscribe to other religions, which may result in religious discrimination disputes that may lead to messy law suits.
2. The existence of two boards in one bank, with one board having apparent superiority of control over the other, may create a serious operating conflict that could have a negative impact on the bank's safety and

soundness. In addition, there can be further conflict if the Shari'aa
Board is paid generously to issue edicts that can create serious conflict-
of-interest issues.

3. Most, if not all, of the scholars represented on the Shari'aa Board do
not have direct experience in banking and finance, and in most cases,
they do not have a proven track record and knowledge of the banking
regulations in the West. They may not even have experience in the local
area in the West where the bank operates. In addition, because many of
the scholars live in other countries, it is difficult for them to appreciate
local needs and challenges, and the regulators may find it hard to exercise their regulatory powers on them.

THE DEVELOPMENT OF SHARI'AA SCHOLARS AND SHARI'AA COMPLIANCE COMMITTEES FOR RIBA-FREE BANKS AND FINANCE INSTITUTIONS IN THE 21ST CENTURY

It is the author's deep-seated belief that the public and businesses in the
West will become greatly interested in the services and products of the
new RF brand of banking. In addition, bankers will be drawn to the concept because it reduces overhead to a reasonable level and keeps loan and
lease losses to a minimum, and because RF banks deal with those people
who are well-known to the bankers who serve them in the local communities. Hence, the banker will be fulfilling the know-your-customer rule of
banking and finance. All these and the trust of the community will expand
the bank's business and increase its profitability. That is why it is important to prepare the groundwork, starting now, for this new brand of
banking.

My vision of the 21st-century Shari'aa Board for an RF bank will be
renamed as a *Shari'aa Advisory Committee*, which will not only include
Muslim scholars but also scholars from the Jewish, Christian, and other
faith-based communities. The idea of a united Judeo-Christian-Islamic approach to banking will make it very attractive and highly credible.

The Muslim Shari'aa Compliance Officer, or the Shari'aa Advisory
Committee Supervisor, will ideally be a scholar who is trained in formal
scholarly sciences in an accredited Religious Studies Department at a major
institution or seminary, such as Al Azhar in Cairo, the Hawzah in Qum
(Iran), the Hawzah in Al Najaf (Iraq), the International Islamic University
in Pakistan, and Aligarh University in India, The King Abdul Azeez University in Jeddah, McGill University in Canada, Princeton University in New

Jersey, or Claremont Graduate University in California. These graduates should not only be well-versed in Islamic Law (Shari'aa) but also in the Jewish Bible, rabbinical laws and traditions, and in the Christian Bible(s) and traditions. These graduates should also have obtained a degree in economics, finance, and/or banking from an accredited university, making them well-versed in finance as well as religious law. It is true that it will take many years to achieve this, but the rewards will be worth the investment of time, money, and effort. This process is reminiscent of preparing securities lawyers in the United States. Securities lawyers specialize in the laws of the Securities and Exchange Commission (SEC) in the United States. Many of them start as graduates from universities in the fields of economics, business, or even the sciences or history. They often work as financial consultants or brokers in an investment bank to gain hands-on experience for a few years, then return to college to study for another degree in law to qualify as a securities attorney.

In addition to the requirements listed above, an operating license in the fields of compliance with Shari'aa should be made necessary, as is done when licensing a stockbroker or a medical doctor in the United States. There are currently a number of pseudo-regulatory organizations like the Accounting and Auditing Organization for Islamic Financial Institutions, also known as AAOIFI, in Bahrain[12] and the Islamic Financial Services Board (IFSB) in Malaysia.[13] My vision for the process of producing the qualified scholar will be the same as that used to produce attorneys, medical doctors, and certified public accountants in the United States. It also involves annual or periodic renewal of licenses to keep all of them informed of the latest developments in the field.

The Central Bank and the Regulatory Shari'aa Compliance Committee

To minimize confusion and conflicting opinions passed by different Shari'aa scholars and different Shari'aa Compliance Boards of different institutes, the Malaysian model of having one Shari'aa Board appointed, run, and supervised as an independent entity in the central bank of the country involved represents an attractive option to emulate. This central bank Shari'aa Compliance Board will issue legal opinions and will be in charge of examining compliance in the same way banks are examined for compliance by the central bank (or the Treasury Department's Office of the Comptroller of the Currency, OCC). However, in this case, testing for compliance will be about adherence to the edicts and legal opinions that comply with Shari'aa as stipulated in the charter of the bank.

NOTES

1. Huston Smith, "Introduction," *The Concise Encyclopedia of Islam*, Harper & Row Publishers, San Francisco 1989, pp. 361–363.
2. Riad Adhami, *Islamic Horizons Magazine*, January/February 2006, pp. 48–50, Maqasid Al Shari'aa.
3. Translations of the Qur'aan were obtained from www.Islamicity.com. Sources used are: (1) Abdullah Yusuf Ali, *"The Meaning of the Holy Qur'an,"* Amana Publication, Beltsville, Md. and (2) The Qur'an, a translation by Muhammad Asad, Andalus Press, Gibraltar 1980. The translation of the Holy Qur'aan by Yusuf Ali is one of the original, and in my opinion, the better translations, because it adds to the meanings a wealth of information on historic references and events and especially on links to Judeo-Christian traditions, making it a wonderful foundation for a Judeo-Christian-Islamic future.
4. The following collections of the Hadeeth are regarded as the most authentic:

   Sahih Al Bukhari, which were collected, strictly and copiously checked, validated, and compiled by Muhammad Ibn Ismail Al Bukhari (from the City of Bukhara, now in Uzbekistan) (194–256 A.H., A.D. 809–870).

   Sahih Muslim by Muslim Ibn Al Hajjaj (202–261 A.H., A.D. 817–876)
   Sunan Abu Dawud by Sulaiman Ibn Ash'ath known as Abu Dawud (202–275 A.H., A.D. 817–888).

   Sunan Ibn Majah by Muhammad Ibn Zaayid (209-303 A.H., A.D. 824–915).
   In addition to these, Muwatta of Imam Malik (93–179 A.H., A.D. 715–795),

   Mishkat Al Masabih of Abu Muhammad Al Husain Ibn Mas'ud (died 516 A.H., A.D. 1122) and Musnad of Ahmad Ibn Hanbal (164–241 A.H., A.D. 780–885) are all well-known authorities.
5. References are as follows:

   1. Imam Jafaar As-Sadiq, founder of the Jafaari or Shi'aa school of thought (madh'hab) in Arabic (80–148 A.H., A.D. 699–765).
   2. Imam Abu Hanifa Numan bin Thabit, founder of the Hanafi madh'hab (80–150 A.H., A.D. 699–767)
   3. Imam Malik bin Anas, founder of the Maliki madh'hab (93–179 A.H., A.D. 715–795).
   4. Imam Muhammad bin Idris Al Shafi'ee, founder of Al-Shafi'ee madh'hab (150–240 A.H., A.D. 767–820)
   5. Imam Ahmad bin Hanbal, founder of the Hanbali madh'hab (164–241 A.H., A.D. 780–855).
6. Riad Adhami, *Islamic Horizons Magazine*, January/February 2006, pp. 48–50 quoted here by permission, The Goals of Shari'ah.
7. Ibid.
8. As ruled by Imam Abu Hanifah.

9. Riad Adhami, *Islamic Horizons Magazine*, January/February 2006, pp. 48–50, Maqasid Al Shari'aa.
10. Please visit Dubai Islamic Bank Web site to read about the role of its Shari'aa Board (www.alislami.ae/en/shariaboard_boardrules.htm); also, read about the Islamic Bank of Britain: www.islamic-bank.com/islamicbanklive/RoleofCommittee/1/Home/1/Home.jsp.
11. Ibid.
12. Please visit their Web sites: www.aaoifi.com and www.IslamicBankingNetwork.com.
13. Please visit their Web sites: www.ifsb.org and www.IslamicBankingNetwork.com.

CHAPTER 5

Money and Its Creation

The Federal Reserve System (Central Banks), Interest Rates, and Commodity Indexation

This chapter is about money and, in particular, its use to help the economic growth and prosperity of the community through providing credit. The question is how to reward those who own, in order to entice them to invest within the community. Chapter 2 concluded that the Judeo-Christian-Islamic tradition and lifestyle prohibits the charging of a rate or fee for the use of money (i.e., usury, which is now called interest). It also concluded that if money is given for helping the poor and the needy, there must not be any increase when it is paid back. In Chapter 3, we discussed how Shari'aa (Judeo-Christian-Islamic Law) requires that when pricing a service or an item, we should use the concepts of *commodity indexing* (using precious metals or food staples as references) and *marking to market* (gauging the value of properties and services according to values on the local market).

Any discussion of the riba-free (RF) banking and finance system, as compared to the riba-based system, should be based on a clear understanding of money and how the U.S. dollar monetary policies are handled. This chapter is a must for everyone who is interested in understanding the way money is created and is interested in popularizing the new way of living using the RF style of Judeo-Christian-Islamic living.

THOSE WHO "MAKE" MONEY AND OTHERS WHO "EARN" MONEY

Money is an important factor in our lives. Many of us say that we work in order to "make" money. We try to save money in order to buy the things that bring comfort and pleasure to us. Others spend money to seek personal satisfaction—perhaps through impressing others, by showing off an expensive new car or watch. Money has become so important that people fight over it, and hate and love because of it; unfortunately, some would be willing to kill for it. It is amazing to witness all this respect and admiration for a piece of paper that may be green, red, blue, or even have an impressive array of colors and designs. This piece of paper may only be recognized and honored in the place it was printed and issued. Not all currencies in the world are as well-known as the major currencies, which represent important world currencies in great demand, such as the U.S. dollar, the euro, the Japanese yen, or the British pound. Money cannot reproduce in the way that "money experts" have been leading us to believe. If one seals one's money in a jar for two years and returns to open the jar, one will find the same pieces of paper—except in most cases the paper will buy you less than it did two years before. It is also fundamental to understand clearly that we cannot eat or drink these pieces of paper called money. However, we can use the money to buy food from those who produce it, so that they can take that money and buy their needs—which may include clothes and medicine in addition to the items needed to produce more of that food. Money is not anything but a medium of exchange—a measuring device.

To realize the American dream of buying a house for which one has insufficient capital, one can go to a banker to seek financing. The applicant fills out an application and passes a few due diligence checking procedures. After appraising the value of the house based on the price at which the most recent sales in the neighborhood were concluded, the banker will arrange for the applicant to get the money. The bank draws a loan agreement that essentially states that it is renting you the money at a rental rate called the *interest rate*, to be paid back in installments over an agreed-upon number of years. As we learned in Chapter 2, interest rate is the cost of (the price paid for) renting the money from the bank. The bank does this mechanically, regardless of whether the deal of buying the house makes economic sense. A buyer might have expected the banker to advise him/her as to whether he/she should proceed to buy a house because it makes economic sense or rent a similar house or apartment because of a prevalent real estate bubble being experienced in the community. That does not happen, because the banker is interested in getting the customer to rent that money in order to make money for the bank. We realize that this scenario does not happen in most cases, because the world is full of honest and decent bankers and wonderful people. Unfortunately, at some time or another all of us can be blinded by the prevailing culture without stopping to think.

As to the "culture of making money," many have forgotten that there is only one entity that can make (i.e., manufacture, print, or coin) money: the government. That is why we should rethink this concept. Money can only be earned when one offers a service. That is why it is important to ask ourselves every night before we go to bed how much money we earned for the services we have offered. It is also important to respect that earned money, which represents time—which is life. As is said in some proverbs, "Money respects and stays with those who respect it." Money is earned when we offer a product or a service that is needed or when it is invested in a productive project that will make an economic difference in our communities by increasing production, creating job opportunities and economic prosperity. If we discipline ourselves to think this way, we will enjoy a new lifestyle that is more productive and less consumptive. We will enjoy living within our means without a heavy burden of debt. This lifestyle is the lifestyle described at length in Chapter 2; the riba/ribit-free lifestyle.

Another important aspect of money over the years has been its purchasing power and how much that power changes over the years. We all have heard our grandparents tell us how cheap things once were. Members of my generation remember that a gallon of gasoline in Texas in 1971 was 20 cents, compared to $2.50 in 2009. This is the same gallon, of the same gas, in the same country, using the very same currency.

The question is, what is money? Is the money revealed in the original Judeo-Christian-Islamic value system and described in Chapter 2 the same as the money we use today? This chapter will focus on this very important issue. This chapter will try, in the simplest terms, to familiarize the reader with money, how it is printed, who decides how much should be printed, and what parameters influence that decision.

What Is Money?

Money is the medium used for the exchange of goods and services. Money is used as a measuring device for the success or failure of a venture that may involve trading, manufacturing, servicing, or construction. The success or failure of the investment is measured in terms of the return reaped at the end of a certain period of time, which is called the *return on investment*. Operators, traders, and investors evaluate the success of their venture by the return on investment. The level of return on investment differs from one locality to another; it is a function of many parameters. A return on investment of 5 percent may be considered a great return in a country with no inflation; however, a return on investment of 15 percent would be marginal in a country that suffers from 25 percent inflation. Riba-banks lend (rent) money to entities at a rental rate called interest. If the interest rate charged on the money is higher than the income generated from the project, to the extent that the borrower cannot pay both the interest and the principal back, then the project is a failure, and it should not have borrowed money anyway. Conceptually, one can look at interest rate as a red line that defines which projects should be financed. If the projected rate of return of a project is higher than the red line, then it makes sense to finance it; if it is lower, financing the project does not make sense. The government sets the foundation of that interest rate by deciding on and adjusting the rate of printing of the money. If the government wants to allow only high-return projects to be financed, it will increase rates. As a result, there will be very few projects that make economic sense. Conversely, if the government wanted to stimulate the economy, it will lower the rates so that less profitable projects can qualify.

The invention of money was one of the important human developments in history. Money has helped develop markets in small villages that attracted many traders and merchants, eventually turning these small villages into small towns, cities, large metropolitan areas, states, and countries. The real value of the idea of money is that it can be transported from one place to another. It can be divided into different denominations, and it can be recognized and accepted by others in other countries, depending on the country or locality that issued it.

The History of Money[1]
Perhaps one of the earliest forms of money was barter: the exchange of one specific good or service for another specific good or service, such as a bag of rice for a bag of beans. Difficulties with this system arose when the bartering parties could not agree what something was worth in exchange, or when one party did not want what the other person had. To solve that problem, *commodity money* was introduced. In the past, salt, tea, tobacco, cattle, and seeds have all been used as money, because of their importance to local economies. As the world developed it was discovered that using commodities as money presented new challenges. Carrying bags of salt and other commodities was difficult. In addition, commodities might have a short shelf life, after which they perished. Around 5000 B.C.E., metal objects were introduced as money because metal was readily available, easy to work with, and could be recycled. Other countries were soon minting their own coins with specific values. Metals such as iron, copper, silver, and gold were used to make coins. The problem moneymakers had was that some metals change as they rust. Only silver and gold kept their condition; these prevailed as the two main metals used for currencies in the world. The demand for gold and silver was driven not only by their practical use, but also by their role as investments and a store of value. The Roman Empire used gold currency called the denarius (or dinar), while the Persian Empire used silver and called it dirham (or drachma). The Muslim state used the gold dinar

and the silver dirham as the official Islamic currency beginning with the Second Caliph Omar Ibn Al-Khattab (634–644 C.E.). The dinar was defined as the weight of 22-karat gold equivalent to 4.3 grams, and the dirham as the weight of silver equivalent to 3.0 grams. At that time the caliph established the well-known standard relationship—seven dinars must be equivalent to ten dirham.

Fiat (Paper) Money

Fiat money is money that has nothing of substance behind it. According to Webster's New World Dictionary, fiat money is "currency made legal tender by fiat (sanction) and neither backed by, nor necessarily convertible into, gold or silver." It is a promise to repay nothing, over an unspecified period. This inconvertible paper currency system gives the central bank the power to issue and circulate paper money, which has no intrinsic value except the full faith and credit of the government of a country that has an economic base to rely on. The government adds its full faith and credit to the currency so its citizens and other governments in the world will accept it. This concept of fiat money also allows the government to create (print) new money at will to pay off government debts, pay government employees, and use the printed money for any other government expenditure.

The first to introduce the idea of offering money at a less-than-pure gold or silver base were the kings of England, who introduced an idea they branded as the *debasement* of money. Debasement is the lowering of the precious metal content of the currency. Debasements were achieved by *recoinage*. In England during the 12th century, one pound of silver was minted into 240 silver pennies; during 1666, one pound of silver was minted into some 700 silver pennies, a decline in the value content of almost 292 percent. By means of their debasements, the kings had created what is known today as fiat money. Fiat money is a token of value . . . its intrinsic value is less than its exchange value. Its exchange value is given to it by *fiat* (order) of the king or the government involved.

Today, precious metal coins are no longer used, and the world deals only with fiat money. The early English bankers produced something of no value (a piece of paper) and gave it the name *one pound*. Some of the earliest known paper money dates to China's Tang Dynasty (618–907 C.E.). During the Ming Dynasty in 1300 C.E., the Chinese placed the Emperor's seal and signatures of the treasury on a crude paper made from mulberry bark.

From the time of America's discovery in 1492 until the California gold rush in 1848, silver dominated in common circulation in America and Europe, while gold came into dominance after the discovery of gold in California and Australia.[2] Under the rule of the British Empire, the British pound sterling and the gold standard were adopted around the world. In 1913, the gold cover for Federal Reserve notes was set by 1913 law to be 40 percent. In 1945, the gold reserves against Federal Reserve notes were reduced to 25 percent, and to continue the inflation spiral, this figure (the 25 percent) had to be reduced to zero. Toward the end of World War II, the U.S. dollar and gold became the principal international reserve assets under the Bretton Woods Agreement. The U.S. dollar became the world reserve currency, and it was treated as if it were gold, because the agreement defined its value to be $35 per ounce of gold.

American Currency Before the Federal Reserve System[3]

The First Bank of the United States (1791) and Second Bank of the United States (1816) were the two precursor banks to the Federal Reserve System in the United States. They were responsible for issuing the small quantity of paper currency that circulated in the early years of the United States. After the Second Bank of the United States closed in 1836, the dominant form of currency became private bank notes issued by state-chartered commercial banks (normally redeemable on demand for gold or silver). The United States did not have a uniform national currency. The system of state-bank issuing of currency notes was confusing and inefficient. By the 1860s, as many as 8,000 different issues of state bank notes were circulating in the United States. With the vast distances to be covered and the lack of efficient means of transportation, banks rarely accepted—at face value—notes issued by banks unknown to them.

During the American Civil War, national bank notes were issued to finance the war and other needs of the different states. Until 1913, these formed the bulk of the nation's paper currency. National bank notes were currency the government gave to nationally chartered commercial banks for them to issue as their own. National bank notes grew out of the government's need to raise money to finance the Union army. Faced with a depleted treasury, and reluctant to raise taxes on northern industry, President Lincoln reluctantly agreed to a plan formulated by his Secretary of Treasury, Salmon P. Chase. Under Chase's plan, the federal government would offer a new type of banking license—a federal, or national, charter. A bank with a national charter would have the power to issue a new form of currency: national bank notes. However, for each note issued, the bank would have to hold a somewhat larger dollar value of government securities as collateral (called a *backing requirement*). The banks could purchase government securities directly from the U.S. Treasury for gold and silver, which were universally accepted money at that time. In effect, the government would receive gold and silver in return for its liabilities (government securities). Chase's plan was embodied in the National Banking Act of 1863. To enhance the prospect that national bank notes would be successful, and to eliminate the competition from notes issued by state banks, Chase also developed a tax that Congress gradually increased until the state bank practice of issuing currency ended. Because national bank notes had to be fully collateralized government securities, the nation's supply of paper currency effectively depended on the government's debt.

The supply of currency expanded and contracted in direct response to changes in the value of government securities in the nation's bond markets, not in response to the needs of the economy. When the government began repaying its Civil War debt, redeeming and retiring securities issued in earlier years, the supply of collateral available in the banking system for note issuance shrank. Currency was inelastic (incapable of adjusting to the public's changing needs and demands), and this led to the money panics[4] that periodically plagued the economy of the United States.

THE FEDERAL RESERVE BOARD OF THE UNITED STATES OF AMERICA[5,6]

The Federal Reserve's power is derived from the Constitution of the United States (Article I, Section 8). The article states: "Congress shall have power . . . to coin money (and) regulate the value thereof . . . " The Federal Reserve Act of 1913 established the Federal Reserve to realize the following objectives:

- Furnish an elastic currency that would respond to the economic needs of the nation
- Serve as a last resort to defend against any run on the banking system of the nation
- Establish a more effective and responsive system to supervise banks
- Improve the efficiency of the national payment mechanism

The 1946 Employment Act established a number of national goals that must be achieved by the Federal Reserve. These goals were expanded in 1978, when the Congress passed the Full Employment and Balanced Growth Act. Following are the expanded goals:

- Full employment
- Increased real income(net of inflation)
- Balanced economic growth

- Balanced federal budget
- Growth in productivity
- Improved balance of trade
- Price stability

The Act also required the Federal Reserve to report to the Congress twice a year on its monetary policies as they related to the goals outlined in the 1978 Full Employment and Balanced Growth Acts.

Function of the Federal Reserve

The three basic functions of the Federal Reserve are:

1. *Implementation of monetary policy:* This is done through the use of three primary control devices:
   a. Setting the reserve requirements of the banks
   b. Setting the discount rate at which the Federal Reserve lends the member banks
   c. Setting the monetary growth or contraction through the activities of the Federal Open Market Committee (FOMC); monetary expansion or contraction is done through the purchase or selling, respectively, of government securities
2. *Providing payment services for the depositories:* These services include loans, check collections, currency insurance, wire transfers, and account settlements.
3. *Serving as a bank for the federal government:*
   a. Supervising and regulating banks
   b. Maintaining the U.S. federal government's checking account
   c. Selling and redeeming interest payments on U.S. government securities
   d. Establishing relations with foreign central banks and foreign exchange trading worldwide

The Federal Reserve was created as a branch independent of the politics of governing. Its shares are owned by participating member banks in proportion to their size. U.S. monetary policy, which includes adjusting interest rates and money supply, is designed and implemented without any political interference from the President or Congress. In such a unique setup, the monetary policy would be implemented for the interest of the nation, and not to promote a certain political party, the Congress, or the President. On the other hand, the President of the United States and the Congress decide on the fiscal policy of the government, which includes the federal budget, taxes, and government spending. The Federal Reserve's structure as an independent central bank is unique among the world's central banks. This adds to the power of the Federal Reserve to influence the U.S. economy and to bring creditability to the U.S. dollar worldwide.

Structure of the Federal Reserve Board (America's Central Bank)[7]

The structure of the Federal Reserve Bank is also unique among the world's central banks. It consists of the following:

- A presidentially appointed Board of Governors with general responsibilities for oversight
- Twelve Regional Federal Reserve Banks that are private institutions nominally owned by their stockholders (commercial banks that are members of the Federal Reserve System)
- The Federal Open Market Committee (FOMC), a 12-member policy-making committee of the Federal Reserve. The 12 members consist of 7 governors appointed by the President and 5 regional reserve bank presidents

The nation's monetary policy is decided at the monthly meetings of the FOMC. To understand how the FOMC operates, let us imagine that people in a community one day find themselves with more paper currency than they wish to hold—for example, when the main Christmas shopping season has ended. If the paper currency is physically convertible (for one ounce of silver, let us suppose), people will return the unwanted paper currency to the bank in exchange for silver, but the bank could head off this demand for silver by selling some of its own bonds to the public in exchange for its own paper currency. For example, if the community has 100 units of unwanted paper money, and if people intend to redeem the unwanted 100 units for silver at the bank, the bank could simply sell 100 units worth of bonds or other assets in exchange for 100 units of its own paper currency. This will soak up the unwanted paper and head off people's desire to redeem the 100 units for silver.

Thus, by conducting this type of open market operation—selling bonds (to take dollars out of circulation) when there is excess currency, and buying bonds (to put dollars in circulation) when there is too little—the bank can maintain the value of the paper currency at one ounce of silver without ever redeeming any paper currency for silver. In fact, this is essentially what all modern central banks do, and the fact that their currencies might be physically inconvertible is made irrelevant by the maintenance of financial convertibility. Please note that financial convertibility cannot be maintained unless the bank has sufficient assets to back the currency it has issued.

The Federal Reserve banks are directed by nine-member boards of directors. Congress also stipulated a unique structure for those boards to ensure that the selection process does not favor bankers and allow them to become a majority on any given Federal Reserve Bank board. The Congress, in doing so, wanted to ensure that the views and concerns of all economic interest groups would be expressed and heard during the development of monetary policy.

The nine-member board of directors of a Federal Reserve Bank is elected as follows:

- Member commercial banks elect three members from the banking community and three members from agricultural, commercial, industrial, services, labor, and consumer communities
- The Federal Reserve Board of Governors appoints three directors on its own (it also appoints the Reserve Banks' presidents)

For a detailed description of the operation of the Federal Reserve and the process used to adjust and manage interest rates, please read David H. Friedman, *Essential of Banking* (American Banking Associations, 1989).[8]

The above discussion clearly indicates that interest rates, especially related to the U.S. dollar, are reflections of the way the Federal Reserve Board manages its monetary policy in response to many other factors.

Who Owns the Federal Reserve Bank?

All national banks in the United States own shares in the Federal Reserve Bank in proportion to their capital. In addition, other financial institutions, like some state chartered banks and other major financial institutions, can own shares in the Federal Reserve Bank if their boards decide to become members of the Federal Reserve System. This way, the bankers in the system can have a voice in the process of developing the monetary policy of the country. Chapter 7 includes more details on this subject.

Credit Creation in the Modern Banking System[9]

T-accounts are abstracts of a bank's balance sheet that show only the changes in the bank's assets and liabilities.

For the sake of simplicity, assume, in this T-account example, that:

- All the deposits created by banks stay in the banking system
- Demand deposits are the only form in which newly created funds are held
- Banks lend out every available dollar

These assumptions do not by any means reflect reality. Some deposits created by banks leak out of the banking system into non-bank financial institutions and money market instruments. Consumers and businesses typically convert some newly acquired demand deposits into cash.

Banks do not usually lend (or invest) every available dollar—not because they do not want to, but because the pace with which deposits flow in and out of banks on any given day is often so rapid, the volume so large, and the net effect of check collections so uncertain, that only at the end of the day do banks know just how much they have in net funds to support new loans.

Nonetheless, these simplistic assumptions do not distort the fundamental process by which banks create deposits, which take place in the following sequence of steps:

1. Assume that Bank A receives a cash deposit of $10,000 from a customer for credit to the customer's transaction account. Under Federal Reserve requirements, the bank must hold an amount of reserves—vault cash or deposit balances at a Federal Reserve Bank—equal to a fixed percentage of its deposits (assume 10 percent). Thus, Bank A must hold $1,000 in required reserves against its new $10,000 deposit, and has $9,000 in excess reserves. These excess reserves can support a new $9,000 loan and the creation of $9,000 in demand deposits entailed by such a loan. See Exhibit 5.1.
2. When Bank A makes the loan, both its assets and its liabilities will temporarily increase to $19,000, reflecting the addition of the loan to its earning assets portfolio and the addition of the newly created demand deposit to its total liabilities. However, as soon as the borrower uses the newly created funds, Bank A's assets and liabilities will decline to their pre-loan level as an inevitable result of the check collection process.
3. Assume that the borrower writes a check for the loan amount to a manufacturing company that has an account at Bank B. When the borrower's $9,000 check clears, Bank A will have to transfer $9,000 of its cash

EXHIBIT 5.1 Assets and liabilities of Bank A

Assets			Liabilities
Cash Assets	$10,000*	Demand Deposits:	$10,000
New Loans	$9,000	Demand Deposits	

(*Created for borrowing*) $9,000
*Required reserves $1,000 (10 percent of deposits).

EXHIBIT 5.2   Assets and Liabilities for Banks A and B

Bank A	Assets		Liabilities	Bank B	Assets		Liabilities
Cash	$1,000	Demand	$10,000	Cash	$9,000	Demand	$9,000
Assets		Deposit		Assets*		Deposit	
Loan	$9,000						

*Required reserves $900—excess over reserves $8,100.

assets in payment for the check to the presenting bank (Bank B). Bank A will also strike the $9,000 demand deposit liability carried for the borrower from its books. Thus, after check clearance, Bank A has $10,000 in assets and $10,000 in liabilities. Note, however, that the composition of its assets has changed. Before the loan, it had $10,000 in cash assets; now it has $1,000 in cash assets and $9,000 in loan assets. The $1,000 in cash assets meets the assumed 10 percent reserve requirement ratio against transaction account liabilities. See Exhibit 5.2.

4. The $9,000 in deposit created by Bank A is now a demand deposit on the books of Bank B, increasing that bank's liabilities. Bank B also received a transfer of $9,000 in cash assets when it received payment for the check deposited by the manufacturing company. Bank B, subject to the same 10 percent reserve requirement as Bank A, must keep $900 (10 percent) against the deposit, but can use the remaining $8,100 to support a new loan and the creation of a new $8,100 deposit.

5. When Bank B makes the $8,100 loan, its assets and liabilities will increase initially and then decline to their pre-loan level in response to the collection of the borrower's check. Assume that the borrower writes a check for the loan amount to pay for a corporate service and that the corporation deposits the check in its account in Bank C. Bank B's newly created $8,100.00 will now reside as a liability in Bank C, together with the $8,100 in cash assets Bank B had to transfer in payment for the check. (See Exhibit 5.3.)

EXHIBIT 5.3   Assets and Liabilities of Banks B and C

Bank B	Assets		Liabilities	Bank C	Assets		Liabilities
Cash	$9,000	Demand	$9,000	Cash	$8,100	Demand	$9,000
Assets		Deposit		Assets*		Deposit	
Loan	$8,100						

*Required reserves $810—excess over reserves $ 7,290.

6. Bank C, in turn, will now be able to create demand deposits equal to 90 percent of its new cash assets. If it does so, it will give still another bank the ability to create new deposits.

In theory, this process of bank deposit creation can continue through hundreds of banks, generating, in this example, a total amount of deposits on all banks' books 10 times greater than the $10,000 in cash deposits that started the process. The *multiplier*, or expansion coefficient, is the reciprocal of the reserve requirement ratio. In this example, because the reserve requirement ratio is 10 percent, the multiplier is 10. This simple multiplier is valid only in the context of this example. In the real world of banking, there are separate reserve requirements for different types and amounts of liabilities. This multiple expansion of bank-created deposits is characteristic of banking systems, but not of individual banks. No bank can create deposits in any amount greater than its excess reserves. If it did, it would find itself in a reserve deficiency as soon as the borrower's check cleared. This act violates the Federal Reserve rules, and the bank would be subject to several federal stipulations, controls, and penalties.

THE DOLLAR MADE AS GOLD! WHAT A WONDERFUL PLACE TO BE!

A Brief History of the Bretton Woods Agreement, Which Changed the World of Money[10]

By 1944, the political leaders of the West knew that somehow trade protectionism and currency warfare had crippled the world economy in the 1930s and helped bring on WWII. The British government called upon Lord Keynes to help design a structure of international finance that would help avert WWIII. The Bretton Woods agreement was the design of Lord Keynes and the undersecretary of the U.S. Treasury, Harry Dexter White. Keynes wanted a world bank, as if there were one world government. Participating nations would have their own currencies, but they would be fully convertible to one another through this world bank, which Keynes called a Clearing Union. The bank would issue its own currency, the *Unitas*, and would maintain its value not by tying it to gold, but by the "wisdom" of its directors. The Keynesian notion of a world bank that could expand credit without the restraint of a gold standard was rejected. The opposite argument by Undersecretary Harry Dexter White, who believed in the "hard money" approach using the gold standard rather than the "soft money" approach of Lord Keynes, was accepted because the United States owned $24 billion in gold; the United States got its preferred hard money currency. The Bretton Woods Agreement and U.S. economic might after WWII gave the United States and the U.S. dollar undisputed dominance.

The system would work perfectly as long as the Federal Reserve Board of the United States enforced sound monetary operations by stopping the printing of dollars when people showed up with dollars demanding gold. The U.S. monetary and Federal Reserve authorities naturally would not be able to accommodate a huge run on U.S. gold; however, if such a circumstance was handled promptly and wisely, and if the U.S. authorities could convince the world of the United States' sound policies, then a crisis could be averted. The world economy would always have precisely the right amount of money.

In 1953, when President Eisenhower tried to boost the U.S. economy out of recession, instead of cutting tax rates, he leaned on the Fed to print dollars. Because all currencies were fixed together, the surplus flowed around the world. The printed dollars reduced the U.S. gold reserve by the same amount.

The system did break down. To run a dollar standard, the United States certainly did not need $24 billion in gold bullion, for the value of gold is not as a medium of exchange, which requires tonnage, but merely as an error signal to alert administrators when too many dollars are being printed. By 1965, the United States had depleted Fort Knox of approximately $12 billion of its gold tonnage, mainly to the Europeans and, in particular, France. A media story of the time reported that the weight of the gold accumulating on the second floor of the London Metal Exchange building was so heavy that the floor gave way.

In the spring of 1971, as the Fed tried desperately to expand the U.S. economy by flooding it with dollars, the rest of the world came demanding gold. On August 15, 1971, President Richard Nixon ordered the gold window closed, ending the international currency's link to gold.

An attempt to rebuild Bretton Woods around gold at $38 per ounce instead of $35 was made with the Smithsonian Agreement. Later, the gold-dollar window was shut permanently, and what Keynes suggested in 1944 became a reality. Economists around the world projected a dramatic increase in the price of oil and other commodities; another interesting twist in the accepted folklore that claims that oil prices increased because of the 1973 Arab-Israeli War. It is important to note that inflation of the 1970s was not caused by the Organization of the Petroleum Exporting Countries (OPEC) but rather was caused by the breakdown of Bretton Woods. No country could escape the impact of inflation. Commodity prices skyrocketed between 1966 and the spring of 1974. Here are some examples:

- Oil prices rose 344 percent, from $2.9 to $10 per barrel
- The price of rice climbed 375 percent, from $8 per cwt to $30 per cwt
- Wheat prices rose 322 percent, to $5.80 from $1.80 a bushel
- Lead went up by 233 percent, from $12 per cwt to $28 per cwt

After President Nixon closed the gold window and currencies started to float, the world changed. Companies with costs in one currency and revenues in another needed to hedge exchange rate risk. In 1972, a former lawyer named Leo Melamed[11] was clever enough to see a business in this; he launched currency futures on the Chicago Mercantile Exchange. Futures in commodities had existed for more than a century, enabling farmers to insure themselves against lower crop prices. But Mr. Melamed saw that financial futures would one day be far larger than the commodities market. Today's complex derivatives are direct descendants of those early currency trades.

This same scenario with different players has repeated itself ever since. The Soviet Union was disassembled in the early 1990s. Iraq invaded Kuwait, and the United States subsequently liberated Kuwait. A heinous terrorist attack on American soil occurred on September 11, 2001. The United States invaded Afghanistan to fight terrorism and simultaneously invaded Iraq to change the regime. In 2008–2009, the financial markets in the United States and the world suddenly collapsed, supposedly because of reckless lending and banking practices. There was a subsequent stock and credit market collapse in October 2008, which led to the U.S. government's rescue of Bear Stearns and AIG Insurance by pumping almost $110 billion dollars into them. It also led to the bankruptcy of Lehman Brothers, an icon of investment banking in the United States and the world. Lehman Brothers's collapse took with it the capital of many countries and individuals who had trusted the government to have supervised these banks properly. For the first time in the history of the capitalist world, there was a massive government effort to rescue banks by owning them outright (which happened in Britain) or owning a minority share (which happened in the United States and all European countries). Additionally, the United States approved a $700 billion rescue plan for its financial system. After all was said and done, more than $1.2 trillion was allocated to rescue the system. And, of course, we do not yet know what more will come upon us.

All we know is that the only way to come up with the needed amount of huge rescue money is simply to create it by "printing it." In other words, the Fed will increase the money supply in the system, as discussed earlier. If the Fed uses—as an example—wheat, rice, or gold as money, there is no way the Fed can produce that wheat, because it takes time and effort to produce it. The same applies to rice and gold. In fact, there is a limit to what we can do to increase the production of agricultural commodities, let alone prospecting, finding, and mining gold. However, it takes almost no time at all to print a lot of money. That has spelled a lot of trouble in the past, because this conceptually means that the price of reference commodities (gold, silver, rice, wheat, and others) will have to go up in paper money (dollars) because there are more dollars in the system compared to the limited production and supply of the commodities. That spells big trouble down the road. That trouble is called inflation, as we saw in the 1960s and 1970s.

The Fed Fund Interest Rates Setting Regime
The Taylor Rule[12,13,14,15]   This section attempts to summarize how the U.S. Federal Reserve Board decides on a suitable level for the Fed Fund interest rates (the interest rate charged by banks to each other for overnight borrowing to balance their books, which is set by the Fed). The Fed Fund rate is one of the important tools used by the Fed to decide on interest rates, which set the policy of money supply in order to influence U.S. monetary and economic policy. It is important that RF bankers understand the foundations upon which these decisions are made and the mechanical procedures followed. This information reveals that the Fed Fund rate set by the Federal Reserve is a tool by which the monetary authorities manage the money supply; it is different from the usury or interest prohibited by the injunctions of Judeo-Christian-Islamic Law, or Shari'aa.

Professor John Taylor of Stanford University in California formally introduced the Taylor Rule in 1994 to model the process by which the Federal Reserve System sets a suitable Fed Fund rate. He suggested that the two primary factors that drive the model are the gross domestic product (GDP) gap and the inflation gap.

Intuitively, these two factors have economic bases. This policy rule states that if the economy is growing beyond its potential, or if the inflation rate is greater than the Fed's assumed target of (say) 2 percent, the Fed will increase the Fed Funds. Professor John Taylor argued that the Federal Reserve Board can be viewed as setting the target for the Federal Fund rate at a level that is close to, say, 2 to 2.5 percent, with a level corrector mechanism. He recommended that two correctors are added. These are:

1. An *inflation corrector*; called the *inflation gap*. It equals current inflation rates minus the inflation rate targeted by the Fed.
2. An *economic growth corrector*, called the *output gap* (GDP[16] corrector), which is equal to current GDP minus potential GDP.

He also suggested assuming a most likely scenario that the impact of numbers 1 and 2 above is equally weighted, at 50 percent each. Another scenario might call for a different weighting—such as, for example, the allocation of 70 percent for inflation and 30 percent for GDP, or vice versa. This will depend on the situation, the country involved, and the strategic options available to the central bankers. It is important to clarify further that the interest rate component of the equation is a mere rate or percentage; it is conceptually and materially different from the usury (price charged for using money) or interest (the price for renting money). In this context, this rate is in fact a percentage rate that influences the rate at which fiat—money— should be grown (by printing more) or shrunk (by selling government bonds at high rates to absorb the excess liquidity, or by increasing the reserve requirements of the banks). The equation suggested can be written as follows:

Target Short – Term Fed Funds Interest Rate = Rate of Inflation as measured by GDP deflator + Equilibrium Real Interest Rate (defined approximately as prevailing interest rate minus inflation) + an Inflation Contribution + an Economic Growth Rate (Economic Output) Contribution

Please see the definitions of the components of the Taylor formula.

Rate of Inflation: As defined by a basket of products and services in the economy.

Equilibrium Real Interest Rate: Interest rate charged by banks and financial institutions minus inflation rate (approximately).
   The interest rate charged by banks and financial institutions to their customers is in fact the riba we are talking about; it is prohibited in the Judeo-Christian-Islamic value system because it conceptually represents paying a price for the use or rental of money. This rate, as we discussed in Chapter 3 and will discuss in more detail later, should be obtained using the mark-to-market rule, not the rental rate of money.

Inflation Contribution: A percentage of the *inflation gap*, defined as Current Inflation Rate minus Target Inflation Rate, as defined by policymakers. Taylor suggested that we give it a 50 percent weight. However, one can give it a different weight depending on monetary policy goals and strategies.

In the case of the United States Federal Reserve System, the policy targets mentioned above are discussed and agreed on in a special committee, the Federal Open Market Committee (FOMC). The committee discusses the tradeoff between the Fed's goal of price stability through achieving a low inflation rate and the need to maintain maximum economic growth and output, as well as the highest employment possible. To achieve low inflation, Fed Fund rates need to be raised. On the other hand, if the committee wanted the highest employment and economic output, they would adopt a policy that reduces the Fed Fund interest rate. The committee's most important challenge is to decide the most suitable and optimum course of action regarding the Fed Fund rate. In addition, Taylor's equation above shows that the Fed Fund interest rate decided by the Fed is needed to adjust the monetary policy in a fiat (paper) money regime, and is far different from the charging of interest prohibited by Shari'aa, as discussed in Chapter 2. The Fed Fund rate is a percentage sign used to influence policy and to decide how much money to print or withdraw from the system in a world run on fiat money. In the case of the Judeo-Christian-Islamic value system there is a world of difference between the renting of real money (as discussed in the six commodity indexes) and the Fed Fund rate as described clearly by the Taylor Rule.

Real and Nominal Interest Rate   As we read in Chapter 2, the contemporary position of the Roman Catholic Church regarding interest and the time value of money coincides with the position of modern economics and finance. In economics and finance, an individual who lends money for repayment at a later point in time expects to be compensated for the time value of money, or not having the ability to use that money (perhaps more productively) while it is lent, and particularly if it is not returned on time. In addition, owners of capital will want to be compensated for the risks of having less purchasing power when the loan is repaid. These risks are:

- *Systemic Risks:* This includes the possibility that the borrower will default or will be unable to pay on the originally agreed-upon terms, or that collateral backing the loan will prove to be less valuable than estimated.
- *Regulatory Risks:* This includes taxation and changes in the law, which would prevent the lender from collecting on a loan or having to pay more in taxes on the amount repaid than originally estimated.
- *Inflation Risks:* This takes into account that the money repaid may not have as much buying power from the perspective of the lender as the money originally lent, and may include fluctuations in the value of the currencies involved.

Nominal interest rates include all three risk factors, plus the time value of the money itself. *Real interest rates* include only the systemic and regulatory risks and are meant to measure the time value of money. The *real rate* is equal to the *nominal rate* minus *inflation* and minus *currency adjustment*.

The *real interest rate* in an economy is often the rate of return on a risk-free investment, such as U.S. Treasury notes, minus an index of inflation, such as the *Consumer Price Index* (CPI) or *Gross Domestic Products Deflator* (GDP Deflator). This is what we can call the interest rate decided by the Fed, as explained earlier, to run its fiat money policy to the best of its ability. It must be stated that no specific money system is being advocated here, because that is not the subject of this book nor of the RF banking and finance system presented here. All we want to achieve is to familiarize the reader with the fact that the interest rate set by the Fed is in fact a policy tool and it is, in simple layman's terms, a mechanism by which the government decides how much money to print or to withdraw from the market in order to achieve its policy goals about inflation, prices, and employment levels.

As suggested by the equation, if all is kept constant and the FOMC wanted to increase the economic production, they would reduce the short-term interest rate on Fed Funds, and increase the rate if the opposite were true. Of course, real life situations are more sophisticated and involve many other scenarios, permutations, and parameters. However, the fact remains that the interest rate that the Feds use is different from the one prohibited in Shari'aa. It is a calibration tool that adjusts the flow of money in or out of the fiat paper money system.

All those who believe in Judeo-Christian-Islamic values should focus on two important factors in our development of the RF banking and finance system. These factors are:

- The use of the *commodity indexation rule* and approach to ensure fair market pricing, as was discussed earlier and will be further developed later in the book.
- The use of the *marking-to-market* concept to make certain that we are renting tangible and rentable assets, and not money, in order to ensure that we are investing prudently.

Fiat (Paper) Money and the Cyclical Nature of the Fiat Money Economy

Professor Ahmad Kamal Meera[17] authored an interesting book on the economics of fiat money, bank fractional reserves, and interest, in which he concluded that the fiat money interest-based system causes asset bubbles, particularly after the potential GDP levels of an economy have been reached. He described a five-stage process to the creation of cycles in a fiat money-based economy. It is important to state here that the purpose of this discussion is not to criticize the system or advocate changing it—that is not our goal—but rather to throw more light on how the system works, in order to allow for it while operating the RF banking and finance system. It is believed that this can be done to a high degree of success (as experienced in our operations at LARIBA and the Bank of Whittier) by applying the screens of the commodity indexation rule and the mark-to-market rule. If we know the way the system works, we definitely can, to a better extent, identify the formation of a bubble and hopefully have the signals and the decision tools that will allow us to avoid or to leave the bubble before it bursts and causes everyone in the RF banking and finance system great loss of assets, reputation, and credibility.

Following are the five phases:

1. A *Period of Money Creation* without significant inflation. In this period, the Central Bank or the Feds would allow the creation of more money through the tools at its disposal—such as, for example, lowering interest rates (the Fed Fund rate) and/or reducing the statutory reserve requirements at the banks. As money becomes available, people begin borrowing money and buying things. This situation creates a period of economic prosperity without inflation, because the excess capacity goes into an absorption process.
2. An *Inflationary Period* of excess money supply with cheap (low interest rate) funds. This stage follows the drying up of supply of inexpensive products, services, homes, and commercial real estate. People still can borrow at low interest rates, which causes demand to rise and outpace supply. This situation causes a period of inflation of prices. Excess money in the hands of the public begins going into higher salaries, which means more excess cash in the hands of the public, more savings for retirement, and, in the end, excess cash pouring into the stock market, causing it to heat up and rise sharply. Of course, those in the money market and stock market will always give the impression that there is no end in sight for this spectacular growth. It is the responsibility of a wise Central Bank or Federal Reserve Board to arrest the money creation machine at this stage to avoid the growth of the bubble.
3. A *Period of Destruction of Money Supply*, causing an economic downturn with financial distress and bankruptcies. Here, prices keep rising, but prudent investors start looking at their positions and discover that the price-to-earnings ratio of certain stocks is too high to be real and the price of real estate is so high that the debt service is much higher than the potential rent. This is where applying the commodity indexation

rules and the mark-to-market rules will be extremely useful to those who believe in and apply the rules of Shari'aa. They decide to go to cash. This reduces demand and increases supply, causing prices to decline and, in most cases, sharply signaling the bursting of the bubble. In most cases, the price of a real estate property, for example, may be lower than the loan the owners obtained to finance it—as many experienced during the 2008 economic meltdown. In most cases, especially in today's culture, that prompts many to declare bankruptcy to run away from debt, and the banks repossess the properties. Because banks are required to sell these properties as soon as possible, prices decline further in a process of capital destruction. The same process happened on the stock market, especially with portfolios that use *margin* financing (borrowing money against the value of the stock portfolio). Market losses in the Dow Jones Industrial Average—in one day—can reach more than $1 trillion (that is $1,000 billion). During this process, we are witnessing the destruction of the fiat money created at the printing press!

4. A *Period of Transfer of Crisis from the Financial Sector (Wall Street) to the Real Sector (Main Street)*. As the recession sets in, businesses, in their pursuit to cut expenses and overhead, resort to reducing employment and begin laying off employees and reducing production (in industries such as home construction and auto manufacturing), with a resulting deep impact on local economies. This process results in massive economic dislocations and price reductions.

5. A *Period of Recovery that Takes the Economy Back to the First Period* described in number 1, above. At this stage, the government starts a recovery program with the help of monetary authorities, and we head back toward the first stage; money creation begins anew.

The five-stage process that ends with the bursting of the bubble has been witnessed during the inflation of the stock market from 1987 to the year 2000 and from 2003 to 2008. The reduction in interest rates that followed the September 11 attacks caused inflation of real estate prices for a long time, resulting in the 2008 meltdown and the near-collapse of the financial system, not only in the United States but also in the whole world.

It is important to note here that one of the responsibilities of the Central Bankers of the world—including the Federal Reserve of the United States—is to try their best to timely stop the "bubblization" of assets by bursting these bubbles before they become so large that they create a heavy burden on the economy and the whole population when they collapse. It is interesting to note that former Fed Chairman Alan Greenspan preferred to allow the housing bubbles in the United States to fester for a long time. They eventually burst after his retirement, causing the huge damage of financial markets worldwide. Unfortunately, in the 2008 experience we have seen that such a *laissez-faire* approach invites corruption and fraud (witness the persistent regulatory and legal violations of many of the investment bankers and mortgage bankers). The outcome can be devastating in depth and extent, as we saw in 2008.

The big question is, how can an average citizen or an RF financial institution avoid participating in this bubble behavior? The answer is that the bubble can be avoided by applying the following two important RF finance rules:

1. Use commodity indexation
2. Apply the mark-to-market concept

These RF finance rules make certain that we are investing prudently and not participating in a bubble. True, we may be premature in quitting a certain market, and we do not participate in some spectacular speculative (gambling) returns, but as RF bankers we are certain that we deliver the most important value of RF banking to our customers: the preservation of capital and the realizing of prudent returns that, in the long run, will be much higher than such "bubble" and gambling-based returns.

THE PROHIBITION OF RIBA/RIBIT: RULINGS ON RIBA IN FIQH, THE SCIENCE OF SHARI'AA

There are two types or classes of riba:

1. *Riba al nassee'ah* is defined as the increase over the original value of capital given, usually by putting a condition in the loan agreement indicating that the lender would be entitled to an increase over the original value if the borrower asks for an extension of the term of the credit. This type of riba is prohibited by the Qur'aan, the Sunnah (tradition of Prophet Muhammad [pp]), and all scholars, without exception.
2. *Riba al fadl* is defined as selling [real] money for [real] money, commodity for commodity (e.g., food for food) with an increase over the original value except under special rules as will be explained later. This practice is also prohibited by all sources (the Qur'aan, the Sunnah, and all the scholars), because it can lead to riba al nassee'aah. It is given the label of riba as a way to attach it to the real reason for prohibiting it, because it leads to riba al nassee'ah. Prophet Muhammad (pp) said[18]:

. . . do not sell the [silver] dirham (a prevailing currency then) for two [silver] dirhams because I am afraid that you indulge in [the prohibited] Riba.

3. The *Hadeeth* (sayings or pronouncements) of Prophet Muhammad (pp) specifically prohibited practicing riba in six items: gold, silver, wheat, barley, dates, and salt. It was reported that the Prophet (pp) said[19]:

   . . . gold for gold, silver for silver, barley for barley and salt for salt hand to hand [in an on-the-spot transaction without delay] those who increase in buying or selling these items they are considered practicing Riba. This applies to those who take the increased amount and those who agree to give it.

   In another narration by Muslim (one of the compiler of the sayings of Prophet Muhammad [pp]), it was added:

   . . . should the kinds [of commodities] differ, then exchange as you wish, provided that the exchange is hand to hand [on-the-spot].

Reason for Prohibition

The reason for prohibiting riba in dealing with these six commodities is that they represented—at the time—the basic necessities of the citizens; without such basic commodities, they could not live comfortably. Gold and silver, at the time of Prophet Muhammad (pp), were the basic currencies used to buy and sell and to define prices in the market to settle transactions. They were called *tathmeen*: the two commodities used to establish prices in the market.

If riba were practiced in dealing with these items, it would have hurt the interests of the citizens and would lead to a breakdown in the fabric of the society. Shari'aa prohibited such dealing as a mercy to mankind and to protect the interests of the citizens.

From the above discussion, one can conclude that the reason for prohibiting riba in gold and silver was because gold and silver were used to price things, and riba was prohibited on the other four food items because they were food staples. If these qualifications are found to apply on other items, the rule applies. Such items are used as reference commodities in the commodity indexation approach discussed earlier.

Based on this determination, the rule can be extended using the discipline of analogy (*qiyas*). The rule can be stated in general as:

1. If the two items transacted are from the same material and are used for the same purpose (e.g., gold for gold, or wheat for wheat), then both

riba al nassee'ah and riba al fadl are prohibited. The following conditions must be satisfied in order for a like-for-like transaction to be ruled riba-free:

a. The quantity on the buy and sell side must be equal, regardless of quality.[20]

b. The buy and sell must be done on the spot (e.g., hand to hand, as the Prophet [pp] said).

If the two items to be transacted differ in their material but are used for the same application, then the rules of riba al fadl can be invoked on the condition that riba al nassee'ah is not used. Gold can be sold for silver or wheat can be sold for barley, and the transaction must be done on the spot (hand-to-hand), but the quantities do not have to be equal. It was reported that the Prophet (pp) said[21]:

> . . . *it is acceptable to sell wheat for barley and you can get more barley but it has to be hand to hand [an on-the-spot transaction].*

If the two items to be transacted are different in material and in purpose of use, there are no restrictions in applying time in the riba al nassee'ah and excess over the original amount in riba al fadl. For example, food can be sold for silver, and one dress for two dresses, or two cups for one cup. In summary, riba al fadl can be practiced on any item, aside from the two metals (gold and silver) and the food staples (wheat, barley, dates, and salt). The Prophet (pp) emphasized this concept when a companion brought to him an excellent type of dates from Khaiber (a city in what is now Saudi Arabia). The Prophet (pp) asked, "Are all the dates of Khaiber like this?" The man said no, but we barter one volume (a volume measuring unit that was used at that time, called *saa*) of this dates for two volumes (*saa*) of ours (they were lower quality, smaller dates). The Prophet said: "Do not do that, because that is exactly Riba and it is forbidden." The way to do it according to RF rules is to sell your dates for money (silver dirham, gold dinar, or another reference staple commodity except for the same commodity—i.e., not other dates), and buy the good dates with the proceeds.[22] By this rule, one can buy 10 bushels of wheat (food) for 1 ounce of gold on-the-spot [cash price] or deferred at 2 ounces of gold after 2 years. Because the gold is a metal and the wheat is a food, this transaction is halal (divinely allowed). Also, buying seven bushels of wheat for ten bushels of barley is allowed on-the-spot, but increasing the price to seven bushels of wheat for fifteen bushels of barley to be paid (delivered) after one year is haram (divinely prohibited) because both are food items. As a more modern example, if one wants to buy heating oil by exchanging two gallons of fuel oil for one gallon of gasoline, it is not allowed by Shari'aa, because both are used as a source of energy and al fadl can only be applied on two items with different uses. In this case, one can offer to exchange the heating oil for another medium (currency), such as gold or silver, or for food such as wheat or rice. Then one can take the proceeds and buy the gasoline with it at market price. This is what we call in this book the commodity indexation and mark-to-market rules.

When the Islamic state expanded beyond Arabia, many of the jurists were exposed to different environments, economies, monetary systems, and cultures that used essential commodities that were not known in Arabia. To deal with the intricacies of concluding whether such practices were acceptable to Shari'aa, the jurists used the system of analogy (qiyas, as explained in Chapter 3). For example, this analysis allowed them to add other commodities to the six reference commodities identified by the Prophet (pp). Muslims continued for centuries to apply these rulings in their dealings.

Application of Shari'aa using the Commodity Indexation Rule

As discussed earlier, Shari'aa requires that commodities be priced in terms of another reference commodity before being traded for a higher quantity, volume, or weight of the same type of commodity. For example, one cannot trade 100 bushels of good quality wheat for 500 bushels of lower quality wheat, because it constitutes ribit/riba. However, one can sell the 100 bushels for another commodity (e.g., gold or silver) and use the proceeds to buy the lower quality wheat. This way, the markets would be kept in stable condition and in equilibrium. A transparent ribit/riba-free market system is free from both ribit/riba and *gharar* (deception and misrepresentation).

Please note that when it is suggested that one use gold or silver it is not meant nor intended to enter into a discussion of going back to the system of the gold standards. What is strongly recommended here to preserve Shari'aa is to use the commodity indexation rule, which requires that we test the price of things in the economy (e.g., oil, houses, food items) by the use of one of the two types of reference commodities (e.g., precious metals—gold or silver—or food staples—such as wheat, barley, and rice). It is interesting to note that in 1987, then-Secretary of the United States Treasury James A. Baker III told world financial leaders during the 1987 fall meeting of the

International Monetary Fund (IMF)[23] that the Reagan Administration "is prepared to consider" using the price of gold in trying to steer its own and the world's economies. Gold, Mr. Baker explained, could be used in a specially designed index, along with other commodities, to help governments discern inflation and then adjust their policies—by using interest rates or taxes, for example. Professor Robert A. Mundell, a Columbia University economist and proponent of the concept, stated that "this is far from a gold standard." On May 20, 1999, soon after the United Kingdom announced its decision to sell part of its gold reserves, Alan Greenspan, then chairman of the U.S. Federal Reserve, said: "Gold still represents the ultimate form of payment in the world." Dr. Mahathir Mohamad, the former prime minister of Malaysia, also made some very interesting comments in one of his speeches[24] in response to the Asian currency crisis, which resulted from massive hedge fund speculations in Asian currencies. The speculation caused massive devaluation of local currencies in Thailand, South Korea, Indonesia, Malaysia, Hong Kong, Indonesia, and many other countries. Dr. Mohamad discovered that even many of his senior central bankers[25] were not aware of the mechanics of currency speculation—or the way to stop such speculation. The solution offered by many senior finance officers and ministers of finance of these countries was to support the local currencies by selling hard currencies like the U.S. dollar, the Japanese yen, and the euro, and buying the local currencies to create demand for the local currencies to attempt to keep the exchange rate intact. The problem was the huge volume of currencies needed. Many of the countries lost a major portion of their reserves without causing a dent in the exchange rate. The following is a snapshot of what happened to some currencies in a very short span of time. The decline of exchange rates relative to the U.S. dollar on February 16, 1998 compared to June 30, 1998 is shown in Exhibit 5.4.

One interesting but sad and painful case was that of Turkey. The Turkish lira's exchange rate was 108,340 lira for each U.S. dollar in January 1997; it declined by 93 percent to exchange at 1,474,525 lira per U.S. dollar in January 2002. Such massive declines obviously resulted in a reduction in

EXHIBIT 5.4 Decline of exchange rates in Asian currencies relative to the U.S. dollar

Country	Decline
Indonesia	75%
Malaysia	36%
Thailand	48%
Philippines	36%
South Korea	47%

the values of salaries, peoples' savings, pensions, and the price of goods and services. Imagine what a poor farmer in the Philippines would do when the cost of rice in his local currency—the only currency he knows about and is using—increases significantly. Such a sudden reduction in the value of local currencies raised the value of short-term debt of the country involved, usually denominated in U.S. dollars or in euros, and increased debt service. As if this was not enough, the sudden currency devaluation reduced the credit rating of the country involved, which resulted in an increase in the cost of borrowing on the international markets. All these unfortunate results reduced the country's economic activity, resulting in massive increases in unemployment and poverty.

In an effort to test the valuation of different commodities in terms of one another in order to conduct sales and trading at a higher price, as stipulated by Shari'aa, we attempted to price different commodities in terms of gold and other reference commodities. What was intended in this research was to detect the historic trend of pricing a commodity, say oil, in terms of gold or another staple commodity, using the commodity indexation concept, by asking the question: How many barrels of oil can one buy for every ounce of gold, or how many ounces of gold are necessary to buy a home using average home prices in the United States? We have done the same for commodities such as natural gas, wheat, corn, rice, and soybeans.

The exhibits on the following pages are charts depicting the prices from 1967 until the time of preparing this book for publication in 2009. In this approach, we disengaged and tried to neutralize the effects of the use of fiat money, and instead used a reference commodity as stipulated in the Judeo-Christian-Islamic Commodity Indexation Rule detailed earlier. It will be made clear that if we refer the value of each of the commodities to another reference commodity or index commodity, we shall find that the price or market value would be more stable, less volatile, moving within a narrow band, and fair. Exceptions to this general finding are cases that involve changes in production processes, technological developments, political factors, or significant change in lifestyle. The charts also show that regardless of how the price of a commodity changes in terms of fiat (paper) currencies, like the U.S. dollar, the value in terms of a reference commodity are more representative, and that a bubble can be detected whenever the band of price fluctuation is penetrated to the higher or lower side. In doing so, the reader is encouraged to consider using this approach to indexing their own products and services to a reference commodity, in order to avoid participating in an economic bubble like those we have witnessed throughout history—from the tulips in 17th century Holland to the stock market dot-com technology bubble in the 20th century United States to the housing bubble in the beginning of this century, which resulted in the 2008 global financial meltdown.

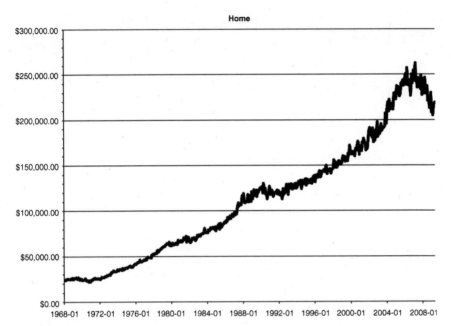

EXHIBIT 5.5 Average U.S. home prices.

HOMES IN AMERICA[26,27]

As shown in Exhibit 5.5, the average U.S. home prices in terms of the U.S. dollar kept rising and have either stabilized, as they did in the early 1980s, declined slightly, as in the early 1990s, or declined significantly, as happened starting in 2006 to 2009.

Looking at this chart in 2005, one can quickly reach the erroneous conclusion that home prices in America must keep on rising. However, in terms of gold[28] (how many ounces of gold are needed to buy an average priced home), Exhibit 5.6 shows the true fluctuation in house prices.

The chart shows that prices are more stable when expressed in terms of gold. The chart shows the average house price fluctuating between 200 and 400 ounces of gold. Whenever the price penetrates the lower level of the envelope, it signals that homes are underpriced; this can be considered a good indicator for investing in homes. If the price penetrates the upper boundary of the envelope, it has signaled over the years that homes are entering a price bubble, and we should be careful in our investments as well as in our financing decisions for homes. The chart also shows that houses in the United States began getting pricy around the late 1990s and peaked in

EXHIBIT 5.6   Price of U.S. homes in gold.

2003 to 2004. It also shows that house prices started to decline after the end of 2005 to reach a bottom, or close to a bottom, in 2008–2009, signaling a good market. It is also important to note that it takes about seven to ten years for home prices to start climbing and for a home's owners to reap a good profit on the sale. In general, 2009 home prices in terms of gold indicate that it is a good time to start buying homes and financing the housing industry. Of course, this data is based on general nationwide data. It is recommended that specific data in specific markets should be used.

The same correlation can be depicted by looking at the price of a home if we were to pay for it in terms of rice or wheat[29] (if the only product of a community were rice or wheat). We will find that the same correlation applies. The reader must be warned that these charts (Exhibits 5.7 and 5.8) are presented here as a directional tool; they are meant to be used by decision makers to gauge the direction of trends in order to avoid participating in a bubble that may result in significant loss of their investments. It is also important to state that it is hoped that a full research effort be conducted along these lines to refine the analysis which is admittedly presented here in the form of the Art of Islamic Finance. One of the questions that needs to be answered is: Why did the prices decline drastically, especially the price of

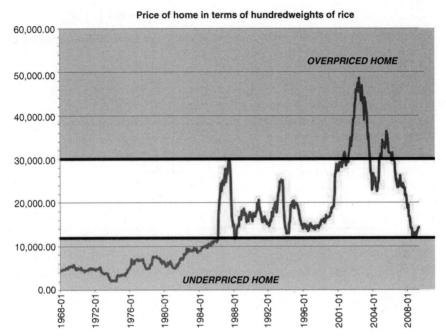

EXHIBIT 5.7   Price of homes in rice.

agricultural commodities, from their pre-1971 levels when the Bretton Woods dollar-gold parity of $35 dollars per ounce of gold parity was discontinued?

PRICE OF COAL

Coal has been used as a source of energy for years. Its production infrastructure, transportation and distribution routes, markets, and uses have matured and are well-developed around the world. That is why we see that the relationship between the price of coal (as a basic energy commodity in the matrix of needs of consumers) and the price of other commodities, such as gold, rice or wheat, fluctuates in a narrower band than that of oil. Please see Exhibits 5.9 and 5.10.

Based on Exhibit 5.10, the price of coal, which kept rising in dollar denomination, went down in real value—in terms of gold—after 1971, and kept fluctuating in a range of 0.06 to 0.1 ounces of gold for every ton of bituminous coal.

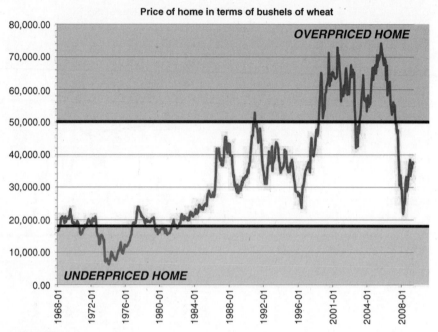

EXHIBIT 5.8   Price of homes in wheat.

PRICE OF CRUDE OIL

The oil market followed the same pattern that we saw in the coal market. Crude oil and the refined products markets have also developed and matured over the years. That is why, as we found in the case of coal, we can safely look at oil price gyrations in the market to try to learn the relationship between the price of oil and that of other commodities. The chart in Exhibit 5.11 is intriguing. It shows that despite the large rise in oil prices in terms of U.S. dollars, in normal times the price of oil in terms of gold is stable, ranging from 0.06 to 0.12 ounces of gold per barrel of oil (10–20 barrels of oil for every ounce of gold), with an average price of 0.085 ounces of gold per barrel of oil (12–13 barrels of oil per ounce of gold). In fact, based on my 14-year experience in the oil industry—ten of these years were with a major United States–based oil company—we considered 10–13 barrels of oil per ounce of gold a fair value. This "technical analysis" was shared by some of the distinguished "technical analysts" at Smith Barney/Citigroup in 1999, and they started using it as an important indicator for oil price trends.

We can see from Exhibit 5.11 that if the value of oil in terms of gold increases and penetrates the upper boundary of 0.12 ounces of gold per barrel

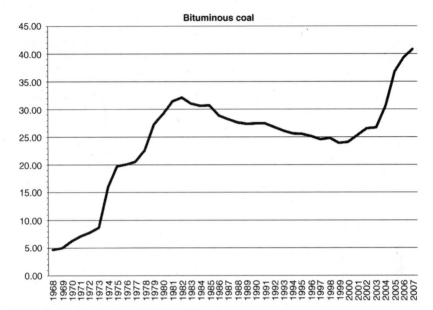

EXHIBIT 5.9 Coal prices, 1968–2007

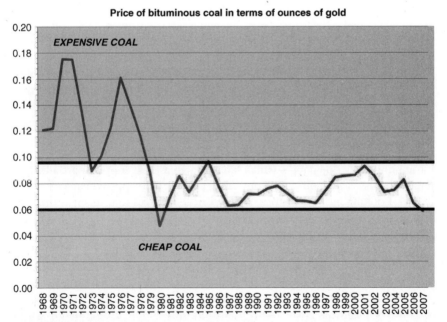

EXHIBIT 5.10 Price of coal in ounces of gold

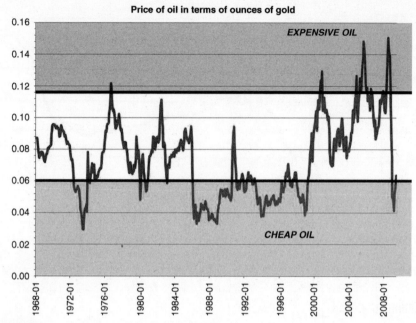

EXHIBIT 5.11   Price of oil in ounces of gold.

of oil (e.g., eight barrels of oil per ounce of gold), oil is overpriced and it is an indicator to sell the oil to avoid participating in a bubble. On the other hand, if the price of oil is low and pierces the lower level of the envelope at 0.06 ounces of gold per barrel of oil (e.g., 17 barrels of oil per ounce of gold), it is an indicator to buy (go long on) oil. It is very interesting to note that spikes in the oil price in terms of gold reflect political and economic changes that occurred over the course of history. For example, before the first oil shock in 1973, the value of oil spiked from 10 barrels per ounce of gold to approximately 35 barrels per ounce of gold, creating hugely undervalued oil and prompting higher demand—which later created a great supply shortfall, leading to the increase in oil price from $2.50 per barrel to approximately $12 per barrel. Looking into the history of this period, one sees that this was the time when most of the oil-producing countries were renegotiating their oil production participation agreements to increase their share of the production and hence reduce the share that would go to the oil companies. This situation created the incentive, on the part of the producing oil companies, to produce as much oil as possible in the shortest time available, flooding the markets with oil and later creating a supply shortfall that nudged oil prices higher. It is interesting to note the clear indication of a bubble during major world events.

At the time of writing this book, the oil price had reached a level of approximately $135 per barrel, while gold has reached approximately $885 per ounce. That is, the value of oil is approximately 6.6 barrels per ounce of gold. Based on commodity indexation discussed above, the price of oil is very high and is overvalued compared to an equilibrium market price. Based on our previous analysis, one expects that this ratio should go back to at least 10 barrels of oil per ounce of gold. At a gold price of $885 per ounce, that would translate to an oil price of $88.50 per barrel. At a gold price of $750 per ounce, and with a most likely oil price index of 10 to 13 barrels per ounce of gold, then one can expect fair value for the oil price to reach $58 to $75 per barrel.

As this book went into printing, the world oil price declined to as low as $35 per barrel and stabilized at about $50 per barrel. This fluctuation depends on the U.S. dollar's value on the international markets; the price of commodities that underlie the U.S. economy (because it is the largest importer of crude oil in the world); and the U.S. government's and Federal Reserve Board's policies regarding the dollar, interest rate, and economic policy (both in the United States and in the major economies in Canada, Europe, and the United Kingdom). Other important factors are the speculative activities of the futures and options markets in the oil, gold, and dollar markets. It is interesting to note the cyclical nature of very high oil prices (overpriced oil) followed by another period of very low prices (underpriced oil). Students of history may find a relationship between capital accumulations by the major oil companies during the overpriced stage followed by an intensive record of negotiating new oil exploration contracts in new areas, coinciding with much lower prices.

The prices of some other commodities are charted in the following sections to give the reader a full scope of the validity of the commodity indexation concept. It is sincerely hoped that a group of researchers will take it upon themselves to research these relationships, not only in terms of relative prices but also in terms of mechanistic analysis, such as determining how much energy is consumed to produce an ounce of gold and how this impacts oil prices. This will not only include the cost of fuel, but also the amount of human energy consumed in exploring for gold, refining it, making it into standardized ingots, transporting it, and storing it.

PRICE OF NATURAL GAS[30]

Natural gas is believed to be the emerging energy source of the future. Its markets, production, and transportation infrastructure are still developing and are not mature yet. There are huge natural gas reserves in the United

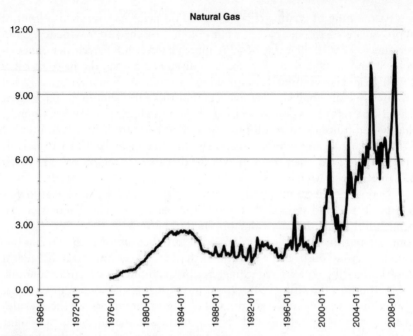

EXHIBIT 5.12   Natural gas prices, 1976–2008.

States, Canada, and the rest of the world, but these are not fully developed. In addition, there is tremendous market potential for substituting natural gas as a fuel for trucks and automobiles. Huge investments in the production, liquefaction, transportation, and distribution infrastructure are still in formation. The chart in Exhibit 5.12 shows the price of natural gas in U.S. dollars; it is volatile, and tends to reach unbelievable peaks mainly due to efforts by speculators to corner the market (as was done by Enron in the late 20th century). However, if we apply the commodities indexation rule, a different picture emerges. For example, the price of natural gas in terms of gold or corn is more stable as shown in Exhibits 5.13 and 5.14. In addition, one finds that the natural gas price has been stepping up every time there is more development in the infrastructure and hence an increase in demand for natural gas.

PRICE OF RICE[31]

Rice is an important staple food in the diet of all Asian countries and most African countries. Exhibit 5.15 shows the history of the price of rice in

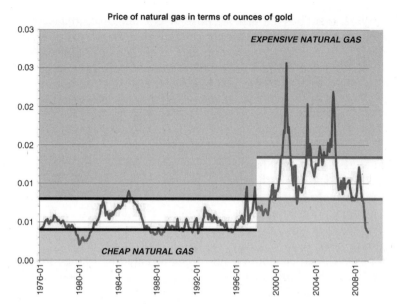

EXHIBIT 5.13   Price of natural gas in ounces of gold—one ounce of gold per MSCF.*
*MSCF = one thousand standard cubic feet

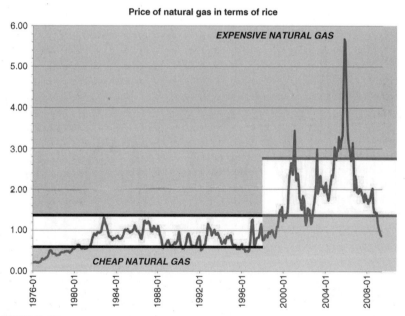

EXHIBIT 5.14   Price of natural gas in rice—one cwt of rice per MSCF.*
*MSCF = one thousand standard cubic feet

U.S. dollars. It is observed that the price in U.S. dollars fluctuated around a mean of about $8 per hundredweight before it rose sharply in 2008. Most of the rice is produced and consumed in Asia. If rice is priced in terms of gold, one would find that the real price of rice declined drastically from its 1969 highs to its lows in the 1980s, and has stayed relatively flat from the 1980s until today—even with the much-advertised commodity price increases of 2007. The real prices of agricultural commodities in the world have been declining. This, coupled with the less expensive agricultural products—mainly wheat—available from the larger developed exporting countries such as the United States and France, has made it less attractive for farmers in the world to produce basic foods such as wheat and rice. Instead, they prefer crops that will provide more cash, such as the farmers in Afghanistan who preferred to cultivate opium over food. Please see Exhibits 5.15 and 5.16.

On the other hand, if we price rice in terms of wheat, we find that the wheat/rice price ratio has been declining. Wheat is mostly produced in Western developed economies, but it is consumed by foreign developing countries. It is recommended that more research be conducted to find out why. Please see Exhibits 5.16 and 5.17 for a comparison.

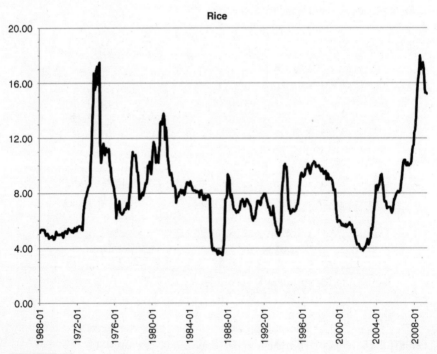

EXHIBIT 5.15   Rice prices, 1968–2008.

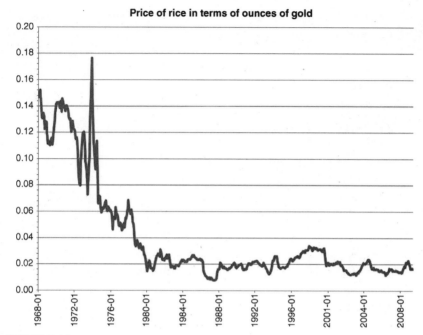

EXHIBIT 5.16   Rice versus gold.

The charts in Exhibit 5.17 displaying price of rice in terms of gold and rice in terms of wheat respectively show how the holders of hard currency in developing nations—in this case, the U.S. dollar—feel the real level of prices of such commodities. The users of wheat and rice in many of the developing countries in Asia and Africa see the real escalation and prohibitive high prices of the staple foods on which their lives depend because they use their local currencies which are pegged or indexed to the dollar and not to the gold. This is not the case in the developed economies because their currencies and prices are tied to the value of gold.

It is sincerely hoped that this discussion will generate enough interest among world leaders as well as international economists and traders to set up a fair pricing system, using the RF commodity indexation principles introduced in this book.

GOLD: THAT AMAZING METAL

Gold is an important metal that has been used over the years as a reference currency and a store of value. This book is not promoting a return to the gold standard; it means to familiarize the reader with the gold market and

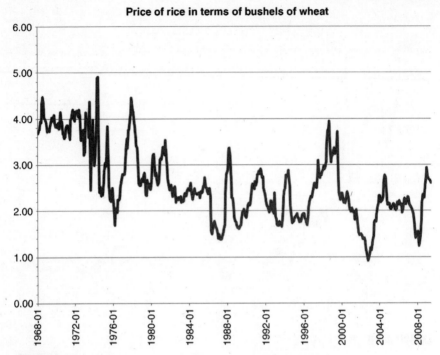

EXHIBIT 5.17 Price of rice in terms of cwt rice per bushel of wheat.

how gold prices are fixed and, in some cases, "stabilized" if not manipulated, by speculators and traders. This brief study should shed more light and give the reader the background necessary to fully understand the RF commodity indexation rule. It is sincerely hoped that a new pricing system for world trade will be established, one that is fair to all the citizens of the world. As we have seen, rice farmers in Asia and other countries were in fact paid less (in terms of gold) for their rice in 2000 than in 1970 despite the fact that they collected more dollars (local currency), and the same is true for farmers of many other agricultural products. This situation makes it difficult to promote farming and food production, especially in many of the developing third-world nations.

Gold was the reserve reference currency of the world before the well-known Bretton Woods agreement set the U.S. dollar as the world reserve currency, in the ratio of 35 dollars to each ounce of gold. Gold has been used as a store of value over the years by central banks as well as by husbands showing their love to their wives, and it is used as a precious metal in industrial applications for its superior conductivity and other physical characteristics. It is well-known that every government's central bank, including the International Monetary Fund (IMF), keeps a certain number of tons in gold reserves. Efforts to exert controls on leading economies in the world to keep inflation under control and to manage their money-printing presses have all pointed toward the use of gold (and possibly other commodities). It is interesting also to note that in 1999, at the IMF/World Bank Annual Meeting, a historic five-point agreement was reached. Fifteen European central banks, including the ECB (European Central Bank), declared their allegiance to the idea of the role of gold in the economy. Willem Duisinberg, president of the ECB at that time, stated that their agreement consisted of the following items:

1. Gold will remain an important element of global monetary reserves.
2. The 15 institutions will not enter the market as sellers of gold, with the exception of already decided sales.
3. Gold sales that were already decided would be achieved through a concerted program of sales over the next five years. Annual sales would not exceed 400 tons, and total sales would not exceed 2,000 tons.
4. The signatories to the agreement agreed not to expand their gold leasing and their use of gold futures and options during this period.
5. The agreement would be reviewed after five years.

Gold Reserves in the World[32]

Analysis of the official gold reserves reveals very interesting results, which are detailed here to familiarize the reader of the amounts of gold that different countries in the world have set aside as reserves. In addition to these gold reserves, many countries add foreign currency reserves. The following is a summary of some observations about the per capita gold reserves[33] of central banks around the world:

1. Switzerland has the highest per capita gold reserve (1040 tonnes), at 4.6 ounces of gold for every Swiss citizen, followed by Lebanon at 2.19 ounces of gold per person. This is followed by the following groups:
   a. The Eurozone countries: 1.16 ounces of gold per citizen (total reserves of 10,866 tonnes)
   b. The United States: 0.86 ounce of gold per citizen(8133.5 tonnes)
   c. Japan: 0.19 ounce per citizen (765 tonnes)
   d. Russia: 0.11 ounce of gold per citizen (523 tonnes)
   e. China: 0.02 ounce per citizen(1054 tonnes)
2. Both Canada and Mexico have negligible official gold reserves per capita (each has 3.4 tonnes)

3. The oil-rich Gulf countries' reserves range from 0.84 ounce of gold per citizen (Kuwait—79 tonnes) to 0.28 (Qatar—12.4 tonnes) and 0.18 (both Saudi Arabia—143 tonnes, and Bahrain—4.7 tonnes)
4. In many of the countries with a growing Islamic banking presence, we find the following reserves in tonnes and in ounces of gold per capita:

	Tonnes of Gold	Approximate per Capita Oz/Citizen
a. Lebanon	286.8	2.19
b. Algeria	173.6	0.16
c. Iran	302.3	0.14
d. Jordan	14.8	0.08
e. Turkey	116.0	0.05
f. Malaysia	36.4	0.04
g. Egypt	75.5	0.03
h. Indonesia	73.1	0.01
i. Pakistan	65.4	0.01
j. Bangladesh	3.5	Negligible

Does the official per capita gold reserve reflect—along with other currency reserves—the economic affluence of a country? This is a question that should be researched in terms of many factors, such as the countries' monetary policies, the contents of the reserves in foreign currency, and the nominal gross domestic product of the countries in terms of their local currencies and how they relate to the exchange rates.

It is believed that the solution is not returning to the gold standard, as some may advocate, but to reflect on the purchasing value of the convenient fiat money in each of the local economies by using the Shari'aa-based commodity indexation rule presented in this book.

The History of Gold Markets and Prices

It is interesting to note that the gold futures market is one of the smallest volume markets in the world. Because it is so small, it can be extremely volatile when exposed to massive short-sale activities. The short position in gold, via derivatives, is the one of the larger positions in the world.

As shown in the gold price chart in Exhibit 5.18, the price of gold stayed relatively stable (and in some periods declined) between the early 1980s and 2005. This has been mainly due to the central banks of many of the worlds' countries selling their gold on paper, and using many commodity-trading

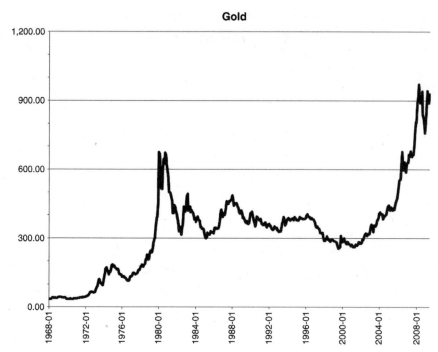

EXHIBIT 5.18 Gold prices, 1968–2008.

techniques. In one of these techniques, called *gold carry*, gold is borrowed (on paper and not physically) from the central banks (of mostly third-world countries) at a low interest rate and is used to flood the market to keep the price down or short gold and make money both ways.

Major players have included hedge funds and central banks of major industrial countries and some oil-producing countries, in addition to investment banks and other private banks. As the chart shows, gold prices stayed at $35 per ounce before August 15, 1971 when the official convertibility of gold into dollars was in force. Exhibits 5.19 through 5.22 also indicate that gold is currently overpriced in terms of coal, oil, rice, and wheat.

Gold Price Fixing

The world center of gold trading is London at the London Bullion Market, operated by the London Bullion Market Association (LBMA).

The practice of fixing gold prices began in 1919. It continued until 1939, when the London gold market was closed as a result of World War II. The market was reopened in 1954. When the central bank gold pool began officially in 1961, the Bank of England (as agent of the pool) maintained an open phone line with N. M. Rothschild during the morning fixing (there was

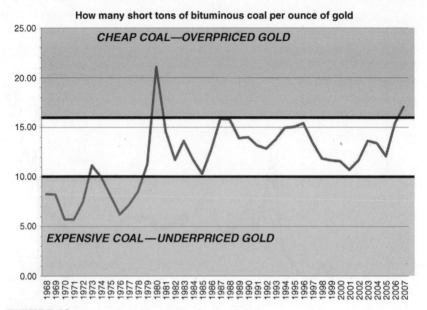

EXHIBIT 5.19 Price of gold in terms of tons of coal.

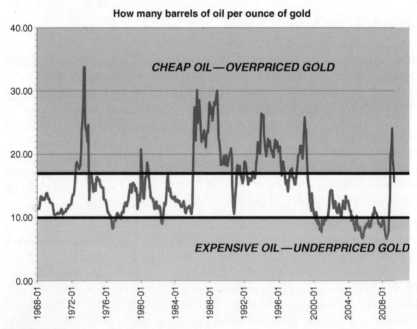

EXHIBIT 5.20 Price of gold in terms of oil.

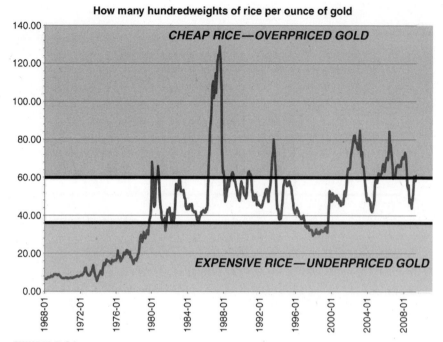

How many hundredweights of rice per ounce of gold

EXHIBIT 5.21 Price of gold in terms of rice.

as yet no afternoon fixing). The objective was to fix the price around the $35/ounce price (as per the Bretton Woods agreement) within a 1-percent band. In its current form, the London gold price fixing takes place twice each business day, at 10:30 A.M. and 3:00 P.M., in the Fixing Room. Five individuals representing each of the following banks sit at the fixing table:

- Scotia-Mocatta—successor to Mocatta & Goldsmid and part of Bank of Nova Scotia
- Barclays Capital—Replaced N. M. Rothschild & Sons when they abdicated
- Deutsche Bank—Owner of Sharps Pixley, itself the merger of Sharps Wilkins with Pixley & Abell
- HSBC—Owner of Samuel Montagu & Co.
- Société Générale

Price fixing is based on balancing supply and demand. Usually, the fixing takes less than 15 minutes. In 1979, when the Islamic Revolution of Iran erupted, the afternoon fixing lasted an hour and 39 minutes, due to price volatility.

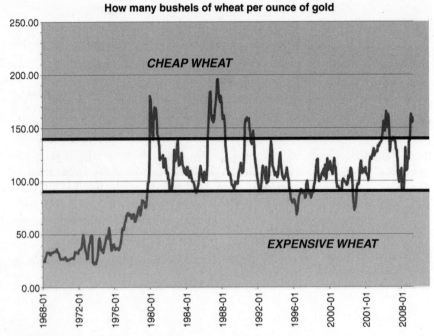

How many bushels of wheat per ounce of gold

EXHIBIT 5.22   Price of gold in terms of wheat.

MARKING THE INVESTMENT TO THE MARKET

The RF banking and finance discipline, in an effort to neutralize the effects of the prevailing fiat currency in the local markets, requires that we first apply the commodity indexation rule to check on the existence of a bubble in the business that we are considering to finance. This process is followed by a mark-to-market approach, evaluating the economic prudence by calculating the real return on investing in this item, using its actual real market rental value. This way, it is affirmed that money is not rented using the prohibited riba—and that the rent is that of the market rent of the facility in the market place. For example, in the case of:

- A *car:* The value for which this car is leased in the market (dollars per day), as obtained from actual operating leasing companies.
- A *house:* The actual market rental or lease rate (dollars per square foot) of a similar house in the same neighborhood. It is important to make sure that this house has essentially the same specifications as those researched. These rates can be obtained live from real estate agents.

- *A commercial building:* The actual market lease rate of the space.
- *A piece of equipment:* The market rental value, in dollars per day.
- *A business:* The lease rate an owner is willing to lease it for in the market.

This rate is used to calculate the rate of return on investment, because RF bankers *do not rent money*—in fact, they invest with and in the customer. If the rate of return is higher than the target return for the institution (which is the return expected in the market from shareholders and depositors), then it makes sense to finance/invest with the customer. If the return is lower, then it does not make sense to finance/invest, and the application is declined. This rejection is applied even if the customer has fulfilled all standard banking requirements from the creditworthiness test, the appraisal test, and the capacity for servicing the financing obligation. We will discuss this process in more detail in Chapters 10 and 13, and examples will be given.

NOTES

1. Davies, Glyn, *A History of Money from Ancient Times to the Present Day*, 3rd. ed. Cardiff: University of Wales Press, 2002.
2. J. Laurence, *The History of Bimetallism in the United States*, Chap. 8, D. Appleton and Company, 1901.
3. David H. Friedman, *Essentials of Banking*, American Bankers Association, 1989.
4. These are episodes of irrational public hoarding and runs on banks.
5. Based on David H. Friedman, *Essentials of Banking*, American Bankers Association, 1989.
6. Yahia Abdul-Rahman, *LARIBA Bank, Islamic Banking, Foundation for a United and Prosperous Community*, 1994. Published by the author.
7. Ibid.
8. David H. Friedman, *Essentials of Banking*, American Bankers Association, 1989.
9. Ibid.
10. This section is based on a comprehensive review of history as outlined by Jude Wanniski, *The Way the World Works*, Touchstone/Simon and Schuster, 1978.
11. A short history of modern finance, *The Economist*, October 16, 2008, pp. 79–81.
12. Professor John Taylor, Stanford University. Please Visit Professor Taylor's Personal Home Page http://www.stanford.edu/~johntayl/.
13. Richard A. Brealey and Steward C. Meyer, *Principles of Corporate Finance*, 6th ed. Irwin McGraw-Hill, London, 2000, p. 49.

14. R. Charles Moyer, James R. McGuigan, and William J. Kretlow, *Contemporary Financial Management*, Thomson One—Business School Edition and Infotrac, pg. 163.
15. For a detailed outline of the many papers, books, and analyses on the Taylor Rule, please visit www.stanford.edu/~johntayl/PolRulLink.htm.
16. GDP (gross domestic product) is a measurement of the national income and output for a given country. It is a measurement of the total value (in local currency or in dollars) of all final goods and services produced in that economy in a given year.
17. Ahmad Kamal Mydin Meera, *The Islamic Gold Dinar*, Pelanduk Publications, Malaysia, 2002.
18. Narrated by Abu Sa'eed Al Khidry.
19. Ibid. Also reported and authenticated by Imam Ahmad and Imam Bukhary.
20. Muslim; the scholar in Hadeeth reported that a person came to the Prophet (pp) to gift him with dates. The Prophet (pp) asked him how he could afford these high-quality, large-size dates and said: "this is not our type of dates." The person said "Oh Prophet Muhammad (pp), we sold two containers of our dates for one container of the better-quality large dates." The Prophet (pp) said: "This is what Riba is!" He proceeded to tell the person: "Return these dates. Then sell it [our dates] in the market for [real] money and use the money to buy the other dates." In another story reported by the scholar Abu Dawood: A person brought the Prophet (pp) a gold bracelet which had beads woven in it, which he had purchased for nine or seven dinars [gold currency at that time]. The Prophet (pp) said: "This transaction must be conducted by separating the gold from the beads. Return it. And price each separately." And the scholar Muslim further reported orders to separate the gold from the beads, and said that the gold should be exchanged for the same weight of gold.
21. By the Hadeeth scholar Abu Dawood.
22. Narrated by Bukhari, one the recognized authorities on the compiling of the Prophet's Hadeeth.
23. Peter Kilborn, "Baker Hints at Gold As Guide on Policy," *The New York Times*, October 1, 1987.
24. Mahathir bin Mohamad, "The Gold Dinar as an Alternative International Currency," Kuala Lumpur, Malaysia, July 1, 2003.
25. Mahathir bin Mohamad: *The Malaysian Currency Crisis—How and Why It Happened*," Pelanduk Publications, 2000.
26. The United States Department of Commerce, U.S. Census Bureau: www.census.gov/.
27. National Association of Home Builders (NAHB): www.nahb.org/page.aspx/category/sectionID=131.
28. London Bullion Market Association (LBMA): www.lbma.org.uk/stats/goldfixg.
29. The United States Department of Agriculture (USDA), National Agricultural Statistics Service (NASS): www.nass.usda.gov/QuickStats/Create_Federal_All.jsp.
30. The United States Department of Energy (DOE), Energy Information Administration (EIA) http://tonto.eia.doe.gov/dnav/ng/ng_pri_sum_dcu_nus_m.htm.

31. The United States Department of Agriculture (USDA), National Agricultural Statistics Service (NASS): www.nass.usda.gov/QuickStats/Create_Federal_All. jsp.
32. Gold sales cost Europe's central banks $40bn - By Javier Blas in London, Published: May 6 2009 23:FT.com, May 6, 2009.
33. World Gold Council; Gold Research and Statistics web site: http://*www .research.gold.org/reserve_asset/*.

CHAPTER 6

Civility and Social Responsibility of the Riba-Free Banking System

In the previous chapters, the faith-based foundation of the riba/ribit-free (RF) banking and finance system was established. This chapter will discuss the important aspect of bringing these values to life by elaborating on the social aspects of this brand of banking and its commitment to community building, growth, and development. The dimension of civility and social responsibility in RF banking and finance will eventually lead to economic growth, new job opportunities, prosperity, and unity, and hopefully to a future of peace, fairness, and justice for all people. The most important foundation of the Judeo-Christian-Islamic value system is justice for all, as defined by the higher authority we all answer to—that is, God, the revealer of the Qur'aan:

> 4:58 God doth command you to render back your Trusts to those to whom they are due; And when ye judge between man[1] and man, that ye judge with justice: Verily how excellent is the teaching which He giveth you! For God is He Who heareth and seeth all things.
>
> 16:90 God commands justice, the doing of good, and liberality to kith and kin, and He forbids all shameful deeds, and injustice and rebellion: He instructs you, that ye may receive admonition.
>
> 5:8 O ye who believe! stand out firmly for God, as witnesses to fair dealing, and let not the hatred of others to you make you swerve to wrong and depart from justice. Be just: that is next to piety: and revere God. For God is well-acquainted with all that ye do.

It is believed that civility and social responsibility in banking and finance is an important foundation for a successful banking operation.

Perhaps the first well-known dramatization of the character of a true RF banker was in Frank Capra's popular 1940s film *It's a Wonderful Life*, in which Jimmy Stewart plays a Building (Savings) and Loan Society manager who helps build comfortable suburban neighborhoods, assisting poorer families to move away from the small, shabby apartments in which they live. The film was released just after the major runs on the banks in reaction to the Great Depression that started in1929. This movie is used regularly as a basic training resource for all RF bankers in the LARIBA system, as will be explained in more detail in Chapter 12.

In October 2008, the world was shocked to hear President George W. Bush and his Secretary of Treasury Henry Paulson talk about the financial tsunami that hit the United States and the world financial systems. This historic compromise of the financial markets and systems, we were told, was caused by the speculative and casino-like gambling behaviors of some "money managers" and corporate executives. This irresponsible behavior lost $4,000 billion dollars of peoples' retirement money and life savings. The speculative activities and economic "bubbles" had been warned against, and had been criticized by many. These objections were ignored and quickly marginalized by former Federal Reserve Chairman Alan Greenspan, who was idolized as the "god" of finance from his appointment in 1987 to his retirement in 2006; he was nicknamed "The Maestro"[2] in a book by the famous investigative newspaper reporter and author Bob Woodward. Only a few voices in the media, to be fair, kept reminding its readers and policymakers about the hazard of inflating the real estate bubble. These were *The Economist*, a financial magazine, and *The Financial Times*, a newspaper—both of which are published in London, UK.

In the 1980s, the Glass-Steagall Act—the most important regulation that translated the lessons learned from the Great Depression—was repealed by Congress. In the 1990s, the Clinton administration and its Treasury Secretary, Robert Rubin, celebrated by approving the merger of an investment bank (Smith Barney), an insurance company (Travelers Group), and a commercial bank (Citicorp). The move was celebrated as a historic development and as the best thing to happen in the American financial services industry in years because, its proponents thought, it offered service integration that would provide banking, investment banking, retirement planning, and insurance services under one roof.

I was personally in the middle of this, because I worked at Smith Barney at that time. I experienced the process by which the financial consultants at Smith Barney (and the whole industry followed) were retrained to become "asset gatherers," whose first responsibility was to gather peoples' money and assets. They would then turn these funds over to "big" money managers, who managed billions of dollars in the mutual funds industry or even

more in the asset management and hedge funds industry. The entire financial consultant and brokerage community was turned into an asset-gather-
ing machine. The broker or the financial advisor would define the
investment objectives, the investment time horizon, and the risk profile of
the customer, and then turn the money over to the so-called "gurus" to take
care of investing it. If a consumer had a bank account at his friendly local
branch of a bank, and he objected to the low interest rates on FDIC-insured
Time Certificates of Deposit, that client would be turned over to another
"investment" representative who offered higher returns. This practice is still
happening in many bank branches at the time of writing this book. Of
course, we were told that the investment advisor disclosed the risks associated with investing in mutual funds, and that the customer was advised to
read the lengthy prospectus before they invested, but unfortunately that was
not the experience of many retired people, who moved their life savings
from FDIC-insured Time Certificates of Deposit to mutual funds. In addition, the financial consultants were pushed to sell annuities as a sure investment that would guarantee investors a safe retirement.

Wall Street became a large casino instead of an instrument to invest in
the long-term growth of the United States and the world (as it was redevel-
oped to operate after the 1929 stock market crash). Talented engineers,
medical doctors, technology experts, mathematicians, and scientists quit
their jobs, in which they had earned a good living through hard work that
added to the real production of the community, so that they could have
more time to "make" money through day trading of stocks, options, and
futures online. It became a national and international obsession to trade
stocks online, to wait in big halls with large computer screens showing market movements, with people in Kuwait, Saudi Arabia, Dubai, Hong Kong,
China, South Korea, Thailand, Russia, Singapore, Malaysia, Egypt, and
many more poor developing countries sitting doing nothing but watching
and seeing how to "make" more money and how to get around the honorable way of "earning" it through hard work. As we learned in 2008, the
insurance companies that were supposed to protect and safeguard peoples'
assets, retirement funds, and insurance premiums betrayed that trust and
speculated with peoples' futures by using structured finance, financial engineering, and loopholes in the laws to avoid the regulators. We learned that
they intentionally broke the spirit of the law while appearing on paper and
on official documents to uphold and respect the laws of the land.

In the end, we witnessed the breakdown of the best and most intricate
financial system, one that was built in a patient and meticulous way over
almost 150 years of America's history. We, the bankers of the United States,
had to stand up embarrassed before the world for what some of us had
done. The United States' financial, monetary, and banking system, which

was trusted by the world to the extent of making the U.S. dollar as good as gold (as stipulated by the Bretton Woods agreement) and making the United States the envy of the world, broke down!

As angry citizens in the United States and the world started asking more questions, the politicians running for election in the 2008 presidential campaign explained that more regulation would be needed. However, they approved more of the same. Merrill Lynch merged with Bank of America; Bear Stearns was bought by J P Morgan Chase; and both Morgan Stanley and Goldman Sachs were turned into bank holding companies in preparation to make them qualified to become depository banking institutions. They started the process of looking for banks to acquire, to realize the model started by CitiGroup. Well, we wish them all the luck in the world, because the culture of a traditional banker (who should be extremely risk-averse, because he/she is assigned the great responsibility of trying to reach a zero risk level to protect the bank's depositors) does not mix well with the culture of risk-taking at all levels displayed in the investment banking business. That is essentially what the Glass-Steagall Act was all about.

Politicians said that the lack of regulation caused this huge catastrophe. That may be partially true, but many respectfully disagree with that sweeping conclusion. All the regulations and laws in the world are good on paper. Good judgment, however, cannot be regulated. These regulations must be respected and applied by the citizens on both sides: the practitioners and the law enforcement. If a citizen does not respect the regulations and is not trained to uphold the laws, then all the regulations in the world would not be enough. The result will be that the law is taken lightly and looked upon as an obstacle that can be overcome by supposedly "intelligent and smart" structures to achieve what one wants. The system then becomes a mockery.

I remember an experience in 1989, after the Islamic Revolution in Iran, when Atlantic Richfield (Oil Company, now part of British Petroleum) lost—through nationalization—250,000 barrels of oil production from Lavon Island in Iran. I was put in charge of trying to secure the supply of as much oil as possible to make up for the loss, in order to meet the feedstock requirements of our refineries. I was fortunate to travel around the world and meet officials in the oil-producing countries in Africa, Latin America, Asia, and the Middle East. On one of my trips, I focused on an important producing country in Africa. Its name will remain untold to avoid any nationalistic sensitivity by its wonderful citizens. I spent more than six months traveling back and forth to develop working relationships with this country's oil executives, to introduce our company, to understand the organizational chart of the country's national oil company and its oil sales laws, and to establish contacts with the President's office and his personal energy advisor. I understood the wonderful legal and operating system of the land and identified the decision makers. I thought that I had a deal.

I forgot to mention, though, that there was one thing missing: the price—or the bribe—needed to get the contract. I want to share with the reader that one thing I never agreed to in my whole life is the use of bribery to get what I want and need. I made that decision early, when I was a young college student at Cairo University. Other students would "bribe" the administrator of the lecture halls to lay down a notebook at a front seat so that the student could get a reserved front seat without having to wake up early in the morning. I disciplined myself to wake up at 5:00 A.M.—a wonderful habit I have maintained to this day—study, and go to the university to get my preferred seat without taking others' opportunities by bribing people in a dishonest way. But let us return to the oil story. Because I refused to pay a "commission" or a "fee," otherwise defined in my book of values as a bribe, I found out later that the contract was given to the Marc Rich Trading Company. Not only had this happened, but to my surprise (one that educated me in the school of "hard knocks" of real life) none of the officials in the wonderful organizational structure of the national oil company were involved. The deal was done in a separate office of a bank run by a tribal leader with the "right" political connections.

Regulations are important if they are well thought out, discussed, and voted on in a proper democratic way within a functioning democracy. However, the citizens and institutions of that democracy should also be socially responsible, civilized, and respectful to each other, and they should uphold the laws of the land. Professor Stephen Carter at Yale University authored a wonderful book on civility.[3] He concluded that if the adults in a community (i.e., the parents and the leaders in business, media, government, political, and religious communities) do not treat each other with civility, this behavior will be reflected by the community's children. "Our children are mimicking the incivility of the adult world. In one survey, an astonishing 89% of grade school teachers and principals [in America] reported that they 'regularly' face abusive language from students."[4] He concluded,

> *Civility, I shall argue, is the total sum of the many sacrifices we are called to make for the sake of living together. . . . Rules of civility are thus also rules of morality: it is morally proper to treat our fellow citizens with respect.*[5]

The moral standard by which the citizens of a community, a city, a state, and a nation live defines the character of that nation. It is also important to note that history has shown repeatedly since its dawn—from the story of Adam and Eve in paradise that not obeying the moral standard set for them by God, which was to not to approach the tree to the knowledge of good and evil, to the story of Cain and Abel, and on to the stories of all God's prophets—that a nation must have a moral standard, ethics, a value system, and a set of rules that are clear to all to live by.

The values of civility, ethics, and morality are taught first at home by the parents, with a spiritual content that is nourished and deepened at the family's place of worship; these values are reinforced at school, by the media, and by the behavior of the political leadership at large. It is unfortunate that many misunderstand the concept of separating church and state. It is believed that this separation rule means the church, or the place of worship, cannot run the government—but it should have the full freedom to produce spiritually and morally qualified leaders who have the proper civility to run every aspect of the society. When the church, the synagogue, the masjid (mosque), and the temples focus on the substance, they will regain their stature in the community.

THE JUDEO-CHRISTIAN-ISLAMIC VALUES: CIVILITY, MORALITY, AND SOCIAL RESPONSIBILITY

As we know from the Torah, the Gospel, and the Qur'aan, God did not create Adam and Eve as separate individuals who each acts on his/her own. He created them as partners: a husband and wife who were entrusted with the well-being of earth and with serving Him and populating earth by multiplying in larger families, villages, tribes, and nations to make the earth a better place to enjoy. In the Qur'aan we read:

> *4:1 O mankind! reverence your Guardian-Lord, who created you from a single person, created, of like nature, his mate, and from them twain scattered [like seeds] countless men and women; —reverence God, through whom ye demand your mutual [rights], and [reverence] the wombs [That bore you]: for God ever watches over you.*

Humanity (male and female) has been reminded that God is closer to us than our jugular veins are. That is, if we were real believers in God, then we have to be careful not to disappoint Him in our behavior, because He is much closer to us than many have disciplined themselves to know, think, and acknowledge. In the Qur'aan God reveals:

50:16 It was We Who created man, and We know what suggestions his soul makes to him: for We are nearer to him than (his) jugular vein.

50:18 Not a word does he utter but there is a sentinel by him, ready [to record it].

We submit our will to the will of God and believe in the Judeo-Christian-Islamic values brought to man by God through all His Prophets—Abraham (pp) and his descendants and subsequent prophets and messengers, including Moses (pp), Jesus (pp), and Mohammad (pp). These prophets of God came to train people to better submit to God's will and to assume the responsibility of becoming custodians/trustees on God's property—the earth and its resources—and to establish justice on earth. This system of justice includes social, economic, political, and legal justice.

It has been established historically that human nature, if untamed and not civilized, is characterized by selfishness, violence, and greed. Religions, including the Judeo-Christian-Islamic system brought to the world by Prophet Muhammad (pp) to continue, deepen, legitimize, expand, detail, and seal the teachings of all prior prophets and messengers, focus on training the individual spiritually and ethically to suppress selfishness and greed and to promote goodness.

Success can be defined by different parameters, such as how much money, power, fame, and control one has attained. In an uncivilized world, success is only measured in a material way, which sometimes loses sight of the value of the rest of the society. In a civilized system, and for a socially responsible citizen (and, for that matter, for RF bankers), success can be defined as the progressive realization of a worthy ideal. Civilized and responsible people consider success to lie in both material achievements and in being virtuous. Virtue implies a positive attitude toward life, toward other citizens in the community and the world, and toward all other beings. The results are peace of mind, contentment, and a sense of security. The true image of success is not how much money one has in the bank or the kind of car one drives. Success is realizing a proven track record and reputation as a pious person who can be trusted and is close to God. Success is manifested by a person who feels for the neediest and the poorest in the community and who takes serious steps to improve their conditions, not only through handouts but through training them and through helping them climb the social ladder from its bottom to higher levels over time. God reveals in the Qur'aan:

2:177 It is not righteousness that ye turn your faces Towards East or West; but it is righteousness—to believe in God and the

Last Day, and the Angels, and the Book, and the Messengers; to spend of your substance, out of love for Him, for your kin, for orphans, for the needy, for the wayfarer, for those who ask, and for the ransom of slaves; to be steadfast in prayer, and practice regular charity; to fulfill the contracts which ye have made; and to be firm and patient, in pain (or suffering) and adversity, and throughout all periods of panic. Such are the people of truth, the God revering.

51:19 And in their wealth and possessions (was remembered) the right of the (needy) him who asked, and him who (for some reason) was prevented (from asking).

The horizon of time in the Judeo-Christian-Islamic value system extends beyond this life to the life after death, the hereafter. Wealth, power, position, and affluence do not come with us to our graves after death. When anyone dies, that person will be remembered by what he or she leaves behind:[6] a family and descendants who perpetuate goodness by following the laws of God; and a permanent contribution that will benefit the community, such as a book, a research achievement, a source of income for the poor and the needy, and/or the development of job opportunities for future generations. It is what we leave behind and its contribution to the community and the world at large that will attain us the highest acceptance by God. It is also believed that the globe belongs to God and it is wide open and full of resources and opportunities. Oppression in one location does not justify acceptance. It is the responsibility of everyone who feels helpless and oppressed to find another location where freedom and human dignity are prevalent. In doing so, a believer, in his/her pursuit of business, carries with him/her the Judeo-Christian-Islamic way of life and values.

A prosperous and healthy society is that which respects hard work and its tangible contributions in terms of quality, creativity, and service. It is a society that discourages and frowns upon gambling, speculation, greed, and fraudulent activities. It is a society that respects the value of education as a means of getting ahead and the value of respecting people's properties, trusts, and assets, and never to speculate with them.

We need to produce for the United States a new breed of bankers: the RF banker, who stands on two important pillars:

- The pillar of faith-based moral, ethical, and spiritual fulfillment
- The pillar of excellence in the quality of products and services offered by the RF bank and its superior operating results, compared to its peer conventional riba-based banks

We need to see a new breed of American RF bankers who are capable of energetically communicating and articulating the values and messages of the Judeo-Christian-Islamic value system to the masses in America and the world.

We in the RF banking system should work hard to build a new system, both in content and extent. We want to present to the United States and then to the world the model of patience, perseverance, and respect for parents and senior citizens.

We want to bring to the United States a new banking world vision, one that shapes a new society:

- A society that is built on intellectual and mental persuasion, in which our mind is the key to knowing God and living by the Judeo-Christian-Islamic values
- A society that believes in the purity of the soul and body
- A society that bans drugs, alcohol, and gambling
- A society that looks at promiscuous activities such as fornication and adultery as filth that should never be condoned
- A society that believes in respecting promises
- A society that believes in volunteering oneself and one's resources to the cause of serving God by serving people
- A society that believes in respecting peoples' properties, dignity, and right to live honorably and freely
- A society that never allows the individual to overburden himself or herself with liabilities, debts, and promises that cannot be fulfilled
- A society that never hoards and never uses riba in its financial dealings
- A society that believes that these goals can all be achieved not through the proletariat of communism and socialism or the selfishness and greed of money changers in an untamed version of what is misrepresented as capitalism, but through the believers and servants of God

THE VISION OF AN IDEAL FAITH-BASED JUDEO-CHRISTIAN-ISLAMIC SOCIETY

We need to remember that the road to this vision is full of challenges and we need to prepare to overcome them:

- We need to learn from the success stories of others in the conventional banking services as to analyze those services' faults.
- We need to expand within our means and focus on human resources, including well-trained RF bankers and administrators, and financial

strength enhanced by voluntarism—and by expanding the market for our services by attracting all people of all faiths to the RF banking services as the preferred banking system in the marketplace.

- We need to stress the requirement of building true partnerships between the customer and community member, the families in the community, the RF bankers and administrators, and the community at large.
- We need to motivate as many youths in the community to study to be accountants, financial analysts, and business managers and to qualify themselves as future RF bankers.
- We need to sign onto a vision of building a standardized nationwide RF banking system that is as good as, and hopefully better than, the conventional banking system.

NEW TRENDS THAT CAPTURED THE IMAGINATION OF THE PAGANS OF THE ARABIAN PENINSULA

When Prophet Muhammad (pp) assumed the responsibility of expanding on and documenting the teachings of all of God's prophets, in particular Moses (pp) and Jesus (pp), and after he was commanded to start building the model community in the city of Yathrib (north of the city of Makkah and the site of the prophet Muhammad's mosque where he is buried), He and his companions started, with the local citizens, to build the new community. The city's name was changed to *Madinah*, which means "the civilized city." The following is a summary of the way this Judeo-Christian-Islamic set of values has captured peoples' imagination and changed the history of the world:

- Protection of property rights and title of ownership
- Abolishment of discrimination and tribalism
- Enforcement of a new set of equal rights and opportunities regardless of tribal connections, race, national origin, gender, power, richness, or poverty
- Recognition of women as equal to men in a united community, and viewing women as important contributors to society who are entitled to inherit and own property (for the first time in history)
- Enforcing of the free market system, which was later popularized in the West by Adam Smith
- Origination of the concept of insurance (*takaful*, which means "mutual benefit and protection")
- Origination of labor rights stipulating fairness to labor and that labor should be paid before the worker's sweat dries from his brow (as pronounced by Prophet Muhammad [pp])

- Prohibition of hoarding (*ihtikar*), deception, misrepresentation of facts about products and services (*gharar*, which means "fraud, cheating, deception, and forgery"), and promotion of transparency
- Promotion of the concept of money not as a commodity that can be bought, sold, or rented at a price called interest rate, but instead viewing it as a measuring device (this concept also states that money does not reproduce if left in a safe vault; it only grows when invested in an economic activity)
- Promotion of the concept that wealth should be circulated and reinvested within the community to help develop that community by creating jobs, economic growth, and prosperity
- Establishment of the Judeo-Christian-Islamic system of economics, finance, and monetary theory, based on three important pillars (described in detail in Chapter 2):
  - Wealth and property (assets) are owned by God; humanity (male and female) is appointed by God in His mysterious and wise ways to serve as trustees and custodians
  - The system of RF banking and finance
  - The system of *zakah*, or alms-giving
  - The system of *miraath*, or inheritance
- Establishment of a standard for behavior and lifestyle, calling for:
  - Followers to live below or within one's means
  - Followers not to waste, not to live in an extravagant lifestyle, and not to overspend, as overspending is defined by the Judeo-Christian-Islamic value system as the work of Satan

ELEMENTS OF THE RIBA-FREE ECONOMIC SYSTEM

Production

The system expects every individual to work and to produce. Prophet Muhammad (pp), as did all prophets before him, teaches: "Never be lazy and helpless." There is no good in an individual who does not want to produce and earn money. It is taught that the unproductive hand is an unclean, impure hand. The system also calls for products to be useful and not harmful as defined in the Law (Shari'aa).

Distribution

In its efforts to do away with discrimination between classes in society based on wealth and affluence, and to reshape the relationship between classes, the Judeo-Christian-Islamic system makes the following points: (1) God owns wealth, power, and natural resources. (2) The individual or the institution is appointed by God as a trustee and custodian to manage them. (3) Every being, human or not, has a minimum requirement of being able to live in dignity. This should be provided by those who are in charge in government institutions to anyone who cannot meet his or her own needs. (4) Private property and ownership are sacred rights and must be protected.

The system is paid back and balanced out through the act of ritual alms-giving (zakah) as one of the pillars of the Judeo-Christian-Islamic system. If these resources are not enough, the government is expected to apply a temporary tax on those who can afford it among the rich and affluent to balance the budget; this additional tax is looked upon as a religious duty (*fard kefaya*).

> 9:103 *Of their goods, take alms, that so thou mightest purify and sanctify them; and pray on their behalf. Verily thy prayers are a source of security for them: And God is One Who heareth and knoweth.*

Zakah is spent and distributed by the government, as explained in Chapter 2, to help the poor, the needy, the traveler (wayfarer), and the administrators, and to help the oppressed indebted to pay off their debts.

> 9:60 *Alms are for the poor and the needy, and those employed to administer the [funds]; for those whose hearts have been [recently] reconciled [to Truth]; for those in bondage and in debt; in the cause of God. And for the wayfarer: [thus is it] ordained by God, and God is full of knowledge and wisdom.*

The RF banker must be trained to feel socially responsible for others in the community. He/she cannot enjoy life while others are suffering. A government that believes in the Judeo-Christian-Islamic values is responsible for the basic needs of every citizen: food, shelter, clothing, education, and health care. The system also calls for a very basic and fundamental understanding that the only road to wealth and achievement is hard work and the assumption of risk, not gambling and speculation. That is why Shari'aa defines exactly how the estate is distributed after death (in a detailed description in the Qur'aan).[7]

> 4:7 *From what is left by parents and those nearest related there is a share for men and a share for women, whether the property be small or large—a determinate share.*

The system of inheritance calls for no one to make a will that attempts to alter the predefined distribution rates as revealed by God in Chapter 4 of the

Qur'aan. In addition, if one wanted to include in his/her will a payout to others outside what Shari'aa defines, this is limited to a maximum of one-third of the total estate. To keep social peace among the heirs, this one-third can only be allocated to benefit others outside the inheritance beneficiaries. This way, money is always distributed fairly and is trickled down through the system.

Consumption

The Judeo-Christian-Islamic RF value system preaches that the citizen should seek a life of moderation and a balanced pattern of consumption. Overconsumption is condemned as the work of Satan.

> 7:31 O Children of Adam! Wear your beautiful apparel at every time and place of prayer: eat and drink: But waste not by excess, for God loves not the wasters.
> 25:67 Those who, when they spend, are not extravagant and not niggardly, but hold a just (balance) between those (extremes);

Spending in the wrong way (bribery, illegal profits, abusing the legal system, and/or reckless spending) and extravagant overconsumption (even of lawful materials) are not allowed. Everyone is trained to plan for the future and to be careful. The story of Prophet Joseph (pp) in the Torah, the Gospel, and the Qur'aan[8]—in which we are told about the seven productive and the seven lean years, and how Prophet Joseph (pp) attained prominence in the house of Pharaoh in Egypt by implementing his long-range plan of saving for the lean years—is an important lesson in long-range planning for all of us to emulate.

THE RIBA-FREE JUDEO-CHRISTIAN-ISLAMIC SYSTEM AND BUSINESS ETHICS

The system calls for profits and services to be maximized legally and fairly in order to realize a better life and living standards, with freedom and independence of the individual and no discrimination, by using interdependence and interaction with other communities and nations. The system promotes free markets and free international trade as the natural mechanism of getting people to know each other; such interactions will promote mutual respect, peace, and prosperity through communications, trading, and mutual benefits.

> 49:13 O mankinds! We created you from a single [pair] of a male and a female, and made you into nations and tribes, that ye may

know each other (not that ye may despise [each other]). Verily the most honored of you in the sight of God is [he who is] the most righteous of you. And God has full knowledge and is well acquainted [with all things].

RF banks are expected to develop new and efficient ways and means to improve the quality of life and preserve the individual's most valuable asset, time. Time is life. Protection of the environment, too, is a sacred duty of every citizen who subscribes to the Judeo-Christian-Islamic values. The RF banker should have the passion to focus on a long-term view of investing in the future without speculation, to help generate long-term job opportunities for generations to come. The RF banker should be the catalyst that will provide flexibility in planning for peoples' futures through strategic planning and training, to prevent business cycles from having a negative impact on the community.[9]

The Market System

The RF banker believes that markets are designed to bring a buyer (end user) and a seller (producer) together to consummate a fair and well-defined and well-documented transaction. Speculation or interference with market forces of supply and demand is not allowed. The RF banker should do his/her best to ascertain that markets are free and open to everyone, provided that Shari'aa and the laws of the land are not violated. Information about products, goods, and services should be readily available, complete, and known to all parties. The RF banker believes that misrepresentations are punishable both by law in this life and according to God's judgment in the hereafter. The RF banker lives and operates believing that full disclosure is a must and that monopoly and hoarding are strictly forbidden and prohibited by Shari'aa and the laws of the land. In an RF banking system, those in charge do their utmost to make sure that prices are set on the basis of supply/demand using the open market system, and that speculation is strictly forbidden.

Management Ethics

The RF banking manager is looked upon as a custodian of God's trust, given to him/her to manage. However, the RF banking manager is also considered a shepherd of his/her subordinates. He or she is expected to provide guidance, vision, and care for his/her subordinates, to maximize their output, and to keep the values of the faith and the system intact. An RF banking manager is chosen with strict qualifications:

- Excellence in professionalism and knowledge
- Performance, track record, trust, and piety
- Good interpersonal relationship skills, as guided by the ultimate example of all of the Prophets of God and by the role models of proven leaders in the community and business

An RF banking manager/owner of a workplace is expected to provide employees with maximum job security through continual training, optimization, and community interrelationships.

Justice and Fairness on Both Sides: The Bank and the Customer

It has been the norm of many who call for social justice to only address one side of the issue, and that is the responsibility of the bankers (or, in other words, those who are in control of the money and who decide whether credit can be extended). By the same token, to be just and fair as ordained by God, we need to remind people in the community of their responsibility toward the promises they make by signing the bottom line of that credit agreement—or any agreement. Fulfilling a promise is the backbone of believing in God. In the teachings of all of God's prophets and in the Judeo-Christian-Islamic value system, we are taught that a person is in fact his/her word and that our word is our bond. In this regard, it is accepted that under normal circumstances—meaning under circumstances that do not include deception, misrepresentation, and high-pressure sales techniques—a person who believes in God should never commit to a promise that he or she cannot fulfill.

People should train themselves to be disciplined. They should not try to predict the future with any certainty. The only one who knows the future is God. We can try to project the direction of the future, but we cannot predict it; if we plan our future based on that (usually) rosy prediction, we end up falling deeper into the hole of debt. This is what happened in 2008, as the housing bubble and the subprime mortgage scandals were revealed. It is also important to note that under severe circumstances that are out of our hands, we can use the safety valves provided by the system to reduce the impact of these circumstances on our lives and the community through reorganization and bankruptcy laws. However, it is not the behavior of a believer in the Judeo-Christian-Islamic system of faith that we sign a promise with the idea that we can get out of it if things do not work out. That is called negotiating and making a commitment in bad faith. I was deeply hurt to watch on television as wonderful couples left the keys to their homes at the front door and said good-bye to their bank. In the Judeo-Christian-Islamic value system, it is the worst offense to not pay one's debt and not to fulfill one's promises and commitments before passing on to God's kingdom. It is known that the first question Prophet Muhammad (pp) asked before he offered prayers unto the dead was: "Did he/she pay off his/her debts and fulfill his/her obligations?" If the answer was yes, he would pray. If the answer was no, he would refuse to pray. That is why it is a standard practice for a Muslim son or family representatives to stand up in the middle of the condolence gathering event and make a public commitment that all the obligations of the person who died (father, mother, brother, or sister) will be the obligations of those who survived him/her.

BANKING AND INVESTMENT BANKING

In the RF banking system, money is an important tool that must be respected and put to good use by investing it prudently. Growth of this money must not be done by looking at money as something that can reproduce as if it were rabbits without investing it in the community.

The RF bankers and customers believe that money must be earned in a proper way, as defined by Shari'aa. There is one underlying holistic concept of producing income: the difference between *halal*, which means divinely lawful, and *haram*, which means divinely unlawful. "Making" money and eating from haram sources are believed to be the same as consuming hellfire, and those who do this will not prosper in this life and will be in the depth of hellfire in the hereafter, when we all face God's judgment.

The RF banking system believes that money must be invested in good productive projects and services that will provide a better, healthier, more productive, more comfortable, and fair lifestyle for all. Unfortunately, some in the community have different ideas about money. Money in the RF system is not considered a commodity that commands a price (interest), as in the riba-based system. It is unfortunate that people are led to believe falsely that money reproduces and gives birth to more money if rented at a price called interest rate. Money is a medium or a measuring device for transacting business. It is used to measure the efficiency of doing business through the use of a yardstick we call in economics the "rate of return on investment."

In an RF banking regime, investment banks are called upon to bring the owner of capital together with the owner of an idea or expertise so that the two may invest together and realize long-term economic growth in the community, resulting in an acceptable return on that investment. The investment bankers' role is education, evaluation, promotion, and follow-up for the benefit of long-term growth, not to realize a commission. The purpose of the RF banking system is to make capital circulate within the community. The Judeo-Christian-Islamic value system prohibits trading paper instruments that do not create wealth but rather transfer it through gaming, speculation, and manipulation. The objective should be long-term investing, not day-trading as if we were in a gambling casino. Some investment bankers like to attract more money by propagating and selling ideas that resemble going to a casino, trying to make 10 or 100 times what one has committed through gambling and betting (which they misname as "investing"). Others may want to do the same by speculating on currencies or day-trading on the stock, commodities, and futures markets, such as what happened during the dot-com stock market bubble, which took the NASDAQ stock market index from almost 1,800 to 5,000, only to crash to 2,100 in 2000 and stay there, with some fluctuations, until it crashed again to almost 1,700 as a result of the burst housing bubble and the subsequent financial tsunami of 2008. Some "investors" made huge amounts of money; others—most of whom unfortunately happened to be the average citizens—lost their life savings and their retirement assets. Worse still, there are others who can make huge sums of money through destroying the economies of whole nations by speculating against their currencies, as we witnessed throughout history. This happened most recently to the British pound in the 1980s and to Asian currencies in the late 1990s. It is important to state clearly that the system has honorable and wonderful men and women who want to do the right thing, but the greed and misguided ambitions of a few have tarnished the whole industry.

In the new brand of RF banking, the RF banker answers to his/her conscience, civility, and social responsibility, because he/she answers to a higher authority (i.e., God). The RF banker is trained to believe in a set of standards as described by the laws of the land and by Shari'aa, as ordained by our Creator. It is God who created us equally, so we might live in peace with each other and to care about each other. The RF banker is disciplined to make a difference in people's lives by investing in them and with them. In doing so, the RF banker evaluates his/her progress not only by how much income was made through commissions and fees but by how many households were added to the family of his/her RF bank and the extent of the improvement the RF bank has made to these families. The RF banker makes sure, before he/she starts the process of financing (notice that I did not use "lending"), that the money-credit-needed will be used in a productive and tangible project that will benefit the community, that it will not involve speculation and/or deceptive activities, that it does not involve investing in socially irresponsible activities—like operating a casino or taking advantage of the poor in businesses such as check cashing, predatory lending, and other similar activities—and that it will be used for environmentally and socially responsible investments. The RF banker should have a passion for serving people, should enjoy helping those who need assistance, and, most importantly, should have a vision for improving the lives of those around him or her in the community. People in the community expect that when their money is entrusted to a bank, it is treated by the bankers as a sacred trust that will be honored. People's money should be returned intact, as is, when it is demanded by its owners. It also cannot be disposed of in the form of a loan or credit facility to others without the consent of the owner.

VALUES AND BUSINESS ETHICS OF THE RF BANKER[10]

Professionalism

Professionalism is the talent of taking power through God, the source of all powers, to love what we do, to improve ourselves, to add to our experiences, and to do the best we can at what we promised to do. Professionalism is making promises that can be delivered and, if possible, delivering them better than promised. Professionalism is believing in and bringing to life the values of the Judeo-Christian-Islamic system. Professionalism is the pride of doing what we know, the strength of being able to say "we do not know" when we do not, and the determination to learn more.

Concentration

Concentration is the ability to focus and listen. It speaks to us quietly above the roar of our mind. Concentration in prayers, in supplication (*du'aa*), in remembering God, and in our work trains us to ignore the extraneous, dismiss the distractions, and avoid the pessimists, and prompts us to focus at will. Concentration is part of worshipping God (*ibada*). It is clarity. It is what keeps our emotions from getting the better of us. Concentration keeps pressure from becoming paralysis, and keeps us away from diluting our efforts by spreading ourselves too thin. Concentration is what keeps our eyes on our goals, allowing us to turn reaction into action, disadvantage into opportunity, and opportunity into success. Our goals should be crystal clear. We need to build the foundation of a worldwide RF banking and finance system, to bring the masses (*alnas*) back to the basic values of trust, humbleness, and sincerity.

Consistency

Consistency is a character trait that makes us unimpressed with a single success. Consistency confers medals only upon those who burn brightly with the repetition of achievement. It is more than a promise. It is performance over time. Consistency means never resting, never taking our talents—the precious gifts of God—for granted. Consistency is the practical proof that we are believers in God.

Commitment

Commitment is what transforms a promise into reality. We need to promise God and the community to build the RF banking and financing infrastructure of our communities worldwide. Commitment is the word that speaks of our intentions and the action which speaks louder than words. Commitment is making time when there is none. Commitment is coming through time after time, year after year, for the whole of our life. Commitment is what builds character. It is the power to change. It is the daily triumph of integrity, of belief in God, and of belief in the future over skepticism.

THE TEN GOLDEN COVENANTS OF THE RF BANK[11]

The RF banker's first and most important responsibility is to serve people in his or her community and to treat them like members of his/her own family. This means knowing the husband, the wife, the children, and the grandchildren. It means that the RF banker becomes familiar with the goals and objectives of the family, who will share with him their dreams and aspirations and view him/her as their financial doctor or expert. It is the responsibility of the RF banker to understand and become familiar with the family's financial situation in great detail, to help the family arrange and position their financial statement (i.e., assets and liabilities) as well as their income statement, to help the family improve their financial status by articulating their dreams and goals and then by restructuring their financial statement when needed. One example is to reduce the family's debts and liabilities and enhance the value of their assets. It is the responsibility of the RF banker to make sure that the family is well positioned and prepared for a comfortable retirement, for unexpected emergencies, and for saving for college expenses for their children and grandchildren. In doing so, the RF banker's prime passion should be the well-being of the family, not the commission or fee generated from the relationship.

In dealing with our own families, we always seek what is best for them. The RF banker would always try to minimize the fees and expenses incurred and charged by the bank and make sure that each transaction is looked upon as an honest-to-goodness investment, with good analysis and prudence exercised to ensure that the purchase of an investment and the taking of credit make economic sense. The RF banker also must have in his or her heart the best interests of the community. He/She will be active in all of its civic activities, including its places of worship of all faiths in which he or she is positioned to serve the worshippers, the school Parent-Teacher Association, the city and town services, and other voluntary activities. The RF banker should be a firm believer in speaking the truth, never betraying or compromising trust, and respecting privacy and confidentiality.

At LARIBA, we set a number of covenants, which we called "Ten Golden Rules for an RF Banker." The following is a listing of these rules:

1. *Do not speculate with people's money and trust.* We place people's trust above everything, including our own interest.
2. *Fulfill our promises.* We never promise what we cannot deliver.
3. *Respect money—money "respects" people who respect it.* We are careful with our costs. We keep them to a minimum.
4. *Do not forget our moral responsibility to local communities.* While our most important concern is to achieve the highest return for our shareholders, we never forget our moral responsibility to local communities. We measure our success by return on assets and by the number of households we have helped open up.
5. *Do not discriminate.* We do not discriminate, regardless of skin color, language, ethnic background, religious beliefs, age, or gender.
6. *Invest in our clients.* We do not look at our business as a money-renting operation. We invest with and in people.
7. *Be socially responsible.* We do not finance alcohol- or tobacco-related businesses, gambling, or any unethical behaviors and activities.
8. *Be sensitive about who we deal with.* We promise to check our depositors, clients, and customers to make sure of the validity of the sources of their funds and the type and quality of their businesses.
9. *Be conservative.* Our most important investment objective is preservation of capital and keeping up with inflation.
10. *Look at our co-workers as our partners.* We aspire to make each one of our co-workers as an important part of the business.

WHERE DO WE START AND HOW DO WE REALIZE THE DREAM?

A young professional in our community approached us when American Finance House LARIBA was started in 1987, as we were pioneering our effort to implement the values of the RF banking and finance system on a small scale. He said, "I respectfully disagree with your attempt to change the order and the seating arrangements on a Titanic-size ship. It will be impossible for LARIBA to do so." We thought deeply about it and we wrote to him stating, "We agree that changing the seating arrangement on a Titanic-size ship in one shot is of course impossible and is in fact unwise and of course would lead to failure. However, our approach is very simple . . ."

Our approach is to take a very small area on that large ship, ask those who are responsible for the space for their permission to rearrange things around without violating their rules and regulations, and offer the rest of the passengers an alternative way of doing things. If we are right, we shall be able to attract more people to notice our new alternative, ask about it, learn more about it, and eventually subscribe to it. This will eventually lead others to change to a better future, as was tested in this pilot experiment. This description is not a pipe dream. It is in fact the lesson of history—of all new civilizations and nations, as described to us in the Torah, the Gospel, and the Qur'aan. All God's prophets started in a small way and grew their base after proving that the new systems they were bringing to the community were better systems. This strategy is articulated in the following sentence: "Start from the possible to achieve the impossible." If we have a good idea that we believe is in great demand by the people, and if we are sincere in our efforts to introduce it to the citizens—one individual at a time—we shall capture the imagination of all people in the community and in the world, and they will eventually follow and subscribe to the new RF banking system.

But the question is, where to begin? The answer is extremely difficult, and in fact was a big challenge for all of us. Our efforts to start American Finance House LARIBA in 1987 and the way we developed it to become a recognized institution in the United States and the world was highlighted in the beginning of the book. Yes, capital is an important ingredient of the process. History has shown repeatedly that money does not make people, but people can earn that money. Experience has shown that the more important factors are belief and trust in God, imagination, and determination to create a clear image of a better but well-defined future. Most important is to attract people who believe in the new RF banking concepts and services and to capture the imagination of educated professionals who are willing to learn RF banking and practice it. Our challenge has been to build the morally and ethically qualified team players and leaders of the future of real RF banking. We believe that if we are sincere and wise in our approach, all else will fall in place by the grace of God.

NOTES

1. *Man* means male and female.
2. Bob Woodward, *Maestro: Greenspan's Fed and the American Boom*, Simon & Schuster, 2000.

  3. Stephen L. Carter, *Civility*, Basic Books, 1998.
  4. Ibid., page 12.
  5. Ibid., page 11.
  6. Hadeeth of Prophet Muhammad (pp).
  7. The Qur'aan, Chapter 4, Nissaa—Women.
  8. Ibid., Chapter 12, Joseph.
  9. Ibid., Chapter 12, Joseph.
 10. Based on a mid-1980s advertising campaign by Shearson Lehman, but adapted
     by the author.
 11. These are posted on the www.LARIBA.com and www.BankofWhittier.com
     Web sites.

CHAPTER 7

The Conventional Riba-Based Banking System

THE BANKING SYSTEM OF THE UNITED STATES

The United States has developed the most sophisticated and highly dispersed banking network and system in the world. The American banking system, when it was developed, benefited from the accumulated body of human experience over history, including many religious values, human experiences, and documented and sophisticated solutions to problems faced while developing the system in the United States and other systems in Europe. The system was and continues to be built using the most capable minds, accounting methods and standards, mathematical tools, and analyses available in the world. It is a project in progress. We are reminded that it would be embarrassing to write about the American banking and financial system after what happened in 2008, when the system failed miserably. It is believed that when the lessons learned from the worst crisis since the Great Depression are applied and the system is modified, it will be better: well-designed, well-positioned, and ready for a better future, not only for the United States, but for the rest of the world. History has shown that a country can have the most sophisticated system in the world, but if some people, who are part and parcel of the system, do not respect it and instead indirectly try to sabotage it by trying to get around the laws, that system is doomed. The United States functioned well with its banking system when Americans at all levels believed in it, respected it, and implemented it, and when we Americans lived within our means.

This chapter covers the U.S. banking regulations, which are considered the most sophisticated banking regulations ever developed in the history of the world. These regulations are included in this book to underline two important facts: (1) These regulations are intended to make sure that every citizen in the United States is treated fairly, and that the money deposited in the depository institutions is protected and safe. This is important, because those who are involved in RF banking and its development need not reinvent the wheel; we can use these regulations as a foundation for future efforts, improving upon or adding to this system of regulations in our effort to develop the RF banking and finance system. The United States' banking regulations are built on a huge body of human experience that was meticulously designed and documented. And (2), many of these regulations have Judeo-Christian-Islamic roots. These roots were tied in with the banking regulations. In addition to the banking regulations, this section attempts to familiarize the reader with the process of regulating and supervising banks. This chapter will focus on the process used by the U.S. Treasury Department's arm responsible for regulating national banks—the Office of the Comptroller of the Currency (OCC)—and how its "Examination of Safety and Soundness" of the national banks is conducted, including my personal perspectives from firsthand experience running the Bank of Whittier, NA, starting in July 2003. The role of the Federal Deposit Insurance Corporation (FDIC) and the Federal Reserve System will also be discussed. Additionally, the role of the Securities and Exchange Commission (SEC) in regulating the investment banking industry will be explained. The goal is to help the reader understand the processes used by the SEC to ensure that the financially uneducated and unsophisticated citizen is not conned out of his/her precious savings and that the process of selling securities (shares of companies, mutual funds, and bonds) is closely scrutinized by the government through the SEC.

To give a historic foundation for our discussion of how banks work and how Judeo-Christian-Islamic values can be applied to them, we need to know how financial institutions in the United States were built, their contributions to encourage community savings and investments, and their contributions to the lifestyle and the economy in the United States. With nearly 99,160 branches[1] and 415,321 automated teller machines (ATMs), the U.S. banking system is the largest in the world. As of the end of 2007, U.S. banks had $13.4 trillion in assets and $7.996 trillion in total loans. U.S. banking is more diverse than in most Western countries. Despite ongoing consolidation, vigorous competition exists within the vast banking community, which includes financial holding companies that operate nationwide, dominant regional banks, and smaller independent banks.

In my many personal communications and meetings with finance and banking officials and bankers in the world, especially in the United States, Europe, the former Soviet Bloc countries, and the developing countries of Africa and Asia, I was amazed to learn that officials outside the United

States are not aware of the real engine of the United States economy: the highly dispersed community-owned (shareholders and board members are from the local community) and operated network of community-based state and national banks, which make it easier for local communities to safekeep their savings and to use these savings to reinvest in the community. Most of the rest of the world is more familiar with branches of a larger bank that serve local communities.

The American banking system is based on a "bottoms-up" approach as compared to that of the rest of the world, which is designed and built based on a "top-down" approach. This basis, in itself, signifies the ideal of the United States banking system, which espouses the democracy of capital distribution. These, along with the many regulations in the system, aspire to make capital available for those who need it. This in itself is a basic Judeo-Christian-Islamic goal. Compare this to many of the countries in Europe and the developed world, which have huge capital resources but have not yet been able to make it trickle down to the masses despite claims, sometimes made by their governments, that they are applying the values of the faith.

It is interesting to report here the results of a survey made by a popular television channel in the Arab world, in which they asked if "Islamic" banks catered to the rich or served the poor and the needy. More than 70% of the respondents said that Islamic banks only cater to and serve the needs of the rich. In fact, most banks in the developing world, including Islamic banks, not only cater to the needs of the rich but also invest large sums of their capital and deposits in projects that are outside their countries. It is sincerely hoped that the United States' banking regulations are studied by the regulators, the religious scholars, and the politicians in these countries in order to make a real difference in the fortunes of the future generations at all levels of the social ladder. This can be done through real economic development, prosperity, social justice, and equal opportunity in obtaining credit and in making sure that the huge fortunes accumulated from the sale of the natural resources are invested back in the local communities through a healthy (and hopefully a riba-free) banking industry that believes making credit available to all people is a basic human right.

TYPES OF BANKING SERVICES IN THE UNITED STATES

The American banking system evolved with the emergence of the United States after the Civil War. There are two types of banks in America: State chartered banks, which are chartered by the state banking department of each state in the Union, and national banks, which are chartered and authorized to operate by the federal government through the U.S. Department of Treasury. One of the reasons Congress created a banking system that issued national currency was to finance the Civil War. Although national banks no longer issue currency, they continue to play a prominent role in the nation's economic life. It is important to understand that banks, be they state chartered or national, are empowered to issue credit facilities that carry the same effect of issuing currency, but only in terms of credit and in the form of a promissory note against the borrowers, as discussed in Chapter 5.

National Banks

Congress has established a number of long-range goals of for the national banking system in America. These are:

- Supporting a stable national currency
- Financing commerce
- Acting as private depositories
- Generally supporting the nation's economic growth and development

The realization of these goals required a type of bank that was not just safe and sound, but whose powers were dynamic and capable of evolving so that national banks could perform their intended roles, well beyond the Civil War. Key to these powers is language set forth in12 U.S.C. § 24 (Seventh), which provides that national banks are authorized to exercise:

> . . . *all such incidental powers as shall be necessary to carry on the business of banking; by discounting and negotiating promissory notes, drafts, bills of exchange, and other evidences of debt; by receiving deposits; by buying and selling exchange, coin and bullion; by loaning money on personal security; and by obtaining, issuing, and circulating notes.*

The national banking system demonstrates the value of applying nationwide standardization by introducing uniform national banking standards to banking activities and products.

State Banks

After the establishment of the United States, each state of the union kept a state-run banking system that was supervised by the individual state banking department. These state banking laws and regulations do not necessarily coincide and are not necessarily similar to the national banking system.

However, the state banking laws and regulations are essentially the same as those of the national banks. State banks are usually small in size compared to national banks; however, there are national banks that are small, with capital of as little as $5 million and total assets of as little as $25 million, and state banks that are large, with capital that can exceed $20 million and assets that may exceed $100 million. It is important to note that state banks can, in general, only operate in the state where they are chartered, while national banks can operate, within regulations, in all states.

To avoid the potential of a conflict that would arise from a particular state regulating a national banking institution that is regulated by the federal government, a dual banking system was invented:

> *It has been a bedrock precept of our [the United States'] constitutional law for more than 180 years, since the Supreme Court's decision in M'Culloch v. Maryland in 1819, that states cannot constitutionally control the powers of entities created under Federal Law. Courts have consistently applied this principle over the years to national banks, holding a variety of state laws inapplicable to national banks, and finding that the federally authorized powers of national banks are not subject to state supervision and regulation.*[2]

In 1861, Secretary of the Treasury Chase recommended the establishment of a system of federally chartered national banks, each of which would have the power to issue standardized national bank notes based on United States bonds held by the bank. In the National Currency Act of 1863, the administration of the new national banking system was vested in the newly created *Office of the Comptroller of the Currency*, or OCC, and its chief administrator, the *Comptroller of the Currency*.[3] The law was completely rewritten and re-enacted as the National Bank Act.[4] That Act authorized the Comptroller of the Currency to hire a staff of national bank examiners to supervise and periodically examine national banks for safety and soundness. The Act also gave the Comptroller authority to regulate lending and investment activities of national banks.

Distinctions between the national banking system and the state banking system are rooted deep in constitutional principles and the history of the United States. These distinctions are essential to the vitality of the dual banking system and are encouraged.

The OCC booklet[5] on the dual system states that each component of the dual (state and national) banking system makes different, positive contributions to the overall strength of the U.S. banking system. In defense of the value and contribution of the *state banking system*, state bank supervisors rightly assert that a separate system of state banks "allows the states to serve as laboratories for innovation and change, not only in bank powers and structures, but also in the area of consumer protection." State banks' supervisors argue that state banks put in action the "smaller is better" model of business. State banks are in general geographically closer to state bank regulators. This provides state banks with greater access to state regulators and gives state regulators greater familiarity with the banks they supervise.

National banks are required by law to become members of the Federal Reserve System. Banks chartered by the states are divided into those that are members of the Federal Reserve system (state member banks) and those that are not (state nonmember banks). State banks are not required to join the Federal Reserve system, but they may elect to become members if they meet the standards set by the Board of Governors of the Federal Reserve System. As of 2007, of the nation's approximately 8,441 commercial banks, approximately 2,459 were members of the Federal Reserve System. Member banks must subscribe to stock in their regional Federal Reserve Bank in an amount equal to 6 percent of their capital and surplus, half of which must be paid in while the other half is subject to call by the Board of Governors of the Federal Reserve System. The holding of this stock, however, does not carry with it the control and financial interest conveyed to holders of common stock in for-profit organizations. It is merely a legal obligation of Federal Reserve membership, and the stock may not be sold or pledged as collateral for loans. Member banks receive a 6 percent dividend annually on their stock, as specified by law, and vote for the Class A and Class B directors of the Reserve Bank. Stock in Federal Reserve Banks is not available for purchase by individuals or entities other than member banks. The Federal Reserve is responsible for supervising and regulating the following segments of the banking industry to ensure safe and sound banking practices and compliance with banking laws: (1) bank holding companies, including diversified financial holding companies formed under the Gramm-Leach-Bliley Act of 1999 and foreign banks with U.S. operations; (2) state-chartered banks that are members of the Federal Reserve System (state member banks); (3) foreign branches of member banks; (4) edge and agreement corporations, through which U.S. banking organizations may conduct international banking activities. Details of the Federal Reserve system are found in Chapter 5.

Credit Unions

There is yet another type of depository institution in the United States that is very close to savings cooperatives. These are called *credit unions*. These are associations of members of a community that are bound together either because they live in the same neighborhood, work in the same company, or worship at the same place of worship. These institutions usually gather assets by selling shares in the credit union and lending to its members at a spread over the dividends paid back to the members. The spread is usually lower than that of larger banks which yield higher dividends for depositors (credit union shareholders). This is because of the smaller size of most credit unions, the lower overhead, and the very low loan losses, because the community knows each other and is close to each other.

Investment Banks

Another important arm of banking in the United States is a category called *investment banks*. They differ from, but complement, the role of depository institutions (i.e., banks). An important role of the investment banks is that they gather funds that are "excess liquidity in the hands of the public and other institutions, like pension and retirement plans" and reinvest them prudently on behalf of the public, mainly in the United States, but also to capture business opportunities worldwide. It is very important to understand this role, because most of the Islamic riba-free banking discussions, especially concerning attempts to operate in the West, mix the roles of depository institutions—banks—and investment banks together. This has been a major source of confusion and a major problem in developing RF banking and finance services in most if not all the developed Western world. The lack of an active, sophisticated investment banking institution and investment bankers who understand the intricacies of reinvesting surplus funds in local economies prudently is an important reason for the flight of capital away from many developing countries. Investment banks are regulated by another U.S. government entity, the Securities and Exchange Commission (SEC), to make sure that the financially uneducated and unsophisticated citizen is not conned out of his/her precious savings, that the process of selling securities (shares of companies, mutual funds, and bonds) is closely scrutinized, and that these activities abide by government rules and regulations.

Licensing a Commercial Bank in the United States

In both types of banks—national and state—an application to start a new bank must detail why there is a need for a banking service in a particular area and the area of service on which this bank will be focusing its services. This area is called the *assessment area*. The bank charter application should include a detailed outline of the business plan, a description of the capital that will be raised and how it will be raised, and the identities of the bank's board of directors and key operating staff, with details on their experience, personal and professional backgrounds, and how they will contribute to the bank's mission of serving the banking and financial needs of the community. The feasibility study should also include a thorough and detailed analysis of the competition and a well-thought-out business plan that justifies the chartering of the bank and demonstrates how the community will be better off chartering and opening the services of this bank. State banks are chartered and authorized to operate by the state regulators, while national banks are chartered and licensed by the federal government through the Department of Treasury of the United States. In case a group wants to buy a controlling interest in a bank—more than 9.9% of the outstanding shares—the group must apply to the regulators for permission to make a change in the control of the bank.

Bank regulators not only review the application in great detail but also perform a detailed check on the background, the police and Justice Department records, and other civil records of all involved to ensure that those who sit on the board or run the bank have a crystal clean reputation before being entrusted with peoples' deposits and assets. It is preferred that the bank's board members come from diverse backgrounds so that they will be able to reflect the different viewpoints of the community. Board members are expected to have received proper training through attending special seminars on banking in general and on how to properly fulfill their responsibilities within the law and the banking regulations in particular. Bank executives and staff members are expected to attend regular training programs to familiarize themselves with all aspects and updates of bank operations and banking regulations. Examples of these training programs will be discussed in Chapter 12. Each board member is required by regulations to risk his or her own money by purchasing at least $1,000.00 worth of stock in the bank. Many will be surprised to know that members of the Board of Directors are not highly paid – in most cases – for their services. The Board fees range between $300 to $2000 (depending on the size of the bank) for each Board of Directors meeting they attend. Members of the Board of Directors not only are responsible for supervising bank operations to make sure that the bank is safe and sound but also are responsible before the law for any lapse in performing their duties of oversight and supervision. The details of all these aspects are not the subject of this book. Only a few samples of the important features of a bank structure are mentioned here, in the hope that such features will be studied, improved upon (if needed), and implemented by RF bankers to build on what is available and to achieve a better future for all.

GOVERNMENT SUPERVISION OF THE BANK

National banks are supervised and regulated by the OCC, which is an arm of the United States Department of Treasury. The OCC regulates and supervises all national banks and federal branches of foreign banks in the United States. These facilities account for nearly two-thirds of the total assets of all U.S. commercial banks.

The OCC's nationwide jurisdiction over banks—from modest-sized community banks to some of the largest banks in the world—also contributes to the agency's ability to develop and maintain highly expert credit examination and risk management capabilities that benefit all banks in the national system. The OCC has a nationwide reach, which enables it to take actions to protect customers regardless of the state in which they reside. The OCC's efforts to combat unfair or deceptive practices and its focused approach to customer privacy issues have had nationally recognized consumer benefits.

The Office of the Comptroller of the Currency[6]

The OCC charters, regulates, and supervises all national banks. It also supervises the federal branches and agencies of foreign banks. Headquartered in Washington, D.C., the OCC has four district offices plus an office in London to supervise the international activities of national banks.

The OCC was established in 1863 as a bureau of the U.S. Department of the Treasury. The OCC is headed by the Comptroller, who is appointed by the President of the United States, with the advice and consent of the Senate, for a five-year term. The Comptroller also serves as a director of the Federal Deposit Insurance Corporation (FDIC) and a director of the Neighborhood Reinvestment Corporation. The OCC's nationwide staff of examiners conducts onsite reviews of national banks and provides sustained supervision of bank operations. The agency issues rules, legal interpretations, and corporate decisions concerning banking, bank investments, bank community development activities, and other aspects of bank operations.

National bank examiners supervise domestic and international activities of national banks and perform corporate analyses. Examiners analyze a bank's loan and investment portfolios, funds management, capital, earnings, liquidity, sensitivity to market risk, and compliance with consumer banking laws, including the Community Reinvestment Act. They review the bank's internal controls, internal and external audits, and compliance with applicable laws and regulations. They also evaluate the bank management's ability to identify and control risk.

In regulating national banks, the OCC has the power to:

- Examine the banks.
- Approve or deny applications for new charters, branches, capital, or other changes in corporate or banking structure.
- Take supervisory actions against banks that do not comply with laws and regulations or that otherwise engage in unsound banking practices.

The agency can remove officers and directors, negotiate agreements to change banking practices, and issue cease and desist (C and D) orders, as well as civil money penalties.
- Issue rules and regulations governing bank investments, lending, and other practices.

The OCC's Objectives   The OCC's activities are predicated on four objectives that support the OCC's mission to ensure a stable and competitive national banking system. The four objectives are:

- To ensure the safety and soundness of the national banking system
- To foster competition by allowing banks to offer new products and services
- To improve the efficiency and effectiveness of OCC supervision, including reducing regulatory burden
- To ensure fair and equal access to financial services for all Americans

OCC Funding   The OCC does not receive any appropriations from Congress. Instead, its operations are funded primarily by assessments on national banks. National banks pay for their examinations, and they pay for the OCC's processing of their corporate applications. The OCC also receives revenue from its investment income, primarily from U.S. Treasury securities.

Insurance of Bank Deposits by the Federal Deposit Insurance Corporation (FDIC)

The FDIC insures the deposits in all member banks in the United States. The basic insurance amount was $100,000 per depositor, per insured bank until it was increased to $250,000 in response to the 2008 financial meltdown. This was done on a limited temporary basis (until 2013) to prevent customers of "shaky" banks from creating runs on those banks (when depositors withdraw their deposits from the bank to avoid incurring great losses of their capital). The FDIC insurance amount applies to all depositors of an insured bank. For more information, the reader is invited to visit the FDIC's Web site: www.FDIC.gov. One of the FDIC rules requires that every bank should have a clear Advertisement of Membership.[7]

UNITED STATES BANKING REGULATIONS

This section covers in detail some of the U.S. bank regulations, which are considered to be the most sophisticated bank regulations ever developed in the world. These regulations are included in this book to underline two important facts: (1) These regulations are intended to make sure that every citizen in America is treated fairly, and that the money deposited in the depository institutions is protected and is safe. This is important, because those who are involved in RF banking and its development need not reinvent the wheel; the existing regulations are built on a huge body of human experience, and it is hoped that RF banks' development efforts can begin by using such regulations as a base for further growth. (2) Many of these regulations have Judeo-Christian-Islamic roots.

In addition to the banking regulations, this section attempts to familiarize the reader with the process of regulating and supervising banks.

Consumer Compliance Management

Every bank in America is required to manage the entire consumer compliance process using an overall *compliance management system*. The system includes a compliance program and a compliance audit function, sometimes referred to as compliance review or self-assessment. The *compliance program* consists of the policies and procedures that guide employees' adherence to banking laws and regulations.

The *consumer compliance audit function* is an independent testing of the bank's transactions to determine its level of compliance with consumer protection laws, as well as the effectiveness of, and its adherence to, its own policies and procedures.

Board of Directors and Management Supervision and Administration

Compliance with U.S. banking laws and regulations at every bank is managed as an integral part of the bank's business strategy. The bank's board of directors and management recognize the scope and implications of laws and regulations that apply to the bank. The *compliance management system* should be designed to ensure that the bank's clients and customers are treated fairly and justly, according to the highest ethical standards, laws, and regulations, to protect the bank. Bank resources are expected to be used effectively to minimize any disruptions in daily activities due to compliance issues.

To ensure an effective approach to compliance, the board and management must take the business of compliance very seriously and make it a top priority. The participation of senior management in the development and maintenance of a compliance program is the pillar of the process. The board and senior management should periodically review the effectiveness of its compliance management system. This review includes reports that identify any weaknesses or required modifications due to changes in laws, regulations, or policy statements. Prompt and capable management response to those weaknesses and required changes is the final measure of the compliance system's effectiveness. The bank's senior management is required to assign a well-qualified staff and the necessary resources to properly implement and administer the compliance program. Participation in the compliance management system at all levels is important to its success.

Compliance Program
Each bank is expected to aspire to have in place a carefully devised, implemented, and monitored program that will provide a solid foundation for compliance. The bank's management will continually evaluate its organization and structure and modify its existing program to ensure that the compliance program meets its specific emerging new needs.

A *compliance committee* is appointed by the board and is headed by a *chief compliance officer*, who has specific responsibilities and authorities.

Compliance Committee
The board is required to organize the committee, which is chaired by the chief compliance officer. A typical committee in a small community bank would include the following members:

- Chief credit officer (deputy committee chairman)
- Chief operations and private banking manager (deputy committee chairman)
- Chief financial officer (deputy committee chairman)
- Manager of loan administration and credit analysis
- Technology coordinator

The bank compliance committee may have the following subgroups, which will focus on specific compliance activities:

- New Accounts, Customer Service, and Information Security and Technology Compliance
- Credit Operations Compliance
- Financial and Accounting Operations Compliance

The committee is expected to meet periodically (e.g., quarterly) or on an as-needed basis.

Duties, Responsibilities, Authorities, and Accountability of the Compliance Committee The consumer compliance committee will be responsible for the following tasks:

- Design, implement, test, proctor, and certify the program
- Develop and continually update all bank policies and procedures
- Develop a continual training and educational program to train the staff, management, and directors on issues pertaining to compliance within the bank training program
- Develop an internal audit program to self-audit different aspects of the compliance functions
- Perform a semiannual risk-based audit program to identify areas of the bank operations that need auditing and the frequency needed to perform the audit
- Develop the compliance audit scope in light of a *risk-based audit program*, and screen outside independent auditors who can perform the audit
- Make recommendations to the board of directors regarding the auditor(s) and scope of each audit; the board of directors has final approval
- Perform internal auditing of the compliance of each subgroup in a *certification program* to ensure that each department has external oversight (e.g., the credit group would audit the operations group; the operations group would audit and certify the financial and accounting group; and the financial and accounting group would audit and certify the credit group)

Clearly, the formality of the compliance program will increase in direct proportion to asset size, complexity, or diversity (including geographic) of operations of the bank. The board of directors and upper management should discuss these needs as they develop and should promptly take action to meet these needs.

Internal Controls
Internal controls are the systems through which the bank provides and ensures continuing compliance. These generally consist of sound organizational structures, comprehensive policies and procedures, and adequate training.

Organizational Structure The ability of the compliance committee to implement the compliance program, administer it, and institute effective corrective action depends on that committee's authority, independence, and role, as perceived by other employees, as well as on the support provided by the board and senior management. The compliance committee should be able to:

- Perform audits across departmental lines
- Access all operational areas
- Ensure that line management implements corrective action/changes in policies and procedures

Policies and Procedures   An effective compliance program includes compliance policies and procedures. Policies provide the framework for the bank's procedures and a source of reference and training for the bank's personnel. Comprehensive and fully implemented policies communicate clearly with all bank personnel the board's and senior management's commitment to compliance. Procedures must be developed to implement the bank's policies. Generally, the degree of detail, specificity, and formality will vary according to the complexity of the issues or transactions addressed by such procedures. Policies and procedures at the bank must be designed to provide personnel with enough information to complete a normal transaction, to the best of management's abilities and taking in consideration the size of the bank. These policies and procedures may include appropriate regulation definitions, sample forms and instructions, and—where appropriate—directions for routing, review, retention, and destruction of the transaction documents.

Training   Education of the bank's personnel is essential to maintaining a sound compliance program. All personnel should be generally familiar with the consumer protection laws and should receive comprehensive education in the laws that directly affect their jobs. They must also be trained in the policies and procedures adopted by the bank to ensure compliance with those laws. The faculty of the training program consists of bank board members, senior management, and invited guest trainers from auditing and training organizations. The training program may use videos and training materials obtained from different sources, such as the American Bankers Association (ABA) and BankersOnline. The training program is detailed in Chapter 12.

Compliance Audit Function   The other component of a comprehensive compliance management system is a *compliance audit function*. It enables the board and senior management to monitor the effectiveness of the compliance program. The audit function tests the bank's compliance with consumer protection laws and adherence with policies and procedures. An effective compliance audit function should address all products and services offered by the bank, all aspects of applicable operations, and all departments and branch locations. Our team at the Bank of Whittier has developed a pioneering risk-based audit analysis computer program, which we use to identify the frequency of each audit in each area of bank operation, based on the many factors that may impact bank operations such as the economy, oil prices, inflation, political developments, and the like.

SUMMARY OF FEDERAL BANKING REGULATIONS IN THE UNITED STATES[8]

The following pages summarize some of the important U.S. banking regulations. These regulations are intended to make sure that the financial system in the United States is streamlined to prevent any excesses or mismanagement and that financial services are performed in a universal and standardized regulatory fashion to regulate the banking business in the states of the United States, which in fact resemble 50 different nations. These regulations are improved on a continual basis in the United States, as we have seen, in response to unfortunate experiences of excess and malpractice. The regulations are built on a vast body of human experience over the years since the dawn of history. As we read in the Qur'aan about justice, discrimination, and fair dealing among people:

> *55:9 weigh, therefore, [your deeds] with equity, and cut not the measure short!*
>
> *10:47 NOW every community has had an apostle; and only after their apostle has appeared [and delivered his message] is judgment passed on them, in all equity; and never are they wronged.*
>
> *11:85 Hence, O my people, [always] give full measure and weight, with equity, and do not deprive people of what is rightfully theirs, and do not act wickedly on earth by spreading corruption.*
>
> *16:90 BEHOLD, God enjoins Justice, and the doing of good, and generosity towards [one's] fellow-men; and He forbids all that is shameful and all that runs counter to reason, as well as envy; [and] He exhorts you [repeatedly] so that you might bear [all this] in mind.*
>
> *42:42 blame attaches but to those who oppress [other] people and behave outrageously on earth, offending against all right: for them there is grievous suffering in store!*

One of the purposes of including some of the important U.S. banking regulations in this book is to introduce the respected government officials and RF (Islamic) banking and finance scholars, executives, and practitioners to such regulations. It is hoped that they will be motivated to study these regulations carefully and learn from them. If we want to develop a specialized set of regulations for an RF (Islamic) banking and finance system, we will not have to start from scratch. Some of these regulations are also included to draw the attention of the eminent scholars to the fact that it is definitely not enough to "devise a financing model" and issue a *fatwa* (an edict) pronouncing that the model is Shari'aa-compliant. Many more aspects of the real spirit of the RF system are based on Judeo-Christian-Islamic values, many of which are catered to by these regulations.

Regulation B: Equal Credit Opportunity

The *Equal Credit Opportunity Act* (ECOA) states that creditors (including banks, retailers, finance companies, and bankcard–credit card companies) that regularly extend credit to customers should evaluate candidates on creditworthiness alone, rather than other factors (such as, for example, race, color, religion, national origin, or sex). Discrimination on the basis of marital status, welfare recipience, or age is generally prohibited (with exceptions), as is discrimination based on a consumer's good faith exercise of their credit protection rights. This regulation is a manifestation of the values of all faiths, including the Judeo-Christian-Islamic faith system, and it forms the foundation of real belief in God. It helps achieve the ultimate goal of the Judeo-Christian-Islamic value system, which requires that credit be a basic human right.

This Equal Credit Opportunity Act must be translated into a policy of fair lending by the board of directors of each bank in the system. Each bank is required to post a special logo that tells all customers that the bank implements the Equal Credit Opportunity Act.

Fair Lending Policy   The bank should extend (and service) all types of credit consistent with safe and sound operational practices. The bank should also originate loans in such a way as to help meet the credit needs of the communities, including low- and moderate-income neighborhoods. All credit decisions must be based on adequate investigation and the application of sound judgment supported by verified facts. The application of credit guidelines and policies must be uniform for all persons and organizations and never based on race, sex, sexual orientation, color, national origin, religion, age, marital status, disability, or any other prohibited basis. This policy is an integral part of each bank's fundamental mission of providing quality financial services to existing and prospective customers.

Banks must realize that in granting credit, they also build customer relationships, and it is only through these relationships that the banks can achieve sustained, long-term success. A bank must be committed to the principle that every applicant for credit receives fair and equal treatment throughout the credit application and approval process. This principle is embodied in the Equal Credit Opportunity Act (ECOA) and the Fair Housing Act (FHA).

General Policy Statement Banks must commit to not discriminate with respect to any aspect of a credit decision on the basis of race, color, religion, national origin, sex, marital or familial status, disability, age (provided that an applicant has the capacity to enter into a binding contract), receipt of income from any public assistance program, sexual orientation, military status, or the good faith exercise of any rights under the federal Consumer Credit Protection Act. Every bank in the system is required to fully commit to the principle that all credit decisions should be made without regard to race or any other discriminatory basis that is prohibited by law. Each bank should recognize that affirmative steps must be taken to ensure that this policy is applied consistently and continuously through all aspects of its credit operations, including product design, marketing and advertising, and application and underwriting processes. Each bank is required to regularly monitor its lending activities to make certain that they comply with this policy. When internal and external reviews suggest that a deviation from the policy may have occurred, the bank is expected and required to act expeditiously to investigate and, if necessary, institute corrective measures.

Advertising Each bank should commit not to engage in advertising practices that would discourage on a basis prohibited by law the making or pursuing of an application for credit and should comply with the requirements of applicable laws relating to the nondiscriminatory advertising of credit. Where required, all advertising, press releases, and marketing materials for the bank's lending activities must include a facsimile of the equal housing lender logotype and legend.

Applications and Information Gathering Oral or written statements that tend to discourage potential applicants on a basis prohibited by law must not be employed with regard to oral or written inquiries and applications. The application process must be neutral in nature and of a type applicable to every applicant desiring the same kind and amount of credit. Credit analysts, private bankers, and other bank employees involved in the loan origination process may not ask prohibited questions regarding:

- A spouse or former spouse
- Marital status
- Familial status
- Military status

- Sex
- Alimony, child support, or separate maintenance income
- Child bearing
- National origin
- Race
- Color
- Religion
- Sexual orientation

Application Processing and Evaluation and Loan Application Second Review Process A bank must not use any information it obtains to discriminate on a prohibited basis. No loan application submitted to the bank will be declined unless the decision to decline is supported by sufficient documentation.

Credit Extension A bank must commit that it will not discriminate on a prohibited basis in the extension or denial of credit.

Notification A bank is required to provide notices of action taken on loan applications in accordance with the provisions of the ECOA and Federal Reserve Board Regulation B, described above.

Record Retention A bank is required to maintain the following information, as required by law:

- Application form
- Written or recorded information used in evaluating an application
- Written or recorded information regarding any action taken concerning a new or existing extension of credit, including a copy of any statement of specific reasons for adverse action
- Information obtained for purposes of government monitoring
- Any claim or accusation of alleged discrimination or other violation of law submitted by an applicant or existing customer

Unless a shorter retention period is permitted by applicable law, the information listed above must be maintained for a minimum of 12 months (non-consumer) or 25 months (consumer) after the date on which the bank notifies an applicant of action taken on an application or of incompleteness of an application.

Government Monitoring Program As required by applicable law, a bank is required to request and maintain information from loan applicants on race, ethnicity, and sex to allow the government to monitor compliance with nondiscrimination laws.

Fair Lending Training   Bank personnel involved in lending are required to receive appropriate training on fair lending laws and regulations periodically from the bank.

Regulation C: Home Mortgage Disclosure Act (HMDA)[9]

The instinct of owning a place in which to live and to produce livelihood is a natural dream for every individual and family.[10] The motor powering economic development throughout history has been the desire to have a place to live and a means of transportation. In today's language, that means owning a house and an automobile. That is why the twin backbones of major developed countries and societies have been the housing and automobile industries. The development of mortgage financing in the United Kingdom, Germany, and the United States has helped propel the economies directly and indirectly:

- Economies are propelled *directly* by increasing demand for the products, industries, and services associated with building homes.
- Economies are propelled *indirectly* by satisfying the citizen's natural instinct for ownership by making him/her feel that he/she owns a house— "a piece of the rock." This feeling of ownership makes the citizen proud of his/her citizenship, deepens the feeling of belonging to the country, and enhances the value of the real estate in general, as owners strive to beautify their owned properties by continually maintaining and improving them. Owning a home strengthens the feeling of responsibility towards the citizens' own families and the community at large.

One of the important parameters used by the U.S. Federal Reserve System, in its decision regarding interest rate and monetary policy, is setting the interest rates (as discussed in Chapter 5) and its impact on the housing and automobile industries.

In an effort by the government to monitor home financing activities in every small town, neighborhood, or city throughout the United States, each home mortgage financing participant—including each bank and mortgage finance company—is required to complete a special government form designed to reveal any implicit or systematic discrimination against any minority when it comes to home financing. This act was designed to eradicate to the best possible ability of the government any discriminationary activity, such as the most well-known scheme (practiced in the 1970s) called *red zoning*. In this scheme, different areas in a city were *red-zoned* to indicate that such areas were high-risk areas and that lending there would be dangerous because of the ethnic character of those who lived there. This practice, of course, made the low-income and poor neighborhoods suffer. The *Home Mortgage Disclosure Act* (HMDA) was enacted by the Congress in 1975 (as amended) and is implemented by the Federal Reserve Board's *Regulation C* (12 CFR 203). HMDA requires financial institutions to maintain and annually disclose data about home purchases, home purchase pre-approvals, home improvement, and refinance applications involving one- to four-unit and multifamily dwellings. It also requires branches and loan centers to display a special HMDA logo on all its communications, publications, Web site, and advertising materials.

Purpose of the Act   The purpose of the HMDA is to provide the public with loan data that can be used (1) to help determine whether financial institutions are serving the housing needs of their communities; (2) to assist public officials in distributing public-sector investment to attract private investment to areas where it is needed; and (3) to assist in identifying possible discriminatory lending patterns and in enforcing antidiscrimination statutes. It was also made very clear in the Act that "neither the Act nor this regulation is intended to encourage unsound lending practices or the allocation of credit."

Reporting Requirements   Financial institutions must report data regarding applications for home purchase loans, home improvement loans, and refinancing, whether originated, purchased, turned down, or canceled. HMDA requires lenders to report information on the following:

- The loan, as to its type, amount, and pricing and whether the loan is subject to the *Home Ownership and Equity Protection Act* (15 USC 1639)
- The property, as to its location and type, and the disposition of the application, including whether it was originated or denied; in case of denial, lenders must report the reason for declining
- The applicant's ethnicity, race, gender, and gross income for mortgage applicants and borrowers
- In case loans are sold, the type of purchaser for mortgage loans that were sold

Denial Reasons and Other Data   Financial institutions regulated by the OCC, such as national banks, are required to provide reasons for denials. Providing reasons for denials is optional for financial institutions supervised by the Federal Reserve and the FDIC.

Disclosure   As the result of amendments to the HMDA incorporated within the *Housing and Community Development Act* of 1992, an institution must make its disclosure statement available to the public at its home office within three business days of receipt.

Training and Oversight Responsibilities   Each loan officer is required to attend HMDA training at least annually.

Regulation Q: Prohibition Against Payment of Interest on Certain Deposit Account Types

Regulation Q prohibits banks from paying interest on *demand deposit accounts* (DDA). Banks, however, may pay interest on *negotiable order of withdrawal* (NOW) checking accounts offered to consumers and certain entities (but not to commercial enterprises, other than sole proprietorships).

This regulation is very interesting for Islamic bankers and RF bankers, because it stipulates *not to pay interest*. I am stating this because in many of the applications made by Islamic bankers to operate in the West, one of the main negotiation issues has been the payment of interest on some deposits and the requirement of many of the Islamic banking eminent scholars to expose the bank deposits to bank profit and loss, with the possibility of losing depositors' money. We will discuss this issue further in Part Two of this book.

Regulation D: Reserve Requirements for Depository Institutions (Banks)

As we discussed in the section on Regulation Q, banks are not allowed to pay interest on their *demand deposit account* (DDA) checking accounts. Regulation D was devised after the introduction of what are known as NOW (*negotiable order of withdrawal*) accounts, which were allowed to earn interest in order to allow banks to compete with investment banks, whose banking products included interest-bearing money market mutual funds that offered interest on invested cash (deposits that are not FDIC-insured). The regulation was devised in an effort to limit frequent withdrawals from these accounts, which may cause the bank to undermine its long-term investment commitment in the community (by keeping a larger percentage of its assets in cash to meet these unexpected withdrawals). Following are the objectives of Regulation D:

- To establish reserve requirement guidelines
- To regulate certain early withdrawals from certificate of deposit accounts

- To define what qualifies as *DDA/NOW* accounts (please see Regulation Q regarding eligibility rules for interest-bearing checking accounts)
- To define limitations on certain withdrawals on savings and money market accounts
- To establish that unlimited transfers or withdrawals are permitted if made in person, by ATM, by mail, or by messenger

In all other instances there is a limit of six transfers or withdrawals per month. No more than three of these transactions may be made payable to a third party (by check, draft, point-of-sale, etc.).

The bank must close accounts where this transaction limit is constantly exceeded.

Regulation O: Loans to Bank Insiders

This regulation was devised to make certain that bank insiders, such as directors, senior management, and/or principal shareholders, are not getting preferential treatment when they deal with the bank (e.g., by obtaining credit at lower rates than the public), are not given preferential credit standards when they apply for credit (e.g., by receiving higher rates on their deposits), do not have access to other customers' private information, and do not "front" others in making business decisions based on their preferred position and insiders' information.

Regulations P and S

Regulation P requires all banks and financial institutions to safeguard all personal financial information given by the customer and not to release any such information to a third party, be it an affiliate, an advertising agency, or even a government agency, unless authorized by that customer. In addition, the financial institution is required to mail all its customers a letter—on an annual basis—detailing the institution's *privacy policy*. A copy of the letter sent by one of the community banks is shown below.[11] It is also interesting to note that if a wife opens an account in her name only, her husband cannot get any information about that account without the approval of the owner of the account (the wife).

This regulation is considered to be an important expression of the Judeo-Christian-Islamic value system, which has at its core a fundamental and keen intent to respect and guard private and personal information. In fact, this kind of policy is an important feature of the Law (Shari'aa) that should be highlighted to RF banking scholars, as they expand their efforts to establish a universal set of regulations that will truly express these values of the Judeo-Christian-Islamic system. Many countries claim they apply Shari'aa as the source of their legal systems or as the foundations of their legal systems, but they have no respect for the private domain of their citizens. In these countries, financial, personal, and corporate information is compromised easily and privacy is violated without a court order or even allowing those whose rights were violated any legal recourse.

Please see Box 7.1 for a sample privacy letter that the Bank of Whittier sends to its customers.

BOX 7.1: A SAMPLE PRIVACY LETTER SENT TO ALL CUSTOMER AT LEAST ONCE A YEAR[12]
BANK OF WHITTIER, NA RIGHT TO FINANCIAL PRIVACY POLICY

BECAUSE YOUR TRUST IS SO IMPORTANT

Your trust is the cornerstone of our relationship. This is why we work diligently to safeguard your privacy. The information that you provide us is kept in the strictest confidence. We have no intention of selling personal information about you, the Customer(s), to any third-party businesses. We are proud to make this commitment to our Customers, because your trust is the foundation of our business. The following privacy policy explains how we use and protect information about our Customers. Please read this very important information carefully.

NOTICE OF CUSTOMER'S FINANCIAL PRIVACY RIGHTS

The terms "we," "our," and "us," when used in this notice, are defined as Bank of Whittier, N.A.

We define our "Customers" or "you" as having a continuing relationship through the following types of accounts with us:

- Deposit account
- Loan account
- Safe deposit box

As the Customer of the Bank, you will be notified of any sources for nonpublic personal information we collect on you. We will notify you as to any measures we have taken to secure the information. We must first define a few terms:

Nonpublic personal information is information about you that we collect in connection with providing a financial product or service to you. Nonpublic personal information does not include information available from public sources, such as telephone directories or government records.

An "affiliate" is a company we own or control; a company that owns or controls us; or a company that is owned or controlled by the same company that owns or controls us. Ownership does not mean complete ownership, but means owning enough to have control.

A "nonaffiliated third party" is a company that is not an affiliate of ours.

THE BANK OF WHITTIER, N.A. PRIVACY PROMISE FOR CUSUMERS

While information is the cornerstone of our ability to provide superior service, our most important asset is our customers' trust. Keeping customer information secure, and using it only as our customers would want us to, is a top priority for all of us at Bank of Whittier.

Our promise to our Customers:

We will safeguard, according to strict standards of security and confidentiality, any information our customers share with us.

We will limit the collection and use of customer information to the minimum required to deliver superior service to our customers, which includes advising our customers about our products, services, and other opportunities as well as administering our business.

We will permit only authorized employees who are trained in the proper handling of customer information to have access to your information. Employees who violate our Privacy Promise will be subject to our normal disciplinary process.

We will not reveal customer information to any external organization unless we have previously informed the customer in disclosures or agreements, have been authorized by the customer, or are required by law or our regulators.

We will always maintain control over the confidentiality of our customer information.

Whenever we hire a third party to provide support services, we will require them to conform to our privacy standards and conduct regular audits to ensure compliance.

For purposes of credit reporting, verification, and risk management, we will exchange information about our customers with reputable reference sources and clearing-house services.

(*continued*)

We will not use or share—internally or externally—personally identifiable medical information for any purpose other than the underwriting or administration of a customer's account, or as disclosed to the customer when the information is collected, or to which the customer consents.

We will attempt to keep customer files complete, up to date, and accurate. We will notify our customers on how and where to conveniently access their account information (except when we are prohibited to do so by law) and how to notify us about errors, which we will promptly correct.

THE CONFIDENTIALITY, SECURITY, AND INTEGRITY OF YOUR NONPUBLIC PERSONAL INFORMATION

We restrict access to nonpublic personal information about you to only those employees who need to know the information to provide products or services to you. We maintain physical, electronic, and procedural safeguards that comply with federal standards to guard your nonpublic personal information.

THE NONPUBLIC PERSONAL INFORMATION THAT WE COLLECT

We collect nonpublic personal information about you from the following sources:

- Information we receive from you on applications or other forms
- Information about your transactions with us
- Information about your transactions with nonaffiliated third parties
- Information we receive from a consumer reporting agency

THE NONPUBLIC PERSONAL INFORMATION THAT WE DISCLOSE

We do not disclose, nor do we reserve the right to disclose, any nonpublic personal information about our customers or former customers to anyone, except as permitted by law.

Regulation Z: Truth in Lending Act

This regulation is one of the most important consumer protection regulations in the United States, as well as to RF (Islamic) bankers around the world. Prior to its enactment, banks lent money at a purportedly low interest rate, but they would charge a number of additional fees that, if added up, would result in a much higher implied interest rate. It was imperative to legal experts and regulators to create a standardized "yardstick" by which the consumer could compare various banks' offers to finance his/her needs. That was the motivation behind Regulation Z, which requires that whenever money changes hands between two persons or entities, the return realized should be expressed in terms of an "implied" interest rate, and that in calculating it, all pertinent fees and costs should be included.

Regulation BB: Community Reinvestment Act (CRA)

The Community Reinvestment Act (CRA) requires banks to define an assessment area that they will be serving. Based on this, the regulators monitor the bank's lending activities to make sure that:

- The bank's loan to deposit ratio is at least 50 percent.
- The bank's loan portfolio has at least 50 percent of its loans extended to entities in the declared assessment area.
- The bank lends to all segments of the community that reside in the assessment area without discrimination and in a way that reflects the demographic nature of the communities residing in these areas.

This is an important regulation that is needed for most, if not all, of the developing countries of the world, including those which have a thriving RF banking industry. One of the most important revelations of God to all of us in all His messages and through all of His messengers, as taught by the Judeo-Christian-Islamic value system, is to reinvest in the communities to which one belongs and from which banks gather their deposits. This regulation is very important, because in my travels throughout the world, both in the developing non-Muslim and Muslim countries, I was sorry to see the public underserved. The banks collected peoples' savings and reinvested them in financing projects that were only short term in nature; most of the financing was done to facilitate imports-related businesses, rather than long-term development and strategic projects. I also discovered that in most of these countries, most banks' loan-to-deposit ratio is 50 percent or less. If this happened in a bank in the United States, the bank would be cited by the regulators for not implementing the CRA and would be required to increase its financing activity in the community. If the bank did not comply within a limited time, its license to operate would be revoked.

Another disappointing fact is that banks in many of these countries invest the liquid money left over in their coffers outside the country, which results in two violations. The first is violating our covenant with the higher authority, God, to reinvest in our communities and to change the fortunes of all people to a better future. The second violation is a violation of the Community Reinvestment Act, CRA. One time, I was visiting a country in North Africa and during a meeting with local bankers, I shared with them the aspects of the CRA applied in the United States. It was a great revelation to them. I told them that in the United States, according to this CRA, all insured depository institutions are required to reinvest in the communities they serve. It was also suggested that government regulators should require banks there to spend documented efforts with measured acceptable results in an effort to increase banking and credit services to all people, including low- and moderate-income areas, communities, and individuals. Insured depository institutions in America must display and make available to the public a CRA notice describing their activities and efforts to serve local communities. To meet that requirement, each bank branch must have a current CRA public file or access to it via the company's intranet. The bank has 10 days to provide the information to any questions on CRA if asked in person or via mail.

Regulation DD: Truth in Savings Act

Regulation DD requires all banks and other depository, savings, and investment institutions to be truthful when they advertise the interest rate they promise to pay the customer who deposits and/or saves with them and the return on investment realized when a customer invests with one of these institutions. Some banks and financial representatives, in their pursuit to attract as many deposits and investments as possible, quote and/or promise higher "interest" or "returns" in their advertising. Regulation DD requires the bank to be complete in advertising the interest rate based on a universal standard format that is used to calculate the interest on deposits, so that the customer can make a fair comparison. This standard will help the consumer make an educated decision when he/she decides to invest or save. For example, the bank must disclose the method it used when it calculated the promised rate—for example, whether the advertised rate was a *compounded* or a *simple* rate.

Fair Credit Reporting Act

This act requires all financial institutions and banks to exercise great care to be accurate and truthful while reporting their customers' credit history and pattern of paying back their debts and commitments to credit reporting agencies. It is a known fact that consumers' credit ratings are of prime importance when a bank decides whether to extend credit to and/or to do business with a customer. That is why the regulation stipulates detailed methods, ways, and means to ensure protection of the consumer and correction of errors if these errors occur, as well as charging penalties if the report was erroneous—particularly if it was intentional.

Anti-Money-Laundering Program

To enhance domestic security following the terrorist attacks of September 11, 2001, Congress passed the USA PATRIOT Act, which contained provisions for fighting international money laundering and blocking terrorists' access to the United States and global financial systems. The provisions of the USA PATRIOT Act that affect banking organizations were generally set forth as amendments to the Bank Secrecy Act or BSA, which was enacted in 1970. The BSA requires financial institutions doing business in the United States to report large currency transactions and to retain certain records, including information about persons involved in large currency transactions and about suspicious activity related to possible violations of federal law such as money laundering, terrorist financing, and other financial crimes. The BSA also prohibits the use of foreign bank accounts to launder illicit funds or to avoid U.S. taxes and statutory restrictions. The U.S. Department of the Treasury maintains primary responsibility for issuing and enforcing regulations to implement this statute.

However, the Department of Treasury has delegated to the federal financial regulatory agencies the responsibility for monitoring banks' compliance with the BSA. The Federal Reserve Board's Regulation H requires banking organizations to develop a written program for BSA compliance. During examinations of state member banks and U.S. branches and agencies of foreign banks, Federal Reserve examiners verify an institution's compliance with the recordkeeping and reporting requirements of the BSA and with related regulations, including those related to economic sanctions imposed by Congress against certain countries, as implemented by the Office of Foreign Assets Control or OFAC. It is beyond the scope of this book to detail such regulations.

Bank Examination for Safety and Soundness by Bank Regulators

Every bank in America is examined on a regular basis (if it is a large bank, the OCC would have permanent examiners on site throughout the year) or on a cyclical basis (in the case of smaller banks, the cycle would be from 12 months in the case of banks that need closer supervision to 18 months for banks that are known to have wise management and a proven track record). The following is a typical letter from the regulators to the bank president (in this case, it was me at the Bank of Whittier, NA[12]) to prepare all the documents needed to examine the bank. The reader will appreciate the detailed nature of the examination as shown in the letter; it is usually conducted by five to eight examiners over a period of two to four weeks—or more, depending on the size and the condition of the bank. After concluding the examination, the bank is rated by the OCC according to each of five important parameters: Capital, Assets, Management, Earnings, and Liquidity (CAMEL). A bank with a rating of 1 or 2 is considered superior, and of medium status if it is rated 3. A bank that is rated 4 or below is required to agree to a *Memorandum of Understanding* (MOU) with the regulators, in which the bank makes promises about how it will operate and fix its problems according to a preapproved time table in the future. Or if the bank is in bad shape, it get a *Cease and Desist* order (C and D), and if not fixed, its charter is revoked. It is also important to note that not all regulations are tested every year and that in some years a particular focus is taken (for example, if there is a high historic risk of flooding, the OCC examination adds a close focus on flooding compliance). It is also interesting here to recommend that compliance with Shari'aa could be a part of this examination process in cases when a bank chooses to include RF banking services as part of their service to the public.

Box 7.2 is a copy of what a bank receives from the regulators in order to prepare for the annual regulatory examination.

BOX 7.2: OCC REQUEST LETTER: FROM THE OCC OFFICE TO THE BANK'S PRESIDENT:

In order for us to prepare effectively for this supervisory activity, we are asking you to provide the information listed in digital format. If this is not practical or becomes inefficient for you, please provide copies of the requested documents. Other large items may be provided in hardcopy form for return to the bank. Please indicate which items should be returned to the bank.

Please make available the following upon our arrival on (date of exam). Please forward any items marked by a check (X) to our Southern California–North Field Office by [*deadline for submitting the requested documents*].

MANAGEMENT AND SUPERVISION

Unless otherwise stated, please provide the most recent information on the following:

- The Board packet. Any information included in the packet and requested below need not be duplicated.

- Current organizational chart.

- If any changes have occurred since the last examination, a list of directors and executive management, and their backgrounds, including work experience, length of service with the bank, etc. Also, a list of committees, including current membership.

- A list of officers' salaries and compensation.

- If any changes have occurred since the last examination, a list of related organizations (e.g., parent holding company, affiliates, and operating subsidiaries).

- Most recent external audit reports, management letter, engagement letter, and management's responses to findings (including audits of outside service providers, if applicable).

- The internal audit schedule for the current year, indicating audits completed with summary ratings, and in process.

- Most recent internal audit reports, including management's responses. Include (20XX) audit reports covering loan administration, funds management and investment activities, Bank Secrecy Act program, risk based capital computations, information processing, and any audit areas that were assigned a less than satisfactory rating.

- Brief description of new products, services, lines of business, or changes in the bank's market area.

- List of data processors and other servicers (e.g., loan, investment). The detail of the list should include:

  a. Name of servicer.

  b. Address of servicer.

  c. Contact name and phone number.

  d. Brief explanation of the product(s) or service(s) provided.

  e. Note of any affiliate relationship with the bank.

  f. For example, services provided may include the servicing of loans sold in whole or in part to other entities, including the service provider. OCC examiners will use this list to request trial balances or other pertinent information not otherwise requested in this letter.

- Minutes of board and major committee meetings (e.g., Audit, Loan, Asset/Liability Management, Fiduciary, and Technology Steering Committee) since our last examination.

(continued)

ASSET QUALITY

Please provide copies of the following [*dated as of XXXX*]:

- List of watch list loans, problem loans, past-due credits, and non-accrual loans.
- List of the ten largest credits, including commitments, made since the last examination and the new loan report for the most recent quarter.
- Concentrations of credit reports.
- Policy, underwriting, collateral, and documentation exception reports.
- List of insider credits (to directors, executive officers, and principal shareholders) and their related interests. The list should include terms (rates, collateral, structure, etc.).
- List of loan participations purchased and sold, whole loans purchased and sold, and any securitization activity since the last examination.
- List of overdrafts.
- Analysis of the allowance for loan and lease losses including any risk rating changes from the most recent quarter.
- List of other real estate, repossessed assets, classified investments, and cash items.
- List of small business and farm loans "exempt" from documentation requirements.
- Latest loan review report, including any responses from the senior lending officer, account officers, etc.
- List of board-approved changes to the loan policy and underwriting standards since the last examination.
- The loan trial balance.
- The bank's loan policy including a description of the bank's risk rating system.

FINANCIAL PERFORMANCE

Unless otherwise stated, please provide the most recent information on the following:

- Most recent Asset Liability Committee (ALCO) package.
- Most recent reports used to monitor and manage interest rate risk (e.g., gap planning, simulation models, and duration analysis).
- Most recent liquidity reports (e.g., sources and uses).
- List of investment securities purchased and sold for [20XX] and [20XX]. Please include amount, seller/buyer, and date of each transaction.
- Most current balance sheet and income statement.
- Most recent strategic plan, budget, variance reports, etc.
- Current risk-based capital calculation.
- Securities acquired based upon "reliable estimates" authority in 12 CFR 1.3(i).
- Securities acquired using the bank's lending authority.
- The pre-purchase analysis for all securities purchased since the last examination.
- A summary of the primary assumptions used in the IRR measurement process and the source.
- Current contingency funding plan.
- Investment portfolio summary trial, including credit ratings.
- The list of board-approved securities dealers.
- List of shareholders and ownership.
- Most recent annual and quarterly shareholders' reports.
- Most recent Report of Condition and Income (call report).
- List of pending litigation, including a description of circumstances behind the litigation.
- Details regarding the bank's blanket bond and other major insurance policies (including data processing–related coverage). Provide name of insurer, amount of coverage and deductible, and maturity. Also, please indicate the date of last board review and whether the bank intends to maintain the same coverage upon maturity.
- Summary of payments to the holding company and any affiliates.
- Bank work papers for the most recent call report submitted.

CONSUMER COMPLIANCE

The consumer compliance examination is being conducted under the authority of 12 USC 481. However, it also constitutes an

(continued)

investigation within the meaning of section 3413 (h) (1) (A) of the Right to Financial Privacy Act. Therefore, in accordance with section 3403 (b) of the Act, the undersigned hereby certifies that the OCC has complied with the Right to Financial Privacy Act, 12 USC 3401, et seq. Section 3417 (c) of the Act provides that good faith reliance upon this certification relieves your institution and its employees and agents of any possible liability to the consumer in connection with the disclosure of the requested information.

Unless otherwise stated, please provide the most recent information on the following:

- A list of approved changes to the bank's compliance policies and procedures since the last examination.
- A description of the bank's training programs and criteria for ensuring that employees receive job appropriate compliance training.

FLOOD DISASTER PROTECTION ACT
Bank's policy and procedures applicable to compliance with the FDPA:

- A copy of bank contract(s) with third parties performing flood determination services.
- Flood maps used to determine whether a property is in a standard flood hazard area (SFHA), if available.
- A copy of flood notices.
- List of all loans located in special flood hazard areas.

EXPEDITED FUND AVAILABILITY ACT
- The bank's Reg. CC policy.
- Copy of your funds availability disclosure.
- Hold reports and/or records from the main office and branch office(s) for the past month.

PRIVACY OF CONSUMER FINANCIAL INFORMATION
- Copies of privacy and information security policies and procedures.
- Describe key internal controls that ensure compliance.

- Copies of privacy notices (initial, annual, revised, opt-out, short-form, and simplified).

- List of affiliates and nonaffiliated third parties to whom the bank discloses nonpublic personal information about consumers, customers, and former customers:

  - Outside of the regulatory exceptions (Sections 13, 14, and 15); and

  - Under Section 13, including joint marketing agreements

- Describe how the bank ensures that nonpublic personal information received from nonaffiliated financial institutions is reused and redisclosed according to regulatory requirements, and describe such sharing activities.

- Any records supporting the bank's categorization of its information sharing practices under Sections 13, 14, and 15, and outside the regulatory exceptions, if available.

- Information sharing agreements and contracts between the bank and its affiliates and between the bank and non-affiliated third parties.

- A list of consumers who have opted out of the disclosure of nonpublic personal information to nonaffiliated third parties.

- Consumer and customer complaints regarding the treatment of nonpublic personal information.

- Nonaffiliated third-party complaint logs, telemarketing scripts, and any other information obtained from nonaffiliated third parties, if available.

- Compliance and audit work papers related to privacy.

- Training program information and materials.

RIGHT TO FINANCIAL PRIVACY ACT

- Policies and procedures on the Act.

- Requests for customers' financial records received from federal government authorities since the last examination.

Bankruptcy Laws[14]

One important and often abused privilege of U.S. citizens and businesses is the ability of the person or entity that obtained a credit facility to stand before a special bankruptcy judge in court to present the reasons why the person or the entity cannot meet their obligations by paying back what he/she owes the bank or the financial institution. These bankruptcy laws are called different names depending on the nature of the problem and the solution. If there is an economic slowdown and demand declines, resulting in lower sales and hence lower net profits, the owner of the business can file for a request to the court to protect him/her and his/her business against foreclosure by creditors. The owner of the business would be requested to present the court with a plan to reorganize that contains a reduction of the monthly payment on a loan and/or partial loan forgiveness as well as a time-table to get out of this dire situation. Another purpose of the bankruptcy laws is to maximize returns under adverse conditions by providing an orderly distribution of assets and debts.

This facility is considereded an important development and a fair "safety valve" in the business of giving credit and in financing. Very disturbing situations and penalties have been reported regarding the failure of a borrower to meet his/her obligations to a bank for good and justifiable causes in other countries—including Islamic countries. Borrowers who do not fulfill their credit obligations are systematically jailed by the government, which resorts to throwing the business owner in jail and taking over the facility. In most cases, the facility is pillaged, the employees are laid off, and the facility is sold for next to nothing. Many developing countries practice such painful and unproductive "therapy." I understand that this action can be condoned, and that this approach should be applied for those who defraud others by lying on an application for credit, intentionally misusing and siphoning funds outside the company or country, and/or outright racketeering. This must be done by following due process according to the law and in the courts of law. On the other hand, the world has seen wonderful, honorable business people end up in jail in one country or another in Africa, Asia, or the Middle East, and their facilities—along with the households of many of their employees—are shut down just because the economy is in decline or a government official wants to settle a political grudge. That is another area that needs pioneering and dedicated work among the RF (Islamic) banking scholars who believe in applying the credible and attractive Judeo-Christian-Islamic value system to the RF banking system that we all aspire to grow. It is strongly recommended that similar provisions be included in Shari'aa guidelines by which RF banks operate.

NOTES

1. Source: American Bankers Association (ABA), Private Communication: As of the end of 2007, there are 42,386 national (commercial) bank branches, 42,895

state commercial bank branches, 9801 national savings banks, 4067 state saving banks (savings banks used to be called savings & loan associations and financed homes and apartments), and 11 foreign banks.

2. Comptroller of the Currency Administrator of National Banks: National Banks and The Dual Banking System, September 2003.
3. Ibid.
4. Ibid.
5. Ibid.
6. For more information about the OCC, contact the Office of the Comptroller of the Currency, Communications Division, Washington, DC 20219, via telephone at 202-874-4700, or via the Web at www.OCC.Treas.gov.
7. As stipulated by the authority of regulation 12 U.S.C. 1818(a), 1819 (Tenth), 1828(a): Part 328 describes the official sign of the FDIC and prescribes its use by insured depository institutions. It also prescribes the official advertising statement insured depository institutions must include in their advertisements. For purposes of part 328, the term "insured depository institution" includes insured branches of a foreign depository institution. Part 328 does not apply to non-insured offices or branches of insured depository institutions located in foreign countries.
8. Banking regulations are labeled by an alphabetical letter, starting from A to Z and then AA to, say, CC. For a detailed listing and description of these regulations, please visit the U.S. Treasury Department Web site.
9. Pronounced "Hamda."
10. Yahia Abdul Rahman and Abdullah Tug: "Towards a LARIBA (Islamic) Mortgage Financing in the United States Providing an Alternative to Traditional Mortgages," Harvard University School of Law, October 9–10, 1998 (Presentation).
11. Privacy letter sent annually by Bank of Whittier, NA. This letter is a copy of the 2007 edition of that letter.
12. Ibid.
13. The Request Letter sent by OCC to Bank of Whittier President in March 2008 to request documents that will help in their examination of the bank.
14. www.uscourts.gov/bankruptcycourts/bankruptcybasics/discharge.html.Chapter 7: The chapter of the Bankruptcy Code providing for *liquidation* (i.e., the sale of a debtor's nonexempt property and the distribution of the proceeds to creditors). Chapter 9: The chapter of the Bankruptcy Code providing for reorganization of municipalities (which includes cities and towns as well as villages, counties, taxing districts, municipal utilities, and school districts). Chapter 11: The chapter of the Bankruptcy Code providing (generally) for reorganization, usually involving a corporation or partnership. (A Chapter 11 debtor usually proposes a plan of reorganization to keep its business alive and pay creditors over time. People in business or individuals can also seek relief in chapter 11.) Chapter 12: The chapter of the Bankruptcy Code providing for

adjustment of debts of a "family farmer" or "family fisherman" as those terms are defined in the Bankruptcy Code. Chapter 13: The chapter of the Bankruptcy Code providing for adjustment of debts of an individual with regular income. (Chapter 13 allows a debtor to keep property and pay debts over time, usually three to five years.) Chapter 15: The chapter of the Bankruptcy Code dealing with cases of cross-border insolvency.

CHAPTER 8

What Is the Difference?

Comparing Riba-Free Banking and Conventional Riba-Based Banking

THE RF BANKING BRAND: HISTORY, DEVELOPMENT, AND STAGES OF GROWTH

Riba is prohibited in Judaism, Christianity, and Islam (as detailed in Chapter 2). The riba-free (RF) banking system was started in the time of the Prophet Muhammad (pp); it reinforced the teachings of Moses (pp) and Jesus (pp) in the seventh century and helped the growth of international trading, but it declined over the years and was dismantled completely after World War I and the disassembly of the Ottoman Empire. The RF banking and finance system was left behind as the riba-based banking system grew and developed in a more sophisticated way to meet the ever-growing volume and diversity of world economy and trade. New economic, monetary, political, and social systems were developed in Europe to cope with the changes of the Renaissance and, later, the Industrial Revolution. After World War I, most the Muslim lands were occupied by the British and the French. It is believed by some that this was God's plan to wake up the people of these lands, to expose them to the Western world and bring them quickly to the latest developments of the 19th and early 20th centuries. As a result, many young men and women were educated and became aware of the new world and its progress in the fields of education, medicine, social relations, and science. A new generation of more educated and sophisticated Muslim leaders came in contact with Europe and began dreaming of catching up with its progress. At the same time, many Muslim religious leaders were sent to Europe—mainly to France and England—to obtain higher education and get exposed to the lifestyle and culture there. These students were sent from Egypt and India (now India, Pakistan, and

Bangladesh). Many were graduates from religious schools such as Al Azhar (the oldest Islamic seminary and university in the world) and other religious schools in India. They obtained post-graduate degrees from the leading universities in Europe and went back to their countries, aspiring to build the future by telling people what they had seen and how they had lived, sharing their experiences and dreams about the future of their land. They started motivating people to work hard in order to catch up with Europe and its Renaissance. They were positioned in responsible posts in the government, such as the ministry of education (to develop a better education system for the future generations) and the ministry of finance (to help streamline and plan state finances and budgets). Many became famous newspaper editors and authors of books in general and about Islam and Prophet Muhammad (pp), using a new research-based approach with documentation and analysis in the way they had learned in Europe. Many of them started new political and civic movements to bring back the long-forgotten glory of the teachings of Islam—which is called in this book the Judeo-Christian-Islamic value system.

One of the first books I read back in 1964 was a small paperback titled *Bonook Bela Fawa'ed*, which means "banks without interest." It was a small book authored by the late Professor Eissa Abdou, a professor of commerce and economics at the second largest university in Egypt, Ain Shams University. I enjoyed reading the book; it was my introduction to a new world of banking. I understood its social objectives, intent, and implications, but did not know much about its banking applications, because I did not even have a bank account yet. Bank accounts were luxuries, reserved for the rich and affluent professionals and millionaires.

The modern, practical Islamic banking movement started in Egypt around the early 1960s as a microlending finance operation in a small village in the Nile Delta. It was started by a young German-educated Egyptian—Dr. Ahmad Al Naggar (this is how it is pronounced in the Egyptian accent, but in the proper Arabic pronounciation it is Al Najjar) who came back to Egypt with his German wife after finishing his education. He was distressed to see the poor farmers in his small village of Zefta/Mit Ghamr in the Egyptian Nile Delta lacking the funds needed to finance the purchase of seeds, farm animals needed to plough the land, cattle, animal feedstock, and simple pumps—even to finance their subsistence and basic needs until the crop was cultivated and sold on the market. The bank expanded its operations throughout the Egyptian farmland and became very popular until it was nationalized by the government of the late president Nasser[1] and renamed Nasser Social Bank (*Bank Nasser Al Ijtmaii.*). Dr. Ahmad Al Naggar was instrumental in training a new generation of Islamic bankers; he started the Institute of Islamic Banking Training in Cairo and then moved it to Cyprus, which was politically less restrictive to many of the students, who were former bankers and accountants from all over the world. In the last years of his life, he became very critical of the direction taken by the Islamic banking industry at that time, because it concentrated more on form and less on substance and because it abandoned its social responsibility of assisting and building the local communities that needed urgent help and instead focused on serving the rich.

The 1973 Arab-Israeli (*Ramadan–Yom Kippur*) war instigated the first oil crisis. The increase in oil prices from less than $2.40 per barrel to almost $12 a barrel brought large sums of cash to the oil-producing countries in the Gulf. This money generated a new class of dollars: petro-dollars. Many in the banking industry spoke about the absorptive capacity of the economies of the Gulf's oil-producing countries, describing the inability of their economies to absorb these sums of money. In an effort to create good use of some of this huge cash flow, King Faisal (died 1975) of Saudi Arabia set a goal for his country to develop Islamic banking and to develop cooperation among Muslim countries. He started the Islamic Development Bank, IDB, and initiated a new vision of an Islamic banking system. In Dubai, a futuristic leader by the name Sheikh Saeed bin Lutah started the Islamic Bank of Dubai. In Kuwait, Sheikh Bazee Al Yaseen headed a new Islamic finance company called the Kuwait Finance House (KFH). KFH attracted huge deposits and built a strong customer base. KFH started its financing activities with auto financing and later became active in commodity trade finance and real estate financing for homes and commercial buildings.

In Saudi Arabia, two Islamic finance companies were started. One was started by King Faisal's son, Prince Muhammad Al Faisal. It was registered in Switzerland and named Faisal Finance. Its headquarters were located in a wonderful high-rise building near the Geneva airport. From Geneva, they invested in commodities like gold (cash and carry contracts as well as commodities funds), and unfortunately lost a lot of money. Prince Muhammad Al Faisal also received a full-service banking license to operate an Islamic bank in Egypt under the name Faisal Islamic Bank (*Bank Faisal Al Islami*), which grew into one of the larger banks in Egypt, with more than 700,000 customers and many branches throughout Egypt. The other company was started by Sheikh Saleh Kamel; he called it *Dallah Al Baraka*. Sheikh Saleh Kamel started branches, offices, and investments in London, France, Egypt, Malaysia, Pakistan, Bangladesh, Turkey, Tunisia, Morocco, Algeria, and the United States. He also received a full-service banking license in Egypt and he opened the Egyptian Saudi Finance Bank (*Bank Al Tamweel Al Misry Al Saudi*). The bank now has many branches in Egypt. In the mid-1980s, he bought a small bank in London and operated it as the first Islamic bank ever in the United Kingdom. The bank was later asked to discontinue its operations by the British Financial Services Authority (FSA) because of a number of operating shortcomings and because the owners (Al Baraka) did not have a chartered bank in Saudi Arabia. It is interesting to note that Saudi Arabia did not have a full-service Islamic bank operating inside its territories until the mid-1990s. In the 1980s, Turkey got a new prime minster, the late Turgut Ozal, who had a keen interest in developing the fledgling economy of his country and ridding it of its tight-gripped military rulers. He started by developing strong relations and economic ties with many of the cash-rich Gulf oil-producing countries, especially Saudi Arabia and Kuwait. His government encouraged investments and export to the Gulf countries. He also helped pass legislation to start what are called in Turkey *finance houses*, a code name for Islamic finance companies that operate like banks but are not called "Islamic" because of Turkish politics. The *finance house* name was arrived at in order not to create sensitivities around the long-standing Turkish policy coined by President Kemal Ataturk, the founder of the Republic of Turkey. The long-standing Ataturk doctrine that made Turkey a secular and non-religious country is still in effect today. Two finance houses were authorized. These were Faisal Finance (belonging to Prince Al Faisal's operation in Geneva) and Al Baraka Turk Finance House (belonging to Al Baraka in Saudi Arabia). All Finance Houses had a minimum ownership of 50 percent by local Turkish shareholders, as stipulated by Turkish law.

In the 1960s, Malaysia started a savings program to help its Muslim citizens perform pilgrimage (*Hajj*). It is interesting to note here that in Malaysia and Indonesia, Muslims believe that the most successful and blessed marriage is one which is consummated during the *Hajj* season in Makkah (close to the *Kaa'bah*, the first house ever built to worship God by Prophet Abraham and his son, which is close to the port of Jeddah, Saudi Arabia). They started a new savings organization to deposit parents' savings so that they could plan ahead, accumulating the cost needed to finance the *Hajj* trip over the years from the time their child is born. This way, when the child grew up and was ready to get married, there would be enough money to perform *Hajj* and consummate the marriage. The savings organization, called *Tabung Hajj*, gathered huge savings from devout Malaysian Muslims. It is important to note that most of the Malaysian Muslim religious leaders received their religious education in the 1950s and the 1960s in Cairo, at Al Azhar University. There, they were taught about the prohibition of riba, which was called also interest (*fawa'ed*). Tabung Hajj began investing these funds in the proper riba-free way according to the Law, Shari'aa, in huge palm tree plantations and in real estate projects in Malaysia and Indonesia; they realized great returns. They started an Islamic bank called *Bank Islam Malaysia*. Since that time, Malaysia has become the leader in Islamic banking activities. In another development, after Malaysia became independent in the mid-1950s, tens of thousands of Malaysian students were sent for higher education in Egypt, England, Europe, and the United States. These graduates came back with big ideas.

I must share with the reader here that I spent a few years of my life traveling extensively to Malaysia and getting to know its people at all levels very well. I was amazed to find out how bold the Malaysians were in their dreams and their aspirations, and how courageous they were in not being afraid of implementing the boldest ideas very efficiently. Their achievement is in fact a manifestation of what people say: "you are as big as your dreams and goals." With these big dreams, the availability of the petro-dollars from the Gulf oil-producing countries, and the interest of Japan and the United States in developing the Asian markets, Malaysia became a prime player in the world economic development matrix—and the Islamic banking movement in Malaysia grew with it. The central bank there—Bank Negara Malaysia (BNM)—pioneered a new approach to help support Islamic banking. They started to run two books: one book for Islamic banks and another for conventional banks. The government encouraged teaching Islamic banking at the International Islamic University Malaysia (IIUM) and started many training and research institutes in the field. They also established a Council of Scholars at the central bank level to establish the central bank's Shari'aa Board to operate according to the rules and regulations of the Law (Shari'aa). They also developed new RF banking products and services that complied with Shari'aa and offered alternative Islamic banking services and products that could substitute and compete with those offered by riba-based conventional banks. The scholars in Malaysia were criticized severely by the scholars in the Arab Gulf countries for their liberal views, especially in the area of Islamic bonds—now called *sukuk*. (The word *check* in English originated from the Arabic word *sak*, or a promise to pay. The plural of *sak* in Arabic is *sukuk*.)

In the West, new efforts were initiated to serve the British Muslim communities in the mid-1980s. HSBC and the United Bank of Kuwait (now part of Shamel Bank of Bahrain) started offering home financing services. HSBC called its services (which are now available in many parts of the world) Amanah. United Bank of Kuwait called its home mortgage finance program Al Manzil; it is still in use in the United Kingdom. The UK FSA authorized the Islamic Bank of Britain (IBB) as a full service bank with some stiff requirements and guarantees from the shareholders, who come mostly from Qatar with a small shareholders position from Bahrain. In the United States, two companies started operations in 1987 to meet the growing demand among the expanding American Muslim community. These were American Finance House LARIBA, which financed all community needs, like cars, homes, and businesses, and Muslim Savings and Investments (MSI), which financed mostly homes. LARIBA grew and its shareholders acquired a full-service bank in 1998, as will be detailed later. MSI experienced significant losses in the housing development business and was later closed down after its contract for home financing was challenged in a Texas court (the case was settled out of court for an undisclosed sum of money paid by MSI). In the late 1990s, the United Bank of Kuwait began to offer its home financing in New York, along the same model it offered in the United Kingdom, but after almost two years of operations it was closed down. In the early 2000s, HSBC started offering home financing in New York and offer services through a wholly-owned subsidiary they called Amanah, but it was not able to compete and was curtailed. A new home mortgage finance company called Guidance Residential Finance was started in 2001, and with LAR-IBA, this company became a major home mortgage financing company. Guidance relied in its sales and promotion campaign on the reputation and endorsement of a religious heavyweight advisor who was a chief religious justice and a former mufti in Pakistan.

Perhaps the most historic moment in the operations of RF financing of home mortgages came in 2001, when Freddie Mac approved LARIBA. In 2002, Fannie Mae followed. The support of Freddie and Fannie helped the growth of home mortgage financing using RF finance models in America. Instead of LARIBA being able to finance a home every two or three months, they were able to finance as many as 50 homes per month after the investments from Freddie and Fannie became available. Another first in the history of the United States was the issuing of RF mortgage-backed securities (RF MBS) by LARIBA with Fannie Mae. These RF MBS securities were based on RF mortgages produced by LARIBA with Fannie Mae. In 1998, some of the LARIBA shareholders acquired the Bank of Whittier, National Association (NA), and in 2003 a new RF banking team came to run the bank in an RF format. The bank offers financing of cars, homes, commercial buildings, businesses, churches, mosques (*masajid*), and schools. Bank of Whittier also offers all of the standard banking services offered by any bank in the United States in an RF format. The bank offers timed certificates of deposit, which derive their income from the RF credit portfolio of the bank. Two other community banks entered the business by offering an Islamic banking window (mostly for home mortgages). These are Devon Bank of Chicago, Illinois, and University Bank of Detroit, Michigan. These banks meet the growing demand for RF banking and finance services in many parts of the United States.

AN OVERVIEW OF RF BANKING

RF banking is a faith-based and socially responsible brand of community banking. It is faith-based because it bases its financing models, its operations, and the moral and ethical values of its staff, management, board of directors, and shareholders on Judeo-Christian-Islamic values, as detailed in Chapter 6. It is socially responsible because it applies the values of social responsibility of all those associated with it according to the same Judeo-Christian-Islamic values. For example, it looks at money not as a "thing" that can be rented at a price (the interest rate), but as a measuring tool to measure the success or failure of investing. It is also concerned with the type of investment in which it invests its money. For example, RF banking does not invest in alcohol-related businesses, gambling and related businesses, promiscuous activities, or in businesses that are not environmentally and socially responsible. It also does not invest in businesses that are unfair to its labor and customers. RF banking does not finance speculative activities that are focused on making money out of money, based on speculations in the different financial, commodities, and real estate markets. It is community banking at heart. It believes in community development. It considers its role to be a qualified professional entity that is sound, safe, responsible, and trustworthy to attract the deposits and savings of the community.

RF bankers work hard to reinvest these assets in the community by financing projects that will create economic prosperity, job opportunities, and most importantly, peace and harmony within the community. RF banking does not discriminate, because discrimination in service and financing and in dealing with others is a major sin in all Abrahamic faiths. The RF banker is trained to have the interest of the customer and the community at large as his/her prime responsibility and passion. RF bankers are trained to serve their customers from a real concern for what is beneficial and good to the family and for the preservation and growth of the family's wealth and assets. The RF banker believes that his/her role is in fact not to generate as many loans and as much lending volume as possible for his/her bank, but rather to consider financing as a process of investing in and with the customer. This approach puts a great burden on RF bankers, because any investment must be prudently conceived and well thought out, and it must make economic sense. That is why all applications for financing are thoroughly studied, prudently analyzed, and evaluated in light of the best interests of the family, its nature, and its prior experience, as well as the prevailing economic, social, and political variables in the community and the country at large.

Misnomers in RF Banking

When RF banking was first presented in the early 1950s by Muslim scholars and activists, they attempted to popularize it by calling it *interest-free banking*. The early scholars believed that RF banking's most fundamental requirement was that both parties—the bank and the investor/depositor—participate in the profit and loss of the project they undertake. This made many newcomers who were engaged in the development of this new brand of banking focus on how to resolve two main issues. These were: (1) the removal of the word "interest" from the vocabulary of Islamic banking and the language of the contracts used, and (2) the restructuring of the transaction to make it appear as a buy/sell transaction, and that the financing institution should own the property—even for seconds—in a back-to-back agreement. An army of riba-based conventional bankers, banking and tax attorneys, and scholars in Shari'aa spent years in the second half of the 20th century developing contracts and models that were focused on trying to resolve these two important issues. The buy/sell and ownership aspect of the transaction were added later, because in the Qur'aan we are taught that riba is not the same as buying and selling. The Qur'aan reveals, as quoted below, that they are different because God made riba divinely prohibited (haram) and buying and selling divinely allowed (halal).

> *2:275 Those who devour usury will not stand except as stand one whom the Evil one by his touch Hath driven to madness. That is because they say: "Trade is like usury," but God hath permitted trade and forbidden usury. Those who after receiving direction from their Lord, desist, shall be pardoned for the past; their case is for God (to judge); but those who repeat (The offence) are companions of the Fire: They will abide therein (for ever).*

Many scholars, attorneys, bankers, and practitioners invested valuable resources to fix the form, but not the substance and spirit of the intent of removing riba from peoples' lives, as required by the Judeo-Christian-Islamic value system. It is interesting to note that the interest-free banking brand, which was used in the early years of Islamic banking, gave consumers the wrong impression and in many cases created a false conclusion. People thought that money would be given away by the Islamic bankers to be used to buy homes and businesses without expecting any increase or profit. Many of my friends in the West would ask me how an Islamic bank could survive if it did not charge interest. How can the bank pay its employees' salaries? What incentive was offered to the shareholders, who expect to receive decent returns on their investments? In the early days of Islamic banking, bankers arrived at an expedient solution: replace the word "interest" with one of a variety of words, such as "service charge," "rent," "profit," and the like. This approach may have helped the form of making the contract and operation "look Islamic," but in fact interest was still being charged, just under a different name. Such contracts were devised by well-trained and experienced attorneys in the West and riba-based conventional bankers.

However, when some customers lost the money they had invested with "Islamic" banks, they were told by the bankers that—and I quote—"this proves that there is participation in profit and loss, and it shows that it is Islamic!" In fact, an Islamic finance company that lost the money of its investors in a number of ill-conceived real estate projects on the east coast of the United States—because they simply had no prior experience—exclaimed "thankfully" that this proved the concept of participation in profit and loss, and the president of the company called it "the cost of being a Muslim"— and even gave it an acronym, *COBM.* This concept and term is still being used by many practitioners of "Islamic" banking, including professional American conventional bankers who in fact know better. These bankers stated many times in public conferences on Islamic banking in America that their motivation was to meet the market demand. We at LARIBA were privileged to have started a movement in the late 1980s to use the term riba/ ribit-free banking—RF banking—instead of interest-free or Islamic banking.

What Is RF (Islamic) Banking?
Some have defined "Islamic" banking as conventional banking minus the word "interest," with a new contract that does not include the word "interest" and that is structured in a convoluted version of buy/sell, in which the seller changes ownership to the bank or finance company and then the bank sells it to the eventual buyer. Many participants in "Islamic" banking business thought, with good intentions, that these guidelines made the contract Islamic. Others conceptualized "Islamic" banking by using the expression of socialism, minus state control, plus God to give it needed faith-based credibility.

The following are believed to be the true conceptual fundamentals of the RF brand of banking, which is based on the Judeo-Christian-Islamic value system.

RF Banking:
- Believes in the fact that giving credit is a basic human right.
- Is socially responsible and ethical banking, designed to deliver services to the community according to the guidelines of the Judeo-Christian-Islamic value system. For example, RF bankers cannot finance alcohol-related businesses, gaming, gambling, polluting businesses, or other unethical activities. RF banks finance businesses in a fair and just way and serve all customers of all backgrounds. RF banks scrutinize the businesses they finance to ensure that the business owners treat their employees fairly and without discrimination.

RF bankers believe in equal financing opportunities without discrimination, because discrimination is a sin in the Judeo-Christian-Islamic value system. No one is too small to serve and work with. Every community member is encouraged to live within his/her means.

- Enjoys the advantages of low overhead, lower risk, and lower loan losses, because the RF banker knows his/her clients, as he/she is active in the community.
- Is built on asset- (and services-) based financing. This requires that a commodity, tangible asset, and/or service must change hands at a fair market value—one that is gathered from the live market—using the concept of *marking to the market.*
- Is not a moneylending operation. It is involved in actual financing of and investing in tangible assets and services. It finances economically viable projects. If the project is not economically viable for the customer, it will not be financed. There is no "name" lending allowed in RF banking.
- Invests in specific activities and projects to make a difference in peoples' lives. RF financing requires that the RF banker/financier knows what the applicant will use the money for and that the agreement involves the exchange of assets/properties/businesses or the leasing of such.
- Believes that speculation and its tools—like trading in risk—and paper trading are divinely prohibited (haram).
- Believes in financing for community development. Promotion of community development and reinvestment in the community is of prime importance.
- Believes that wealth should be circulated within the community to create jobs, economic growth, and prosperity. It uses the power of congregations and networks in places of worship and in social organizations to enhance its market penetration at the grass roots, thus fulfilling the financing and banking rule of "know your customer." This approach minimizes losses due to ill-conceived financing of the wrong project with people who may not meet the needed prerequisites for a successful venture.
- Believes that one of its prime objectives is to remove riba/ribit from peoples' behavior and lives, one step at a time. RF bankers must start from the possible to achieve the impossible.
- Does not intend to remove or "destroy" riba-based conventional banks and systems. The aim of RF banking is to develop an alternative system that serves all people, regardless of faith or background.

- Measures success by return on investment, the number of households financed, and its achievement in making a difference in the lifestyle of the family and in the community.
- Believes that fiat (paper) money is not a commodity that commands a rental fee (interest rate). It also does not reproduce. It only grows when used in an economic activity. Money is a manmade measuring device. It is a "thing." It cannot be rented. It is only useful if invested. *Riba* can be defined in today's terminology, and in light of riba-based financing activities, as renting money at a predetermined price called interest. RF bankers cannot merely take the interest rate of the day and charge it under the names *rent*, *service charge*, *index*, or *profit*. Financing should be based on renting assets and services at the actual prevailing market rental/lease rate commanded by the market forces of supply and demand—not on the rental of money.
- Believes that the value of different things in fiat (paper) currency must be related to one of the reference commodities using the commodity indexation system, as detailed in Chapter 5. For example, economic bubbles can be detected by relating prices to a precious metal or a staple commodity, and investment practices can be adjusted to avoid loss of assets and properties.
- Believes in full transparency as a must. Full disclosure is required as part of the contract, because deceptions, ruses, and/or attempts to misrepresent (called *gharar*) are haram (divinely prohibited).
- Believes that it must comply with the laws of the land without violating God's Law (*Shari'aa*). RF bankers are not in business to change the laws of the land, to be elected to a high office using the power of money, to influence, or to discredit others. RF bankers do their best to educate and guide government banking regulators, politicians, and the public at large about the RF system and its values and benefits.
- Prepares and offers to the community RF bankers who are trained to believe that their ultimate goal is not to sell and make commissions, but to serve to earn a living and, eventually, win paradise.

What Is the Difference Between Riba-Based Conventional Banking and RF (Islamic) Banking?[2]

- *Dominant attractor*
  - Riba-based: Money
  - RF: Life as prescribed by God in all Abrahamic faiths, as ordained in the Judeo-Christian-Islamic value system and way of life
- *Defining purpose*
  - Riba-based: Use money to make money for those who have money

- RF: Employs available resources within its means to meet the basic needs of everyone without extravagance
- *Bank size*
  - Riba-based: Very large (e.g., mega-banks)
  - RF: Small and medium-sized
- *Ownership*
  - Riba-based: Impersonal, with absentee shareholders' role in most cases
  - RF: Personal, with shareholders playing an active role in bank direction and procedures
- *Financial capital*
  - Riba-based: Global, with no borders
  - RF: Local/national, with clear community reinvestment borders and assessment areas
- *Purpose of investment*
  - Riba-based: Maximize private profit and wealth
  - RF: Increase beneficial output to the community to make it prosper
- *Role of profit*
  - Riba-based: An end to be maximized
  - RF: An incentive to invest productively in the community
- *Coordinating mechanisms*
  - Riba-based: Centrally planned by mega-corporations
  - RF: Self-organizing markets and networks of communities around temples, synagogues, churches, masajid, and other social congregations and networks
- *Cooperation*
  - Riba-based: Among competitors, to escape the discipline of competition and in some cases to avoid regulations
  - RF: Among people and communities to advance the common good for all
- *Purpose of competition*
  - Riba-based: Eliminate the unfit and capture markets
  - RF: Stimulate efficiency and innovation
- *Government's role*
  - Riba-based: Protect the interests of property
  - RF: Advance the human interest, as revealed in all God's messages
- *Trade*
  - Riba-based: Free, but for the benefit of mega-corporations
  - RF: Free, but fair and balanced
- Political orientation
  - Riba-based: Elitist, democracy of the money (greed is good!)
  - RF: Populist, democracy of persons

NOTES

1. President of Egypt (1956–1970), a leader of the Egyptian Free Officers Revolution of 1952 and a pan Arab leader of Arab Nationalism.
2. This comparison is based on a comparison originated by Professor David C. Korten. It was adapted by the author to compare conventional riba-based banks with riba-free banks. David C. Korten, *The Post-Corporate World*, a copublication of Kumarian Press Inc. and Berret-Koehler Publishers, Inc., 1999, p. 41.

CHAPTER 9

Islamic Banking in the 20th Century

The efforts to start Islamic banking and finance in the mid-1970s resulted in the development of a major model, which became very popular because it was very close to the conventional riba-based financing model. The model is called the cost-plus (*murabaha*) model, which, as described in Chapter 3, includes the following steps:

1. The finance institution buys the item at the order of the ultimate buyer (who wants to finance it) at a certain price.
2. Then the financial institution sells the item back to the ultimate buyer at the original price plus a profit element. The profit element usually reflects the accumulated *implied interest*—called profit—that would accrue over the period of financing.

The model focused on the fact that there is a buy/sell transaction and that interest is not charged, as required by the Law (Shari'aa). This model was very convenient to the new and emerging Islamic banking industry, because it was a straightforward application of the interest-based model used in conventional riba-based banks. It was also applied in many of the newly established financial institutions at that time, such as Kuwait Finance House (KFH), Dubai Islamic Bank, and Dallah Al Baraka Finance Company,[1] and later in Malaysia. (In Malaysia, the model is not called *murabaha* but it is called by what it does, which is to sell at a delayed payment price called in Arabic *al bai' bithaman aajil*, or *BBA*.) It was later adopted by many of the operating Islamic banks that emerged in many of the Muslim countries.

A number of challenges appeared to the Islamic bankers who began practicing the murabaha approach. These were:

1. How should one calculate the profit element that will be added to the original purchase price? As a solution to this problem, the finance companies were allowed by some scholars to use the prevailing interest rate as an index to be used to calculate the profit. Because the London money markets were accessed and used by most of the former British colonies in the Arab world (including the Gulf oil-producing countries) and Asia (including Malaysia), the scholars agreed on the use of the London Interbank Offering Rate (LIBOR) or local prevailing interest rates as the reference interest rate. This step was the source of frustration, confusion, disillusion, and disappointment for many young and dedicated RF bankers—Muslim and non-Muslim alike—whom I met all over the world, in Turkey, Malaysia, Egypt, Saudi Arabia, Kuwait, the Emirates, Pakistan, Europe, and the United States. "What is the difference?" they asked. "My boss asks us to survey the interest rates in the market and he ends up using it and we call it a 'profit' or 'rental' rate."

2. What will the "Islamic" finance company or the bank do with the one-step capital gain that results from reselling the item at this huge added "profit" (cumulative interest), which is added to the original price the bank paid to buy that item? In the beginning, the profit was booked on the income statement as an income from transactions, resulting in great performances for the Islamic banks. Later, after the involvement of many international audit firms familiar with international accounting standards (like the Financial Accounting Services Board, or FASB, in the United States) and the establishment of AAOIFI (Accounting and Auditing Organization for Islamic Financial Institutions), profit was spread over the life of the facility (amortized) in the same way a loan interest income is booked in a conventional banking operation or as in the case of an origination fee, which is handled by the FASB accounting standards (FASB-91).

3. What will the "Islamic" finance company do with delinquencies in payments? The original conditions (required by Shari'aa) of the cost-plus (murabaha) model were to not increase the profit element added to the original price in case of delinquency or inability to pay the periodic payments or the payoff in time, because increasing the profit would be considered a clear violation of RF values (*riba al nasee'ah*). This rule was abused by many of the customers of "Islamic" finance companies and banks. To resolve the situation, some scholars issued an edict (*fatwa*) that allowed the "Islamic" banks and the financial institutions to charge penalties to those who are chronically late in making their payments without an acceptable legitimate and reasonable excuse. A small loophole was left open by the fatwa, and that was to use the principle of

mercifulness (*tarahum*) in case the customer had a legitimate excuse. This small loophole created many lawsuits and many legal attempts to help borrowers who dealt with "Islamic" banks. In addition, the edicts ruled that the late payment fees cannot be added as an income. These fees—in the form of penalties—are booked in a separate account and are paid as donations to legitimate charities.

When Islamic banking proponents started considering the implementation of the murabaha approaches in the West, they met with many additional challenges. These were:

- The banks (depository institutions) in most Western countries are not allowed by the laws of the land to own properties unless the property was foreclosed on by the bank and was classified as *Other Real Estate Owned* (OREO). In this case, the bank is encouraged to sell OREO properties as soon as practical. This stipulation made it difficult for a bank to buy an item, change the title from the seller to the bank, then sell it to the ultimate buyer by changing title again from the bank to that ultimate buyer to satisfy the buy/sell rule called for by Shari'aa, as discussed earlier.
- If the Islamic financing institution was structured as a finance company, then it could—in some jurisdictions—buy properties and hold title to these properties. However, finance companies in the West discovered that when the company buys a property in its name at a price (X) and turns around and sells it at original price (X) plus a profit (P), then a tax event is created, because the tax authorities considered the profit (P) a capital gain that must be taxed. In addition, in some countries (particularly in Europe), a tax is charged every time title changes hands, creating unnecessary additional expenses.

The real challenge came when the Muslim communities in the West—mainly in the United Kingdom and the United States—wanted to obtain RF financial services. The effort to provide RF financial services was pioneered by Al Barak Bank in London in 1988, when it tried to come up with a home financing contract that would fit the requirements of the banking laws in the West in general and in the United Kingdom in particular and that would be compliant with Shari'aa. A number of meetings between scholars, attorneys, and bankers were held. This resulted in the birth of a new "Islamic" financing model based on the lease-to-purchase model (*Al Ijara Wal Tamaluk* or *Ijarah Wal Iqtina*—these Arabic terms both mean *lease to own*). This model is now becoming more popular because the "Islamic" banking attorneys—most of whom had Western training, experience, and credentials—

were able to adapt it in a way that makes the financing closer to the requirements of Shari'aa and to expand its use in the development of the "Islamic" asset-based bonds (*sukuk.*)

ISLAMIC BANKING MODELS

The following is analysis of the Islamic banking models designed to fit the existing conventional finance contracts to make them Shari'aa-compliant.

The Cost-Plus (Murabaha) Model

This mode of financing (in Malaysia it is called *Al Bai' Bithaman Aajil*, or *BBA*) was developed to finance trade transactions in a riba-free format. *The Institute of Islamic Banking and Insurance* magazine (London, the United Kingdom)[2] responds to reservations and criticisms made by many Shari'aa scholars, as well as users of murabaha "Islamic" finance models and contracts, by stating that we should not " . . . ignore that the basic Islamic finance structures adopted today were used primarily in trade in the early Islamic period." The article further states that

> *Murabaha [cost-plus], in its original Islamic connotation, is simply a particular type of sale, not a mode of financing. The only feature distinguishing it from other kinds of sale is that the seller in Murabaha [cost-plus] tells the buyer the cost incurred and the profit (mark-up) on the cost.*

The magazine also quotes retired Justice Muhammad Taqi Usmani:

> *There are two essential points which must be fully understood in this respect: 1) it should never be overlooked that, originally, Murabaha [cost-plus] is not a mode of financing. Therefore, this instrument should be used as a transitory step . . . and its use should be restricted only to those cases where Musharaka [joint ownership with diminishing equity] is not practicable; 2) the Murabaha [cost-plus] transaction does not come into existence by merely replacing the word of "interest" by words of "profit" or "mark up."*

The article further states that:

> *Murabaha [cost-plus], though not an ideal model in Shari'aa compliant finance, was adopted initially for home purchase in the UK in the late 1990s, as pure Musharaka [joint ownership with*

diminishing equity] and other models were not well suited for mortgage transactions.

In response to concerns voiced regarding the added cost resulting from capital gains taxes levied by tax authorities in the United States for a sale and buy back at a higher price, the scholar Dr. Hamoud issued an opinion to the author when we, at LARIBA, started applying the cost-plus financing concept in the United States in 1987, allowing the company to appoint the customer as an agent (*wakeel*) to buy the property on the bank's behalf. The opinion of Dr. Hamoud was the basis for the fatwa issued by the First Conference of Islamic Banks (Dubai, 1997). *This fatwa—based on an opinion of the Maliki jurist Ibn Shubruma[3]—stated that an Islamic financial institution may require its customers to sign a binding promise that he or she will purchase the financed property on credit (with an agreed upon mark-up) once the bank buys it based on his order.* It is important to notice here the use of the term "binding promise" or *waad* in Arabic. The word *promise*, some scholars stress, is different from the word *contract*. The reason for this distinction to be made, with customers signing a promise to buy back rather than a contract to buy back, satisfies some of the scholars' demands. That is because of a clear ruling by the Prophet Muhammad (pp) that prohibits including two contracts (a contract to buy and another contract to sell back to back) in one contract to purchase the property. The resulting contract came to be known[4] as *Murabaha Lil Aamiri bil Shira'aa* (meaning: *cost-plus sale to the one who ordered the original purchase*).

The mechanics of a murabaha financing transaction sometimes blur the boundaries between interest-bearing riba-based conventional loans and credit financing. In fact, cost-plus is sometimes called the bridge between riba-based conventional financing methods and the RF financing domain. Many of the puritans who were looking for RF financing criticized this mode of financing severely when it was first introduced in the United States because it was similar to riba-based financing. This perspective challenged us at LARIBA to research and try to come up with other methods of financing, which led us to innovate and develop the LARIBA RF financing model.

In murabaha transactions,[5] the customer is appointed as the financier's buying agent (*wakeel*). Thus the customer may proceed as the financier's wakeel to purchase the property on the financier's behalf. Subsequently, the ultimate buyer also acts as the financier's selling agent to sell the property to himself. Technically, jurists argue,[6] the financier in fact owns the property during the period of time between the two agency sales and bears the risk, for instance, of its destruction by lightning. Unfortunately, close scrutiny of the process used in this mode of transaction indicates that the bank or the finance company takes all precautions to ensure that the buyer will not go back on that promise, so that the financing entity will not end up owning the property. In addition, Shari'aa defines the transaction based on the intention (*niyah*) of the transacting party. It is a fact that the financing entity never intends to buy and own that property.

In our efforts to evaluate the cost-plus model used in the United States for "Islamic" Shari'aa-compliant mortgage financing, we shall share with the reader important glimpses of the procedure used and the contract supplied by one of the banks in America that advertises its "Islamic" "no-interest" mortgage financing program, which uses the cost-plus (murabaha) model. We are deeply indebted to a friend in the community who financed his home using the services of this bank and was kind enough to share with us the details of the process he went through. Here are our observations:

- It is claimed that no interest is charged, despite the fact that the bank uses the prevailing interest rate of the day of the agreement as a base for calculating the added "profit" element in the cost-plus (murabaha) scheme used and uses the same mortgage amortization program. Would that be considered a violation of consumer compliance and advertising regulations mandated by the federal and state banking laws?
- It is claimed that the bank buys the property and that the customer promises to buy it back from the bank in a simultaneous back-to-back operation. Upon researching title of the property, we found out that the bank used very restrictive language to ensure that the customer would not change his/her mind and that he/she would proceed with the buy-back from the bank. The customer signs a contractual form, not just a promise. We found that the bank never changed title of the property to its own name, and the title was recorded in the name of the buyer. In fact, even the down payment was paid by the ultimate buyer and not by the bank, which was supposed—at least on paper—to have been the buyer of the property.
- Upon further investigation and research, we discovered that the bank in some cases has formed a special purpose vehicle (SPV) in the form of a limited liability company (LLC) that would "synthetically" purchase the property and sell it back to back to the ultimate buyer. In this case, the buyer is charged all the costs associated with this scheme.
- The buyer signs a promissory note for the original price and the accumulated interest together. This makes the buyer liable for the whole amount (the cost plus the profit (interest) charges).
- The bank required the buyer to sign a rider stating that the buyer will be responsible for any capital gains taxes that may be levied by the tax authorities should the buy/sell agreement produce—in the opinion of the tax authorities—an implied capital gain.

■ The contract was mostly similar to a regular finance contract, and the note was also mostly similar to a standard note but without the word *interest*.

■ The bank charged the customer for the additional expenses involved in this "circumvented" transaction.

Another attempt at Islamic banking was made by a major mortgage finance company which is now owned by the U.S. government, but was then (before the 2008 financial meltdown) classified as a GSE (government-sponsored entity) active in mortgage financing. The GSE was kind enough to seek the opinion of the author about its newly developed Islamic home mortgage financing model and structure. The proposed contract claimed that the customer would be charged zero interest and it had to post, in the contract, a table that translated the "Islamic" finance terms used in the contract to the regular riba-based finance language that is used in standard riba-based mortgage finance contracts. The GSE was informed that this contract should not carry the name of this respected GSE, because it is in fact a regular conventional contract dressed up to make it look compliant with Shari'aa. The GSE was also warned that this kind of contract can be challenged in the courts of the law, as happened in other instances in Malaysia, the United Kingdom, Saudi Arabia, and in the United States (with MSI Company of Houston, Texas). The GSE did not go further with such a contract.

It is surprising and troubling to experience these attempts at circumventing Shari'aa using such ruses. Bank regulations in the United States (as well as in the United Kingdom) have plenty of detailed consumer compliance laws that disclose the finite details of the transaction and the total charges levied by the bank in a finance transaction, as required by the "truth in lending" regulation (Regulation Z in the United States) and the regulation that gives the buyer the right of rescission of the deal. But most amazing of all is the fact that the cost-plus (murabaha) model is used by tens of banks that employ many of the "superstar" scholars on their Shari'aa Boards. Most important of all, it is noted that there is no mention of the method that is used to calculate the markup (profit) in the murabaha model. The fact of the matter is that they use the prevailing interest rate used by all banks in the conventional riba-based system, call it rent or profit, and claim that this interest (usually LIBOR-based) is looked upon as an index.

Financial Engineering and Shari'aa

One of the most controversial issues and sources of contention among scholars in Shari'aa has been the transfer of ownership or title of the property first from the seller to a special purpose vehicle (SPV), in the form of a limited liability company (LLC) created by the bank in order to create a synthetic buy/sell transaction without violating the banking laws. While many scholars have allowed the appointment of the buyer as an agent (wakeel) in the back-to-back buy and sell, there are a few who refused to accept it. For example, in a cost-plus transaction, the bank or the financial institution would first buy the house and record title in its name; then it would immediately turn around and sell the house to the real buyer. However, U.S. government banking regulations prohibit banks from owning real estate properties (except those foreclosed on due to nonperformance, which are classified as OREOs on the balance sheet). Regulators press banks to sell such OREOs as soon as practical. To abide by these laws, and to circumvent Shari'aa in order to have a transaction that appears to be compliant, the bank would start by incorporating a new company (i.e., an SPV in the form of an LLC or a limited partnership) that does the buying and the selling in a back-to-back instant way. This would eventually make the process look—in form—as though it were legitimate with Shari'aa because the title of the property changed hands, making it a sale. However, this method forgets the real purposes and spirits of the Law (*shari'aa*) which are:

- Not to rent money at an interest rate
- To transact a true prudent investment in the property by marking the property to the market

Many Shari'aa scholars have condemned the use of deceptive financial engineering techniques used to circumvent the Law by focusing on the form of the transaction and the contract (on paper) rather than the substance! Dr. Elgamal[7] states:

> . . . *Al Shatibi concluded that cynical adherence to classical contract conditions in order to achieve form and not substance using ruses and deceptive tricks (even if these tricks are classified as Hassan heelah—or a good trick) to circumvent [the Law] Shari'aa may violate it* . . . *"Legal ruses—al-heyal—in religion are rendered as generally illegal. In this regard, legal provisions—al-amaal al-shar' iy'ah—are not ends in themselves but means to legal ends, which are the benefits intended by the Law [Shari'aa]. Thus, one who keeps legal form while squandering its substance and intent does not follow the Law [Shari'aa].*

It is troubling to see the bank or the financing entity form an SPV with the intention of abandoning it just to make the deal look compliant with Shari'aa. Conceptuallly, it is not much different from signing a marriage contract as a matter of convenience with the intention of divorcing after the purpose of that contract has been achieved. It is believed that this renders the contract null and void. Such an approach stands in fact as a mockery of the real purpose, intent, and wisdom of the prohibition of riba or the culture of renting money. These SPVs cost money to conceive, design, and register—a cost that some call COBM (the cost of being a Muslim), to our surprise! We believe that wasting money, however small or insignificant, on such kinds of ruses does not fulfill the basic objective of Shari'aa, which is the pushing away of what is harmful and the bringing of benefits to the community. It is also important to note that such schemes have not yet been challenged in the courts of law or by the tax authorities. It is strongly believed that we should use wisdom to keep our community members out of harm's way by not following such unnecessary ruses.

The Lease-to-Own Models (Al Ijarah Wal Iqtina or Al Ijarah Wal Tamaluk)

In response to the many reservations and criticisms leveled against the model described above, another effort to develop new models was started, based on the lease-to-purchase transaction. The first model was developed by a group of scholars from the Arabic-speaking Middle Eastern countries for Al Baraka Bank in London in 1990.[8] The second was a modification of the Al Baraka model developed later by (retired) Justice Taqi Usmani and detailed in his book[9] for an "Islamic" mortgage finance company that has operated in the United States since 2001. The third model, which will be detailed in Chapter 10, is the LARIBA model, which improves on the Al Baraka model by applying the *mark-to-market* principle and the *commodity indexation rule*, explained in Chapters 3 and 5.

The Al Baraka Bank of London Shari'aa-Compliant Model[10]

This model was devised to fit the mortgage financing requirements in the United Kingdom in order to offer RF mortgage financing by the first Islamic bank to operate in London, Al Baraka Bank. It was the first serious attempt to offer solutions to the British Muslims' demand for mortgage financing according to Shari'aa. The author was closely involved with the growth of Al Baraka Bank's operations and experienced at close range the last few weeks before it was closed down by the Financial Services Authority (FSA). The closure was mainly because Al Baraka Bank owners did not have a chartered bank in Saudi Arabia, its country of domicile, but also due to regulatory violations in its operations. In general, the model calls for three steps:

1. The financing entity and the customer buy the property as a joint venture (*Musharaka*).
2. The share of the financing entity in the property is sold to the customer at the outset. This allows the ultimate and real buyer of the property to receive and record title immediately.
3. The financing entity would retain ownership of the "right to use the property" in terms of the lease rate it would produce if it were rented. In lieu of that, the financing entity would receive a lien (implied co-ownership) on the property and collect its share of the rent income as stipulated in the agreement/contract. (In many cases, Shari'aa scholars mistranslate the word *lien* as *rahn*, which means *pawn* in Arabic.) This issue will be discussed in further detail by researching the definition of lien (as an implied co-ownership) compared to pawn (complete arrest of the property to the pawn holder).

A series of edicts and opinions (*fatwa*)[11] were issued by a group of highly placed, recognized scholars. These edicts formed a milestone in the "Islamic" finance ways and means. Here are some of the important issues discussed and the edicts issued:

- *The use of the word interest*[12]: The word "interest" can be used in a contract to satisfy local legal requirements as long as riba is not practiced during the transaction. The fatwa states:

> *Applying the principle for reviewing transactions, stipulating that what matters in contracts are the intentions and the substance—not words and forms—we have reached a consensus that there is no objection to using the term "interest" as an alternative to the term "profit" or "rate of return." In this regard, it is imperative to ensure that the term "interest" in the sense described above is used only in the forms required by entities other than the bank, e.g. tax declaration forms for depositors, or special forms used in various financing cases. However, if the intent is to change the nature of the transaction to make it an interest-bearing loan, then such transaction will be fundamentally impermissible.*[13]

- *Developing the lease-to-own model to comply with the banking regulatory requirements of the United Kingdom's FSA.*[14]
  - *Registering the house's title in the partner's name*, based on trust, from the inception of the contract is permissible under Shari'aa. Registering the property's title in this manner does not contradict

the agreed-upon partnership, especially since the partner's ability to sell the home is restricted until his full ownership of the property is established. In this regard, we took into consideration the fact that this registration of title is a form of documentation insured by the officially established lien on the property, according to the conditions agreed upon with the partner.

■ *Making the partner alone responsible for all [closing costs like] registration, survey, and other documentation costs* associated with the jointly owned property from the inception of the contract, and absolving the bank from responsibility for such costs, is permissible if the partners agreed accordingly. This is particularly appropriate, since the partner will ultimately become the sole owner of the property at the end of the financing contract.

■ With regards to insurance, the default ruling would require that *both partners bear responsibility for insurance premiums* as a shared burden of the jointly owned property. However, the bank may take that into consideration when determining the rental of its share of the property, and include appropriate compensation for the appropriate share of insurance costs.

■ The default ruling in joint ownership is *sharing profits and losses in proportion to ownership*, based on the principle that entitlement to profit must be commensurate with risk exposure. In this regard, since the regulatory framework requires that the bank should not be exposed to the possibility of losses when the partnership is dissolved, the model should be altered such that the order of the transaction proceeds as follows:

  ■ The bank and the customer share in purchasing the home according to the agreed-upon proportions.
  ■ The bank sells its share in the physical property ownership (milk al-raqabah) to its partner, while retaining its share of ownership of the right to use it (haq al-manfaʿah) until the time its partner pays the remaining portion of the price.
  ■ The bank collects an annual rent in accordance with the actually paid portion of the property's price.
  ■ If the partner is delinquent in paying the installments for which he is obligated, the bank has the right to keep the sale agreement intact and collect its right to the remaining portion of the price according to the obligatory performance clauses of the lien; or the bank may void the initial sale and take full ownership of the property, if the partner agrees. In the latter case, the bank should pay back to the partner whatever he had paid previously, as a revocation of the sale from its

inception. (This item was agreed upon by a majority of the participating scholars.)

The South Asian Diminishing Musharaka Shari'aa-Compliant Model[15]

This model was developed by retired Justice Muhammad Taqi Usmani, a world-renowned Shari'aa scholar who specializes in Islamic financing. In 1998, he authored a book on the subject.[16] The step-wise approach and methodology recommended by Justice Taqi Usmani were essentially the same as the ones described above in the Al Baraka model (1990), but without splitting the rights to a property into the right of ownership (title ownership) and the right of using the property (usufruct). Following is a summary of the model based on the book authored by Justice Taqi Usmani, which is titled *House Financing on the Basis of* Diminishing Musharaka (*Joint Venture*). The proposed arrangement is composed of the following transactions:

1. Create a joint ownership in the property between the buyer and the financing entity in the form of joint venture (*Shirkat-al-Milk* in Arabic)
2. Rent the share of the financier in the property to the client[17]
3. Get the promise (*notice the use of the word "promise" and not "contract"*) from the client to purchase shares owned by the finance company
4. Have the buyer gradually buy back the shares of the finance company
5. Adjust the rental paid by the buyer gradually, in proportion of the ownership by the finance company

The following is an analysis of each ingredient of the arrangement based on the model description as detailed in Justice Taqi Usmani's book. In general, the steps recommended in this model are not much different from the earlier model used at Al Baraka Bank in London, but with a number of changes. Contrasting the South Asian model with that of Al Baraka yields the following:

1. The finance entity leases its share in the house to its client and charges him/her a monthly rent. This is the same process that the Al Baraka model calls for. But the Al Baraka model is clearer and more defined, as it divides the rights of the owner in the property to two rights. These are the right to own title (*milk ul raqabah*) and the right to lease or rent the use of the property (*haq al manfa'aa*).
2. The South Asian model states that the client buys "units" of the "undivided" shares owned by the finance entity, compared to selling all the

finance company's shares outright at the beginning. as in the Al Baraka model. This step is a very serious step and has created a number of issues, because:

a. In this model the buyer and the finance entity continue to own the property, which requires that the title be recorded in both names. However, in the Al Baraka model, the buyer buys back the shares in ownership from the finance entity, which allows the buyer, according to Shari'aa, to record title in his/her name only.

b. If the finance entity sells back its shares over a period of time, the price of these shares cannot be fixed ahead of time in the beginning of the transaction, because that would be like a sale and buyback at a future date with a fixed predefined price. This type of sale is called in Shari'aa the sale of *eena*. This type of sale is clearly prohibited, because it represents a ruse or a deceptive trick to circumvent the Law. This model may imply that the model proposed accepts that the parties agree that the price of each share is fixed in the future. Sheikh Ali Al Salous,[18] an established scholar in the field of Islamic finance, recommends that in cases in which the finance entity sells shares to the customer over a period of time in the future, these shares should be sold at the prevailing market price of the property and the price cannot be fixed ahead of time. After discussing with him the difficulty of establishing a share price every month, he suggested that when the customer is billed, he/she should be told clearly—through proper and clear disclosure on the billing statement—that the shares he/she is buying back from the financing entity are offered at a certain price, and that he/she has the right to accept it or refuse it. Of course, the client's refusal to buy the shares at the offered price will trigger other actions as stipulated in the particular contract. Justice Taqi Usmani agrees with this and states so clearly in the conditions listed in the book, but he provides a way out:

It will be preferable that the purchase of different units by the client is effected on the basis of the market value of the house as prevalent on the date of purchase of that unit, but it is also permissible that a particular price is agreed in the promise of purchase signed by the client.

However, the signing by the client of a fixed price in the future—as done in many of the contracts we have seen—does not make the agreement compliant with Shari'aa, because it makes it a definite *eena* sale. That is why Justice Taqi Usmani states in his conditions that " . . . at the time of the purchase of each unit, sale must be affected by the exchange of offer and acceptance at that particular date."

    c. To get around the problem of having two sales contracts in one, the South Asian model uses the word "promise" to describe the action of the customer toward the financier without putting it in writing in the form of a contract. If this occurred, it would again be a sale and future buyback, with a predefined price or *eena* sale which is prohibited by Shari'aa. It is important that the steps recommended by the models are done independently, as Justice Taqi Usmani states in his book:

> It is clear . . . that each one of the transactions . . . is allowed per se, but the question is whether this transaction may be combined in a single arrangement. The answer is that if all these transactions have been combined by making each one of them a condition on the other, then it is not allowed in Shari'aa, because it is a well settled rule in the Islamic legal system that one transaction cannot be made a pre-condition for another . . . the proposed scheme suggests that instead of making two transactions conditional to each other, there should be a one-sided promise from the client, firstly to take share of the financier on lease and pay the agreed rent and secondly, to purchase different units of the share of the financier of the house at different stages. . . . It is generally believed that a promise to do something creates only a moral obligation on the promisor, which cannot be enforced through courts of law . . . [the] most the promise can do is to compel the promisor through court of law to fulfill his promise and if the promisor is unable to fulfill the promise, the promisee can claim actual damages he has suffered because of the default. This makes it clear that a separate and independent promise to purchase does not render the original contract conditional or contingent. Therefore, it can be enforced.

    It will be left to the reader to decide if this "promise" is in fact a contractual agreement or not. One fact needs to be made very clear. The contracts used by those banks and financial institutions do obtain clear and firm agreements from the customer to buy back the property—not just a promise. Based on our detailed research and in-depth evaluation of the documents used—at least those used in the United States—no bank or financial institution would act on a mere "promise." The financier makes sure that the customer not only gives a binding contract, but also pays the down payment of the house he or she wants to buy. In addition, it is known that the financing entity does not intend in the first place to buy the property and that it would have never embarked on the step of the "claimed" purchase of the property (as required by the model) without making sure that the client was fully committed and contractually obliged to buy the property back.

We have tried to understand the benefits to the client or to the financing entity of following all these "synthetic" steps, and we found that there are no benefits. It is important to note that this South Asian model requires that the finance entity devise new contracts, mortgage agreements, and promissory notes that may not be different in content, intent, and spirit from the standard riba-based ones, without adding any economic or real legal benefit to the customer. If these newly formulated—nonstandard—contracts are litigated in the courts of law, it exposes the customer to the risk of confusing the court and to liabilities that may be leveled against the financing entity or its parent bank or company. It is understood that this may be a remote possibility, but in the legal system, we learn from history that what may be considered remote today can be messy and greatly complicated and involved when a smarter attorney starts challenging it.

In contrast, the Al Baraka model solves the above problems in an elegant, straightforward, and more practical way, which is acceptable by Shari'aa. It does not need to resort to establishing the LLC or SPV, because of the direct sale back to back and the registration of the title in the customer's name at the outset of the transaction. It simply states that the finance entity sells all its shares directly at the outset to the customer. The sale proceeds are paid by the customer—without any Riba/interest—over a period of time that is agreed upon between the finance entity and the customer. Against this trust, the client proceeds to record title in his/her name and proceeds to share in the rent that the two parties have agreed to in the proportion of ownership. The financing entity keeps a lien on the property. The lien is settled, title is *reconveyed*, and the implied joint ownership by that lien is released when the shares of the financier have been completely paid back.

Application of the South Asian Shari'aa-Compliant Model To examine the practical application of the South Asian model, the methods and procedures used by an American-based Islamic mortgage finance company that uses the model will be examined below. This "Islamic" mortgage finance company came to market in late 2001 and was heavily promoted as the real solution to the problem of providing "Islamic Shari'aa-compliant" financing to "Muslims and others" in the United States by the company that uses it.[19] In general, the procedure used by the company is based on the South Asian model described in the previous section.

The company advertises and publishes on their Web site a copy of the fatwa signed by the Shari'aa Board of the company, which includes (retired) Justice Taqi Usmani. The company states that the purposes of the model are to:

- Assist Muslims and others to acquire homes in compliance with Shari'aa
- Help buyers to enjoy tax benefits
- Allow the company to securitize their ownership investment in homes

The company goes through the following steps:

1. The mortgage company forms a limited partnership as a special purpose vehicle (SPV) with the customer. They agree to purchase the property together and to record title in the name of the customer and the company jointly. The cost of forming the SPV is charged to the customer (approximately $1,400 to $1,500) and its monthly maintenance cost (usually $18 to $20) is also charged to the customer. The company makes the following disclosures about the use of a "Bankruptcy-Remote Limited Liability Company" (LLC—a special purpose vehicle) as co-owner: " . . . the LLC [has a] separate legal entity that prohibits co-owner from incurring debt other than the financing of the property." This may be an advantage, in that it limits the customer's ability to use his home as a credit card. Despite that fact, we have seen in practice customers who have still taken a home equity line of credit on homes financed by this model—but only from that company, because it has the customer captive through its joint title ownership. In fact, the company that uses this model has been advertising to encourage members of the American Muslim community to take a home equity line of credit to finance *Hajj* (pilgrimage.) It is known that Shari'aa requires that the Muslim pays off all debts before he/she goes on Hajj and not to borrow to go on Hajj. It is not clear whether the Shari'aa Board approved such an invitation to take a loan to go on Hajj, which first stands opposite to the condition required by Justice Taqi Usmani and second is in violation of Shari'aa. The LLC that serves as co-owner may also serve as co-owner with other consumers in up to 10 separate properties with 10 separate consumers.[20] The LLC mortgages the property to the financier ("the company"). The company also discloses that there will be an ongoing LLC fee of $18.75 per month to be used to pay for unaffiliated third-party expenses. The company also states that it may adjust the ongoing monthly LLC fee in the future to reflect any increase to the current fee. The LLC fee is part of the financing costs, but is not reflected in the net monthly payment.

2. The SPV would proceed to rent the property back to the customer at a rate agreed between them using the prevailing (interest) rate as the rent of the property—making it, in fact, a process of renting money and not the property. This rent is exactly the riba interest rate charged in the market. It is well known that renting a property depends on the neighborhood, the specifications of the house, and any other special features the house may have. The actual rent of the property on the market can in fact be drastically different from what the company defines as rent using the interest rate at that time. The name of the SPV company stays on title until the buyback is completed. At that time, title is transferred to the customer. This feature limits the freedom of the customer to act without the approval of the joint holder of title. In other cases, it may represent a liability to the customer, in case the company faces challenging times.

3. The buyer would agree to buy back shares from the partnership, representing the payback of the principle. Since the units of property will be purchased by the consumer under this arrangement at cost and without increase, the company claims that there is no element of eena in this arrangement. As stated earlier, eena is defined as a sale with a promise to buy back at a later date at a pre-agreed-upon price. The buyer should be offered these shares at the prevailing market price, but that is not what happens.

4. The company states that the consumer will make monthly payments comprised of *profit payments* and *acquisition payments*. The acquisition payments, the company states, represent the consumer's payments for his/her acquiring the co-owner's interest in the property. It is noticed here that there is a lack of the full disclosure as required by Justice Taqi Usmani. The scholar makes the condition that for the model to be compliant, the company must offer its shares in the joint venture for sale at a true prevailing market price, and not just bill the customer to pay the acquisition payment (principal).

The company that uses this model discloses that this model or mortgage product conforms both to the practices of the U.S. mortgage regulation and the principles of Shari'aa. Therefore, the use of the terms *interest*, *principal*, *borrower*, and *lender* are mandated by law, and the model is subject to the same disclosures as a regular mortgage loan, such as a good faith estimate, the truth in lending disclosure, and so on.

It was also noticed that the company claims that both parties benefit and bear the risks of their respective shares in the property throughout the contractual arrangement ("term of the financing"). The customer benefits from the fact that he/she is participating in what is presented as a "Shari'aa-compliant" contract. However, the customer has to go through a number of extra steps without reaping any economic or religious benefits—like joint venturing with an LLC, paying extra costs, and accepting a joint title ownership that may result in future undefined risks. One of these risks, for example, is a case in which the company—the joint owner of the title—experiences legal difficulties. The other concern that can be made about this model is the claim that this model allows both the customer and the company to bear the risks of their respective shares in the property. Upon further detailed analysis, it can be safely concluded that the risk carried by the company is even less than the risk assumed by a conventional bank or a financing entity doing a riba-based transaction. It is also concluded that this method exposes the consumer to many risks, especially the risk of getting involved in a nonstandard mortgage structure with nonstandard contracts and notes that has not been tested in the courts, as compared to the standardized mortgage finance contract offered in the United States. The other risk is the unfamiliarity of judges and participants in the legal system with such contracts, let alone the extra legal expenses that would eventually be incurred in case a lawsuit is brought to court as compared to a standard and simple administrative process in the case of a standard contract.

It is important to state that regardless of the objections voiced about the contract and the circumventive ruses and deceptive tricks used, it is believed that God will reward those who have made an attempt to develop it in good faith and those users who trusted these claims and were willing to pay more to avoid participating in riba because He knows their intention to not violate the Law.

COURT CHALLENGES TO THE SHARI'AA-COMPLIANT "CONTRACT FITTING" ISLAMIC FINANCE APPROACH[21]

It is important to note that the use of Islamic banking as a financing alternative was challenged in many courts in the United Kingdom, Malaysia, the oil-rich Gulf countries, and the United States. Many of the lawsuits were settled outside the court, and the details on all of these cases may not be readily available. Many of these lawsuits were brought to the Courts of the Law (Shari'aa) in Muslim countries in which such courts operate—in most cases—outside the realm of the civil laws that prevail in many countries of the world. Such courts exist, for example, in many of the Gulf oil-producing countries, such as Saudi Arabia. Details of the lawsuits and how such suits were settled are not available. However, in most cases, and based on reports from friends who live and work in these areas, a religious judge presiding over a Shari'aa court may rule that the interest owed on a loan is forgiven because it is considered riba.

Malaysia and the United Kingdom courts have litigated many of these cases. Most of these cases involve financing deals that used the cost-plus model (murabaha, or BBA in Malaysia). Philip T.N. Ko, Esq.,[22] a practicing attorney in Malaysia, has documented a number of cases that were brought to British and Malaysian courts.

These cases are quoted here to alert those who think that Shari'aa-compliant financing in the United States may not one day be brought to and challenged in court to please think again. All these LLCs and SPVs and sophisticated structures present a smarter attorney with wonderful opportunities to challenge all such schemes, ruses, and claims—most importantly, that the claim of *"Shari'aa* compliance" can be coupled with a discrimination claim. These claims can cause damages ranging from expensive settlements that may bankrupt the institution to negative publicity that may have far-reaching negative effects on the operation of the institution (s) involved.

The following are examples of such cases.

Cases Litigated in the U.K. Courts
In *Shamil (Islamic) Bank of Bahrain v. Beximco Pharmaceuticals*,[23] the defendant (Beximco) argued that obligations on them are enforceable only if valid under both Shari'aa and English law. They argued further that the cost-plus (murabaha) arrangements were merely a disguise for interest-bearing loans which are not unenforceable under Shari'aa.

The court held that reference to the Law (Shari'aa) was intended to mean that the bank held itself out as doing business in accordance with Islamic principles and was not intended to trump the application of English law.

There have been many other litigations and court cases in Malaysia regarding the same subject.[24] In a case that involved the application of the different schools of thoughts—*Sunni* and *Shi'aa*—the judge,[25] after conducting a survey of differing sects of branches of *Sunni and Shi'i*, described the issue as "a mind boggling minefield awaiting lawyers and judges alike."

Resolutions Taken By "Islamic" Banks to Avoid Lengthy Trials
In response to these cases, and to reduce the confusion of the judges in different courts and in different countries (especially non-Muslim countries), many Islamic banks and finance companies have resorted to modifying their "Islamic" contract to include some of the following sample statements[26]:

■ "This Agreement shall be governed by and be construed in all respects in accordance with the laws of the State of Malaysia not being Islamic Law

(Shari'aa) and the parties submit to the jurisdiction of the Courts. . . (not being the Shari'aa Courts or any Courts implementing Islamic law or Shari'aa) in all matters connected with the obligations and liabilities of the parties under the security document."

■ "Nothing in this Agreement shall be invalidated and no rights powers remedies and security of the financier created under the Security Documents shall be affected in any way if any of the provisions herein . . . or the enforcement thereof contravenes or is prohibited by Islamic Law, Islamic tenets and/or 'Shari'aa.'"

It is also interesting to note that in many of the "Shari'aa-compliant" contracts that are supposed to be "Islamic," we find similar statements, most famous of which is: " . . . this is a finance contract and in case it is brought to court it will be handled as a regular interest-bearing financial transaction."

CONCLUSION

It is amazing to have gone through all these statements, claims, models, and references, in addition to the hundreds of millions of dollars spent and the valuable energy invested to develop such models, to end up traveling a full circle. We read that in a court of law, the contract is to be handled as a regular (riba-based) contract. This is the same good old riba-based contract that many of the Shari'aa-compliant efforts made since the 1970s were trying to change. There is another amazing observation having to do with the complete and deafening silence about two very basic aspects of RF financing. These are the marking-to-market principle and the commodity indexation rule, which were discussed in Chapters 3 and 5.

NOTES

1. The Cost-Plus model was used by American Finance House LARIBA in the Southern California area in the United States when it started its operations in 1987; it was used until 1989. However, after severe criticism from many of the community members based on the fact that it was very similar to riba-based transactions, LARIBA started searching for another model. In late 1989, LARIBA started using the new model, which was based on a lease-to-own approach developed for home financing for Al Baraka Bank in London. However, it was further developed by the author to include in it the marking-to-market principle, as will be discussed in a later chapter.

2. *Institute of Islamic Banking and Insurance (IIBI)* magazine: New Horizon; www.NewHorizon-IslamicBanking.com, issue number 170, January–March 2009, p.38.

3. Cited in Mahmoud Elgamal: *Islamic Finance—Law, Economics and Practice*, Cambridge University Press, 2006.

4. Ibid.

5. Ibid.

6. Muhammad Taqi Usmani, *An Introduction to Islamic Finance*, Karachi: Idarutul Ma'arif, 1998, pp.152–153.

7. Mahmoud Elgamal, *Islamic Finance—Law, Economics and Practice*, Cambridge University Press, 2006, pp. 44 and 129.

8. Fatwa of Al Baraka available at www.lariba.com/fatwas/index.htm and in Arabic: www.lariba.com.eg/karadawy.htm.

9. Muhammad Taqi Usmani, *An Introduction to Islamic Finance*, Idaratul Ma'arif, Karachi, Pakistan, 1998, pp. 85–91. Also available online at www.lariba.com/fatwas/usmani.htm.

10. Fatwa of Al Baraka available at www.lariba.com/fatwas/index.htm.

11. Al-Baraka Annual Edict (Fatwa) Meeting of Islamic Finance Scholars—Meeting Number 6: (pp.77–78) Algeria 5–9 Sha'baan 1410 A.H./2–6 October 1990 C.E. Sha'abaan is the eighth month of the Islamic calendar, and A.H. (which stands for After Hijra) denotes the Islamic calendar system. (*Hijra* means immigration of the Prophet Muhammad (pp) from Makkah to a northern city in the peninsula called Madinah, where the early pioneering Muslims started the foundation of the Islamic civilization and where the Prophet Muhammad is buried.) The Islamic calendar has 12 months, but it is based on the lunar system, which is 11 to 13 days shorter than the Gregorian system. That is why, for example, the month of fasting—Ramadan—rotates through all seasons. The calendar does not have a "short" month concept, as in the Jewish and Asian lunar calendar, to adjust for the seasons. For more information, please visit: www.islamicity.com/science/islamic_calendar.shtml.

12. Ibid., pp. 81–82.

13. Ibid. The fatwa also states: "This opinion is based on the view that what is intended here is not to effect Riba, which is forbidden in the Law (Shari'aa). Thus, following our deliberations, we reached the following conclusion: 'Despite the fact that interest, as conventionally used in banking transactions, coincides precisely with the Riba that is forbidden in the Law (Shari'aa) to pay or receive, and regardless of whether the underlying transaction is a consumption or production loan, we have found that there is no objection to the use of the term "interest" in the cases related to those dealing with Al-Baraka Bank, London, aiming to benefit from the financial advantages given to interest in various cases of deposits and financing.'"

14. Ibid., pp. 84–87.

15. Muhammad Taqi Usmani, *An Introduction to Islamic Finance*, Idaratul Ma'arif, Karachi, Pakistan, 1998, pp. 85–91. Also available online at www.lariba.com/fatwas/usmani.htm.

16. Ibid.
17. Ibid: Justice Taqi Usmani states of the Shari'aa foundation: " . . . there is no difference of opinion among the Muslim jurists in the permissibility of leasing one's undivided share in a property to his partner. If the undivided share is leased out to a third party, its permissibility is a point of difference between the Muslim Jurists. Imam Abu-Hanifa and Imam Zubair are of the view that the undivided share cannot be leased out to a third party, while Imam Mali and Imam Shafi', Abu Yusuf, and Muhammad Ibn Hasan hold that the undivided share can be leased out to any person. But so far as the property is leased to the partner himself, all of them are unanimous on the validity of 'Ijarah.'" It is interesting that he does not call the leasing its proper classification and name as the "right to use." He also stays silent about his position on the subject of dividing ownership into the title and the right to use.
18. During a number of meetings with him at his home in Cairo and via telephone conversations.
19. Guidance Residential Finance.
20. It is interesting to note that company representatives claim that the LLC monthly fee is paid to the state, that it costs $35 in the state of Florida, and that the customer pays half of it and the company pays the other half.
21. Philip T.N. Koh, *Islamic Financial Instruments: The Civil Law and the Sharia Confluence or Conflict?* Presented at the fifth Islamic Finance Conference, Monash University, Kuala Lumpur. Philip T.N. Koh, FCIS is an advocate and solicitor for the High Court Malaya; his degrees include: LLB (Hons) (University Malaya), LLM (London), MA (Theology) (Australian Catholic University).
22. Ibid.
23. Ibid. *Shamil Bank of Bahrain v. Beximco Pharmaceuticals* [2003]2AllE R (Comm) 849 (Ch); [2004] 2 Lloyd's Rep 1 (CA).
24. *Bank Kerjasama Rakyat Malaysia Berhad v. EMCEE Corporation Sdn Bhd* [2003] 2MLJ 408; *Affin Bank Bhd v. Zulkifli b Abdullah* [2006] 3MLJ 67; *Bank Islam Malaysia Bhd v. Adnan B Omar* (1994) 3CLJ 735; *Bank Islam Malaysia Bhd v. Shamsudin bin Hail Ahmad* [1991 1 LNS 275; *Arab-Malaysian Merchant Bank Bhd v. Silver Concept Sdn Bhd* [2005] 5 MLJ 210; *Tahan Steel Corp Sdn Bhd v. Bank Islam Malaysia* [2004] 6MLJ 1, 33,34.
25. J. Suriyadi, in *AMMB v. Silver Concept.*
26. Philip T.N. Koh, *Islamic Financial Instruments: The Civil Law and the Sharia Confluence or Conflict?* Presented at the fifth Islamic Finance Conference, Monash University, Kuala Lumpur.

CHAPTER 10

RF Banking Model for the 21st Century

Developing the Shari'aa-Based Finance Model

This chapter will detail the unique financing model that we pioneered at American Finance House LARIBA, which we based on the Law (Shari'aa) in contrast to the "Shari'aa-compliant" approaches discussed in Chapter 9. This unique and pioneering model embodies the true spirit and substance of the RF (riba-free) system.

In 1987, we started a humble effort by establishing LARIBA (American Finance House). We started our finance operations by using the Cost-Plus (murabaha) model, because we did not know better. We simply started with the interest rate of the day, calling it a "profit" index based on opinions and edicts (*fatwa*) by some of the Islamic finance Shari'aa scholars at that time. We would calculate the value of the dollar amount to be borrowed and compound it at the "index" (interest rate) to create an equivalent sale price at the end of 15 or 30 years, depending on the term of financing. The company would agree to sell the house back to the ultimate buyer at the original price plus a profit element, so that the total cash paid would be equal to the compounded value arrived at—just as if it were a regular interest-based transaction.

Many of us were not very comfortable with this approach, despite the fact that it was sanctioned by most of the well-known Islamic finance Shari'aa scholars at the time. At this juncture, the value of the educated and sophisticated believers in the Judeo-Christian-Islamic value system became useful. The educated and analytical members of the community objected to the system, because it did not make sense to change names, use the same exact approach used by riba-based conventional banks, and then claim that we are providing Islamic finance services just because the name was different. We were severely criticized by many of the puritan and educated members of the community, who asked repeatedly: "What is the difference?" In fact, we concluded that they were right—there was not much difference. Within our first year of operation, we began to develop a model that is truly beneficial to the user and that follows Shari'aa. We call it the Shari'aa-based model or the LARIBA model, as it is known worldwide.

Through our development of this model, we asked a fundamental question: "Why does the RF system prohibit riba or the act of renting money for a price (the interest rate)?" We reasoned that if we stopped renting *money* and started looking at the rental rates of the *items* financed in the actual marketplace, then we were in fact investing in rent-producing cars, properties such as homes and commercial buildings, and businesses. If the transaction is profitable because of the rent it generates, then it makes prudent economic sense to invest in it with those who come to us for finance. We also concluded that based on the fact that money is a fungible thing that cannot be rented, then giving it to a customer in the form of debt financing (*dayn* in Arabic, compared to *qard*, or *loan*, as explained in Chapter 2) is actually as if we are investing with this customer.

THE PUZZLE AND THE CHALLENGE OF DEVELOPING RF BANKING AND FINANCING

It is useful to document the many challenges we faced while trying to solve this puzzle with the humble tools and the limited resources available at the time. The intention is to document what our team did for the record and for the benefit of future generations. When we started, our goal was to come up with a solution to the problem of living a full American life without violating the laws of Shari'aa and to uphold the laws of the land without participating in the culture and practices of riba/ribit. It may have been easy to articulate that goal; in practice, though, it was a big and daunting challenge and a hard dream to realize!

The following sections comprise a review of the many currents faced in developing an RF financing and banking regime.

Legal and Financial Categories

First, let us review what we learned in Part One in each category of the subject that had an impact on the development of the RF financing and banking brand.

The Law (Shari'aa)

- Shari'aa has as its main goal the protection of the self, the family, the assets and wealth, and the faith in the community.
- Shari'aa focuses on the intent and not the form. The real test is the outcome.[1]
- The main objective of Shari'aa is to maximize the benefits to the family and the community at large while pushing away what is harmful.
- Shari'aa requires those who make edicts (*fatwa*) to be knowledgeable of the faith, the community, and the local conditions and systems where the edict is solicited and applied.
- Shari'aa states that if it (the Law) cannot be applied in full, that does not give believers an excuse to abandon it completely without attempting to the best of one's abilities to apply whatever is possible.[2]
- Shari'aa does not allow the use of ruses (deceptive tricks, *heelah*) or circumventive structures that look Shari'aa compliant but in fact ignore the intent and spirit of Shari'aa.

Money

- Money is a thing and is fungible, like an apple or a loaf of bread. Fungibles cannot be rented because the minute they are given to another, they become an "investment" that is entrusted with those who accept it.
- Money cannot be rented by paying a price for using it. In the past, the payment of a price or the use of the money was called *usury*; now it is called an *interest rate*.
- Money is a measuring device and is useful only if invested. It can only be invested in a useful activity, such as the purchase of an asset, a service, or a business. Money does not grow on its own if not used. It must be invested in a productive activity that produces a useful outcome.
- Money cannot be loaned, except in the form of a good loan to those who need it. A loan is conceptually looked at as a bite (*qard*) out of the assets of those who have a lot of money; it is to be given to the poor and needy without expecting any increase.
- Money is a measuring tool that is used to measure the value of the product or service produced by this economic activity. The success or failure of that activity is measured by how much value—measured in money—is produced by that asset. The concept of *return on investment* is a measurement of the success or failure of that investment.
- Money must be real money, and real money must be a base commodity. It can be gold, silver, or a basic food staple. Paper (fiat) money can be used as a convenient tool of exchange and trade, but it must be related

and indexed to these basic real money reference commodities. That is, one can use U.S. dollars, British pounds, and/or the euro, but such currencies must be referred and indexed to a reference commodity to be fair to all by keeping fair pricing and free and balanced markets without deception (*gharar*).

- When basic commodities—that is, gold, silver, and food staples like wheat, rice, corn, salt, dates, and the like—change hands, they must be exchanged for the same amount if they are of the same element. That is, gold is exchanged for the same amount of gold, and corn for the same amount of corn. The exchange must be done on the spot, hand to hand. If the exchange involves two commodities that are different but used for the same purpose—for example, gold and silver, which are used as a pricing reference (real money), or corn and wheat, which are used as a food staple—the exchange can be made with an increase but it must be done on the spot. For example, it is allowed to exchange one ounce of gold for seven ounces of silver because both are used as pricing commodities, or one bushel of wheat for three bushels of barley because both are used as a food staple. The exchange must be done on the spot. No delayed delivery is allowed. If the two commodities are different in element and in use, they can be exchanged for an excess amount, and the exchange can be done on the spot or for delivery at a later date for a different price. However, if delivery is not completed at the agreed-upon date for a legitimate reason, such as a change in the economic environment or climate conditions, no increase over the agreed future exchange ratio is allowed to compensate for the delay in payoff, because it is considered riba. For example, an ounce of gold can be exchanged for seven bushels of wheat hand to hand; subject to agreement between the two parties it can be exchanged for fifteen bushels of wheat after one year. If the wheat is not available after one year for reasons that are considered *force majeure*, no further increase is allowed. This concept was introduced in Chapter 5 as the *commodity indexation rule*.

- In case one wants to exchange an item for another item of higher quality—for example, exchanging small oranges for larger, higher quality oranges—the exchange must be done in equal quantities. However, to perfect the exchange, the small oranges should be first exchanged in the market for a different element, such as gold or corn; then the gold or corn can be used to buy the larger oranges. This way, markets are kept fair and fair pricing is achieved without deception (*gharar*). This concept, called *marking to market*, was introduced in Chapter 3.

Interest Rates

- Interest can be defined as an excess—riba (in the Qur'aan) or ribit (in the Jewish Bible and the Old Testament)—over the original amount of the capital given as a loan (*qard*). The increase is divinely prohibited (*haram*) in case of a qard to the poor and needy. Any increase in whatever form—be it in the form of excess money, compensation through free and unpaid labor, the free use of the borrower's facilities, or publicizing the borrower's indebtedness—is not allowed.

- In a *fiat* money regime, the interest rate used by central bankers to decide on the policy of how much money to print or to withdraw out of the market—called the Fed Fund rate in the United States—is different from the riba prohibited by Judeo-Christian-Islamic values.

- Interest charged as a price for renting money to those who do not have it is what the prohibition of riba (and usury) is all about. Interest charged for a transaction that implies the renting of money to a user of money for credit (*dayn*) without marking it to market is considered riba or ribit, and is not allowed by Shari'aa.

Money and Commercial Transactions

- The original teachings of the Judeo-Christian value system focused on the abuse exercised by the rich against the poor in agrarian societies in order to expropriate their land, crops, and properties and render them slaves in their own originally owned land. The Judeo-Christian-Islamic value system reinforced that ruling, which prohibited *usury* (or *interest*), the act of charging for the use of money, which is considered an act of riba or ribit. The system encouraged helping those who need money through the system of *qard hassan*, a good loan that does not charge any increase over the original amount in any shape or form.

- As commerce developed, the Judeo-Christian-Islamic system expanded upon the Judeo-Christian system to allow buying and selling at different prices, but not renting the use of money (*usury*, now called *interest*). Buying and selling transactions that involved an increase due to profit making are not like charging riba by charging for the use of money, as revealed in the Qur'aan. For buying and selling to be perfected, the title of the item to be acquired must change hands from the seller to the buyer in a documented buy-sell agreement. Different models developed to put this rule in effect were used during the Muslim reign and adapted in the 1700s by the rabbis in the eastern European areas in their "*Hetor Iska*" models (also known as *Musharaka* or Joint Venture in Islamic RF banking applications).

- To perfect the buy-sell transaction, the two parties must participate in all risks (including profit and loss) as defined by the buy-sell contract.
- The buy-sell contract must be fully documented, free from any deceptions or undefined parameters and risks, and should be transparent. The concept is called *gharar-free* (which means deception-free.) *Gharar-free* rules also require that trading in risk, as in cases of sale with a guaranteed buyback at a future date at a predefined price (called *eena* in Shari'aa), uncovered short sales, naked options, and futures, as well as financial derivatives, involve major aspects of *gharar*, and they are prohibited.
- Future sale prices cannot be set ahead of time because such practices interfere with the free market system as defined by the Judeo-Christian-Islamic value system. Only God knows the future. That is why a contract that includes two sales (i.e., buying a property from someone at a price and promising to sell it back to him/her at a future date in the same contract at another prefixed price—an eena sale), is prohibited. Contracts of this type are considered divinely prohibited (*haram*) contracts and a means of gharar.
- If the person who was entrusted with the money cannot make the payments for legitimate reasons, such as unexpected changes in the economy or a sudden war—*force majeure*—foreclosure is not allowed unless one of the parties committed fraud or deception. In this case, the asset is sold and the proceeds are distributed between the contracting parties as per partnership agreement.
- In a joint venture, a predefined profit is not allowed. However, the percentage participation in profit and loss, or the rent for the use of the property, or the service between the parties can be agreed upon between them.
- One cannot sell what one does not own.
- Ruses and circumvention (*heelah*) of the rules of Shari'aa are not allowed.

Banking and Securities Laws and Regulations

- In the United States, these regulations are rooted in the Judeo-Christian-Islamic value system of fairness, transparency, full disclosure, truthfulness, trust, and preservation of people's assets and properties. These regulations encourage the people to reinvest their savings in the community, thus generating job opportunities and economic prosperity and allowing equal opportunity for all, regardless of faith, skin color, gender, marital status, language, national origin, social status, and/or relationships.

- The laws and regulations are designed to supervise, identify, and discover abusers of the system and to examine the safety and soundness of the institutions entrusted with people's hard-earned deposits, investments, and assets.
- The laws and regulations are based on the vast body of recorded human experience throughout history.
- The laws are designed to prevent fraud by those who attempt to defraud people in the marketplace and those who want to take advantage of people who do not have knowledge, are not educated, or are not well informed, by insisting on full disclosure, transparency, and fair representation.
- The regulations are in continual development because they are adapted to correct previous faults in the design of the system, with an objective to reach perfection as closely as is humanly possible.
- The laws and regulations require that any financial transaction must be translated into an implied interest rate (as required by Regulation Z in the United States) that includes the effect of all fees and expenses so that the consumer can make a fair comparison and an educated decision in his or her financial dealings.
- The regulations do not allow depository institutions (i.e., banks) to own properties except in cases where these properties are owned by default, such as foreclosure (this concept is known in U.S. banking as *other real estate owned*, or OREO). Banks are encouraged to dispose of these properties as soon as practically possible.
- The laws and regulations include a safety valve that gives borrowers who cannot meet their obligations ways and means to restructure and reorganize in an orderly fashion without destroying their facilities or their investments, which might cause the loss of jobs and create more problems (U.S. bankruptcy laws).
- The laws prohibit the payment of interest on bank demand deposits (Regulation Q in the United States). Interest-paying accounts are only allowed with strict conditions and limited withdrawals (see Regulation D in the United States).
- The regulations offer standardized, frequently used, and fundamentally needed contracts, such as those used to finance home mortgages or automobiles. This cohesiveness helps maintain quick settlements of disputes and avoids lengthy and expensive legal proceedings.

Participants in the Development of Modern RF Banking

It is important to recognize all the wonderful people from different professions, with diversified training in many fields, Muslim and non-

Muslim alike, who did and are still doing their best to bring full life back to the "Islamic" RF banking industry. This effort has not been attempted nor tried since the 19th century, in a world that has seen quantum leaps in the business of riba-based banking and finance since that time.

The following is a listing of the different professionals and customers who actively and sincerely participated in the development or the use of services of modern Islamic banking and finance since it was first conceived in the second half of the 20th century.

Muslim Puritans   The word *puritan* is advisedly used because of its American roots.[3] It was used first in England to describe a group of early American settlers who immigrated to America so that they could apply the true spirit of the Judeo-Christian values as articulated by the Protestant reform leader Martin Luther to their daily lives. The Muslim Puritans emigrated from many Muslim countries around the world to the United States to escape persecution in their own former lands and/or to seek new opportunities in America. It is believed that the first responsibility of the RF banking brand is to help this category of citizens solve the problem of living the American dream without the use of riba/ribit. The challenge that RF bankers have to resolve is how to convince these puritans that an RF banking approach is acceptable, in order to bring them into mainstream America and get them to move out of small apartments they do not own and into a nice home that they do own in a nice neighborhood. This, it is believed, could help them and their families become viable and effective U.S. citizens, because they will get to know their neighbors, send their children to neighborhood schools, and become fully involved in the American way of life. They would eventually transform, becoming owners of a "piece of the rock." We have had the honor of meeting wonderful professionals who have lived a puritanical life in the United States, without borrowing with interest or depositing their money in conventional riba-based banks to earn interest on a time certificate of deposit, because they believe that doing so is haram (divinely prohibited). Many of these families lived in humble crowded apartments for more than 20 years to avoid taking a loan with interest to buy a home. They went on saving as much as they could to pay for their dream home. In fact, when we started LARIBA, some of these wonderful new Americans had saved up to 80 percent of the price of their home and contacted us so they could finance the rest riba-free. Because of their meticulous attention to detail regarding the RF models and procedures used, and their commitment to not participate in any religiously prohibited transaction, many of these puritans wanted proof that the techniques used were sanctioned by a fatwa from a recognized and trusted scholar. We were happy, patient, and delighted to meet that challenge.

To satisfy the needs of these customers, we wanted to expose them to all the edicts and Shari'aa opinions (fatwas) by displaying these fatwas in full on the www.LARIBA.com Web site. We urged our customers to read these edicts carefully before they decided to use our services. We also made it clear on the Web site that including these edicts on our Web site did not mean that these scholars have given us an edict to sanction our own model, and that we shall never use the names of the scholars to sell our products and services. In addition, we made our Shari'aa supervisor available to answer any questions from these customers. The Shari'aa supervisors used to spend approximately 3,000 minutes a month on their mobile phones answering questions about Shari'aa and the details of the LARIBA finance model. This strategic decision proved to be an important one, because it made us serve and meet those highly analytical, deeply religious, and intellectual customers who are interested in reading and analyzing. They are disciplined to reach their conclusions on their own, without being influenced by superstar names or persuasive marketing and advertising. It also was very fortunate that they were so well-disciplined, because of the highly diverse nature of the many scholars (some of whom are self appointed), who have opinions that in many cases differ from one scholar to another, depending on their country of origin and the religious subgroup they represent. This situation made us address the customer base in a direct and transparent way.

Monetarists[4,5,6]   These research-oriented Muslim scholars in the field of monetary theory believe that the use of *fiat* money and credit creation in the modern banking system through the multiplier effect, as explained in Chapter 5, are the main reasons for the ills of the international riba-based conventional monetary and finance systems, and that truly Islamic banking should not be part of these. They sincerely believe that Islamic banking scholars and practitioners should start a serious effort to use gold as a monetary base. Efforts toward that goal were attempted in the late 1980s with the introduction of the gold dinar in Malaysia. The prime minister of Malaysia, Dr. Mahathir Muhammad, was one of its supporters. Many of these monetarists believe that Islamic banking in a *fiat* monetary regime is in fact a mere change of names and brands without resolving what they believe to be the fundamental problem of *fiat* money and riba-based conventional banking monetary expansion techniques. It is believed that resolving this major concern will take a very long time, and it would not be practical to wait until it is resolved, because it involves major structural changes in the world's monetary and political systems. It is the duty of RF bankers to develop wise solutions that can be applied now to benefit all people by applying the tenets of Shari'aa in an intelligent, prudent, and productive way.

This approach will achieve our goal of helping people transact their business in an RF way, according to the values of the Judeo-Christian-Islamic system, and hopefully in a way that will normalize the effect of such a variable and major concern.

To attempt to meet this important challenge without having to wait for a solution that may take many years to achieve, we followed what is believed to be two wise solutions that are based on Shari'aa. One was an ideal solution in which we would apply the *commodity indexation rule* described in Chapter 3. The approach was to replace *fiat* money with a reference commodity, such as gold or silver or even a staple food commodity like wheat, rice, or soybeans—or a combination of all of these, as James Baker, III recommended in 1987 and which is detailed in Chapter 3. However, this solution would be complicated and impractical. It would take years and the support of many of the countries that command strong economic, diplomatic, and military power—exactly as happened in 1948 in the Bretton Woods agreement. That is why it was decided to use these reference commodities as a tool to decide, in a macro way, whether an economic bubble is perking in the type of asset we intend to finance (by this we implicitly mean "to invest in"). The other solution we use is to *mark the property to market* using the rule described in Chapter 3. Applying the mark-to-market rule normalizes the effect of *fiat* money and its growth by evaluating the return on the investment in the property at hand based on its actual lease or rental rate in the marketplace. Doing it this way—going to the live market and researching the lease that such a property or a business could command in the open market—enables us to evaluate the economic viability of the capital investment. This way we can ascertain that the actual market rent or lease rate of this property is used, and not interest rate, which is the rent of money.

Religious Leaders   We deal with many categories of religious leaders. These differ not only by their role but also by their country of origin and the school of thought in Shari'aa they subscribe to. They are:

Popular Thought Leaders in the Muslim World   These recognized leaders write extensively on many religious, social, political, international, and jurisprudence issues that have to do with Islam in general and business transactions and finance in particular. They became recognized and highly respected stars in the field of religious leadership over the past 50 years. Because of their status, they were the first to be contacted by those who wanted to develop Islamic banking practices. These leaders did the best they could, based on the knowledge on hand at the time, to start the "engine" and get it going. Their biggest challenge was their lack of understanding and education in the fields of banking and finance. However, their religious knowledge was complemented by the Muslim and non-Muslim professionals who worked in the riba-based conventional banks as bankers, attorneys, and entrepreneurs. They were able to lay down the foundation of what is now documented as a set of opinions that are based on Shari'aa.

Perhaps one of the more significant, pioneering, and influential efforts was the annual symposium that was pioneered by Dallah Al Baraka[7] to "Islamize" different banking products and services. The annual symposium pioneered by Dallah Al Baraka was by invitation only and was attended by most of the recognized religious, banking, and Shari'aa experts in the world. Sheikh Saleh Abdullah Kamel, a visionary leader in the field of RF finance and the founder of Dallah Al Baraka in Jeddah, Saudi Arabia, must be recognized for the historic effort that laid the foundation for the growth and globalization of RF banking and finance. Many of the tools, techniques, edicts (*fatwa*), and research centers at Al Azhar Seminary, Al Azhar University in Cairo, and other universities in Saudi Arabia, Malaysia, and Pakistan that are available today were pioneered and generously financed by the important and historic effort of Sheikh Saleh Abdullah Kamel. Most of the invited scholars came from the Arabic-speaking world in Egypt, the Sudan, Jordan, Syria, the Gulf oil-producing countries, such as Saudi Arabia, Kuwait. and Bahrain, and English speaking countries like Pakistan, India, and Malaysia. These scholars have since served as active members of the Shari'aa Boards—a new profession pioneered by Sheikh Saleh Kamel in most of the Islamic banks around the world. As these scholars became involved, their reputations increased and respect for them grew, from the wealthy banks in the oil-producing nations of the Gulf to the masses at large (particularly in the Indo-Pakistani subcontinent and Bahrain). Their services were solicited by 40 to 70 different Islamic banks around the world. As a result, it became both difficult and expensive—if not impossible—to obtain a famous name (super star) religious scholar to sit on the Shari'aa Board of an Islamic bank, to approve a product, or to issue a fatwa that would sanction and legitimize the activities of a new Islamic bank or finance company.

Local Community Religious Leaders, or Imams   The imams are the leaders of the community masajid (mosques). *Imam* means *prayer leader*, and in particular the leader for Friday congregational prayers. Imams are also considered religious leaders who act as counsels for the community. Most of them are qualified scholars in the Qur'aan and the *Hadeeth* (pronouncements and sayings of Prophet Muhammad [pp]), but few of them have a good command of the details of Shari'aa, especially in topics having to do with riba, business transactions, banking, and financing. They rely on the easy way out by honestly stating that riba is haram and that they cannot recommend a certain model because they are not familiar with the details. Others rely on the opinion of the scholars discussed in the previous category.

Some of these local leaders are first-generation immigrants from the Muslim world, and they usually resort to checking with their teachers in their home country. Communication, translation, and familiarity with the local norms, cultures, and ways of doing business in the United States, Europe, and the West in general are a real challenge with this group. Others, who can be considered the new generation of American (Western) imams, are either raised or are born in the United States. It is our sincere hope that these imams will bring a new dimension to the study and implementation of Shari'aa that will be useful and beneficial to all.

Community Leaders   These are professionals who took a keen interest in organizing the communities in general and religious services for the communities in particular. These professionals became the heads of the national Islamic organizations in America and in the European countries, and the heads of the local communities in major American states and in countries such as the United Kingdom, France, Germany, and the rest of Europe. They mostly are self-educated in religion and are well read. Some of them have even decided to go to religious seminaries to learn more about the Qur'aan; in some cases, they memorize all of it and decide to be further educated in Shari'aa. They usually take a neutral, well-advised position of not sanctioning any commercial activity, business, or company, because they are afraid of the repercussions that may impact the whole community if the company or bank they recommend fails or uses practices that result in the loss of the community's investments and assets.

Academics and University Professors of Economics and Finance   These university professors and recognized research scholars in the field of finance and economics have invested their life in research in the field[8] of finance and economics at the highest academic levels. Some of them, by the nature of their discipline in research and analysis, have attained a very high level of proficiency and scholarship in the field of Shari'aa and in particular the science of commercial transactions and business. Many have been critical of the models used in Islamic banking (the Shari'aa-compliant models developed in the 20th century) as it is practiced in the world. They concluded that the methods and contracts used may fulfill the requirements of Shari'aa on paper and in form, but these solutions do not achieve what the spirit and intent of RF financing was instituted to do.

Dr Abdul Hamid Ahmad Abu Sulayman,[9] formerly Rector of International Islamic University—Malaysia and a Saudi Arabian religious scholar, stated:

Islamic Banking is a good example of a field where basically the Western system has been partially "Islamized," but in many aspects

"Islamic" names have been given to various transactions that do not truly reflect the goals or vision of Islam. The result of this frame of mind is called al–hiyal al-shari' yah, "shari'aa tricks," where forms, terms, and words are changed rather than the substance when the need is really for a new vision.

In fact, a new term was coined by one of the distinguished academic researchers in the field and the first professor to hold a Chair in Islamic Finance and Economics at Rice University, Professor Mahmoud Elgamal.[10] The term he uses is *Shari'aa arbitrage*, by which he means that a new arbitrage has been created for Shari'aa scholars' sanctioned models. Such arbitrage does not really add anything to the transaction. It only adds an increased cost due to the fees and added cost of legal maneuvers and ruses (*heelah*) used to make the existing riba-based contracts compliant—at least in form—with Shari'aa. Professor Elgamal complains bitterly about the added cost and sophisticated structures that have been used with one benefit in mind—keeping the form intact without trying to preserve the spirit and intent of the riba-free value system. As a matter of fact, legal fees may have been very high for the first few deals, but as the contracts were standardized and used in a large number of transactions, the costs became much lower. It is believed that the concern should not only be about the cost, but about the real economic benefits of going through the many sophisticated ruses, deceptive tricks, and special-purpose limited liability companies (LLC) that have no economic or even structural or legal benefit except to make things look Shari'aa compliant. It is the responsibility of the academics to reveal, through dedicated and thorough research, the real benefit of the RF system to rescue all people from a lifestyle that may mean a bleak future for all of us. We need to focus on the spirit and intent of the RF value system.

Politicians   The attitude of political leaders toward Islamic banking varies depending on the country, the region, and the political orientation of the leader. In many of the Arabic-speaking Middle Eastern countries, Islamic banking has been a big challenge to many of the politicians. Some are afraid of giving the Islamic political groups or political parties added legitimacy and power that may undermine their ability to rule. Others have resorted to allowing it as an expedient political solution, but with many limitations and restrictions. Other politicians in the West have been sensitized by politically motivated lobbyists who are interested in casting the Muslims as terrorists and disloyal. Another concern has been the creation of a back door to implement the Law (*Shari'aa*), which is frequently criticized as being backward and medieval. In the oil-rich Gulf countries and in some Asian countries (Malaysia, Indonesia, Pakistan, and Bangladesh, for example),

Islamic banking is offered side by side with riba-based banking to meet the growing market demand for Islamic banking.

To meet this challenge, LARIBA organized an annual seminar on RF financing, which included a prestigious awards dinner to recognize outstanding contributors to RF banking from all countries in the world. We invited local and national politicians to the dinner, as well as religious and community leaders, diplomatic core representatives, and the press in Los Angeles. In one of these galas, we recognized the Prime Minister of Malaysia, the honorable Dr. Mahathir Muhammad, in Chicago for his unique efforts to rescue the economy of Malaysia during the 1997–1998 Asian currency crisis and for his support of RF banking in Malaysia. These efforts have helped us introduce many in the political arena to what we are trying to do, increase their understanding of RF banking, and help them feel comfortable about the integrity and worthy ideals RF banks stand for. This effort has had a definite positive impact on the acceptance of RF financing in the United States.

The Media   We were contacted and were covered by many media outlets, including television, radio, newspapers, and magazines. These outlets included organizations such as ABC News, National Public Radio, Voice of America, Malaysian TV, *The Wall Street Joutnal*, *Time* Magazine, *The Los Angeles Times*, *USA Today*, *The Dallas Morning News*, *The Washington Post*, *The New York Times*, the *Chicago Tribune* and many other newspapers and magazines. It was very difficult to explain to the reporters what we do, because it is very involved and required a lot of attention and concentration. We learned that reporters are looking for "sound bites" and simple, fast statements. We also learned how to do that, but we insisted that they get a piece of paper and a pencil, and we went through the LARIBA model from A to Z. Many of them were impressed. In fact, the coverage we received was the envy of many in the field. Our competitors asked who was our public relations officer. The fact of the matter is that we never had one. We received all these calls from all these reporters without even seeking or expecting them. They must have been a gift and recognition from the "higher authority."

The most interesting experience was a call we received from a senior business reporter, Elliot Blair Smith, at *USA Today*. The newspaper had published at least three articles about LARIBA. When we took the call, Smith explained that he had spent more than a year in Pakistan investigating money laundering and transfers involving terrorists. He wanted to investigate and know more about LARIBA. We explained to him in great detail what LARIBA is and what we have done at LARIBA, as a responsible American finance company that abides by Judeo-Christian-Islamic values.

The phone call lasted more than 60 minutes. At the end of the call, he said, "Can I come to visit you?" He flew from Washington, DC to meet everyone at LARIBA in Pasadena, California. Over lunch, he told us that he was looking for "blood" and illegal activities and that he was extremely impressed with what he experienced. He published a wonderful article about us at LARIBA in *USA Today* on the front page of the Money section.[11]

Bank Regulators Bank regulators are required by law and their job description to make sure that the depository institutions (banks) under their jurisdiction operate according to regulations and that the laws of the land are upheld to the fullest in a safe and sound way to preserve the assets of the citizens and the reputation of the system. Regulators have been willing to listen graciously and with great interest, and to entertain new products and service ideas.

The first attempts to engage the banking regulators were made in the United Kingdom, when Al Baraka Bank was started in London in the mid-1980s. The charter was withdrawn later by the U.K. bank regulators because of a number of violations and the fact that the owner entity—Dallah Al Baraka in Saudi Arabia—though licensed there to operate as a finance and investment company did not have a licensed operating banking institution that was chartered by the central bank of the country of origin, Saudi Arabia.

Another attempt was later made by a Kuwaiti bank (United Bank of Kuwait) at its U.K. branch in London and its U.S. branch in New York. The New York branch representatives explained to the regulators—the OCC, in this case—how their finance scheme and model for home mortgages, called *Al Manzil*, worked.[12] After long evaluation, research, and deliberation, the OCC concluded, based on the detailed supporting documentation supplied by the applicant, that there was no difference between the scheme and the regular interest-based contract, and pronounced it acceptable.

When an entity (like Fannie Mae, Freddie Mac, the IRS, or the OCC) decides that a new product or scheme looks fine, they list it under the category of *exceptions to the norm*. This term was used by Fannie Mae and Freddie Mac in order to accept the modified Shari'aa-compliant contracts. That is well and good in good times, but that "exception" can be taken away any time, rendering the RF bankers' many years of effort worthless. That is not what we are aiming to do. The challenge, for those who believe in RF banking and way of life, is to devise legal documents that abide by the laws of the land, using ways and means that comply with the regulations and the laws of the land while not violating the basic values of the Judeo-Christian-Islamic value system.

Professionals Who Serve and/or Benefit from the New Islamic Banking Industry

Shari'aa Scholars   Shari'aa scholars come from diversified backgrounds; they have accumulated a respectable body of knowledge and command the respect of all. The demand for Islamic finance Shari'aa scholars has outstripped the available supply, which elevated many of the scholars, especially those who have a good command of the English language, to the level of "superstars." In RF banking, the Shari'aa scholars serve three important operating functions.

1. Developing the proper models to be used in financing
2. Developing Shari'aa-qualified banking products and services
3. Ensuring that the bank operates according to Shari'aa (religious compliance)

The Shari'aa scholars also serve another important function, and that is the marketing of the bank they represent. The Islamic bank with the most superstars scholars on its Shari'aa Board will carry more credibility to its operations and will attract more depositors and customers. Shari'aa scholars also participate in and attend seminars, symposia, and international conferences to represent the banks they work for and the products they developed. They hold training courses, give television and radio interviews, and go on talk shows (some are beamed live to the United Kingdom and the United States), which brings a lot of customers to do business with the banks they represent. For example, as a prerequisite for their success and their ability to sell their shares to the public, new Islamic banks make sure that their *Shari'aa* Boards include some of these superstar scholars. A typical Shari'aa Board member commands an annual retainer of approximately $50,000 (or more) and a first-class plane ticket and accommodations when he travels. Scholars with this superstar status sit on the Shari'aa Boards of an average of 50 to 70 banks. This raises very serious conflicts of interest, confidentiality, and insiders' concerns and issues. It is hoped that a major effort will be designed to increase the supply of these scholars by producing a new generation of scholars to serve in the future.

Attorneys   Many Western attorneys became involved in the field of Islamic banking, because world banking laws and regulations are set according to Western standards. Most of the attorneys involved specialize in tax planning, business structuring, and financial engineering. These disciplines are important because the attorneys invited to "Islamize" the banking agreements, finance contracts, deed of trusts, promissory notes, and arbitration were requested to improvise these legal documents so that they would be acceptable to both Shari'aa experts and to Western countries like the United

States, the United Kingdom, France, Germany, and other countries in Asia and the Middle East that use these laws. The author has participated in, attended, and was exposed to many of the meetings between representatives from Islamic banks or finance companies and specialized lawyers. The time spent by the lawyers, and the fees charged, were unbelievably high. Once one of my attorney friends telephoned me after concluding one of these contract "Islamization" programs—and earned a handsome seven-figure fee. He asked me, "Why are you Muslims doing it this way? You end up with a contract that looks Islamic on paper but it does exactly what any other standard conventional finance contract does—but of course it costs a lot more just to remove the word interest from the contract to make it look as if it is a buy/sell agreement, which it definitely is not."

Riba Bankers   These are professionals with a proven track record and experience. In the early stages of the development of "Islamic" banking, they brought the products, services, and techniques of the riba-based conventional banking system to the Islamic banking arena. They are useful in explaining the conventional banking business to the scholars, which helps them create Islamic products and services that comply with Shari'aa. They also brought their experiences in conducting efficient banking operations.

Organizers for Seminars, Industry Group Conferences, and Training Programs   In the beginning of the Islamic banking movement, seminars were organized by semi-government and government organizations—mainly in Malaysia and Bahrain—to discuss, promote, and present papers on new products and services that are RF qualified. Professionals who were known to make true and pioneering contributions to the field of RF banking and finance based on their research work were invited to present their papers at these conferences, seminars, and workshops.

As the business of training conventional bankers on "Islamic" banking grew, and demand increased from many banks throughout the world, commercial seminar organizing companies took over the business. These seminar and training companies organized educational training programs and (promotional) conferences in the field of Islamic Banking and Finance. These conferences were run for profit, which is why the organizers invited a predefined roster of superstar scholars and speakers to attract participants, who paid thousands of dollars to register in these seminars. These seminars were turned into marketing forums for large investment banks and conventional commercial banks, which paid to speak or participate in a panel. Fees paid to include the name of the company on the program and to invite the company to speak in the conference ranged from $10,000 to $100,000. These entities would present their new, revolutionary, and extremely profitable "Shari'aa-compliant" products, which were designed and approved by no less than the superstar scholars, who were of course present at the conference as speakers and as supporters of the "marketing and sales" cause.

After this practice became the norm, LARIBA's board of directors decided not to participate in any conference that required that we pay to speak. Our position has always been that we do not believe in the practice of "pay to play." We consistently told the organizers that if they thought we could add value and substance to the seminar or the conference because of what we achieved, we would be happy to participate. The result was, of course, that not many of these organizations invited us to such conferences.

RF Banking Consumers and Potential Users

Four types of customers have contacted us for RF financing:

1. *The puritans.* These customers "shake in their boots" when the word riba is uttered. They contact us because they are looking for an RF solution to a financing situation. They are willing to pay more to save themselves from participating in the haram act of dealing in riba. These are the best customers any financial institution would hope to add to their books. They have some of the best credit scores and are devout customers who are the best in fulfilling their contractual obligations. However, it takes extreme patience and knowledge of the products and services, as well as a long time, to explain the models used and to convince them of (and make them comfortable with) the true RF nature of the transaction.
2. *Average consumer.* These are customers who would be interested in RF financing if it were made available at competitive prices, costs, and terms as compared with conventional riba-based banks. These customers can be Muslims or non-Muslims. At LARIBA and the Bank of Whittier, we have had the great honor of adding many of these customers, who come to us from all faiths and backgrounds through referrals because they appreciate the unique, sincere, and high-quality service as well as the added value of the RF bankers.
3. *Customers who claim that they are coming to RF banks because they want RF finance*, but after further investigation it is discovered that they have been to every bank to seek financing, and after they failed to get it, they came to us, the RF bankers, to see if we could help. These customers need to be handled with great care and scrutiny. One such experience was a potential customer who had a printing shop. He stated that he liked RF financing because the RF bank "participates" in the

profit and loss. After scrutinizing the application and exercising prudence, we found out how much loss he had. We declined the financing (i.e., the investment).

4. *Educated and sophisticated customers.* These are the young American-educated and trained professionals who are used to asking questions and who are keen on getting straight convincing answers that make sense. They respect the opinion of scholars, but they want to know why things are done in a certain way and how the scholars arrived at their edicts (*fatwa*). They want answers that appeal to the mind and to the intellect. They demand answers that prove that the RF finance makes economic sense and offers advantages over the alternative conventional riba-based system. They are savvy, Internet-conversant, and sophisticated in analysis and in reaching conclusions. These customers are, in fact, the best customers for a bright RF banking future.

SHARI'AA AND THE LAWS OF THE LAND

The many different and sometimes opposing undercurrents, mainstream constraints, and varying participants detailed above make the process of developing a true RF banking operation a huge challenge. These challenges had to be met and resolved wisely, and all the pieces of the puzzle had to be put in place to pioneer *the art of Islamic banking and finance* in the United States. It was a huge challenge. Here is a list that gives an overview of the major issues:

- Where should we start? We did not have the capital to apply for a bank charter, and even if we did, how could we apply for the charter of a bank run without riba in a business environment that only knows and recognizes riba-based conventional banking and finance transactions?
- Who would run the bank or the financial institution? There are very few experts and practitioners in the field. It was also challenging to know that those with banking experience are employed by established banks and are paid high salaries. Bankers with Islamic banking expertise are employed with very high salaries by the well-capitalized and rich Islamic banks in the Gulf oil-producing countries.
- Where could we find an attorney that had the expertise and was affordable, given our limited resources?
- What financing model should we use, and would it comply with the laws and regulations of the United States—our country—without violating Shari'aa or the Judeo-Christian-Islamic set of values?

Developing the Art of Islamic Banking and Finance

The art of Islamic banking and finance is the process by which all of the undercurrents described earlier are put together to come up with a new brand of banking. The RF banking (riba-free banking) brand merged all of these undercurrents to produce a banking service that would be able to satisfy the market demand. The goal was to develop the RF banking system as an optimum and meaningful financing approach that would benefit all people and help them to live a life free from riba.

The Approach Used to Develop the Art of Islamic RF Banking

The challenge we faced was how to develop an RF bank (with the limited knowledge we all had then; please note that in 1987 we called it *interest-free Islamic banking*) that would abide by Shari'aa and at the same time would comply with the laws of the land. In trying to do so, a prior experience I went through in 1972 in Dallas, Texas was useful. At that time, I was the chairman and one of the imams (religious leaders) of the first organized Islamic Center in Dallas (and maybe one of the first in the state of Texas), the Islamic Association of North Texas, or IANT. One of my responsibilities was to perform weddings according to Islamic Law (Shari'aa). The Board of the Association asked me to start working on getting Texas state officials to recognize an Islamic wedding contract, instead of the state-sanctioned civil marriage license. Our group talked to lawyers, state officials, and to the clergy in the Christian and Jewish faiths. Soon we learned that other faith leaders had tried earlier, but it was not possible. A wise religious leader shared with us the fact that the civil marriage certificate carries with it the weight of the law of the land in order to protect the two parties in the marriage contract. In addition, the civil marriage contract can be signed by a civil official (e.g., a justice of the peace), which makes it civil, or by a religious leader, which makes it religious. Without the power of the state's legal system, law enforcement system, and legal codes, this leader pointed out, no institution would be able to prevail in case of a dispute.

It was a personal experience that made us see the light. One day I performed the wedding of a wonderful young lady who had come to the United States from a Muslim country to study. She met a young man, and they decided to get married. I officiated the wedding using a "homemade" Islamic wedding contract. Six months later, the young lady contacted me with tears in her eyes and told me that her husband had left her and disappeared. We tried to help by calling the police. I showed the police the "Islamic" marriage certificate. We were told that it might be a useful document, but it did not carry the weight of an official civil marriage certificate issued by the municipality involved. After searching my heart, I concluded that we should use the civil marriage contract. We concluded that what makes a marriage Jewish, Catholic, Methodist, Protestant, or Islamic is not only the religious vows and the signature of the religious leader. What makes it any of these things is what the parties do at the time of dispute. The couple can go to the religious leader (e.g., the rabbi, priest, or imam) to preside over an arbitration process that is conducted according to the tenets of the faith, and that will make it religious. Or they can go to a civil court and that will make it civil. After this experience, which deeply touched us all, we recommended to all Islamic Centers in the United States and Canada that no imam or certified community leader be allowed to perform a wedding without a civil marriage certificate, in order to protect each party. This ruling stands today.

Our team at LARIBA reflected on this experience when we started looking for ways to bring RF banking to America, in order to solve the puzzle and optimize the process of merging the many currents and players in the field. We were concerned and troubled by the standard approach used by many "Islamic" bankers who were interested in establishing an Islamic bank in the West. It is sincerely hoped that this frank discussion will not offend any of the wonderful, well-intentioned, and believing Islamic bankers in the world—Muslims and non-Muslims—who want to use this approach. The standard approach used starts by requiring local authorities in other non-Muslim countries to change their laws, regulations, and procedures to fit the requirements of the Shari'aa Board of those banks. Your author was privileged to have been exposed to many of the detailed discussions that led the U.K. Financial Services Authority (FSA) to license an Islamic bank (*The Islamic Bank of Britain, IBB*). The legal costs involved, the compromises arrived at, and the monetary guarantees offered could only be done by a very rich entity that could afford it and would be capable of providing the guarantee from the central bank of the country involved. We respectfully ask those who use this approach to reverse roles. Imagine that a bank in the United Kingdom comes to a Muslim country, presents itself as a Christian bank, and calls itself "The Christian Bank of Country X"—and demands that the laws of the Muslim land be changed in order to transfer large sums of money and open that bank. It does not require much imagination to project the reaction of the country. It is wished that this attitude will be changed, because it may be temporarily accepted by some non-Muslim countries' officials to achieve a short-term goal, like securing "Islamic" funds for an "Islamic" bond (*Sukuk*) in a European city. Alternately, it will be accepted from those who happen to have the funds to spend today, but after the funds dry up then there will be no more guarantees and the license is withdrawn or the special conditions are removed. It is also important to note here that complying with the United States banking regulations and satisfying the regular periodic examinations conducted by the bank regulators is a very important and essential aspect of running a viable bank—both RF and conventional—in the United States and most other Western nations, as well as other nations in the world.

In our efforts to establish a viable RF banking operation in the United States, we started by realistically listing the facts. Here is a list of what we came up with:

- The OCC[13] ruled that the Islamic banking models of cost-plus (*Murabaha*) and lease-to-own (*Ijara wa Iqtinaa*) proposed by the United Bank of Kuwait—which follows the Shari'aa-compliant model—are in fact regular finance transactions with different names.
- Almost all Shari'aa-compliant contracts we reviewed and analyzed were in fact similar to the regular finance contracts, but with different names and procedures that make them look "Islamic" on paper. In fact, the contracts stated implicitly that they are indeed regular finance contracts in case they are brought to the courts of law.
- There is sensitivity associated with the mixing of religion with business and also the stereotyping of Muslims in many Western societies. These sensitivities intensified after the heinous attacks of September 11, 2001.

While developing an RF finance model in the United States, we decided that our goal was to find a workable solution that would abide by Shari'aa and would not violate or attempt to change the laws of the land. We drew on our experience in developing the Islamic marriage procedures and contracts in the United States. There were many reasons for us to adopt this strategy. The first is that we do not have the money, the human resources, or even a standardized and universal working legal code that we could present as a foundation. The basis of our strategy was to achieve small successes in our endeavor to prove the viability of this new RF banking and finance system, and not to limit our growth and success potential by trying to achieve impractical and unrealistic goals. We started from the fact that the United States has, as described earlier in the book, the most sophisticated and fair banking system representing the fruits of many years of improvisation; it is rooted in the fairness of the Judeo-Christian-Islamic set of values. In our efforts to develop RF banking and finance, we decided that we should not start from ground zero and reinvent the wheel, but should draw on the huge body of human experience in banking and finance, which cannot simply be ignored or thrown away, as that approach would not be fair and wise and indeed would have been counterproductive. Our priority was to prove to ourselves first that we had a working concept with proven success and to chart a track record for applying this new brand of banking and finance. We knew that this approach would require a lot of hard work to raise capital; to put systems in place; to locate, identify, recruit, and train human resources; to clearly understand how conventional riba-based banking works; and to develop models and products that are easy to understand by the RF bankers and customers and that comply with Shari'aa while at the same time upholding the laws of the land. Most importantly, we wanted to develop an investment (loan) portfolio that proved that we have a small but viable and proven alternative. We firmly believed that American Muslims as a minority—and, for that matter, the minority of all minorities in America—must be humble, respectful, and understanding in this effort to develop RF banking and finance without violating Shari'aa but while also upholding the laws of the land.

An important aspect of the RF banking business is its faith-based credentials. History has shown us time and again that religious fervor, when instigated, can be very strong; it can be the source of great emotional energy, which can be used for marketing products and services. It has happened in the United States, when religious groups (including some Muslims) raised capital from innocent and trusting members of their communities, promising them great returns in this life and God's acceptance in the hereafter, only to see the trusting customers lose everything when the promoters disappear. One recent episode was the Madoff hedge fund, which attracted money from many Jewish nonprofit organizations as well as many wealthy investors and banks all over the world. It turned out, apparently, to be a type of Ponzi scheme that lost its investors billions of dollars.[14] Another episode was that of Sunrise Equities, a Chicago, Illinois company that not only offered "Islamic" investments but also had its own "Shari'aa Board," which the company had imported from India to add legitimacy to its operations. In one of the financing applications we received from a customer, we noticed an investment certificate from Sunrise Equities that promised the investor 15 and 20 percent annual returns on investment. We met the representatives of the company during a New York conference in October 2007, took them to the side, and told them that what they were doing was wrong, illegal, and damaging—not only to themselves and their victims but to all of us in the new and emerging RF banking and finance industry. They shrugged their shoulders and walked away smiling. Earlier that year, a delegation from LARIBA had flown to Chicago to discuss the matter with their "scholar" and his team and to alert them to what was being done in the name of religion. We were discounted. It was saddening to learn that in September 2008 the Indian Muslim community—mostly from Hyderabad—lost all of its investments, and the "bearded" and "turban-dressed" religious business "leader" disappeared with his staff. Episodes like these, which have also been experienced in Egypt, Turkey, and many other places. We at LARIBA have disciplined our operations from the time we began in 1987 to go slowly; to have prudent; never to use faith in our advertising; to learn systems, techniques, and operations from the pros in conventional banks; to attract professionals to join our team; never to promise what the return will be, because only God knows the future; and to always underpromise and overdeliver. These are, in fact, some of the aspects and character foundations of the Judeo-Christian-Islamic value system that make RF banking a uniquely positioned brand name in banking.

In conclusion, we decided to first understand the laws of the land and to try to apply these laws in the same way that the civil marriage process was developed in the United States.

MAJOR OBJECTIONS OF SHARI'AA SCHOLARS TO THE CONVENTIONAL RIBA-BASED FINANCE CONTRACT

Most modern Islamic finance scholars who reside in some of the Muslim countries made the following recommendations to change the riba-based conventional banking system:

- The contract must be changed to fix some of the noncompliant features it suffers from. The Shari'aa-compliant contract (as ruled by these scholars) must:
  1. Not show the word *interest*. As discussed in Chapter 7, this stands against Regulation Z (the Truth in Lending regulation). As discussed in Chapter 9, there is a clear edict (*fatwa*) from the most senior and respected scholars which states that if the laws of the land require using the word interest, then it can be used. This fatwa is conditional on not using interest—money renting—in the actual process of financing.
  2. Show a buy-sell transaction in which the bank buys the item from the seller, then sells that item to the buyer. As discussed in Chapter 9 and in many parts of this book, U.S. banking regulations stipulate that banks cannot act as buyers of properties. In addition, in most Western systems, any buy-sell transaction triggers a tax event, and the profits are taxable. In addition, as was concluded in Chapter 9, all the buy/sell schemes are synthetic in nature and are in fact ruses and deceptive tricks (*heelah*) used to get around and circumvent Shari'aa.
  3. Late payment fees cannot be applied unless the payments were intentionally made late without an acceptable excuse. These late payment

fees should be paid out to a charity, and should not be added to the bank's profit. This was an easy requirement to implement.

4. Any income realized by the bank due to an unavoidable interest source must be paid to charity and not added to bank profit. This condition is also achievable.

5. In a lease-to-purchase model, insurance premiums must be shared by the two participants in the transaction in proportion to their ownership. Most scholars suggested that the monthly payment of the buyer be increased to reflect that cost, and add the portion of the insurance premium to the monthly payment. Per U.S. bank regulations and for the sake of transparency and straightforwardness, the bank must disclose in full the payments made and what they were used for. In response, it was decided that if an RF bank uses the LARIBA Shari'aa-based RF model, the bank must tell the customer openly that he or she is responsible for the insurance; because he/she own the shares from the beginning and that he/she is the one benefiting from the use of the facility in an operating lease.

6. Maintenance must be shared. Again, because the buyer uses the facility, regular maintenance is not only required, but must be paid by the user to keep the property in the best of all shapes.

7. Customers' deposits must be exposed to bank profit and loss. Investment products cannot guarantee a certain interest rate or return. It is believed that it is unfair, in a banking scheme that offers Federal Deposit (FDIC) insurance on funds, that peoples' hard-earned savings and deposits are exposed to the risk of loss. We are aware of the scheme used in the United Kingdom, in which the customer must be offered the guarantee *and* offered the option of refusing it in order for that condition to be applicable.

8. The bank should have a supervisory board that specializes in Shari'aa to ensure that the bank's products, services, and operations are compliant with Shari'aa. The Shari'aa Board is given the power to render bank operations not compliant. That condition can be implemented as a part of, and a complement to, the annual onsite regulatory examination conducted by the concerned regulatory authorities. As discussed earlier in the book, many of the aspects of the regulatory onsite examination ensure compliance to regulations. It must be frankly admitted that the bulk of the regulations, which are in fact Judeo-Christian-Islamic in nature, are not even considered by the Shari'aa Boards of the Islamic banks in many of the Muslim countries. As an example, the fairness of treating expatriate workers needs to be closely examined and evaluated by the Shari'aa Board of the bank or finance company. Another example is applying the basic

human right of obtaining credit in a host country. The Shari'aa Board in the setting we propose should complement the onsite regulatory supervision to make sure that the models used are in fact the same as advertised and that these models comply with Shari'aa and that the bankers and their representatives apply Shari'aa when they "sell" these products and services. Unfortunately, the extent of the Shari'aa Board's involvement in the operations of many Islamic banks has been minimal, and their job ends at sanctioning a model or a product. Unfortunately, the "Islamic" bankers use the names of these respected scholars to advertise and seek acceptance in the market. The question we have is: Does every light bulb we buy have to have the signature of Mr. Thomas Edison to make it an acceptable light bulb?

■ It is interesting to note that the focus of the scholars was concentrated on the legal aspects of the contract but did not include some of the basic requirements that define the substance and spirit of the true RF banking and finance system. For example:

1. Very little is mentioned about the aspect of social responsibility of "Islamic" RF finance. It is true that the rules put forward by many Shari'aa Boards and scholars prohibit participation in financing the businesses that involve the manufacturing or selling of intoxicants, gambling, illegal activities, or promiscuous activities, as well as socially irresponsible activities such as environmentally damaging industries, businesses that do not treat their employees and customers fairly, and institutions that use false advertising to con their customers. However, one would notice little or no mention of the responsibility of the RF banker to local communities by investing the deposits gathered from a community back into that community—as in the U.S. Community Reinvestment Act (CRA)—before allowing bank deposits to be invested outside the communities (and in some cases, outside the country), depriving the local communities of the opportunity to help their citizens grow and prosper and to create job opportunities for all. Also, it is noticed that there is no mention of treating people equally, without discrimination based on national origin, wealth, tribal ties, skin color, gender, or language.

2. There was no significant sign that the scholars of the Shari'aa and the "Islamic" bankers tried to benefit from the vast body of bank regulations that deal primarily with fairness and respect of human rights in the communities, as well as to protect those who experienced unexpected and unfortunate circumstances beyond their control, as we see in the bankruptcy law and codes in, for example, the United States.

3. It is peculiar to note the posture of most of the Shari'aa finance scholars, who ignore what is believed to be the basic revolutionary aspect of the RF finance system: the *commodity indexation rule*, which neutralizes the effects of *fiat* money fluctuations, and the *mark-to-market rule*, by which each of the items to be financed is marked (compared) to the market to identify any market bubbles and help investors make prudent investment decisions. We believe in prudently evaluating the potential investment in terms of *return on capital* invested, by pricing, for example, cars, homes, or equipment based on the actual lease rate they would command in the open market system. It is believed that these rules are the most important, and add fundamental unique aspects to the RF financing approach. There is no mention, for example, of paper (*fiat*) money and how it may lead to unfair and deceptive aspects of a transaction.

In conclusion, it is believed that in a fair and viable RF banking regime, all the banking regulations that were discussed in Chapter 7 should in fact be part of Shari'aa requirements. It is the real intent, and not merely the words in a convoluted contract, that in fact makes the RF banking and finance system unique and beneficial. Many of the Shari'aa-compliant contracts are in fact designed by force-fitting the conventional riba-based contract into language that "complies" with Shari'aa in form, but that in most cases does not satisfy the real spirit and substance of why Shari'aa prohibited riba.

We want to share with the reader a personal experience that we hope will shed more light on the unfortunate practice of some of the "scholars" who have in fact risen to positions of fame despite very little being known about their education, training, research, scholastics, and/or any proven track record of documented, debated, and critically reviewed research.[15]

At LARIBA, we once decided to engage a well-educated economist who had completed a Ph.D. in economics in the United States, had authored a number of books on "Islamic" economics, presented himself as a scholar in Shari'aa, and acted as an advisor to some of the most prominent law firms active in "Islamic" finance legal services. We wanted this economist to evaluate the LARIBA Shari'aa-based RF model as a foundation and develop a set of documents that he would feel satisfied what he believed to be the Law (Shari'aa), in his opinion. We gave him the fruits of our 27 years of research, supported with references and research papers to read. He came back with a big smile on his face, saying, and I quote, "This is really unique and is different. I think you have something that will be very useful." We gave him our instructions, which consisted of making sure that the research we documented was included and articulated in his efforts and ensuring that we had followed the laws of the land and the norms required by the U.S. banking regulations—something we later discovered that he knew very little, if anything, about. He asked us to supply him with copies of the standard deed of trust and promissory note used in standard banking transactions. After a few weeks, he e-mailed us his products. Upon investigation, and after matching the Microsoft Word documents using the edit-tracking facility, we can summarize what he did as follows:

1. Replaced the word *interest* with *rent* or *profit*. We had told him that we take care of that in the process of finance preparation, and that doing it this way creates a completely different set of documents that will require us to obtain an exception to receive detailed approvals from the regulators, which would expose us to a lengthy and expensive process. We also stated that this approach might compromise the interests of the customer, especially in a court of law where it would result in utter confusion among the judge, the prosecutors, the defense attorneys, and the jury. We also stated that it does not matter—based on many references in Shari'aa—what you call that percentage as long as it does not imply the "renting" of money, indicating a riba-based transaction.

2. Made the process look like a buy/sell agreement. We told him that in a buy/sell transaction—based on the laws of the land and Shari'aa—we should include a documented and properly recorded transfer of title from the seller to the bank (the buyer), which violates U.S. bank regulations and credit policy, and subsequently from the bank to the ultimate buyer. In addition, this claimed buy/sell step is, in reality, synthetic, because we know that the bank never intended to buy the property and that the process is done this way to make it look Islamic. We told him that metaphorically, it reminded us of a man who wanted to enjoy a few nights with a lady. He proceeded to marry her with the intention of divorcing her after he got his pleasure— definitely a deceptive trick designed to make the process look religiously acceptable on paper, though the intention was anything but! We also told him, based on our long-time banking experience, that this approach might open the bank (as a buyer of the property) to punitive actions by the regulators and a potential capital gains tax that could be significant. He said, to our amazement, that changing title was not necessary, because at the time of Prophet Muhammad (pp), there was no change of title! We told him that we obviously were no longer living in that age. We also told him that it would be counter to our claims to be trying to uphold Shari'aa if we did not tell the truth, which is one of the most important foundations of any faith, let alone the Judeo-Christian-Islamic value system.

3. Included in the documents was a very interesting disclosure, in which he stated, and I quote: "This is a finance contract . . ." Our response was, "If this is the real intent, what is the point? Why go through all these changes and maneuvers?" He said that we needed this to be done in order to be compliant with Shari'aa.

We canceled his consulting contract. He reacted by saying that he was not surprised, because he felt that we had no respect for scholarship! He is still being invited to teach scores of European and Western bankers in training seminars, short courses, and conferences on how to structure "Islamic" contracts that would "comply" with Shari'aa. These are the same seminars organized by the same groups that have controlled the "Islamic" banking promotion domain with one goal in mind: presenting scholar participants who will help promote the "Shari'aa-compliant" banking that conforms to the methodology promoted and signed on by the very Shari'aa scholar "superstars" created by such promoters.

In another experience, one of our staff members was sharing the challenges we face as a minority in the United States with another "scholar." The staff member shared with the scholar that we all should be wise, honest, and creative in order to offer true RF banking that would be based on Shari'aa without violating the laws of the land and the U.S. banking regulations, while at the same time offering real economic substance and an advantage to the user of RF financing techniques. This scholar's advice was that we get ourselves a good lawyer who is well connected with the regulators and/or a retired regulator—as they had done earlier, in another European capital—and all would be taken care of. We shared with this scholar that in the United States, it is not the usual practice to buy your way in; even if you were successful, it would cost you a lot of money and result in many restrictions—as happened in the aforementioned European country—that would render RF financing a "joke," something that satisfied the form but not the spirit and the substance of the Judeo-Christian-Islamic value system based on Shari'aa.

While developing this LARIBA Shari'aa-based RF model, we had to come up with solutions to the many challenges discussed previously in this book and we had to merge many of the opposing undercurrents. The following is a list of the major guidelines used to develop the model:

- It should reflect and embody the real spirit and substance of Shari'aa.
- It should be based on Shari'aa (notice here the phrase *based on*, not *compliant with*) and not force-fitted, as is done in the Shari'aa-compliant approach.
- It must reflect the benefit to the user when compared to the models used by the riba-based system and the Shari'aa-compliant system.

- It must enforce and abide by the laws, regulations, and standards of the banking and financing system in the United States.
- It must be appealing to all users, regardless of their faith, skin color, national origin, ethnicity, gender, or language.
- It must be convincing to the educated and sophisticated users, offering a real economic advantage and benefit and not relying solely on the reputation of a famous religious scholar's endorsement.

BUILDING THE SHARI'AA-BASED FINANCE MODEL

After a thorough analysis of the Islamic finance models available on the market and used mostly in the oil-rich Gulf countries and in Malaysia, it was concluded that these "Shari'aa-compliant" models were in fact not much different from those used by the conventional banking system. What reinforced our conclusion was the ruling passed by the Office of the Comptroller of the Currency (OCC) in response to the application of the New York branch of United Bank of Kuwait to allow "Islamic" banking using the cost-plus (*Murabaha*) and lease-to-own models. The OCC concluded that these products were the same as interest-based financing. This fact made us conclude that we do not need to obtain special government approvals and exceptions that require a huge investment of time, money, and effort. We felt that what is needed is a system that would truly implement the Judeo-Christian-Islamic values of Shari'aa to benefit all.

Many attempts were made to devise a model that would satisfy our requirements. After a long search and extensive analysis, the effort focused on an analogy to our community's experience with the development of marriage procedures and contracts in the United States. A marriage contract is considered in the Judeo-Christian-Islamic system as the most solemn, most binding, and "thickest" of all contracts (Qur'aan 4:21). Based on our community's earlier experience with the development of an Islamic Shari'aa-based marriage system and procedures that utilize the civil marriage contract, we can draw a wonderful parallel with our efforts to develop a Shari'aa-based RF finance system. As is normally the case in marriage, a standard process is used. In this process, a number of preparatory steps must be followed before signing the standard civil marriage contract. For example, the two families would meet and agree on the details of the marriage agreement (e.g., the dowry), and the wedding details (e.g., the religious leader (the rabbi, priest, preacher, or imam) who will officiate the wedding). Then, the couple to be wedded would apply for a standard civil marriage license that has a space in it for a religious leader's signature. The religious leader would meet with the two families and the couple to be wedded to explain in full detail the meaning of the marriage contract according to the rituals and processes of the faith and to consult with and agree upon the details of the process. It was also reasoned that what makes a contract Islamic, Catholic, or Jewish is not only the religious ceremony and the religious wedding vows and rites pronounced, but also where the couple goes if they have a dispute. If they seek religious arbitration, that makes it a real faith-based marriage; if they seek the civil courts, that makes it a civil marriage.

There are two important considerations that need to be included in the development of the Shari'aa-based RF finance system:

1. That money is not rented. This stipulation is met by ensuring that the property is marked to market.
2. That, in the case of a dispute, the contracting parties use a board of arbitration that abides by Shari'aa. This makes the contract "faith-based," depending on the faith involved.

Another important parallel experience of the American Muslim community and its development was our 1969 attempt to make available to the American community *halal* (divinely permissible) meat products from chicken, cattle, and animals in general that are slaughtered according to the rules of Shari'aa. I tried to arrange for the famous Oscar Mayer meat company in Madison, Wisconsin to give us beef that was slaughtered according to Islamic rites, as it is conceptually done for kosher meat.[16] I went to Oscar Mayer's general slaughterhouse and participated in making the slaughtering according to Shari'aa and witnessed firsthand a rabbi doing the same for kosher meat. In an effort to systemize this process, one can state that the meat production involved a number of subsequent steps. These are:

1. *The Preparation* of the animal. It had to be clean, clear of any illness, and able to pass the standard regulatory tests of the veterinarian.
2. *The Faith-Based Action* to slaughter the animal, which differs by faith.
3. *The Processing*, which includes proper slaughtering and cutting and complete drainage of the blood; the details of this process also differ by faith.
4. *The Packaging* can include the label *kosher* (for Jews) or *halal* (for Muslims) in addition to the U.S. Department of Agriculture (USDA) label and emblem, which are required to sell the product according to the laws of the land as described in the universal standards set by the USDA.

Our strategic group reasoned that this process, too, could be copied and used in the development of RF financing without the need to incur huge expenses in trying to reinvent the wheel.

Applying this vision based on the analogies and the stepwise approach described above, we reached the following process as it pertains to RF financing:

1. *The Preparation:* This step includes taking an application from the customer and processing it by evaluating the customer's credit scores to check on his/her credit character profile, to learn where the property is in order to be ready for an appraisal, and to learn the customer's financial details.

2. *The Faith-Based Qualification:* This step includes the application of the LARIBA Shari'aa-based RF finance model to decide whether investing in and buying the property makes economic and prudent sense.

3. *The Processing/Underwriting:* This step includes the analysis of all the information gathered, the assembly of all the documents needed, and the decision as to whether we should join in investing in the property with the customer.

4. *The Documentation:* This step includes documenting the agreements according to the standard and universally used documents that follow the banking laws and regulations of the United States. To record the process we used, we developed what we call the LARIBA Agreement. It is a rider that is added to the agreements and contracts. It describes in detail the prohibition of riba, the process that was used, and the U.S. banking regulatory reasons why the phrase *implied interest* was used.

We are aware that others in the field of Shari'aa-compliant "Islamic finance" in the United States and other parts of the world—in their sincere attempts to comply with Shari'aa—have used expensive lawyers and costly and sophisticated structured corporate vehicles for the purpose of "financial engineering." We are also aware that others use ruses (*heelah*, or deceptive tricks and practices) to make the financing agreement look Shari'aa-compliant on the surface, but when the intent, the fine print, and the methods used are investigated, one can clearly and readily conclude that the contract is intended to circumvent the Law (Shari'aa). Based on thorough research in the original sources, on our consultations with many scholars in Shari'aa since 1987, and our soul searching, we decided to be fully transparent about the LARIBA model methods and not to mislead or misrepresent facts by using "financial engineering" techniques such as the use of a special purpose vehicle (SPV) as discussed in Chapter 9.

It was also decided never to use the names of the eminent scholars in Shari'aa for advertising purposes to make it easy to "sell" our products and services. We feel that doing so takes away respect and eminence from those respected scholars and, in fact, is counterproductive, because it is important that educated and sophisticated users understand the concepts used in order to be responsible for his/her actions and decisions in this life and the life after.

The Unique Features of the LARIBA Shari'aa-Based Model

As described earlier, in today's banking terminology, one can conceptually define riba as the rent on money and/or lending to rent this money at a price or rate called interest rate. Riba-based conventional financing may involve unsecured and noncollateralized credit that is not asset- or service-based. The riba-based conventional financing system uses an index called interest to define the cost of "renting" money to the customer. In an RF finance setting, the bank's financing activity is looked on as an investment by the bank in the individual (or company), in order to help that entity acquire tangible assets and/or services. In this capacity, the RF finance officer makes sure that the finance facility has economic merit by measuring the return on investment using the market rent of the facility, the service, or the business. Please note that in RF financing, we prefer to use the word *finance*, not *lend*, because the financing is looked upon as a true investment with the customer. The only loan in Shari'aa, as detailed earlier, is *qard hassan* (a loan that is returned with no additions to the original value, which is made for a good cause).

The other important aspect of an RF banking transaction is that there is no predetermined value measurement for the renting of money, called *interest* in riba-based conventional banking transactions. In an RF banking transaction, the return on investment is obtained as a result of the investment process or the leasing process of the asset in question. That return on investment is the real measure of the value of the investment activity, with its unique characteristics. In doing so, the RF banker marks the item to be invested to the local market, instead of using a unified interest rate to rent money at a predetermined level throughout the country. For example, a house rent should reflect the value of that house and not a *capitalization* rate, as is done in most leases and in many models used by some "Islamic" bankers. The rent of two similar homes—one in Alabama, which has a smaller economy, and another in California, the eighth largest economy in the world—should be different, because of the difference in the economic characteristics of each state. That difference should be reflected in the financing process by the lease rate of the item to be financed in each state, as dictated by the market forces of supply and demand.

The following are some of the unique features of the LARIBA Shari'aa-based RF finance model:

1. The RF model is based on a belief that can be articulated as "*We do not rent money; we invest in you.*" Applying this model requires that the RF banker approach each transaction as an investment (using The Declining Joint Venture Lease-to-Own Model) instead of lending. The RF banker advises the customer, to the best of his/her abilities, as to whether the transaction is a good investment or it is better for the customer to rent. This process prevents the buyer and the finance company/ bank from participating in an economic bubble and from buying an overpriced facility or business.

2. The RF model requires that the RF banker does not calculate the monthly payment by starting from an interest rate, as is done in riba-based finance. Homes, cars, and businesses can be rented at a fair market value that is defined and agreed upon by the RF banker and the customer after studying the market. The monthly payment is based on the market rental value of the property to be financed. The rental value is determined by going to the market—both the customer and the RF bank finance officer independently—to measure the rental rate of a similar property in the same neighborhood by asking real estate agents in the area. The fair rental value is determined by mutual agreement between the customer and the RF finance entity. In this process of *marking to the market*, the house buyer calls three different real estate agents to get the actual market value of the rent of a similar house, if it were to be used as an investment property. In addition, the RF bank finance officer does the same. This way, the RF bank obtains a marked-to-the-market, agreed-upon property market rent that the RF bank finance officer subsequently uses in its calculation of the rate of return on investment to decide whether buying the property makes prudent economic sense. Prudence in investing is an important ingredient of the spirit of RF financing.

3. The RF model requires that the RF bank or finance company work with clients in a humane, merciful, and fair way (*tarahum*) in times of trouble. To do this, the RF bank helps families that are in trouble by counseling them and offering them the facility of an RF *qard hassan*, a "good loan," without any increase or interest, from a nonprofit organization that can assist in making part or the whole of the monthly payment until the difficulty is eased—for example, when the husband gets a new job to enable him to resume the payments.

The Stages Used to Implement the Shari'aa-Based LARIBA Model of Financing

The LARIBA Shari'aa-based RF finance model is based on the original and pioneering fatwa and model developed for financing homes in the United

Kingdom by Al Baraka Bank in London. However, the model has been modified and expanded to include in it the two basic foundations of the true spirit of removing riba from financing transactions: the *commodity indexation rule* and the *mark-to-market rule*.

The process consists of three major stages:

A. Formulating the riba-free Shari'aa-based agreement

B. Documenting the RF financing for compliance with U.S. laws and banking regulations by transforming the agreement into a U.S. government–sanctioned and standardized financing (mortgage) note and contract

C. Signing the *LARIBA Agreement*, which explains the prohibition of riba, the terms in the standard U.S. contract, and the process used to mark the property to the market so the transaction is Shari'aa based

A. Formulating the Financing According to Shari'aa

Fatwa There are a number of edicts (*fatwa*) issued by some of the highest-placed scholars in RF banking and financing (detailed in Chapter 9). The edict used by the LARIBA model is based on that developed for use by Al Baraka Bank of London. In this model, the scholars divided the property rights of an item into two rights: The first is the right to own title of the property (*milk ul raqabah*), and the second is the right to use/operate the property—such as the use of a home, a car, or a business (*haq al manfa'aa*, meaning usufruct).

The procedure used by the model goes through the following stipulations:

1. The model allowed the RF finance institution or the RF bank to assign the buyer to act as an agent (wakeel) of the bank and to proceed to negotiate the purchase price and other conditions on behalf of the RF bank.

2. The RF bank agrees to form a conceptual partnership with client to buy the property together, with the following stipulations: Registering the title of the item to be financed (home title, for example) in the partner's name, based on trust, from the inception of the contract is permissible under Shari'aa. Registering the property's title in this manner does not contradict the agreed-upon partnership, especially as the partner's ability to sell the home is restricted until full ownership of the property is established. In this regard, the scholars took into consideration the fact that this registration of title is a form of documentation insured by the officially established lien on the property, according to the conditions agreed upon with the partner.

3. The bank would finance the purchase jointly with the buyer in the form of a joint ownership (Musharaka):

   a. The RF bank would sell its entire share back to the buyer immediately and record the property (the house or the car) in the buyer's name.

   b. The RF bank would exercise and perfect a lien that makes the RF bank a lien holder, and get a contractual promise from the client to pay back the bank share over a certain period of time (the term of the buy back) by the customer. In this step the buyer would be the owner of the title (milk ul raqabah).

   c. The RF finance company or the RF bank would participate in and share in the benefits of using the property (haq al manfa'aa)—in the case of a car, it is the lease rate of the car; in the case of a house, it is the lease rate of the house—over the years in the proportion of its changing implied ownership (the RF bank's implied ownership—through the lien—and hence the share in the usufruct declines as the buyer progressively pays back his owed part of the purchase price).

   d. The bank or the finance company can use the word interest to satisfy the laws of the land to describe the payments share of the rental of the property. However, the opposite (taking interest and calling it profit) is not allowed.

The word *lien* has been mistranslated to Arabic as *rahn*, which means *pawn*. There is a world of difference between the two in legal definition. In general, in case of *rahn*, or pawning the property, the property itself and its use are both arrested and placed in the custody of the pawn holder. That means that the right to use the property (haq al manfa'aa) is confiscated until the riba loan is paid back. If it is not paid, then the rahn-holder would take over the property (milk ul raqabah) without legal action, because it is in the possession of the rahn-holder.

DEFINITION OF PAWN[17]

Verb: To deliver personal property to another in pledge or as security for a debt or sum borrowed.

Noun: A bailment of goods to a creditor as security for some debt engagement; a pledge; a deposit of personal property made to a pawnbroker as security for a loan. That sort of bailment when goods or chattels are delivered to another as security to him/her for money borrowed of him/her by the bailor. Also, the specific chattel delivered to the creditor as a pledge.

DEFINITION OF A LIEN

Lien is defined as the right to take and hold or sell the property of a debtor as security or payment for a debt or duty.

It is also defined as a claim, encumbrance, or charge on property for payment of some debt, obligation, or duty.[18] Additionally, it is defined as a *qualified* right of property which a creditor has in or over specific property of his debtor as security for the debt or charge or for performance of some act. It is further defined as a right or claim against some interest in property created by law as an incident of contract. It is also defined as:

- Right to enforce charge upon property of another for payment or satisfaction of debt or claim
- Right to retain property for payment of debt or demand
- Security for debt, duty, or other obligation
- Tie that binds property to a debt or claim for its satisfaction
- A charge against or interest in property to secure payment of a debt or performance of an obligation

The Meaning of Establishing a Lien Based on the definitions of pawn and lien, one can establish that liens, which could not have existed without a searchable title database in order to make sure that the property is free and clear and that there are no unknown claims against it, are a form of ownership right that is different from the classic pawning (*rahn*) contract. Here are some facts to support our conclusion:

- A lien is defined in the dictionary[19] as "a conveyance of title to property that is given to secure an obligation—as a debt or promise to perform a financial obligation—and that is defeated upon payment or performance according to stipulated terms."
- An acid test of the above consists of the response to two events: The first is that when the house experiences damage of some sort, the insurance company issues the check in the name of the title owner and the co-mortgage—or lien—holder. Second is the fact that the process of releasing the lien is called "re-conveyance" of title.

Based on these facts, the conceptual definition of a mortgage and the perfection of a lien in favor of the RF bank is like a *diminishing partnership* (*musharaka mutnaqisah*) between the two entities—the property (home or business) buyer, called the mortgagee, and the RF bank or RF finance (mortgager) entity.

As a result, it can be concluded that there is no need for the creation of an SPV or the incurring of additional expenses and significant legal complications and confusion that would render RF financing more expensive and liable to complicated legal suits in case of a dispute.

We significantly modified the Al Baraka model described in Chapter 9. This modification produced the model known as the Shari'aa-based LARIBA RF finance model,which is based on Shari'aa in contrast to the other approach and models, called *Shari'aa-compliant*, which have been used since the latter part of the 20th century. As was discussed in Chapter 9, the Shari'aa-compliant proponents use the approach of force-fitting the existing riba-based models to Shari'aa. In contrast, the LARIBA Shari'aa-based RF finance model uses the commodity indexation rule to normalize the effects of paper (*fiat*) money regimes (to avoid participating in an inflated economic bubble as discussed earlier) and the mark-to-market rule to introduce, for the first time, the real spirit, intent, substance, and wisdom of modern Islamic RF banking to the finance field. Following are the modifications introduced by the LARIBA model to the Al Baraka model:

1. LARIBA Model *Modified Step 1*. In this step, the actual rental rate of a similar property (a car, a home, or a commercial building) or a business in the same neighborhood and with similar specifications (in case of a home or a commercial building, in terms of dollars per square foot) is researched in the market by contacting automobile or real estate agents active in the area. The customer and the finance officer each come up with three documented estimates. The average of the six estimates, or a mutually agreed-upon rental value, is used. This rent is used to evaluate the rate of return on the investment, using the patent-pending LARIBA model. This way, the bank and the investor act as if the purchase of the car, the home, or the business is an investment. This will be discussed later in further detail.

2. LARIBA Model *Modified Step 2*. The costs, including recording fees, maintenance, and other fees are booked to the account of the customer, who now owns the facility and is its operator. The insurance is not shared, because of the strict consumer compliance requirements that demand full disclosure of the items involved in every payment. (The recommendation made in the original fatwa could not be applied.) This way, the customer will have the freedom to choose his/her own insurance provider.

Monthly payments include an installment to repay the capital forwarded by RF bank and a rental component:

1. The monthly repayment of the RF bank capital invested with the buyer is paid back, on a monthly basis, on an agreed-upon schedule and on an interest-free basis. This component is called the *return of capital* and was given the acronym *RofC* (pronounced "rofsee"), which is called in riba-based financing the payment of principal.

2. The rental component is the RF banker's share in the rent, based on the proportion of the capital returned to the RF bank. This component represents the profit or income the RF bank collects as a benefit in co-owning the right to use the property. This is called in the RF finance model *return on capital*, and its acronym is *RonC* (pronounced "ron-see"), which is called in riba-based financing the payment of interest. It is important to note here that the RonC is based on the actual market rent of the property, not the rent of money, in contrast to the portion of payment in a riba-based conventional banking setting in which the interest is really calculated using the rent on money (riba), which is prohibited by the Law (*Shari'aa*).

It is important to note that the above steps are done independently without preconditions, and none of the steps is a precondition for the other to take place. If the process is not done this way, it will not be based on Shari'aa, because it may be considered as "two sales contracts in one contract," as explained in cases of the sale of eena in Chapter 9.

Calculation of the Economic Viability and Prudence of the Investment   An important and truly unique aspect of the LARIBA Shari'aa-based RF finance model is prudence in investing one's assets. It is the responsibility of the RF banker to act as a wise and prudent investment adviser, preventing the customer from digging a deeper hole of debt for himself and his family by investing in a property, a business, or a house. If it would not make prudent economic sense to invest in if it were rented to a third party as an investment, it would not make prudent sense for the customer.

Appraising the Property or the Business   There are two approaches to appraising the property. The first approach is that obtained by the standard appraisal, based on the last few sales in the neighborhood. But this approach may be extremely misleading in an inflated market, like the ones experienced in Houston, Texas, during the 1980s housing and commercial real estate bubble, in Silicon Valley in the 1990s, and during the nationwide bubble experienced in the United States for housing and commercial real estate, which reached its peak in 2006 and burst in 2008.

This is the real spirit and real intent of the prohibition of riba/ribit in the Jewish Bible, the Christian Bible, and the Qur'aan. In fact, based on the LARIBA model, LARIBA may be the only finance company that would decline financing a property or a business if the return on investment based on the actual market rent of similar properties were not attractive, using market parameters that will be detailed later.

Applying the Rule of Marking the Property to the Market   Each property has a market value, which is best defined by what its lease value would be if it were leased on the open market. The model assumes that the property is leased at fair market value, as defined by the location and specifications of the property, and as mutually agreed-upon between the client and RF bank. Here is the detailed procedure:

1. The customer is asked to research the actual long-term rental of a home, car, property, or businesses with the same specifications and in the same neighborhood. This can be done, in case of buying a house for example, by calling three different real estate agents in the area and documenting the findings. The RF bank officer does the same.
2. Based on the six data points collected above, the customer and LARIBA agree on a *fair market rent* value of the property.
3. The RF bank calculates the customer's monthly payment. This monthly payment consists of two parts: the RonC (portion of the rent that belongs to the RF bank for renting its share of the usufruct of the item) and the RofC (repayment of the capital paid as interest-free credit to the customer).

The Unique Features of the LARIBA Shari'aa-Based Model   In a riba-based conventional banking setting, the customer will approach the bank to ask, "If I take a loan of $240,000, and repay it over 20 years to finance the purchase of a house, how much would the monthly payment be?" The riba-based banker would look at the interest rate of the hour on that day and tell the customer that if he or she qualifies, the bank can lend them $240,000 at an interest rate (money rental rate) of, say, seven percent. The riba banker would start an amortization computer program and input the amount to be financed, the number of years, and the interest rate. The unknown here is the monthly payment.

When the unique LARIBA model is used, the customer will be told that the RF bank cannot calculate the monthly payment before we know the location of the property, its specifications, and its rental/lease rate on the open market—based on the rent of comparable properties in the same area—because we do not rent money (which is riba/ribit), but we rent properties and businesses. We also assure the customer that if the investment makes economic sense based on our RF finance model, the monthly payment will be competitive with that offered by the conventional riba-based banks. To evaluate the economic viability of owning a property in contrast to not buying it and instead renting a similar property, the RF banker inputs the monthly rent obtained from the market survey process described above, the number of years to pay back, the purchase price, and the down payment into the patent-pending and copyright-protected LARIBA computer program. The unknown here is the rate of return on invested capital, which is called the *implied interest rate*. It is actually the rate of return on investment for this property. This rate of return is compared with the expected rate of return by the investor in the RF bank or finance company. There are three possible outcomes:

1. *The rate of return on investment, based on the actual market rental value of the property, is higher than the RF return on capital expected by investors.* In this case, the RF bank would inform the property buyer that the property purchase makes economic sense and that because the investors (those who invest with the RF bank and its shareholders) are looking for a lower return to compete with the riba-based conventional banks, the RF bank will unilaterally reduce the agreed-upon rent so as not to hurt the community member who wants to abide by Shari'aa. This makes RF financing competitive with the rest of the market.

2. *The rate of return on investment, based on the actual market rental value of the property, is very low compared to the return on capital expected by investors.* In this case, the RF bank officer advises the prospective buyer that the property market in this neighborhood is extremely inflated and is experiencing an economic bubble. The RF bank informs the customer that it cannot finance the property. In fact, some markets in northern California, Arizona, Nevada, Washington, D.C., and Massachusetts have been suffering from this problem since late 2005 to mid-2006. The appraised value by sales comparisons is acceptable, but the economic viability based on the unique LARIBA marking-to-market RF finance model is not valid. The LARIBA model may make the RF bank the only RF finance institution that would reject financing, despite the fact that the buyer may be a great customer for any bank to deal with—because investing in the property does not make economic sense. It is important to state that we, at LARIBA, have saved many customers in the aforementioned states from participating in the most recent real estate bubble. In fact, because of this feature of

the model, we have realized the following achievements at LARIBA and the Bank of Whittier:

a. The mortgage portfolio produced by LARIBA and the Bank of Whittier was rated as one of the best 64 performing portfolios in the United States. This was reported to us by United Guaranty Insurance Co.

b. Fannie Mae informed us that our mortgage portfolios with them were one of the ten best-performing portfolios in the Western region, which extends from Colorado to Hawaii.

c. The delinquency and foreclosure rate is a fraction of the national average.

It is interesting to share with the reader the experience we had when LARIBA's bankers first met with Freddie Mac to allow their representatives to inspect and look into what we do, so that Freddie Mac could proceed with its fact-finding and approval process. We explained our model to the four representatives. The head analyst asked us, "Do you really mark the house to market?" We said yes. He asked to review the files. He was impressed. It took Freddie Mac six weeks to approve LARIBA, compared to the national approval time needed of six months. Later, Fannie Mae followed Freddie Mac's lead.

3. *The rate of return on investment, based on the actual market rental value of the property, is marginally lower than the return on capital expected by investors:* In this case, the RF bank officer and/or credit committee would advise the prospective buyer to try to renegotiate the price to render the investment economically viable. At LARIBA, we have had a number of successful experiences where we helped a number of community members negotiate a lower price for the home.

Our customers may sell the property at any time and pay back the remaining capital owed to LARIBA (the balance of the financing amount). Partial prepayment may also be made at any time. Partial payments are applied against the purchase installments in inverse order of maturity, and the rental component is reduced proportionately.

B. Documentation of RF Financing for U.S. Compliance The banking and financing laws and regulations in the United States are among the strictest in the world. RF financing in America is offered using two approaches:

1. Start with the conventional riba-based banking product and devise ways and means to "force" fit it to an "Islamic" solution that would comply with (or at least look like it complies with) Shari'aa, using intellectual and expert help from experienced riba bankers, attorneys, and ex-regulators. One of the techniques is the creation of a special purpose

entity (SPE) or a special purpose vehicle (SPV), which would buy the property and either sell it back, in a Cost-Plus (Murabaha) scheme, or lease it back, in a joint venture with declining equity (Musharaka Mutnaqisah) scheme. The other idea, used in Musharaka Mutnaqisah, is to register the title of the property in both the financial institution's name and that of the property or business buyer to make the transaction appear to be a true joint venture.

2. Start with the LARIBA RF model to test the prudence of the investment and to calculate the monthly payments, based on the actual rental value researched in the market (by applying the mark-to-market rule). Financing contracts are drawn up according to the U.S. federal banking laws and regulations. The contract is supplemented by a propriety "rider" called the LARIBA Agreement. The LARIBA Agreement explains the prohibition of riba and the process used.

It is believed that this second approach is a true manifestation of the Judeo-Christian-Islamic values because it is based on Shari'aa. Here are the reasons why:

1. The LARIBA RF finance model uses the standard mortgage documentation required. This documentation and its associated contracts have been in continual development by the U.S. banking and finance authorities since the Great Depression of the 1930s.
2. It can be easily compared to the conventional riba-based approach. This way, the customer can make a fair comparison (apples to apples) in his/her pursuit to make the right decision.
3. It offers protection of the customer, because it conforms to standard U.S. financial and banking industry norms rather than to special considerations that may require lengthy court deliberations in case of a dispute.
4. In the case of RF mortgage financing, the LARIBA RF financing model offers the customer the advantage of being able to deduct the rent-based payments as implied interest, using the statutory mortgage reduction laws in the United States. In comparison, the Shari'aa-compliant model uses an IRS Opinion Letter, which does not carry the weight of the law and is usually temporary in nature. It can be withdrawn and/or nullified at any time.
5. Because the LARIBA RF Shari'aa-based model records title in the name of the customer, it protects the customers. Companies that use the Shari'aa-compliant models require that the title be in the names of both the buyer and the financial institution. Recording title in both the name of the customer and the finance company or bank may expose the customer to any risks assumed by the finance companies.

The LARIBA RF finance model uses the following documents:

- *Promissory Note* that indicates the amount of financing, the agreed-upon monthly payments, and the imputed (implied) interest rate of the transaction
- *Deed of Trust*
- Other required regulatory documentation relating to truth in lending, non-discrimination, servicing of the financing, and so on
- The unique, copyright-protected *LARIBA Agreement*

C. The LARIBA Agreement   The RF Shari'aa-based financing process (as is done at LARIBA) uniquely supplements the above standard documents (which use the word interest) with a specially devised rider called the LARIBA Agreement. This Agreement documents the process used in the LARIBA Shari'aa-based RF finance model to calculate the monthly payment using the market measured rental value agreed upon between the customer and the RF bank or financial institution. The LARIBA Agreement clearly declares that riba/interest charging and/or receiving is divinely prohibited (*haram*). It also summarizes the proprietary process and model used. In addition, it states that the calculated and agreed upon rate of return, using the actual market rental rate of the property, is called an *implied interest rate* in order to comply with the U.S. Regulation Z (the Truth in Lending Act, detailed in Chapter 7).The RF bank issues an Internal Revenue Service (IRS) U.S. form 1098 to allow for the deduction of the rental portion of the payments (as an implied interest) in the case of home mortgages, which is calculated at the beginning of the transaction and converted to an implied interest rate on the promissory note, as explained above.

Monthly Billing   LARIBA has created a new billing format that, we believe, is a historic development in the RF movement. LARIBA's monthly billing breaks down the monthly payment in terms of RofC (called principal payment in the riba-based finance industry) and RonC (called interest in the riba-based industry). A copy of the monthly billing is shown in Exhibit 10.1.

Servicing the Financing Facility (*The Loan*)   Servicing of the credit facility (loan) is the process of maintaining the finance facility after it has been funded. It includes billing the customer on a monthly basis, responding to customer inquiries, resolving any issues faced by the customer, escrowing taxes and insurance for the property, and maintaining records according to consumer compliance government regulations. Many finance companies and banks "sell" the servicing to outside companies, some of which are located outside the United States, for a handsome fee. This practice may

LARIBA
American Finance House

750 EAST GREEN STREET STE 210
PASADENA, CA 91101
PH: (626) 449-4401
FAX: (626) 449-5319
LARIBA@LARIBA.com

ABCD

750 E. Green Street Suite # 210
Pasadena, CA 91101

www.LARIBA.com

Your community owned Bank; the Bank
of Whittier, N. A. is offering: SHARI'AA-
COMPLIANT FDIC-Insured Certificates
of Deposit (CDs) at competitive rates of
return from income derived from Shari'aa
Compliant Financing Portfolio.

Bank of Whittier's holding company is
offering 500,000 shares at $10 per share to
Qualified Accredited Investors. This is the
first RIBA- FREE Bank to be owned by our
community in the history of the USA.

Please call Mr. Mike Abdelaaty (626)
348-4393 or Dr. Yahia A. Rahman. (626)
818-0855.

Account Information:

Account Number:	310610601
Statement Date:	7/21/09
Payment Due Date:	**8/1/09**
Property Address:	

Balance:

Principal: (Unpaid capital)	283,300.18

Year-to-Date Summary:

RofC* Paid (Repaid Capital):	699.82
RonC* Paid (Implied Interest):	2,113.79
Late Payment Expenses Paid**:	.00

Payment Information:

RonC* Paid (Implied Interest Rate):	4.87500 %
Monthly Payment (RofC* plus RonC*):	1,502.95
Escrow Payment (Taxes, Ins. or PMI):	.00
Number of Past Due Payments:	0
Past Due Payment Amount:	.00
Unpaid Late Payment Expense**:	.00
Unapplied Payments:	.00

Total Payment Due:	**1,502.95**

For Billing Inquiries Please Call:
1-888-LARIBA-1 Ext.112
1-888-527-422-1 Ext.112

**Late Payment Expense (Late Charge) of 30.06 will be applied if
payment is not received by 8/15/09 (as explained in the Financing
Note). This is the estimated administrative cost to LARIBA for
handling overdue payments.*

*The RofC amount stated on this invoice represents the Repayment of Capital using our conceptual Lease-to-Purchase model of financing. The RonC
amount represents the Return on Capital calculated using our conceptual Lease-to-Purchase model of financing. It is presented as an interest rate
for purposes of conformity with Federal and State laws, and is intended to be mortgage interest under the Internal Revenue Code and similar tax laws.

Please detach and return the bottom portion of this statement with your payment using the enclosed envelope. (Allow a minimum of 5 days for postal delivery.)

LARIBA
American Finance House

PAYMENT COUPON
*Please include your account number on your check

Account Number:	310610601
Statement Date:	7/21/09
Due Date:	8/1/09
Total Due:	1,502.95

Additional RofC*:	_____
Additional Escrow:	_____
Total Amount Enclosed:	_____

AMERICAN FINANCE HOUSE - LARIBA
750 EAST GREEN STREET STE 210
PASADENA, CA 91101

Return portion

☐ **AutoPay** check here and fill out the back to pay all
your future payment automatically

☐ **Change of billing address**
Check here and make change on the back

EXHIBIT 10.1 LARIBA monthly billing.

expose the customers to customer service personnel and managers who are
not from their community, are not familiar with RF finance, and are not
trained in the moral authority required by the Judeo-Christian-Islamic value
system. It is believed that this may not be permitted by Shari'aa. The

Shari'aa-based LARIBA RF model requires that the RF institution service the RF facilities it originated and that it cannot sell the servicing of those facilities to another company. When the RF institution services its facilities, community members who are well-trained and who understand the RF finance concepts, community values, culture, and languages are not only ready to serve and respond to inquiries, but also trained in the important Judeo-Christian-Islamic value of mercifulness and kindness (*tarahum*) to those in need.

Sources of Funds Used in RF Financing   One of the biggest challenges to our effort to popularize RF financing in the United States has been the availability of capital. When we started in 1987, it was very difficult to raise the necessary capital. We were faced with many challenges. The first and most important challenge was the novelty of the effort. Many members of the community had talked about having a bank or a financial institution that serves our community, which is one of the most underserved by the banks and financial institutions because of the prohibition of riba. However, when many of these community members were contacted to invest, they politely regretted, with many excuses.

The other approach we thought of trying was to start a public drive to raise capital. That option was very expensive because it required the use of very expensive attorneys and SEC registration fees, which we could not afford. In addition, we did not have a proven track record of a working model with tangible results. It was simply a venture capital project that needed high-risk capital—and it is known that high-risk capital comes at a very high price.

We also thought of starting or acquiring a bank. This would have been a wonderful solution, because all depository institutions are allowed to take deposits that can be used to finance different projects. However, that was a formidable task because we did not have the capital or the qualified staff that could be certified and accepted by the regulators.

On another front, we went through the process of applying to start a credit union and we were very close to receiving a charter. However, after reading the details of how a credit union works, we found that every depositor is considered a shareholder. We found that regardless of the size of the deposit, each individual represents a vote. We became very concerned due to prior experiences in the field of political manipulations of elections and voting in many nonprofit organizations. We discussed the matter and decided to back off.

We finally decided to start a small finance company, organized as a small—Subchapter S—corporation. This option had its advantages and disadvantages. The main advantage was the flexibility of raising the capital needed and the avoidance of double taxation. That means that the company's profits are not taxed at the company level. The profit is distributed to the shareholders, and they pay taxes according to their own situation. The disadvantages were many, but we had to start from what was possible to achieve what is impossible. The first disadvantage was that the number of shareholders was limited to a small number (it was 35 members when we started in 1987; as of 2009 it has expanded to 120 shareholders). In addition, a Subchapter S company cannot solicit funds from the public because that would require registration with the Securities and Exchange Commission (SEC). We started LARIBA in 1987 with a small capital of $200,000 which we had gathered from close, lifelong friends in the United States. We had humble means, but our dreams and aspirations were greater. We started a Web site (www.LARIBA.com) that became very popular throughout the world. We financed cars, homes, and small businesses. It is true that we only did one or two financing deals per month, but those deals helped us to start a balance sheet, an income-expense statement, a financial ledger, and a successful track record for the company. The biggest challenge was the huge demand we received from the community. We were heartbroken to say to prospective customers, "We are sorry, but we do not have enough capital." We asked our friends who we knew could afford to participate but they refused. They indicated that they would be more comfortable if their funds were federally insured by the FDIC, something that was impossible at the time. We used to finance homes with a 40-percent down payment and a term of seven years. This financing term could only be afforded by a few, who were mostly the believing affluent puritans.

It may prove useful to share with the reader the size of the problem of raising the necessary capital by focusing on one aspect of the business, mortgage financing. If we wanted to finance only 50 homes a month at $200,000 each, that would require that we come up with $10 million a month or $120 million per year. Knowing the community, we did not have this kind of money available. Some recommended that we contact the oil-rich countries. We tried, but the competition had gone ahead of us, promising returns of 20–50 percent rather than the more realistic numbers we, as responsible bankers and business people, projected with no guarantees. Of course, they put tens of millions into the companies that promised high returns but not into us. We decided to remain patient and never to compromise our standards and values.

Around the turn of the century, in 2000, demand for our services was so large that we could not meet it because of the lack of capital. One of our executives suggested that we close the company down because we could not meet the demand. My reaction was simple. I told him, with tears in my eyes, that all God asks from us is to do the best we can with what we have. In a few months we received an e-mail from a person who used to work with Freddie Mac — Mr. Ahmad Elshal. He told us that he had visited our Web site and that he liked it. He called to inquire about the details of what we do at LARIBA. He asked one of the Freddie Mac executives at that time, Mr. Saber Salam, to contact us. The rest is history. As stated earlier, LARIBA received early approval from Freddie Mac, and we were elated. New problems erupted but they were much sweeter. Now, our problem was how to organize ourselves to serve the growing demand.

Freddie Mac and Fannie Mae were originally organized as government-sponsored public companies (GSEs, which stands for government-sponsored entities) by the U.S government to provide necessary liquidity to the housing market in the United States. To accomplish this goal, Fannie Mae and Freddie Mac provide the liquidity to the institutions that finance homes (called mortgage companies) and banks, by authorizing the companies to act on their behalf to finance homes according to universally set but strict guidelines, and proceed to exchange the note for cash. The GSEs assemble the notes in the form of asset-based fixed income securities (bond-like) called mortgage-backed securities, or MBSs. The GSEs offer these securities for investment to institutions looking for high-quality asset-based bond-like investments that yield a higher interest rate. This way, the GSE generates cash to reinvest in mortgages.

In April 2001, LARIBA was the first ever RF finance operation in the West to be approved for investing Freddie Mac's money using the LARIBA Shari'aa-based RF home finance model. In 2002, LARIBA became the only U.S.-based Shari'aa-based RF finance company to be approved by the largest mortgage investor in the world, Fannie Mae. Later, LARIBA became the only RF finance company that issues—with Fannie Mae—RF MBSs.

It is also important to state for the record that LARIBA—and, for that matter, any RF finance company or bank—is not allowed by Shari'aa to borrow money with interest from Freddie Mac, Fannie Mae, and/or other investors. Freddie Mac and Fannie Mae are looked upon as investors in the RF LARIBA Shari'aa-based mortgages. In fact, we evaluate the financing of each home as an investment and we offer it to Freddie or Fannie online as investors in the LARIBA-financed homes. If approved, they indicate to us the expected return they need to realize as investors. This is the rate we use to measure the economic prudence of the investment (using the rate of return on investment based on the actual market rent, as explained earlier). If approved, LARIBA forwards the money from its own funds to purchase the house and is paid back within a week or less by Freddie Mac or Fannie Mae. Freddie Mac and Fannie Mae were the real major source of capital for all "Islamic" finance companies in the United States. We were fortunate at

LARIBA to have acquired a national bank—the Bank of Whittier, NA—which accumulated the deposits needed for financing.

Another important aspect of dealing with Freddie and Fannie has been the documentation used in the RF financing process. Such documents must follow the same standards called for by the industry and regulations. Our LARIBA Shari'aa-based RF finance model paid us a wonderful dividend, because we did not have to receive a special exception from the GSEs or regulators to be approved. The risk of receiving an approval with an exception is that this exception can be taken away when times are not suitable. While others went through expensive legal maneuvers to make the documents look "Islamic," then diluted the Islamic content to bring it back to the standard codes, we at LARIBA started on the right and straightforward track. It is important to note here that the LARIBA Agreement described earlier is a required part of the documentation called for by the GSEs. Many of the "Islamic" MBS companies, which are based on Shari'aa-compliant models, were designed for sale to the "Islamic" banks in the Gulf and Malaysia. In contrast, the LARIBA RF MBSs were designed to be offered for investors and all entities in all markets, and are of the highest quality. These MBSs are "manufactured" by us at LARIBA. That is why they are not a mere "black box," like other MBSs, because we simply know the components of each of the LARIBA RF MBSs.

Other sources of capital are the share capital of the company and investments from accredited and qualified high net worth and sophisticated investors. It is important to note here that not a single investor or shareholder has lost a penny since we started our operations at LARIBA in 1987. In addition, we consistently distributed dividends and profits that were at least one to two percent higher than what any riba-based institution would offer on a time certificate of deposit.

Advantages of the LARIBA RF Shari'aa-Based Model and Procedures

1. Applies the fundamentals of the RF Law (Shari'aa) of the Judeo-Christian-Islamic system. It does not use ruses (*heelah*) nor financial engineering and structuring techniques that are usually used in the Shari'aa-compliant models.
2. The LARIBA Agreement clearly spells out the bases from Shari'aa upon which the relationship, the process of financing, and the process of calculating the monthly payments are built.
3. It is universal and designed to benefit all people of all faith.
4. It is not based on renting money at a price called interest rate. It is based on the actual market-measured rent of the items to be acquired as measured—live—in the marketplace by the customer and the finance

company/bank. It helps the customer make the decision to buy a property—or not to buy it, and instead rent until it becomes more economically sound to buy it.

5. It normalizes the monetary problem of paper (fiat) money by marking the property to the market, as called for by the mark-to-market rule, and by relying on pricing the property in terms of a reference commodity, as called for by the commodity indexation rule. Using this approach helps us to identify economic bubbles before they fester and become speculative bubbles. In this way, we avoid participating in such a bubble. We detected the real estate bubble in many states in the United States as early as 2005 and 2006. This raised a red flag that stressed to our underwriters the necessity of exercising diligent caution when evaluating the "investment" based on the mark-to-market rule and the commodity indexation rule.

6. It benefits the customer and the financing entity, because its method is based on investing in a property or a business and not on renting money. It reveals the economic value of the purchased property which insures prudence in investing and protects against participation in an economic bubble.

7. It relies on arbitration using experts who are well versed in Shari'aa that are chosen by each side.

8. It uses the standard financing documents and notes. This makes it fulfill the U.S. banking regulations, meets the requirements of bank examiners, and makes it seamless in case other government requirements are implemented. This also helps the consumer and the financing entity settle any dispute before U.S. courts without confusion or misinterpretation that may cost a lot of time, money, and frustration. Using the standard finance document and notes allows the customer to declare its finances in an understandable and U.S. government–compliant way that benefits the customer in preparing and reporting their taxes and in reporting and complying with government agencies like the Labor Department, pensions, and/or retirement plans.

9. It records the title of the property in the name of the customer directly. The model does not call for the title to be recorded in both the customer and the company's name, as is required in some Shari'aa-compliant schemes. Doing it this way may expose the customer to the unknown liabilities and unknown corporate future of the financing entity/bank, and it limits the freedom of choice of the customer.

10. It services the financing facility (servicing means billing, collection of monthly payments, escrowing of insurance and tax payments, and resolving any problems) and it does not sell servicing to an outside servicing company. The Shari'aa-based model requires that the RF finance

entity/bank keep the servicing in house, with the work done by community members. This practice helps the customers if a problem occurs,
especially in cases when the customer loses his/her job or is temporarily
disabled. The concept of mercifulness (*tarahum*) is applied. The customer is turned over to a nonprofit assistance organization to help meet
the needs of the family until the problem is resolved.

THE RESULTS

The most important feature of the Shari'aa-based RF finance discipline and
principles is that the investment decision is based on the actual market rates
of rent of the property or the business, as measured by both the customer
and the finance officer. The process does not take the rental rate of
money—riba—and calculates the monthly payment. Because the process of
buying a home, a car, a business, or a service is looked upon as an investment that must be prudent, not just as a buying exercise that obtains money
by incurring debt at an interest rate. In this regard, the RF finance company/
bank considers itself as an implicit co-investor in the activity as implied by
the application of the lien.

That is why investing according to the Shari'aa-based LARIBA RF finance model has had superior results compared with the results experienced
by conventional riba-based banks and other "Islamic" finance organizations that use the Shari'aa-compliant model. This success is because the RF
banks rely on evaluating the prudence of the investment. It is clear that due
to using the LARIBA Shari'aa-based RF finance model, delinquencies are
essentially nonexistent—almost 1 in a 1000—compared to a delinquency
rate as high as 10 percent—100 in a 1000—in some cases, as experienced
by riba-based banks and financial institutions.

One day, after the revelations of the economic meltdown of 2008 and
the subprime mortgage debacle, we received a call from the assistant editor
of a major U.S. news magazine.[20] She had been following our progress since
her first interview with LARIBA in 2002. She asked about our portfolio performance and how we were doing in the difficult market conditions. We
told her that we are doing very well, and we shared with her the fact that
LARIBA mortgage portfolio delinquencies are a small fraction of the national average.

Fannie Mae representatives were impressed by the performance of the
home mortgage portfolio underwritten using the RF LARIBA Shari'aa-
based model and process. Fannie Mae analysts explained to us that our
portfolio is among the top ten performing portfolios in the Western region
of the United States. We told them that the reason for our success is our

disciplined approach of marking every home we attempt to finance to the market. If the investment does not make economic sense based on the actual market-measured rental rate of a similar home in the same neighborhood, then we do not proceed with the financing, as explained earlier. It is also interesting to note that a United Guaranty insurance company representative came to visit us, asking how we at LARIBA could increase the size of our portfolio that is insured with them, because our portfolio—based on their analysis—is one of the best-performing portfolios among the top 64 U.S. companies and banks they underwrite for private mortgage insurance (PMI, the insurance required by industry standards if the down payment of the customer is less than 20 percent of the appraised value, as called for by standards and underwriting requirements). In addition, Bank of Whittier, which uses the LARIBA Shari'aa-based RF financing model, was rated a five-star bank (the highest rating by Bauer Financial; www.Bauerfinancial. com) because of its performance at a time when major banks were failing due to the 2008 economic meltdown.

NOTES

1. The Prophet pronounced in the Hadeeth: All deeds are dependent on the intentions (Niyat) and each will realize his/her real intention.
2. A well-known rule in Shari'aa (*mala yudraku Kulluhu la yutraku Julluhu*, in Arabic).
3. Yahia K. Abdul Rahman and Abdullah S. Tug, Towards a LARIBA (Islamic) Mortgage Financing in the United States – Providing an Alternative to Traditional Mortgages, Paper presented at The Islamic Finance Program, Harvard University School of Law, October 9 and 10, 1998; and Yahia Abdul Rahman, Mike Abdelaaty, and Gary S. Findley, The Challenge of Offering a LARIBA Financial Services Window in an American Bank, A Research paper presented at the Harvard Islamic Banking Symposium, Harvard University, October 1, 1999.
4. Tarek Diwany, *The Problem with Interest*, Kreatoc Ltd., London 2003. This is the most useful and educational book on the problem of charging interest and paper (fiat) money. The book has published two editions and was translated into Turkish, Bhasa Malaysian, and Arabic. Dewany is a thought-provoking researcher and a prolific author who disagrees with the approach that uses form over substance in Islamic banking.
5. Tarek Diwany's Web site is www.Islamic-Finance.com.
6. Ahmad Kamal Mydin Meera, *The Islamic Gold Dinar*, Pelanduk Publications, Malaysia, 2002.
7. For example: Fatwa of Al Baraka, available at www.lariba.com/fatwas/index. htm.

8. For example: M. Nejatullah Siddiqi, *Muslim Economic Thinking*, Islamic Foundation, Leicester, England, 1981. Professor Siddiqi was responsible for this highly praised work, which included for the first time some 700 references of works in English, Arabic, and Urdu in the field of Islamic Economics. He is a prolific author and was a LARIBA Fellow in Islamic Banking and Finance at UCLA, California.

9. Philip T.N. Koh, *Islamic Financial Instruments: The Civil Law and the Sharia Confluence or Conflict?*, presented at the 5th Islamic Finance Conference, Monash University, Kuala Lumpur.

10. Mahmoud Elgamal, *Islamic Finance—Law, Economics, and Practice*, Cambridge University Press, Cambridge, England. Professor Mahmoud Amin Elgamal holds the first ever Islamic Economics Chair at Rice University. He is a gifted researcher in economics, mathematics, game theory, and Islamic law, economics, and practice. He authored a pioneering book in the field. His bitter frustrations about the practices of scholars have landed him a lot of resistance and, in many cases, isolation by many conference organizers. In fact, some scholars refuse to appear in the same conference programs in which his name appears. He coined an interesting term, "Shari'aa arbitrage," by which he means the added premium charged in Islamic banking and accepted by some banks and customers that create an arbitrage between the Islamic banking techniques and the conventional banking methods. His thesis has been that the methods used in Islamic banking sanctioned by many Shari'aa scholars focus on form and lack the real spirit and substance of the original Shari'aa sources, and that these methods are inefficient and costly while in fact they are the same as conventional banking.

11. *USA Today*, Web site posted 2/24/05 and updated 02/25/2005: www.usatoday.com/money/perfi/general/2005-02-24-islamic-finance-usat_x.htm.

12. OCC, Interpretive Letters #806 (1997) and #867 (1999). Please visit www.OCC.treas.gov. These letters were written regarding the United Bank of Kuwait's Al Manzil Program: The OCC has issued two opinion letters, one on Murabaha and the other on Ijara home financing by the United Bank of Kuwait (UBK), which has since been merged into what is now Shamel Bank in Bahrain; the federal branch was closed in the early 2000s, only two years after it started offering these contracts.

13. Ibid.

14. Bernard Lawrence "Bernie" Madoff (born April 29, 1938) is an American businessman, and former chairman of the NASDAQ stock exchange. He founded the Wall Street firm Bernard L. Madoff Investment Securities LLC in 1960 and was its chairman until December 11, 2008, when he was charged with perpetrating what may be the largest investor fraud ever committed by a single person. Prosecutors have accused financier Madoff—the alleged mastermind of a $65 billion Ponzi scheme—of intending to transfer up to $100 million worth of assets to protect them from seizure, and they want him locked up immediately. Madoff was sentenced in June to 150 years in prison after admitting the fraud – the largest in history.

15. I had the good fortune of moderating a session on Shari'aa that was attended by some of the superstar scholars. As customary, I asked them to give me their CVs. I am sorry to state that they did not have enough formal education in Shari'aa to qualify them to assume that role. I am sorry but I cannot name them in respect for their privacy.

16. This occurred when I was in charge of the Muslim Students Association (MSA of the USA & Canada, now called Islamic Society of North America, ISNA) near Madison, Wisconsin, in 1969.

17. Henry Campbell Black, MA, *Black's Law Dictionary*, 6th edition, West Publishing Co., St. Paul, Minnesota, 1990, p. 1128.

18. Ibid., p. 922.

19. Black's Law Dictionary editor: Bryan A. Garner.

20. Ms. Temma Ehrenfeld, Newsweek, private communication 4/16/2008.

CHAPTER 11

Starting an RF Bank in the United States

Acquiring and Restructuring a Troubled Bank and Operating It Riba-Free

INTRODUCTION

This chapter covers the efforts we went through to acquire and operate a full service bank in the United States. This chapter is a must for anyone who may be interested in buying and operating a bank in America. It is also a useful step-wise discussion that should benefit those who want to re-structure a troubled bank and bring it to a healthy and a profitable condition. Finally, this chapter is important for those who are interested in operating a riba-based bank in America and the West in a riba-free (RF) format without having to go through the lengthy and expensive process of trying to obtain exceptions from the regulators. As was stated earlier in the book, RF banking is not about changing words and using circumventive techniques to make the contracts "compliant" with the Law (Shari'aa). RF banking is a new brand of banking that applies the spirit and substance of Judeo-Christian-Islamic values. It is about the use of principles that would save the consumer and the businesses from participating in an economic bubble like that of 2008.

One of the options we considered in 1987 when LARIBA was started was to organize it in the form of a depository institution (meaning a bank). We reasoned that this option would offer us the ability to take deposits and to offer insurance on deposits through the Federal Deposit Insurance Corporation (FDIC). However, we knew nothing about the business of starting a bank in the United States. We were told by many of our friends that the process of starting or buying an existing bank is called change of control of that bank. Acquiring an existing back is an expensive, involved, and lengthy process. In addition, it requires the organizers to be well-known to the banking regulators and the founding shareholders to have sufficient capital. As detailed earlier, we did not satisfy many of these prerequisites:

- We did not have a lot of capital.
- We did not have a lot of money to spend on pre-organization and pre-operating expenses, such as legal, organizational, administration, and application fees and expenses.
- We were not known to the regulators; we were offering a new brand of banking which at the time was foreign to all people. For that matter, the RF banking and finance system was not only foreign to the banking regulators but also to Muslims and non-Muslims in general.

We simply did not know where to start.

That was why we started by licensing LARIBA as a finance company regulated by the State of California Department of Corporations.

After operating for almost three years and interacting with customers and users of our services, many of our customers and community members indicated that they would love to transfer their bank deposits to us, but they could not, because deposits at LARIBA are not insured as in banks by the FDIC. We told them that we, at LARIBA, could not accept deposits anyway, because LARIBA is not a U.S. government-chartered depository institution; it would be illegal for us to accept deposits. However, this thought planted the seed of the idea of owning a full-service bank in the United States that would serve the community in an RF mode. The dream we had was to start or buy a bank that would eventually be operated according to Shari'aa while upholding the laws of the land.

Our strategic vision was to design this bank to serve people of all faiths, and not Muslims only. That is why, later on, when we developed the bank, its advertisement, its business development campaigns, the Internet site, and the presentations we gave were all designed for all people of all faiths. In our focus groups, people in the community were asked a simple question: "Would you prefer to go to a small crowded Asian or Middle Eastern store? Or to go to a large, clean, well-stocked and -organized supermarket that offers international foods?" The answer has always been the supermarket.

Another important strategic decision made was how to present our services. Many others that came to the market focused only on the Muslim community. We decided to focus on the United States first, and hopefully the world. Calling something Islamic does not necessarily make it so. It is the way one conducts business, deals with people, and conducts his or her life that defines who that person and that institution is. Calling a model of financing by a "foreign" name does not make it Islamic; what makes it Judeo-Christian-Islamic is the substance and spirit by which it offers unique and measured advantages over other conventional banking models. In summary, we made sure that we do not "wear our religion on our sleeves."

BENEFITS OF OFFERING AN RF BANKING ALTERNATIVE IN AMERICA

1. It applies the strict conventional U.S. banking regulatory and supervisory environment and practices enjoyed by U.S. banks to RF banking practices, products, and services. This adds more credibility to the RF banking approach and will make its product more reliable and acceptable in the market.

2. It creates a larger pool of bankers of all faiths, training, and experience who are well-versed in both conventional riba banking and RF banking. This will bring a large pool of banking experience, expertise, and creative abilities to manufacture new products and services for the RF banking industry. It will also provide the emerging RF banking industry with RF bankers who can show the real difference by the mode of service they offer and be able to explain it well. This will help us achieve our long-term objective of creating the foundation for a new banking service, RF banking, that is offered nationwide.

3. It offers consumers the choice between conventional riba-based banking services and RF banking products and services. The consumer will enjoy the ability to choose from a wide variety of banking, financing, and saving products and services.

4. It encourages the members of the faith-based communities that believe in a riba-free lifestyle, including the American Muslim community, to participate fully in the U.S. economic system, integrate with it, and become important contributors to American life without violating their religious beliefs. This will have a great social impact on the growing American Muslim community and faith-based communities at large, and will encourage savings and entrepreneurship.

5. It creates an atmosphere of healthy competition between the riba-based conventional banking products and services and the RF banking products and services. This competition should be beneficial to the consumer.

RIBA-BASED CONVENTIONAL FINANCING VERSUS RF FINANCING

To contrast the approach taken in a riba-based conventional financing with RF financing, let us consider a case study.

A family wants to buy a car for $30,000. They only have $6,000 of the purchase price. They approach a bank to help them finance the car. The following is a comparison between how the process would likely go in a riba-based banking setting as compared to RF banking setting.

Riba-based conventional banker:

1. Evaluates the application form.
2. Concludes that the family derives a good income and that they have a good balance sheet, and a good credit history. Also, the banker finds that the family's cash flow could help them pay for a larger car or even to take a bigger loan without putting the $6,000 down. The reason is that the banker is interested in "selling" a larger loan to increase the profitability of the bank.
3. Decides to lend the family (i.e., rent them) money at a certain rate [interest rate] over a period of time. In fact, the banker may encourage the family—especially if they have a good credit history—to stretch the repayment period for a longer time. The repayment period defined by the banker can even be longer than necessary, because (the banker says) he or she wants to help improve the family's surplus cash flow. In fact, it also helps the bank derive more interest income from a good, qualified family as the loan repayment is extended.
4. The riba-based conventional banker may convince the family to buy a bigger and more equipped car. This is because the larger loan amount will only represent a small addition to the monthly payment, and it will be taken care of by prolonging the financing period (term of the loan).

RF (riba-free) banker:

1. Evaluates the application form.
2. Concludes that the family derives a good income and that they have a good balance sheet, good credit history, and good tax returns. Also, the banker finds that the family cash flow is enough to cover the monthly payment for the car purchase.
3. Calls around to ask car leasing agencies—such as Hertz and Enterprise, as well as manufacturers' leasing agencies, such as the Toyota, Ford, and GM fleet leasing divisions—about the utility value of the car measured by the lease rate charged in the market.

4. Draws up an agreement with the family that complies with the RF finance legal requirements.

In this agreement, the family acts as the agent of the RF bank to buy the car. The transaction is structured such that the family would own 6,000/30,000, or 20 percent, of the car, and the RF bank would (temporarily) own 80 percent of the car. The family agrees to buy the bank's share of the car for the same value, or $(30,000−6,000=) $24,000. This way, the bank does not own the asset (as based on Shari'aa) and is in compliance with the U.S. banking rules and regulations. The family, based on their cash flow, agrees to pay back the bank's share, interest-free over a period of (for example) three years, or $8,000 per year. This is called the *Return on Capital (RonC)*. In lieu of the promise to pay back *RonC*, the family gives the RF bank a lien on the car. In lieu of the joint ownership of the right (perfected by the lien) to use the property, the family and the RF bank divide the income from the lease among themselves in the (changing) proportion of unpaid capital.

The family and the RF banker independently survey the market to find a fair leasing rate for a similar car in the same market. They negotiate a fair lease and agree to it. Here, the lease is divided between the family (20 percent in the beginning, rising to 100 percent over three years) and the bank (80 percent in the beginning and declining to 0 percent over a three-year term). This is called the *Return on Capital (RonC)* for the RF bank. The proprietary computer program developed by LARIBA is mechanically not much different from a regular amortization schedule. The difference is that the variable in the LARIBA program is the car lease rate defined by the market, while the riba-based amortization schedule uses interest rate—the rental rate of money—as an input parameter. In other words: In the riba-based conventional banking model, the unknown is the monthly payment. In the RF banking service, the monthly payment is calculated based on the lease rate using the declining equity model, and the unknown is the rate of return on investment.

The family and the RF banker, in order to satisfy the laws of the land, sign a promissory note that documents the repayment of the debt (*dayn*—no time value of money) and the declining lease rate in a total monthly payment. To comply with the laws of the land, the RF banker plugs in the monthly market measured and agreed-upon rent of the facility representing the lease rate, the purchase price, the down payment, and the number of years to pay back into the LARIBA proprietary computer program. The program calculates the rate of return on investment, which is called in the RF system "implied" interest rate. This rate is disclosed to the client to comply with the "truth-in-lending" Regulation Z.

Please note that the resulting "implied" interest rate is not uniformly the same. It differs from one car to another, based on the leasing rate the same car would bring in the relevant market. If the rate of return on investment is higher than the rate of return expected by the investors, the RF banker encourages the family to buy the car and would unilaterally reduce the monthly rental rate obtained from the market so that the monthly payment would compete with that offered by riba-based conventional banks. If the rate of return on investment was calculated to be much lower than that expected by investors, the RF banker would inform the family that buying this car is not a good investment, and the financing would be declined.

In the RF banking environment, the RF banker encourages the family to pay their car off as quickly as possible in order to reduce the burden of debt on the family's cash flow and free more money to save for the future.

LOOKING FOR A SUITABLE BANK TO ACQUIRE

In 1989, we started searching for banks available for sale. We stumbled into a report called the *Findley Report*,[1] which is published by a prominent banking law firm in Southern California. The firm was started by a leading California attorney who specialized in helping communities obtain charters for community banks. The *Findley Report* is an amazing source of banks' financial information and great reading material for me. We all pored over it and studied the financials and profitability of many banks.

In 1989, after feeling more comfortable that the concept of RF financing works and that there was demand for RF financing—and knowing that we were really hurting for more capital—we began to consider buying a small bank. We called for a meeting with Mr. Findley, Sr. He invited us to his rather humble office in the city of Yorba Linda (in Orange County, California) and sat us down. After the niceties of introducing ourselves and briefing each other on what we do, he looked us in the eyes and shocked us by saying, "There are three reasons that I know why someone would like to own a bank: The first is that he/she is stupid, the second is that he/she wants to put hands in the 'cookie jar' and taste from it—" (by this, he meant using the bank money for personal benefit) "—and the third is that they are genuinely interested in serving people in the community without expecting any rewards or recognition." I was quiet for a few seconds and came back directly by saying that we belonged to the third group. We told him that our passion was to build a bank that will serve the community. He apparently believed us, and introduced us to his son, who was also an attorney in the same field—the honorable Gary Steven Findley, Esq. who runs the firm today. We became good friends and developed mutual trust and rapport.

Throughout my life, I can attest to the fact that when God wanted to help me achieve a goal, He would create an event that made a change in the scene or brought a certain person in my life to help me do so. When I started thinking of LARIBA, God created the reasons for me to meet the distinguished pioneer; Sheikh Saleh Abdullah Kamel, the founder of Dallah Al Baraka Group in Saudi Arabia. This man was then (when I met him in 1987)—and still is until today—one of the most influential, visionary, and busy Islamic bankers in the world, and one of the most difficult people to get an appointment with. He happened to be visiting Los Angeles in mid-1987 and attended a congregational prayer, which I was leading as an imam. He liked my ceremony, approached me after I finished, and he said that he wanted to know me. He introduced himself. I had no idea who he was and what he did. He politely asked that we meet. I agreed—as I always do with people who approach me. Later, I asked about him and the person who briefed me did not believe that this influential Islamic banker had asked me for an appointment. We became very close family friends. Our mutual respect and appreciation for each other continues today. I learned a lot about the concepts of Islamic banking and finance from him and from the many distinguished and highly accomplished and qualified scholars he was able to assemble from most of the Muslim world to get RF financing off to a good start in the Gulf, Europe, and the United States. As if God wanted to add to that gift to help us in our efforts to realize the vision of popularizing RF banking in America, God created the reasons for me to meet the father and son banking attorney team of Mr. Gerald Findley, Esq. and his son Mr. Gary Steven Findley, Esq.

When we started looking to buy a bank in America, we considered offering an RF finance window into a regular riba-based conventional bank. This idea was extremely controversial when it was first implemented in Malaysia. The issue of major concern was how one could justify, from the point of view of Shari'aa, owning a financial institution that dealt with the forbidden riba while at the same time claiming to be active in offering an RF banking window. In fact, many of the puritans and strict Muslims believe that this is a clear case of hypocrisy that should never be allowed. This problem has been investigated at length by a number of jurists and scholars. It was first investigated in Malaysia and then in the Middle East.[2] However, after many conversations and "spot" opinion checks with leaders in the community, we decided to abandon the idea of opening an RF banking window in a riba-based bank. The problem of dealing with riba-based (conventional) and RF financing models in the same institution troubled many of the Muslim scholars of Shari'aa and many members of the American Muslim community.

The U.S. banking system has emerged from a community-based banking network to become the most sophisticated banking system in the world.[3] The system offers products and services that meet the traditional needs of the community. At the same time it is active in many other services, such as in developing new products that are technology based or focused on expanding the type and quality of financial services and products. While the U.S. banking system is primarily based upon tradition, to a certain extent this banking system has only recently recognized the financial and banking traditions of a significant segment of the American population—the American Muslim community. The faith-based communities of all faiths have been endowed with a reservoir of highly qualified professionals, entrepreneurs, business executives, successful scholars, and distinguished students. Most of the community members are compelled to violate one of the most basic requirements of their faith: dealing with interest, or riba/ribit. The Community Reinvestment Act (CRA), which played an important part in the American banking system in the 20th century, was originally introduced to allow community banks to gather community savings and reinvest these savings into the community and not outside it. CRA has helped many communities develop their housing, consumer, and business needs and has also helped in creating job opportunities for the members of the community.

MAKING HISTORY: ACQUIRING THE BANK OF WHITTIER, N.A.

To look for a bank, we sat down to list the characteristics of the bank we wanted to acquire in order to offer in it RF banking and finance services. The following is the list we came up with:

1. *Capital* required to buy the bank should not exceed $1.5 to 3.0 million.
2. *Loan portfolio* should be very small so that it could be reviewed thoroughly by our team on a loan-by-loan basis.
3. *Type of charter* we preferred was a National Association (N.A.) Charter, which would enable us to serve other states in addition to California.
4. *Bank location* should be somewhere in the center between Los Angeles County and Orange County (in California).

It took us almost eight years to locate the Bank of Whittier as our target bank for purchase. During this long time, we would identify a bank, and then Gary Findley and our group would go to visit its president, to get a feel for the bank management's reaction to the idea of its being acquired, and to take a closer look at the bank. Upon our return, we would assemble a team to evaluate our impression from the first meeting and to make a decision as to whether we should proceed. We looked at six banks in the period between 1990 to 1997.

At the end of 1996, we took another look at a bank we had considered earlier. The Bank of Whittier, NA was chartered in December 1982 and was owned by a holding company structure called the Greater Pacific Bancshares (the letters NA stand for National Association, which means that the bank is chartered by the U. S. Treasury Department's OCC—the Office of the Comptroller of the Currency).

In March 1997, Gary Findley and I went to meet the chairman of the Bank of Whittier at that time, Mr. N. Ghannam (87 years old at that time), who was a first-generation American of Lebanese descent. His father had immigrated to the United States after World War I. Mr. Ghannam was in the printing business. He told us that he owned a few shares of the bank, but the share price kept going down because the bank was not run well and the shareholders wanted out. He went on buying more and more shares in the bank. He had assembled a small board of directors to help him run the bank. As a result, at the time we met him, Mr. Ghannam owned about 55 percent of the shares. We had a number of meetings with him, and agreed that he would sell the bank. What he did not understand clearly was the meaning of the word "sell." He thought that he would be selling his 55 percent share. We advised him that there are many rules and restrictions regarding his other shareholders, and that fiduciary responsibility required that he sell his other shareholders' shares before his. He impulsively said that meant all the bank's shares must be sold. We (some of the shareholders of LARIBA) agreed to buy the shares, and ended up owning almost 93 percent of the shares of the holding company.

The Bank of Whittier offered us the best opportunity to meet the strategic parameters we set for ourselves.

1. It was (and is) a national bank.
2. The bank was wholly owned by a holding company; Greater Pacific Bancshares. The holding company was (theoretically) traded on the stock market. Of course, at that time, it was traded as a *pink sheet* item. But, we reasoned, as we improved it, increased its capital, increased the number of shareholders, assigned it to a good market maker, and started introducing it to the investment banking community, it would be a good publicly traded stock in which to invest.
3. Its assets amounted to approximately $29 million. In fact, it was one of the last few small, independent banks left in southern California that had not been acquired or merged.

4. Its capital was approximately $2.3 million.
5. Its loan portfolio had been cleaned regularly during the bank and savings and loan crisis of the 1980s and early 1990s. In fact, the bank had stood the test of the 1980s banking crisis and was still in operation.
6. It is located in a city in the center between Los Angeles County and Orange County, which makes it accessible to many community members.
7. The bank's senior staff was essentially out because of their bad performance, but not all were replaced. This situation helped us to participate in the selection of the new management (while waiting for federal approval for change of bank control).

The Bank of Whittier had been in business since December 1982. It offered a unique service environment, with "sit-down" teller stations, and a location on Whittier Boulevard, a major commercial street, in the same complex with the Whittier Community Hospital and at least two medical doctors' professional buildings.

In December 1997, we signed an agreement with the Board of Directors of Greater Pacific Bancshares and Bank of Whittier to purchase up to 100% of the shares of Greater Pacific Bancshares. The Bank was operating under a Memorandum of Understanding (MOU) from the regulators. The MOU required that the management and board of directors improve the board of directors committees and supervision, hire necessary senior staff, increase capital, and not distribute dividends or acquire new companies/banks until approved by the authorities. After reviewing the OCC's most recent bank examination results, we concluded that it was good to note that the examiners were now increasingly positive about the bank because of its new management and the new loan cleanup and classification system installed by the new management. In addition, the feeling was that the MOU might be removed very shortly. The total of adversely classified items, as a percent of the total assets, was 6.6 percent. Out of that, total past-due and non-accrual loans and leases were 5.8 percent of the total gross loans and leases. *ALLL*, allowances for loan and lease losses, were adequate and the analysis used was reasonable. The ALLL totaled approximately $796,000 in mid-1997 and was 4.6 percent of the total loans.

In general, the new management continued its efforts to improve credit quality, credit administration, and risk management. Based on the public information and the audited financial statement of the bank and bank holding company, we came up with the following:

■ *Capital ratios:* Tangible equity capital as a percent of total assets was estimated at 7.8 percent, indicating that the bank passed the capitalization test and was considered well capitalized. However, more capital would be needed to strengthen the bank earnings by deploying new loans into the assets. It was recommended that at least $1 million in fresh capital be injected immediately after takeover. However, a $3 million capital increase (total capital of approx. $5.3 million) would greatly improve the bank's earnings.

- *Earnings analysis:* Net income (after tax) was expected to be 0.64 percent of total average assets. ROAA (Return on Average Assets) was lower than it had been in 1996 (0.86 percent) due to the aggressive loan write-off by the management (in coordination with us while waiting for the approvals). Earnings analysis indicated that the bank had a strong *net interest margin* (NIM). But this NIM continued to be offset by weak assets quality and high overheads. The NIM was 6.95 percent, which compared favorably to peer banks. However, loan losses and deterioration in the Small Business Administration (SBA) and Business Manager (factoring) portfolios resulted in ALLL provisions of at least $380,000 by the end of 1997. Despite this, the bank was expected to be able to earn at least $165,000 in 1997. Overhead expenses, particularly consulting fees, had been very high historically. However, they declined 18 percent in the first 6 months of 1997 compared to the first 6 months of 1996, and were expected to decline further under the new management. Many unnecessary overhead expenses were curtailed or were on their way out; the SBA loans had been brought to a halt, and the Business Manager (factoring) had been canceled and the loan officer in charge removed. It was expected that monthly profitability would improve as a result of management's decision to increase loan volume, primarily through carefully selected loans (we expected these to be RF loans.)
- *Liquidity:* Bank liquidity was satisfactory, and liquidity risk was low. Short-term investments were 24 percent of total assets and included approximately $4 million in Fed Funds sold and approximately $2.4 million in CDs. The loan-to-deposit ratio was 67 percent. This indicated the need for new high-quality loans added to the portfolio. We thought that this was an excellent entry point for our LARIBA portfolios in Pasadena. The fund management and investment strategy needed to improve upon the bank's operating results by establishing a good investment portfolio in which to invest the bank's liquid assets without sacrificing risk and liquidity, while earning the highest return possible.
- *Interest rate risk:* The bank's interest rate risk position was good. The bank's balance sheet was asset sensitive, with rate-sensitive assets (RSA) of $27.2 million, higher than its rate-sensitive liabilities (RSL) of

$17.8 million within a one-year period. The RSA/RSL gap was 1.72 at 60 days and 1.33 at 1 year. The goal was to keep it at 1 to 1.5. A sensitivity analysis showed that with a 100–basis point decline in interest rates, annualized net interest income exposure was $82,000.

We signed the preliminary agreement to be approved by the bank's board and shareholders. We obtained these approvals. We then set out to take a very close look at the details of the bank's operations, its assets, and in particular its loan portfolio. We evaluated the financial statements, the law suits (if any), the loan portfolio (loan by loan), and the operations of the bank. We discovered more about the MOU that the bank was operating under, and the details of the special restriction from the OCC as detailed in the MOU. One of the criticisms the OCC had was that the bank did not have a detailed set of operating policies; there were other criticisms about the bank's operations, its policies, and its profitability. Placing an MOU on a bank is not an action that can be undertaken lightly. The bank management is required to operate according to a plan approved by the OCC, and the bank management must go to the OCC for any decision. This slows down management operations and limits management flexibility, but it is the price that must be paid when a bank's management does not abide by the rules and regulations. This MOU was removed in the early 2000s after fulfilling the requirements of the OCC.

If the readers think that was the end and that we now owned a bank . . . please think again.

The next major and most demanding step was gaining the approval of the United States government's banking authorities for the buyers to assume control of the bank, a process called "change of control." In the case of the Bank of Whittier, government regulators were represented in three entities. These were:

1. *The Office of the Comptroller of the Currency*, because the OCC supervises National Banks. That is why we—as buyers of the shares who would become the control persons of the bank—had to file a full application with the OCC.
2. *The Federal Reserve Bank of San Francisco and the Federal Reserve Board (FRB)*, because the Bank of Whittier was owned by a Holding Financial Services company that was supervised by the FRB.
3. *The Federal Deposit Insurance Corporation* (FDIC), because the bank was a member of the FDIC system.

The application process took a long time. The application forms to change control of the bank required full background information and disclosures that might go back to the childhood of the applicants, their place of origin, their education, their financial details, their criminal records, and their business history, in detail. The application also called for a complete description of the reasons why the new control persons wanted to take control of the bank, how they would operate the bank, what their business plans were for the bank, and how they would serve and improve the bank's service to the community. The regulators also required that the new control group prepare a complete business plan for the bank's future budget and financial projections.

In an effort to reduce legal expenses and the pre-acquisition cost, our team first took the applications from Mr. Findley's office and then would spend very long nights completing them and preparing the plans and reports the application requested. In many cases, some of us were traveling out of the country and would operate via telephone and fax, because the Internet was not popular yet. We would send the completed forms and reports to Mr. Findley, who would edit them and pass them on to the regulators. The regulators would respond with more questions and inquiries for Mr. Findley, who would pass them on to us. We would again prepare the detailed answers to these questions. The word "detailed" here sometimes worked to our detriment because, as we learned from Mr. Findley's office, when we got a question from a government agency, that question had to be answered in a specific fashion, in full and clear details, and in a direct way, without opening new topics or subjects. Not abiding by these rules and course of action triggered more questions. The process took approximately one year of back-and-forth communications that culminated in a telephone meeting in January 1998 (during *Ramadan*) that was attended by:

- The OCC in California and in Washington, D.C.
- The Federal Reserve Bank in Washington, D.C. and the Federal Reserve Bank of San Francisco
- The FDIC in Washington, D.C.
- Mr. Gary Findley and his associate
- Our team

The government agents thanked us—the applicants—for ". . . your patience, perseverance, detailed answers, and your posture as humble professionals. . . ." We, in return, thanked them for their wonderful and refreshing due diligence. I wanted to lighten the atmosphere, so I told them that they now knew more about us than our parents and family ever had. This experience is shared here in great detail to reassure the reader of the quality of the U.S. banking system and the meticulous detail the system goes through to make sure that the regulations of the system are put in effect. What happened in 2008 and before was due to a group of irresponsible people who violated the law, violated the trust placed in them, and ended up hurting all of us.

We thought that this was the end of our challenges and that we now had a bank. The local community paper published the news, and we all were delighted. Frankly, we were expecting the whole community to rush to transfer their accounts to the bank. Well, that did not happen! We also thought that we could run the bank in the same fashion we ran LARIBA, for the benefit of the whole community. We did not know what we were getting ourselves into. The community banking fraternity, we discovered, is an interesting group to say the least. Please enter the new domain called community banking. Many of the community banks were run by veterans who prided themselves in front of others—visitors, customers, other bankers, and auditors—as to how many years of "banking" experience they had. You heard them bragging about their "40 years of banking experience." We ended up with a few of them. I developed an interesting sensitivity scale, in which I raised a big mental red flag whenever I heard that claim uttered. I once told one of them, who really did not have much to offer except that claim to fame, "Did you ever consider the possibility that you were making the same mistakes for 40 years but did not know about it?"

The reader may also find interesting a request made by one of the candidates for president of the bank. After stating his huge salary and benefits request, he asked for two SLX automobiles. Frankly, I did not know what he meant. I asked him why he needed two cars. He said that he wanted one for him and another for his wife. I obviously told him no! I then called my young daughter to ask her what an SLX car was. She said, "Dad, I thought you did not like expensive cars. An SLX is a Mercedes Benz that can cost $120,000." A story like this should give the reader an insight into the state of affair of a few bankers and how it changed compared to the community building and loan society banker we watched Jimmy Stewart portray in the movie *It's A Wonderful Life.*

We tried to work with at least two bank presidents to convince them of the responsibility to reinvest in the community, to care for people, to go out and mix with the community, and to serve people. It was very difficult. We were not treated nicely, because we were looked at as outsiders to the community banking fraternity and as people who did not have "enough" banking experience. We also discovered that any time we shared some of the successes we had experienced at LARIBA, they would directly come back to tell us that it is not doable, because the regulators would not approve. We would come back and show them that other successful banks in the business were doing the same.

Around the year 2000, a bank president sent to the OCC a letter claiming that I was interfering in the management of the bank, which was in complete violation of the banking regulations because I worked at the time for another investment bank—Citigroup/Smith Barney. I committed in writing to the OCC that I would not step foot in the bank again. In fact, from that time until I took early retirement from Citigroup and started managing the bank, I did not set foot in the bank—as I promised—until our management came to run the bank.

It is also interesting to share with the reader what happened to us when we arrived at the Bank of Whittier on July 10, 2003 to take over bank management. Most staff had resigned and we were left with two employees. The bank's total assets were approximately $26 million, and the bank had been losing money. We could not even find an insurance company that would agree to insure our executives and officers against any business mishaps. The bank was going from bad to worse. There were no written policies in any of the bank's operations, and the bank treasury and accounting systems were not well taken care of. There was no experienced operations manager, there were no manuals for the computer systems, the financial ledgers were not properly balanced by the person in charge, and customers had no respect for the new team. One day in our second week of running the bank, two contractors arrived at the bank to cash some checks, and we were very busy. One of them made a loud and noisy scene. I approached him politely to ask him to please lower his voice and to tell me what the problem was. He said, "In this country, American customers expect immediate service," and he proceeded to make some references to the fact that I am an immigrant. I smiled at him and asked him and his partner to step into my office. Then I closed the door and gave him a real piece of my mind. I told the man that I was proud to be a first-generation American—"but I want to assure you that in this great country, I started with nothing, I must have paid much more in taxes than he did, and that he should never demean or put people down again because of their accents or national origin". The man was shocked. His partner apologized and he followed. His partner is still the bank's customer to this day.

After arriving at the bank we decided to clean it up—to refurbish the bank facilities to give the feel of a private community bank with a "family living room" atmosphere. We also obtained board approval to improve the technology and systems so that we could have a fully automated banking operation that would be ready for the 21st century, in addition to a very user-friendly Web site (www.BankOfWhittier.com).

We started looking for associates who could help build up the bank. Another person who was also a gift from God was a young man I met by mere coincidence in one of the community centers. Mike Abdelaaty was a banker with Bank of America at the time, where he had spent seven years of his career. He then moved to Sanwa Bank (now Bank of the West) for ten years, and he spent three years in the one of the Gulf oil-producing countries. While in Los Angeles, I always solicited his support in the banking and finance work that we did at LARIBA. After his return to the US in 1999, he contacted me and decided to join LARIBA as its president.

Another interesting experience we went through was dealing with the audit firm that audited the finances of the bank. We noticed the sloppiness of the representatives who came to collect the bank's information and documents. We went through with the audit in the first year, but were not satisfied; many of us were not comfortable with the results. It was felt that the certified public accountant (CPA) who signed our financial statements did not do his due diligence and did not know the financial condition of the bank. I shared this information with Gary Findley and the board and they authorized a change. We commissioned another CPA firm that we were very happy with and we are using the firm even now.

We started with a very small staff. We had to spend long and hard hours to put together a full set of policies by which the bank would operate. In addition, we started to look for outside auditors who could come and audit—on behalf of the Board of Directors—bank operations, bank compliance with government regulations, the bank loan portfolio, and *Bank Secrecy Act* matters. We went through our first-ever OCC examination as a new team and we received wonderful results. From this humble beginning, we have come a long way. The Bank of Whittier, NA was rated a five-star bank by Bauer Financial during the 2008 financial meltdown.

OPERATING THE FIRST RF BANK IN THE UNITED STATES

As explained in Chapter 2, in today's banking lingo, one can conceptually define riba/ribit-based financing as renting money for financing, secured and unsecured (non-collateralized credits that are not asset or service based). In RF banking, a bank's financing activity is conceptually looked upon as an investment by the bank in the individual (or the company) in order to help that entity acquire tangible and productive assets and/or services. In his capacity as an investor of the bank's money—which is the community's money—the RF bank credit officer makes sure that the financing facility is used for a specific purpose and that the investment is prudent and makes economic merit.

The time has come to publicize and popularize the new *RF banking* brand as a complementary community banking and financing service, to allow the community to make a choice. The free market system will be the judge of the real value of this RF finance and banking system to the average consumer in the United States.

Our Strategic Approach to Restructure the Bank of Whittier

On July 10, 2003, our team of three associates arrived at the Bank of Whittier to take over the management of the bank. We found that the bank was in a very sorry state of affairs. In addition, the OCC requested that we submit to them within a few weeks a detailed plan that documented how the new team would change the fortunes of the bank.

The Bank Restructuring and Workout Plan: Turning the Bank Around

To begin, the management team developed a number of goals that had to be achieved in order to turn the bank around and start operating it as an RF bank. The following is a list of these goals:

1. Rectify any regulatory concerns as soon as possible.
2. Increase the bank's capital.
3. Stress quality in services, and use a new slogan that identified our character as an RF bank: *We Do Not Rent Money—We Invest in Our Customers.*
4. Control bank expenses in a tight, micro, detailed way. For example, we used both sides of the copier paper and recycled paper in the copying machine to save on paper.
5. Hire highly educated and qualified staff.
6. Use the best banking and service technologies available.
7. Improve bank facilities to give a feel of a private bank and a living room ambience in order to attract new clients who would feel like members of our new and expanding bank family.
8. Achieve reasonable and competitive profitability, compared to bank peer group.
9. Increase loan (credit) portfolio to 70–75 percent of total deposits, and then increase deposits and loans in a parallel mode.
10. Improve quality of and expand the bank's loan portfolio using RF financing values and discipline.

11. Do not allow speculation lending.
12. Do not do business with intoxicant sellers, bars, check cashing, pawn shops, gambling casinos, or individuals deriving their income from socially irresponsible sources and activities.
13. Popularize the RF concepts that require that we do not "sell" or "buy" loans. We invest with the customer, and we do not sell our relationships. We service all the financing that we originate.
14. Be fair to all.
15. Be active in serving the community.
16. Offer new RF products and services to attract new deposits and customers.
17. Offer a Bank of Whittier Credit Card Service through a bank that specializes in credit card services, because the bank does not have the staff available to administer credit card services, and it cannot compete with the mega-bank issuers of credit cards. These conditions drastically reduce the credit risk exposure to the bank, while offering an important facility to our customers without the bank getting involved in any prohibited interest charging. The card is a Visa network card that offers credit, but the bank advises the customers to pay within a month to avoid paying riba (interest). This advice is posted in red letters on the front page of the bank's Web site. We may be one of the few banks that strongly encourages its customers *not* to use credit cards as a means of borrowing. The other card is a regular Visa-linked *automatic teller machine* debit (ATM) card that only dispenses money or credit up to the deposits in the account. I know that some call the debit cards "*Islamic*" credit cards! We insist that we call it what it really is.

Specific Action Plan and Steps Taken by Bank Management

After a number of intensive brainstorming sessions attended by the new management and the board of directors the new management recommended (and the board of directors approved) the following list of actions:

1. *Continue to develop a sound corporate image and reputation in the local community, with the business community, and with the regulators.*
   - Better and professional facilities
   - Socially responsible, educated, experienced, friendly, humble, and professional staff
   - Deeper community involvement by communicating with civic associations, faith-based organizations, and surrounding universities

- Training bank staff on credit, business development, communications, appearance, and customer service at the newly innovated Bank of Whittier Open University

2. *Develop strong roots and community relations to increase the bank's client base and its loan (credit) and deposit activity.*
   - Call on existing bank holding company shareholders, friends, and our network of customers and potential customers to bring their business to the bank.
   - Call on medical doctors and professionals in our building and surrounding buildings, including Whittier Hospital, Presbyterian Hospital, and neighborhood fast food restaurant franchises.
   - Call all existing deposit and loan clients and bank shareholders.
   - Actively ask for referrals.
   - Hold in-person meetings with existing clients and prospects, in order to act as their trusted bankers.
   - Hire staff from the bank's immediate service areas and through neighboring colleges.
   - Participate actively in the Chamber of Commerce.
   - Develop personal working relationships with city and county elected officials.
   - Broaden and stress the offering of diversified RF banking services.
   - Cross-sell bank products and services.

3. *Review all bank policies and develop new bank policies and train staff through bank open university.*
   - The following is an abbreviated list of policies developed by the new management team and reviewed and approved by the board of directors:
     - Employee Handbook
     - Credit Policy
     - USA PATRIOT Act Policy
     - Bank Secrecy Act Policy
     - Customer Identification Program, used to open new accounts
     - Anti-Money Laundering Prevention Policy
     - Large Currency Transactions and Kiting Detection Policy
     - Availability of Funds Policy for out of town and area checks
     - Audit Policy
     - Funds Management Policy
     - Liquidity Policy
     - Wire Transfer Policy
     - Investment Policy
     - Information Technology and Information Security Policy

- Emergency Preparedness Plan and Procedure
- Disaster Recovery Plan
- Policy and Procedure for Privacy (Gramm-Leach-Bliley Act)
- Vendors' Management Policy

4. *Improve and enhance the security of the bank facilities, systems, and operations.*
   - Equip the bank with the most up-to-date alarm and security systems.
   - Run drills and emergency tests for different scenarios, such as fire, earthquake, loss of power, loss of computer connection to the central computer processor, loss of server, and loss of Fed-Line Connection.
   - Continue to implement frequent risk-based outside audit programs in all bank operations, loans, consumer compliance, BSA activities, accounting and finance, and technology.

5. *Continue to improve bank quality of services and operating efficiency.*
   - Assemble a strong team of RF bankers and instill a conservative, professional, helpful, and friendly operating culture.
   - Continue to hire highly educated, computer-literate, professionally sound team members.
   - Hire trainees from surrounding colleges to prepare candidates for future employment at the bank and to fulfill the bank's social responsibility of training future generations.
   - Train staff on systems and on high ethical, moral, and professional standards.
   - Streamline management by focusing on specific job functions and the measurement of staff achievements against the board of directors' approved budget, joint planning, goal setting, and comparing results with budget.

6. *Improve the computerization and automation of bank operations and services.*
   - Start using a standard client and prospect management and communications maintenance system on all staff's computers, to keep track of customers, prospects, loan renewals, and reviews.
   - Improve the quality of the bank's computer network.
   - Improve the quality of the hardware used by staff.

7. *Increase bank deposit base.*
   - Continue to improve facilities to increase efficiency and attract customers.
   - Continue to improve service quality.
   - Tap existing network of community members and friends to open new accounts and to add new loans.

- Diversify products and services without having too many products that would confuse customers, using the "Keep It Simple Stupid - KISS" approach.
- Expand customer base through better involvement with family, including children and grandchildren, to keep an evergreen book of clients.
- Expand customer base through asking for referrals.
- Continue to carve and deepen a unique corporate image and culture and promote social responsibility in lending and services.
- Continue to advocate, enhance, and implement a bank policy of cultural diversity among employees and bank customers.

8. *Continue to reduce bank operating expenses.*
   - Control expenses on all fronts by paying attention using a micro-expense review approach.
   - Motivate and reward team members by using productivity-based and bank profitability-based salary and bonus review programs through a system tied to personal production and bank profitability.
   - Insist on thorough and prudent loan analysis to reduce loan losses.
   - Develop steps to achieve close scrutiny and follow up of existing loans in order to solve any problems and fix them, if possible, before they occur.
   - Conduct weekly comparisons between actual expenses and budgeted expenses.

9. *Increase bank income.*
   - Actively pursue the prudent growth of the loan portfolio through deeper penetration of current depository customers and cultivation of new customers through referrals and community involvement.
   - Preserve and retain existing loans.

The following includes strategic steps that were implemented to improve the management process of bank operations.

1. *Open and review all incoming and outgoing mail and faxes.*

   The first step taken by the new management was to find out where the bank was, and what was going on in its day-to-day operations. It is important that we share our management experience with the reader, because this was one of the important steps that helps in understanding what is going on in a newly acquired institution. The new chief executive officer asked that all incoming and outgoing mail and faxes be brought to his office so that he could open the incoming mail, review the incoming faxes, approve the outgoing faxes before they were sent, and read the outgoing mail before the envelopes were sealed, stamped, and mailed. This is done always in the presence of another officer. The management needed to know how the bank was connected to the outside world by, for example, reviewing the incoming invoices and engagement contracts to know who we were dealing with. This step gave us—in three months' time—a great feel for the bank, its pulses, and its operations.

2. *Hire new employees*

We started looking for new employees to help. We needed at least two tellers, a highly qualified credit analyst, and a good accountant. We contacted some of the tellers and loan administration officers who had resigned from the bank, to see if they would come back. Only one teller accepted our offer; all the rest declined. In fact, some of them did not care to return our calls. We then started thinking about a way out of this dilemma. One of the management team came up with the idea of hiring business school students from the surrounding colleges and training them on the job. This proved to be a great idea. We appointed juniors at the business schools of the colleges and universities surrounding the bank as tellers and administration personnel. Later, these student workers became candidates for full-time positions as operations manager and supervisors. As to the training of these new employees, we started looking for a high-quality and experienced auditor of banking operations and compliance. We wanted an auditor who would critique and at the same time coach and train the new staff as he audited the bank. We asked him to come on a quarterly basis and to make himself available for consultation. We instructed all employees to be open to any comments or lack of compliance discovered by the auditor. We assembled them before the audit and asked them to look at the auditor as a teacher and a coach and to be truthful and open when answering any questions. The management team also had a meeting with the auditor and told him that the management and the board of directors wanted to learn in great detail what was wrong in the bank, not simply what was right. We also assured the auditor that we wanted to fix any problems he found as soon as they were recognized.

3. *Familiariaze management and staff with computer systems and outside service providers*

Management also started to familiarize the staff with the computer operating system and with the bank check processing and technology providers in order to know how the business is conducted.

4. *Review all financial ledgers and financial operations*

On the financial front, the new management went through the bank financial statement and ledger in great detail with the chief financial officer (CFO) and asked a lot of questions. This step was the most important, because we discovered many violations and non-posted transactions. For example, every time the CFO had not been able to balance the financial statement, he had assigned the discrepancy to a new bank control account. We discovered more than 30 such accounts. It took us many days and long hours to try to reconcile these accounts and we still were not able to reconcile all of them. That meant that we had to add such discrepancies to the bank losses.

5. *Evaluate the quality of the bank auditors*

After discovering the unfortunate state of affairs of the treasury function at the bank and the fact that the auditors/CPA of the bank never mentioned anything about it in their annual audited financial report, management was very disappointed in the quality and authenticity of the audits. We contacted the bank's CPA and complained about the unprofessional way the bank accounting and auditing system had been handled. He did not have the time, he said, because he was busy with bigger and more important banks. He relied on two young accountants who would come to the bank to pick up the statements from the CFO and leave. Management conferred with the board and the bank's lawyer. We had some concern about changing the bank auditor. We worried that people might suspect that the CPA auditor may have been in disagreement with bank management on some issues and that is why the bank was motivated to change the auditor. Management finally decided to push hard to change the auditing firm because we were sure of the sincerity of our motivations. It took us a long time to find an audit firm that would accept a bank that was losing money and had a new unproven management. I called Mr. Findley, and he found a firm that accepted he job. He kindly put in a very good word about the bank's new management. However, the new firm had a condition: they first wanted to review the bank's condition and then contact the existing audit firm. They did. After numerous contacts and interviews, they decided to become our auditors. We were all very impressed by the quality and depth of their work, and we felt comfortable about this most important bank activity.

6. *Develop the unique RF niche at the Bank of Whittier*

One of the most important steps in rescuing and restructuring the bank was to develop a strategic vision for a niche that would characterize that bank. The following sections give a summary of the process we used to articulate our RF finance system under difficult and challenging conditions.

Strategies Designed and Steps Implemented by the New Management

The following is a list of the strategies developed and the steps that management took to achieve our goal of restructuring the bank and operating it as a successful and preferred riba-free bank.

1. Determine the appropriate optimum size of deposits needed for the bank to serve its clients while reducing the cost of retaining expensive-to-keep deposits. In doing so, we reduced deposits and at the same time increased the loan portfolio to improve profitability and operating ratios. The strategy called for reducing the rates paid on all interest-bearing accounts first, and then, as the loan portfolio grew, we could grow the deposits accordingly. This strategy resulted in the closing of all those accounts that were interest-rate-sensitive liabilities. In a matter of a few months, asset size had decreased from $29.2 million at December 31, 2003 to $25.0 million at December 31, 2004, resulting in reduced interest expense.

2. Renovate the bank's facilities and automate its operations to improve the bank's image and operating efficiency.

3. Improve the bank's Web site and offer full Internet banking, bill pay service, and mobile phone banking, free of charge.

4. Prohibit board members from taking loans or benefiting directly or indirectly because of their position. In this way there would not be the slightest concern of violating Regulation O, which requires close proctoring and disclosure of any insider activity in the bank operations.

5. Offer new Bank of Whittier products and services, like the FDIC-insured Certificate of Deposit accounts, which are insured up to $50 million through a strategic alliance with the Certificate of Deposit Account Registry Service (CDARS).[4]

6. Employ highly qualified and educated employees with extensive banking experience, and train a new generation of bankers by hiring new business school graduates, preferably from the immediate neighborhood and the local universities around the city. In addition, hire tellers who are business school students. They are hired as part-time employees and cultivated to be future bank employees to meet our long-term growth plans.

7. Provide exceptional banking services by splitting the traditional bank "Loan Officer" function into two functions.

   ■ *RF Private Banker*—This function was designed to provide each customer with a well-trained and seasoned RF banker who is well-educated and becomes the point of contact between the client and the bank. In addition, the RF private banker is responsible for knowing the family and its members, understanding their aspirations, and articulating their financial state of affairs. This allows the RF bank to integrate its services with the client's needs. The RF private banker aspires to add new family members to the RF Bank of Whittier's expanding family. The RF private banker is available to serve customers 24 hours a day, 7 days a week.

- *RF Credit Analyst*—The analysts hired are some of the better educated in the field of financial analysis; some have MBA degrees, and all hold business school degrees from some of the better business schools in the United States. The goal of the RF credit analyst is to conduct a thorough analysis of the financing application at hand and to develop a number of scenarios and recommendations for whether or not to finance the proposed financing using the RF discipline. We train our RF credit analysts not only to protect bank interests but also to be in the best interests of our customers. During the Open University training program, we drill the candidates and reiterate that the bank is not in the business of renting money. We are in the business of investing in our clients.

8. Provide all employees with the best training available through in-house training programs conducted by expert bank executives and senior managers, video training programs, Web-based programs, and live training presentations by outside experts. In addition, we train our employees on being socially responsible. Our simple focus is to train every one of our staff to be like George Bailey in *It's a Wonderful Life*. In fact, every employee is required to watch this movie at least twice a year, and it is discussed in bank training forums to improve the spirit of serving our clients. In addition, the bank finances special banking university MBA training programs at some of the best schools and universities in the nation.

9. Expand bank services through a strategic alliance with a major bank. This alliance allows our business customers to access the services of the Bank of Whittier at any of the thousands of the major bank branches in the United States.

10. Expand our business hours; we are open from 9:00 A.M. until 5:00 P.M. every weekday except on Friday when we close at 6:00 P.M. On Saturday we are open from 9:00 A.M. to 3:00 P.M.

11. Develop policies for all aspects of bank operations, as well as a procedures and operations manual.

12. Focus on improving the quality of the loan portfolio. Perhaps this is the most important aspect of the strategy. This was done by:

- Contacting our community members in our Community Reinvestment Act (CRA) assessment area, especially those who have been underserved.
- Closing and declining renewal of loans that were below our conservative credit underwriting standards, and increasing the loan portfolio through cross-marketing the existing customers and our existing network of personal and business contacts.
- Developing new loans using strict and conservative RF underwriting standards.
- Activating RF mortgage financing to attract new customers and increase bank income. The bank pass-through mortgage business has been an important contributor to its income and turn around.

13. Offer integrated banking services on both the asset and liability sides of the customers' ledger. This is done through the services offered by the bank's private bankers and business development managers.

THE STAFF AND EMPLOYEE POLICY: STRATEGY USED TO BUILD UP AND TRAIN BANK STAFF

I felt fortunate but immensely challenged due to the staff situation when I arrived at the Bank on July 10, 2003. I essentially had to staff a new bank, which was good, but the challenge was where to begin, where to find the staff, and most importantly what to look for.

One approach anyone in my situation would do is to contact an employment agency or to put an advertisement in the business papers like the *Wall Street Journal*. However, that was not an option, because of the type of bankers that would apply. They would ask for very high salaries, which the bank could not afford, and in general they would not agree to join a bank that was losing money and was in the shape that Bank of Whittier was in at the time. The other approach, which I tried, was to contact friends in the banking industry to help recommend bankers. I interviewed a few of them. I felt that they wanted a job and a big salary, which they knew was too large for the bank to afford in its state of profitability.

I sat down in a quiet moment to think. I reasoned that I could continue to use the services of the chief financial officer (CFO), but with very close supervision and a lot of patience to accommodate his "energy sapping" remarks and attitude. I would also seek some of the wonderful hardworking associates at LARIBA. I asked my deputy at LARIBA and the secretary of the board to act as the chief credit officer on a part-time basis, because the loan portfolio was very small, and I started looking for a smart, sophisticated, and highly analytical credit analyst. I reasoned that this person did not have to have any banking experience. I called a friend and he recommended a person who was a perfect fit. He had an undergraduate degree in aerospace engineering (which meant to me a very careful approach to analysis), an MBA, and was working on his Certified Financial Analyst certification. He had a very heavy accent, and you had to listen carefully to him to understand his English. I mention this to share with the reader the value of a person that can be uncovered regardless of the accent, the national origin, the faith, the skin color, or the gender.

In this regard I want to share with the readers two experiences. When I was training at Shearson American Express for a cold-calling financial consultant job (telephoning a person one has never met to get to know that person and to offer one's services based on the experience and the service) that required excellent communication skills and clear expression, a co-trainee approached me and said he wanted to give me advice. He said that because of my accent, I needed to apologize to the person I cold-called, telling him or her that if he/she did not understand my accent to ask me to repeat what I said. I looked at him for a minute and said to him that he must be crazy. He thought that he had offended me and started to apologize. I told him that he had not offended me, but that if I had a scar on my face, I was not going to apologize for having it to every person I met. There are things that people cannot do much to change, and that should never be an impediment to their acceptance. In fact, it is all in the mind of the person who has the accent. If he accepts it and tries to improve it, he will be successful. If she feels sorry for herself and feels she is failing because she is discriminated against, she will fail. The mind is like a fertile earth. If you sow rose seeds in it, you'll see roses; but if you sow the seeds of poison ivy, you will be harmed by that poison. In my case, I went on to become the top achiever in the training class, and eventually became a trainer in the Financial Advisory school at Shearson, where I specialized in training people on how to make a cold call.

Another experience I had was with a customer at the bank. A prominent lady in a prominent family in the city had an account with the bank. I knew that the bulk of her money was at another bank. Our private bankers at the bank and I personally tried very hard to encourage her to transfer her banking service to us, because she appeared on the NSF (non-sufficient funds) list every morning. I finally had a private meeting with her. I asked her to tell me frankly why she was not expanding her relationship with us. She said the first thing I needed to do was to hire employees who speak English without an accent. I thanked her for her feedback. She continued to be on the NSF list. At a meeting of the operations department, they all complained about the way she treated them when they called her respectfully to tell her that she had written a check without sufficient funds to cover it. We all were surprised, because she never apologized but was always rude. We decided to ask her to close the account. During my exit interview, I told her that I was sorry about the "accent" problem, but asked her to remember that the United States was founded and built and still is being built and refreshed by people with accents, and I wished her the best.

The New Staff: A Strategy for Defining Whom to Look for and Where to Search

We also decided to home-grow our own RF bankers using two approaches. The first was to announce banking entry positions in the business schools in surrounding universities. We looked for fresh graduates with an excellent scholastic achievement, with a grade point average (GPA) of at least 3.75. We also advertised for part-time tellers in the business schools. The idea was to train these tellers at a young age (sometimes as young as 18) and watch their progress closely in order to recruit our future staff. I knew that this strategy and approach would need time, but I reasoned that this would be the best investment for the future.

To train all of these new and fresh bankers, we pioneered the "Bank of Whittier Open University." The classes are held at least twice a year for 45 days from 8:00 A.M. to 9:30 A.M. and all staff members, including those with prior banking experience, are required to attend. The training program will be discussed in detail in Chapter 12.

This proved to be the most important decision we ever made to change the fortunes of the bank. These smart fresh graduates were like sponges, hungry to absorb information, to learn new banking regulations and techniques, and to create new solutions to the problems we faced. They brought with them vibrancy, fresh ideas, challenges that made me feel younger, and most importantly the ability to be molded to believe in, operate, and serve people in our new brand of banking—the RF banking way.

THE AUDIT POLICY: STRATEGY USED FOR AUDITING BANK FUNCTIONS AND OPERATIONS

At the Bank of Whittier, N.A., we pioneered the use of a risk-based audit program that helped management establish which areas of bank operations needed to be audited in light of the risks associated and the extent of those risks. Management innovated and developed a computer-based program that helped institutionalize this risk-based audit function and determine the frequency of each audit area.

All board members, management, and staff of the bank sincerely believe that the various internal and external audits and the onsite examination are a process of discovery, cleansing, training, and coaching of bank management and staff that will help to improve the quality and effectiveness of bank operations. Bank management trains bank staff to listen carefully, to not argue, to not act defensively, and to learn. They are also trained to take prompt and immediate action to correct any oversight or error pointed out by the auditors. The management asks bank auditors to point out specifically what needs to be fixed so that we can attain the highest level of compliance.

The board of directors' *audit committee* is responsible for establishing and maintaining an effective audit function that satisfies statutory, regulatory, and supervisory requirements.

As stipulated by the standards of government regulators, directors cannot delegate these responsibilities. However, they may delegate the design, implementation, and monitoring of specific internal controls to management and the testing and assessment of internal controls to auditors and other outside vendors. The board of directors' meeting minutes should reflect decisions regarding audits, such as external audit engagement terms (including any decision to forgo an external audit), the scope of audits to be performed, or why an audit of a particular area is not necessary.

Members of the bank's board of directors are specifically responsible for:

- Reviewing and approving audit strategies, policies, programs, and organizational structure
- Monitoring the effectiveness of the audit function

Following are the audit functions to be executed by the board's *audit committee*:

- Facilitation of the appointment and work of the internal and outside auditors
- Analysis and evaluation of their findings
- Recommendation of corrective actions with a specific timeline
- Reporting of all findings and recommendations in the Board's meeting minutes
- Review of financial content of the bank's financial reports to be submitted to stockholders, the public, and/or regulatory agencies
- Recommendation and/or initiation of an investigation of adverse operation results or trends, where applicable

The formality and extent of a bank's internal and external audit programs depend on the bank's size, complexity, scope of activities, and risk profile. The board of directors must carefully consider how extensive the audit program must be to effectively test and monitor internal controls and ensure the reliability of the bank's financial statements and reporting.

The board of directors must strive to ensure that the bank's audit system is efficiently capable to test internal controls in order to be able to identify:

- Inaccurate, incomplete, or unauthorized transactions
- Deficiencies in the safeguarding of bank assets
- Unreliable financial and/or regulatory reporting
- Violations of laws and/or regulations
- Deviations from the bank's policies and procedures

The board of directors is expected to do its best to be aware of all risks and control issues for the bank's operations, including risks in new products, emerging technologies, information systems, and Internet banking. Control issues and risks associated with increasing reliance on technology include:

- Increased user access to information systems
- Reduced segregation of duties
- Potential unidentifiable errors resulting from the shift of operations from paper to electronic audit trails
- Lack of standards and controls for end-user systems
- Increased complexity of contingency plans and information system recovery plans

Engagement Letter for External Auditors

In its efforts to prudently identify the most capable auditing entities for its various audits, the bank's board of directors must invite and request external auditors to submit engagement letters before commencing audit work. Such a letter will be expected to reflect preliminary discussions between the bank's board and/or senior management and the external auditor(s).

The engagement letter(s) will stipulate, among other things, the audit's purpose, its scope, the period to be covered, and the reports the auditor will develop. Schedules or appendixes may accompany the letter to provide the board with more details of the proposed audit. The letter may briefly describe procedures to be used in specific areas. If the scope of the audit is limited in any way, the letter may specify procedures that the auditor will omit. Additionally, the letter would specify if the auditor were expected to render an opinion on the bank's financial statements and/or other bank functions, depending on the type of audit being conducted.

Types and Scope of Various Audits

I. *Risk Assessments and Risk-Based Auditing*

Risk assessment is defined as the means by which the board of directors identifies and evaluates the quantity of the bank's risks and the quality of its controls. An effective risk-based auditing program will cover all of the bank's activities. The frequency and depth of each area's audit will vary according to the area's risk assessment. All areas of bank activities are included in order to establish the frequency of the audit necessary to mitigate any risk in bank safety and soundness and its reputation.

II. *External Audit Function*

The primary role of the external auditor is to independently and objectively review, evaluate, and document its findings about bank activities in order to help the board of directors of the bank and its management maintain and/or improve the efficiency and effectiveness of the bank's risk management, internal controls, and corporate governance.

External auditors must understand the bank's strategic direction, objectives, products, services, operating philosophy, strategy, and processes. The auditors will communicate their findings to the board of directors and to senior management.

III. *Objectives*

The objectives of external audits are:

a. To provide reasonable testing, review, and analysis of the Bank's operations to ensure the effectiveness of internal controls over financial reporting, the accuracy and timeliness in recording transactions, and the accuracy and completeness of financial and regulatory reports

b. To perform an independent and objective view of the bank's activities, including processes relative to financial reporting and bank operations

c. To determine whether the bank complies with laws and regulations and adheres to established bank policies and whether management is taking appropriate steps to address control deficiencies

IV. *Types of Audits*

The type of audit commonly referred to as a Directors' Examination entails specified and/or agreed-upon procedural reviews of the adequacy of internal controls and accuracy of financial information. The independent audit parties can be public accountants, certified internal auditors, certified information systems auditors, bank management firms, bank consulting firms and/or other parties knowledgeable in banking.

Please note that the frequency of the audits suggested below is determined in light of the risk-based audit discussed earlier.

1. *Financial Statement Audit* by a certified public accounting firm, CPA

An independent audit of financial statements should be designed to ensure that the bank's financial reports are prepared in accordance with Generally Accepted Accounting Principles (GAAP) and that the Independent Financial Statements are performed in accordance with Generally Accepted Audit Standards (GAAS). The scope of the audit will be sufficient to enable the CPA to express an opinion on the bank's financial statements.

The following list represents areas for which the board of directors requires an annual audit.

a. Cash and due from banks
b. Loans
c. Allowance for loan and lease losses (ALLL)
d. Premises and equipment
e. Other assets and liabilities
f. Deposits
g. Notes payable
h. Non-interest income
i. Expenses
j. Equity (holding company, if applicable)
k. Tax return

2. *Operational, USA PATRIOT Act, Bank Secrecy Act (BSA), and Office of Foreign Assets Control (OFAC) Audits*

These types of audits include a review of policies, procedures, and operational controls to determine whether risk management, internal controls, and internal processes are adequate and efficient. Operational audits generally include procedures to test the integrity of accounts, regulatory reports, and other aspects of operations. These audits may also include a review of management and employee compliance with bank policies and procedures. The Operational, Bank Secrecy Act, and OFAC audits should be scheduled annually at specific times.

3. *Compliance Audit*

This type of audit determines whether the bank is complying with bank procedures and internal and external regulatory regulations. This audit should be scheduled annually—or as frequently as the risk analysis may call for—preferably in the first quarter of the year but no later than the second quarter of the year. It focuses on the bank's adherence to consumers' compliance regulations to ensure that the bank has adequate systems and control procedures to avoid any violations.

4. *Loan Review Audit*

This type of audit is conducted to assess the quality of the bank's loan portfolio and provide an early alert of problem loans or negative portfolio patterns or trends, as well as the adequacy of and procedure used to calculate allowance for loan and lease losses (ALLL). The ALLL estimation process at the Bank of Whittier is conducted, as discussed earlier, by following a unique risk-based method and a proprietary computer program pioneered by the bank to include in the calculation all risk factors that may have an impact on the various credit facilities. The process will be detailed in Chapter 12.

5. *Information Systems, Technology, and Security Audits*

These types of audits assess the controls over the bank's electronic data processing and computer-related areas. These audits focus on management, development, support and delivery, data security, and physical security. Information system and technology audits also include a review of computer and client services systems, end-user reports, electronic funds transfers, and service provider activities. This type of audit should test the system and should be completed annually in the first quarter of the year. It also helps review and critique security systems used by the bank.

V. *Treasury, Financial, Operations, and Loans Management Monthly Certifications*

The responsibilities of the operations and loans departments are to certify all general ledger accounts as provided by management to the application—DDA, savings, time deposits, and loans. For example: operations staff will be responsible for certifying all loan systems to the general ledger, and the loans department staff will certify all operations applications to the general ledger. The certifications will be completed according to the certification listing and provided to the CFO monthly before the tenth day of every month.

Audit Response by Management

Management will prepare a written response to the board of directors within 21 days from the date of the submission of the particular audit report and its findings. The management response will outline any deficiencies or concerns outlined by the audit, list the corrective actions already taken, and identify specific recommendations, plans, and the expected time of completion for responding to such recommendations to fix the problems discovered by the audits.

The management response will be sent to the firm that completed the audit. In addition, the OCC (usually during the exam time) and other related regulatory bodies, if needed, will be notified by the bank's chairman of the board of directors as to the different audit findings, the corrective actions already taken, and the actions that will be taken, including expected time of completion.

NOTES

1. The founder of the Findley Company was Mr. Gerald Lee Elmer Findley who, from 1952 to his retirement in the late 1980s, was responsible for chartering more than 120 banks in California. Gerald and his son Gary have organized almost 200 banks in their 50 years of business.

2. The Central Bank of Malaysia (Bank Negara Malaysia) sought the views of three jurists on the permissibility of establishing a RF Banking window as an additional but unique service offered by a conventional RIBA bank. The Shari'aa scholars involved were the late (Almarhoum) Tan Sri Professor Ahmad Ibrahim and Professor Dr. Mahmoud Saedon Awang Uthman from the International Islamic University, Malaysia, and Tuan Haji Mohammad Shahir Ahmad from the Department of Islamic Affairs in the Malaysian Prime Minister's Office. These scholars' view was that "a conventional riba-based bank, whose operations are conducted on the basis of interest, *is not prohibited* from operating an RF banking window." The conclusion was based on foundation of Shari'aa. Many jurists and scholars around the world have concluded that owning and operating a conventional riba-based bank that offers RF banking products and services, such as lease-to-purchase financing, is not only acceptable but is encouraged (Dr. Saleh Malaikah, in a private communication dated May 17, 1999; the opinion is based on research conducted by Dr. Malaikah). Scholars like Dr. Al-Qari, and Dr. Abdul-Rahman Serri have concurred with this opinion. This, however, does not make riba-based finance activities permissible according to Shari'aa. The ownership and operation of a conventional bank by Muslims is desirable and encouraged if the intention is to offer riba-free products as a unique service that can compete with the conventional banking products. The gradual approach with a clear plan will allow riba-free banking products and services to be tested by the consumers who will ultimately make the final decision about which products and services they like to use.

3. Yahia Abdul-Rahman, Mike Abdelaaty, and Gary S. Findley, Esq., *The Challenges of Offering a LARIBA Products and Services Window in an American Bank*, presented at the Harvard University Seminar on Islamic Banking, 1999.
4. CDARS stands for "Certificate of Deposit Account Registry Service," which offers CD investments insured up to $50 million by capitalizing on the network of member banks accepting tranches of the deposit and swapping it with a deposit from that bank in the originating bank. This allows the originating bank to access the FDIC coverage of the corresponding bank.

CHAPTER 12

Operating an RF Bank in the United States

A bank—also known as a government chartered (licensed) depository institution—is allowed by government authorities to solicit and accept deposits from the public and institutions for safekeeping and to manage these deposits. Legally, the bank's relationship with its customer is defined by the type of account the customer chooses to open with the bank. As will be discussed later, if the customer uses the bank as a place to keep money safe and to withdraw from it using a checkbook or the Internet, the bank is looked upon legally and according to Shari'aa and the Judeo-Christian-Islamic values as a trustee of these funds. This type of account is called a *demand deposit account* (DDA) in conventional riba-based banking. In RF banking it can be called a *deposit in trust account* (DIT Account, or *Amana*, which means trust). That means that the bank has accepted a legal responsibility and promised the depositor before God and the laws of the land to safeguard his or her funds, in order to make them available on demand. For this service the bank can charge a fee.

On the other hand, the bank is also entrusted by U.S. bank regulations and laws to manage a pool of funds for those customers who choose to invest their money in an investment account, such as, for example, a *time certificate of deposit* (TCD). In this capacity, the contrast between the role of the riba-based conventional banker and the RF banker becomes clearer. In riba-based conventional banking, the objective is to maximize the spread between the interest charged to customers who use the money to finance their needs and the cost of these funds, which is mainly the interest paid on the money deposited (invested) in the bank—mainly TCD. The riba-based banker is trained to make that spread as high as possible within a well-designed portfolio with a risk profile that is approved by the bank treasury, the loan department, and the board of directors of the bank. The riba-based banker who is involved in lending is trained to "sell" loans that will employ the deposited funds in financing different projects. As the funds available to the banker grow—as in the case of the mega-banks—the loan officer of the bank is given a quota that must be met, and in most cases, without proper training on social responsibility, experience shows us that money motivates many such "loan sales people" to sell more loans. This is especially true for loan officers who receive a percentage of the loans booked as a commission. They use their sales training to entice and encourage the consumer and businesses to borrow more money than they need and to create more consumption. This may lead to more loans for the bank and more consumption for the economy, but in many cases it leads to very little real economic production and a deeper hole of debt for the consumer and the business. In addition, the riba-based banker who works in the treasury of the bank can also choose between a number of short-term and long-term investment instruments to squeeze as much interest as possible out of that cash. Because the funds are insured by the FDIC, the riba-based conventional bank management would also use the DDA deposits, which are deposited as a trust and conceptually for safekeeping, to generate more interest income.

In contrast, the RF banker is trained to look at the money deposited in the bank in a quite different way. First and most important is the DIT (*deposit in trust* or *Amana* deposit). This DIT money cannot be invested in any instrument except the Fed Funds, which are, in fact, government instruments that reflect the government's monetary policy in a *fiat* (paper) money regime, as discussed in Chapter 5. The interest given by the government—the Fed Funds rate—is not the same as the interest prohibited by the Judeo-Christian-Islamic value system and by the Law (Shari'aa). In this case, the RF banker becomes the safekeeping holder of this money in trust. The other role of the RF banker is to act as a money manager (*mudharib*) entrusted with the prudent investment of the funds earmarked for that purpose to create real economic production, job opportunities, and prosperity. This is done by investing the money in projects and services that will make a difference in peoples' lives. The RF banker is trained to:

- Encourage people to live riba-free by helping them devise a plan to pay off their debts (especially the riba-based ones like personal loans and credit card debt) as soon as possible in a methodical process and to help them achieve their dreams without overburdening themselves with excessive borrowing
- Help them in restructuring and reducing their obligations and debts
- Encourage them to consume less by living within their means

That is why the RF banker in charge of financing/investing operations (lending in riba-based banks) is not trained to "sell" loans to customers in order to maximize the size of the loan portfolio. The RF banker is trained to think of the process of financing (lending in a riba-based bank) as a process of investing prudently with the customer. The RF bank employees, management, board of directors and shareholders believe in the values of voluntarism and real service to all people in the community. They are willing to forgo some of the short-term higher profits, higher salaries, and "perks" to ensure the success of this new brand of banking. The RF bank staff members are required by bank management to approach their responsibilities not as businesspeople who are interested in squeezing their customers for more cash—by charging fees and other expenses to achieve higher profits. They are trained to be dedicated and believing leaders in their communities for the purpose of developing the community, touching peoples' vision, hearts, minds, and future. The dream of these RF bankers is to apply and bring to life a working RF banking system, on a community level, as one of the pillars of a worldwide RF banking system—pioneered in the United States—which operates according to Judeo-Christian-Islamic values and principles. In this context, the real profits of the RF bank will not only be measured in dollars and cents but also in the number of households served and the extent of that service as it changes peoples' lives and fortunes for the better. The real profits will be the contributions of the bank to a better society and a happier community by opening job opportunities through financing the community's members and businesses. The net result would be more economic activity, healthy economic growth, and an affluent community.

INVESTING IN AND OPERATING A RIBA-FREE BANK IN THE UNITED STATES

Riba-free (Islamic) banking in North America (the United States and Canada) was introduced in 1987 by LARIBA in the United States. So far, it has focused mainly on providing the money needed by the community to invest in home mortgages, commercial buildings, businesses, and automobile purchases. We are privileged at LARIBA to have started this grassroots, purely American movement in 1987 by offering, in a humble way, financing services for the needs of the community in order to strengthen it financially, get its members to live a full and active life in the United States as Americans living by the Judeo-Christian-Islamic value system according to Shari'aa, and to produce a new generation of community members who are qualified bankers and who believe in RF banking.[1]

It is believed that riba-free and gharar-free (*gharar* is deceptive misrepresentation and use of misleading representations) faith-based financing in the United States and Canada (in particular, in the United States, with which I am more familiar) will present the financial capital markets at large with one of the better banking and financing products and services available in the world. The reason is that these products and services comply with the most sophisticated and best designed regulatory standards available in the world—the U.S. banking regulations and the Securities and Exchange Commission (SEC) regulations—to provide the investor with fairness, safety, soundness, full disclosure, and compliance. In addition, corporate governance in RF banking institutions is not only supervised by the U.S. government, but also by a higher authority (i.e., God). It is interesting here to remember the very popular Hebrew National advertisement for kosher hot dogs in the 1960s, which stated, "We Answer to a Higher Authority."

As RF banking expands in the United States and creates demand for more capital from the general global markets (outside the traditional Gulf petro-dollars), it will need to attract new investors who subscribe to its concepts and approaches to invest in its products and services and eventually in its capital. The RF banking industry will have to devise the strategies needed to meet this challenge.

It is important to remember that the foundation of the whole concept of RF banking (riba-free and gharar-free) is to attract community deposits and savings and redeploy these deposits and savings into the community as investments to generate economic prosperity, job opportunities, and a better future for all. This is not much different from the well-known and important U.S. banking regulation called the Community Reinvestment Act (CRA). This act makes certain that the accumulation of wealth from a certain community is largely invested back in the community without discrimination. Investing community assets outside that community has been and still is something that is chronic in most countries, especially the developing ones.

To shape the architecture of the RF banking industry and its capital needs, it must meet the most stringent measures of full disclosure and transparency, and a strict sense of corporate governance not only based on the banking and financial laws and regulations of the land but also on the basic moral and ethical values in Shari'aa and the tenets of the Judeo-Christian-Islamic value system. That means not only relying on supervisory examinations by the regulatory authorities of the U.S. Treasury Department (the Office of the Comptroller of the Currency, or OCC, for national banks; the state finance authorities for state-chartered banks) and the SEC, but also by dedicated organizations that make sure that the foundations of Shari'aa, including moral and ethical values of the day-to-day dealings of all the RF bank's staff, management, board of directors and customers are upheld in all operations.

To recap what has been covered in the book thus far, the following section discusses important aspects needed to strengthen investors' confidence in RF banking and finance and its projected capital market needs.

THE ADDED VALUE OF RF BANKING

New RF banking institutions need to let the market know—through practice, experience, and track record—the answer to a very important question: *What is the added value of investing in RF products and services?*

Here is a brief list of the significant sources of added value that RF bankers need to articulate to the newcomers to the emerging RF banking industry and put into effect in the day-to-day operations of the RF financial institution. These added values are taken seriously by the RF institution's management and staff, who are trained and instructed to be serious and sincere about implementing the following code of ethics and mode of operations in their RF banking practice:

- The ethics of *halal* (divinely allowed) and *haram* (divinely prohibited).
- The discipline of the *know-your-customer* rule in banking and finance, because RF banks serve all people in the community of faith-based congregations, including members of temples, synagogues, churches, and masajid (mosques).
- The deep-seated belief that RF financial services are available to all community members of all faiths and backgrounds without discrimination of any sort, because discrimination is one of the worst offenses against the higher authority we all subscribe to in the Judeo-Christian-Islamic value system (i.e., God).
- The policy of full transparency, proved by full disclosure and full documentation of contracts and all related parties.
- RF banking is:
  - Asset/services-based financing
  - A socially responsible system
  - A system based on the *mark-to-the-market* and *commodity indexation* rules as capital market tools to ascertain prudence in investing and financing
  - Based on the belief that credit is one of the important basic human rights
  - Superior, because it offers lower risk and better return on investment

WHAT IS RF BANKING AND FINANCE?

As was discussed earlier in the book, RF finance is not only about the mechanics of financing. It is a new banking brand, designed for people of all faiths. The Judeo-Christian-Islamic value system prohibits the culture of renting money at a rate called interest rate and the abuse of the power of money. The foundation of the RF banking and finance system (riba-free and gharar-free) is based on the moral and ethical values and behavior of its bankers and employees. It is a system based on:

- Riba-free financing and banking procedures, which means not renting money, but establishing the prudence of investing money in the clients' assets and services and that the rental of those assets/services produces attractive returns on investment
- Gharar-free, which means that it is free from deception and/or misrepresentation of facts and the use of "tricks" or ruses (*heelah*) to circumvent the spirit and substance of Shari'aa and the spirit of Judeo-Christian-Islamic values
- Delivering services that are focused on the substance of the transaction, and not only on its form and its mechanics
- Compliance with the tenets of Shari'aa while not violating the laws of the land

U.S. Banking Regulations and Bank Regulators

The U.S. banking regulations represent the most sophisticated and up-to-date documentation of rules and regulations defining the relationship between the financial institution and the customer. These regulations represent the integration of all accumulated human efforts designed over time to prevent, to the best of our abilities, the illegal, fraudulent, and unfair practices some people attempted to use to enrich themselves over the years by misleading and defrauding the average consumer, investor, and depositor. These regulations are the latest efforts of humanity to ascertain that financial institutions are fair, transparent, and truthful to the unsophisticated and less financially educated customers and communities. In studying these regulations, it can be testified that they are the best tools developed, and they are still being developed. Many of these regulations were discussed in Chapter 7.

U.S. Securities Laws and Regulations

The U.S. securities laws, in general, prohibit the solicitation of funds for investment purposes and/or the sale of securities to the public without full disclosure and proper registration with the SEC. In some cases, funds can be solicited without registration with the SEC, as in the case of a *private offering*. These are allowed to be offered exclusively to *accredited investors*, who are wealthy and sophisticated enough—as defined clearly by SEC rules—to be able to understand the risks involved.

The Spirit of the Riba-Free and Gharar-Free (Islamic) Banking and Finance System

Money is a manmade measuring device, created to help people transact business activities (buying and selling) and to measure the accumulated wealth and the success or failure of a venture. It cannot be rented. Renting money (through the use of the interest rate) is riba and is prohibited by Shari'aa. Assets are considered to be the properties of God, and they are placed in trust by God—according to His infinite wisdom—in different forms and quantities in the custody of each one of us. It is our duty to honor that trust, and when we invest or use these assets, we should do so properly and prudently. Assets and savings of each community must be largely reinvested in the community to create economic growth, prosperity, and job opportunities. The system redistributes wealth through the mechanics of "trickle-down economics" through the system of inheritance and almsgiving.

STRATEGIES USED TO BUILD A VIABLE RF BANKING SYSTEM IN THE UNITED STATES

The following is the set of strategies we used when we started RF banking services in the United States, first in the form of a finance company—LAR-IBA—in 1987, and then as a full-service national bank in 2003.

- RF banking and finance proponents' ultimate goal is to offer an alternative banking and finance service, not to discredit and/or dismantle the existing riba-based conventional banking system.
- The RF bankers' attitude is not to grow as quickly as possible by using capital or sources of money from outside the community. RF bankers believe in putting their money where their mouth is. We state that it is wiser and more prudent to grow methodically with our own money and the community's money to develop community ownership. Our commitment is simply to develop trust between our community members, and to start with what is possible to achieve what may be impossible, as we learn from the Sunnah of our beloved prophets Abraham, Isaac, Ishmael, Moses, Jesus, and Muhammad (pp.). It is not shameful to say today that we are small because, God willing (*inshaa Allah*), we aspire to be bigger by the blessings of God.
- The RF bankers' goal is not to change the laws of the land. The goal is to adhere and uphold these laws without violating Judeo-Christian-Islamic values and the tenets of Shari'aa (the Law). RF bankers need

to remember that the most overriding goal of Shari'aa is to bring what is beneficial and useful to the community and to drive away any harm.

- RF bankers are out to popularize our RF financing and investing to all people of all faiths and backgrounds. The goal is to present what we believe through the quality, style, and dedication of the financial services our dedicated RF banking pioneers provide.

- The RF banking motto is: *We Do Not Rent Money—We Invest in Our Customers*. The RF bankers' philosophy and disciplined training programs, as well as RF banking operating policies, should reflect the belief that an RF banker's primary job, as the customers' preferred banker and advisor, is not to dig a deeper hole of debt in the customer's life but rather to find ways and means to optimize that debt, to establish to the best of their abilities that it is used for financing rewarding and prudent investments and businesses, and to help customers get out of it as soon as possible. RF bankers are trained to look at customers as true members of their families. In times of need and difficulty, the RF banker is trained to practice the concept of merciful caring, helping, and assisting (known as *tarahum* in Islam).

- RF bankers' operating challenge is not to take existing riba-based products and services and dress them to make them look riba-free (and gharar-free). In fact, doing so may bring unforgiving harm to all of those involved in the RF banking industry, as well as the community, and will destroy the work that many dedicated servants of the community have spent their lives to develop. The approach used in Shari'aa-based RF banking and finance is to do the exact opposite, by conducting the RF banking business according to the Law (Shari'aa), then dressing it up to fit the laws of the land. And yes, one word of great caution for all those who are focused on marketing in the name of God and faith: Violation of and noncompliance with, as well as toying with, the financial laws of the land may take time to uncover, but when it is discovered, these offenses bring immediate, swift, irreversible, terminal, and global punishment to the perpetrators.

- The RF bankers' job is not to try to use non-English words to brand products to make them appear foreign to the English-speaking public. The real challenge is to choose names that make it easier for the English speakers (or, for that matter, speakers of whatever the local language is, anywhere in the world) to understand what these products are and what their function is. For example, instead of only using *murabaha*, the RF banker can use cost-plus; for *musharaka* one can use joint venture, and so on. RF bankers need to remember that the goal is to benefit people by helping them understand and use RF banking. We need to popularize the RF banking services to people of all faiths and make it easy to compare RF banking to the existing riba-based conventional banking products.

■ The RF banker does not live lavishly, because the money he or she manages is in fact the trust of our customers—a trust hanging from our necks before God. RF bankers refuse to travel first class, stay in expensive hotels, or live a luxurious lifestyle, squandering their customers' and shareholders' money on expensive advertising campaigns. RF bankers believe that money respects those who respect it.

■ RF banking grows by word-of-mouth referral from satisfied customers.

The net outcome of all these values and modes of operation for this new RF banking service is superior service, solid products, lower risk, and higher returns because of lower default rates and lower overhead. Naturally, more customers will come to the RF bank to be served, and many more investors will keep coming.

Key Internal Controls at the Bank

The following committees were created to establish the key internal controls that ensure compliance. Committee proceedings are reported to the bank's board of directors:

■ The *Bank Secrecy Act (BSA) Committee* meets on a regular basis to discuss Currency Transaction Reports, Suspicious Activity Reports, Wire Transfers (domestic/international), Office of Foreign Assets Control (OFAC), Financial Crimes Enforcement Network reports/findings, and other BSA matters. Minutes of the meeting are maintained.

■ The *Credit (Loan) Department Committee* meets on a regular basis to discuss issues pertaining to credit approval and related matters. This includes the current loan portfolio, loans in progress, and the status of credit memos. In addition, the performance of each loan is evaluated to assess the level of risk. Minutes of the meeting are maintained.

■ The *Information Technology/Security (IT/IS) Committee* meets on a regular basis to discuss all matters pertaining to the computer and information technology (IT) systems' viability and security. The committee reviews, on a regular basis, any attempts to penetrate the computer system, data security, network server, computers, software, security cameras, telephones, online banking, and disaster recovery.

■ The *Daily Operations Committee* meets on a daily basis to discuss issues pertaining to operational activities. This includes non-sufficient fund activities, non-posted transactions and items, stop payment orders, wire transfers, and basic management of daily reports and transactions.

In addition, the following are samples of the bank policies developed by management and approved by the board of directors:

- Employees are restricted from entering other departments' areas, the vault, and the Fed wire and computer room.
- Faxes sent and received must be checked by the CFO, CEO, or a qualified officer. All faxes must be approved before sending.
- Opening/closing bank doors may only be done by designated bank officers who have a set of keys to open the bank. The officer who is opening and/or closing the bank must follow a specific procedure for searching/clearing the facilities and sign a logbook located next to the vault. A log for keys handed out to employees, as well as other keys, is also kept.
- The vault is opened by two officers; each officer has half of the combination. Both officers must sign the Opening/Closing Vault log next to the vault. Vault access is limited by time clock as well as by authorized personnel.
- The ATM/Night Drop needs to be opened every day by two employees, one of whom must be an officer. The night drop is opened twice a day, once in the morning and afternoon. The ATM is opened daily in the afternoon.
- All information for an outgoing wire transfer needs to be approved by CEO, CFO, or Vice President. All wire transfers are entered and verified under dual control and registered in a special log.
- Employees are required not to use work e-mail for personal use, and all incoming and outgoing e-mail is monitored, read, and reviewed by the chief security (executive) officer.
- All mail sent and received by the bank is checked by an officer, and all shipments received through special delivery (UPS, FedEx, Messenger, etc.) are logged into the book and opened by two persons, one of whom is an officer.

Creating True RF Private Bankers and RF Credit Analysts

The conventional riba-based approach to developing a loan portfolio has been to attract an employee from another bank who can bring with him the customers who borrowed money from his current bank to grow his new bank's loan portfolio. In addition, these banks train their bankers to bring in loans to the bank, prompting the banker to be a "salesman" of loans and to encourage prospects to rent money at a "lower" interest rate. In fact, in many cases the salesman mentality prompts many bankers to practice what is known in the banking business as "bait and switch," in which the loan officer quotes a very low interest rate but intentionally does not talk about details such as fees, administration costs, loan origination fees, and other expenses. The customer thinks that he/she has gotten a low rate, only to discover at the time of signing the loan documents that the implied interest rate of the loan is much higher than promised. This is because Regulation Z requires that all loan costs and fees be added to that interest rate. That is why we always ask our community members and clients to insist that they get these offers in writing, so that they can read all the fine print in these loan proposals.

Many of these loan officers carry expensive brief cases, wear designer suits and expensive watches, and drive expensive cars; they carry inflated banking titles with no meaning, like "Senior Vice President—Loans," "Senior Vice President—Business Development," or "Senior Vice President—Loan Adviser." They use these "attractive" interest rates as sales and bargaining tools to meet the weekly target production expected by management. In their pursuit to meet the bank's targets, many families end up in a deeper hole of debt which they cannot serve. The subprime mortgage loan crisis in America is a case in point! While some banks de-emphasize the value of providing highly trained account officers who are supposed to serve and guide honest and hard-working families and business owners, RF bankers choose a different course of action. In addition, while many banks replaced their "loan" officers with computerized credit scoring, Internet-based operations officers, and a retail (mass production) approach to corporate banking, RF bankers chose an opposite course of action.

At the RF-operated Bank of Whittier, N.A., we took the basic approach: we determined what our customer base wanted, and we simply gave it to them in an RF format. We promoted and delivered concepts such as the idea that "we do not rent money—we invest in our customers," honesty, caring, service, family feeling, family values, the comfort of talking with a sincere and concerned advisor, local decision-making authority, tailor-made business banking services, and professionalism. It was thought that separating the lending/underwriting decision from the banking services and advisory responsibility would be a more efficient, credible, and prudent way of delivering true RF banking. This separation helps isolate the emotional attachment of the loan officer to the customer, an attachment that may lead to reaching the wrong credit decision. That is why we have introduced two new important but complementary activities at the RF bank. These are the *RF private banker* and the *RF credit analyst*.

The RF Private Banker The *RF private banker* function was designed to provide each customer with a well-trained and seasoned community banker who is well-educated, responsible, and reputable in the community to become the point of contact between the client and the RF bank. The RF private banker is responsible for maintaining continual contact with bank customers to understand who they are, and to get to know their families, their businesses, and their detailed financial situation including any changes that might come up in the future. The RF private banker is trained to become the "financial doctor" of the family, responsible for the articulation of the family's current financial situation and their goals and aspirations. He/she is responsible for guiding the family towards its financial goals, be it their retirement, the children's education, or financial independence and business growth. The RF private banker aspires to add new family members to the bank's expanding family. The RF private banker makes sure that he/she is available to serve our customers 24 hours a day, 7 days a week.

The person best suited to being an RF private banker is a professional in his/her mid-career who has decided to change his/her career or has lost his/her job. These staff members are handpicked from the community, were extremely successful in what they did before they joined us, are active in the community, are responsible, with high moral and ethical values, and have wisdom and life experience. The ideal RF private banker is a person who is real, sincere, and who is believable and trustworthy.

The RF private banker is trained to read financial statements, financial newspapers, and publications like: *The Wall Street Journal*, and *The Financial Times* (London). Naturally, the RF private banker will not be the expert who recommends how to finance things, but he or she will be the trusted guide who holds the clients' hands and presents the client to qualified bank experts in the needed fields.

The RF Credit Analyst The role of the *RF credit analyst* is to conduct a thorough analysis of the credit application, using the most sophisticated tools in financial analysis and applying RF financing models that use marking-to-market techniques. The RF credit analysts draw on their business, analytical, and banking expertise to reach the most educated and well-thought-out recommendation on whether to approve or decline the credit application.

It is also important to note that the objective of the analysis is to make sure that the customer will be able to service the debt and that the investment the customer wants to embark on makes—in our best judgment—prudent investment sense. The most important factor in the credit analysis step is to make sure that we do not "help" the client dig a deeper hole of debt for him- or herself. We want the client to succeed, and the bank will be an important factor in that success story. In fact, we at the RF bank believe that the success of the customer will lead to our success through new referrals.

To ensure that the RF credit analyst has all the information needed to recommend a course of action, the RF private banker helps the customer understand the purpose of the application process and the usefulness of properly completing forms and promptly supplying all needed documents so that the RF credit analyst can carry out a fair and thorough credit analysis. The RF private banker also acts as an advocate for the client. The RF credit analyst, on the other hand, takes the role of the "hard-nosed" analyst and makes sure that serious questions are asked and issues are raised during client conferences. These conferences are attended by both the RF private banker and the RF credit analyst, and are moderated by the chief credit officer and/or his/her deputy.

In the credit department, we train our associates to believe in the following:

- We are not in the money "renting" business. When we evaluate a credit application, we look at the customer's total situation, including their families, their businesses, and their goals and aspirations, and we provide true total financial advice. The RF bankers pride themselves on investing their time in prudent analysis before they invest the bank's money.
- The best credit is that which is cultivated and developed by the RF private banker.
- The walk-in credit applications are to be reviewed very thoroughly to ensure that the RF bank is not one of the many banks tried by a walk-in customer after he/she has been rejected by other banks.
- We do not accept brokered loans and/or deposits.
- We are not in business to look for participation loans in which to invest the RF bank's money. We are in business to cultivate, develop, analyze, and originate credit transactions, with the purpose of participating in the success, prosperity, and growth of the community.
- We give priority to the community. We gather our deposits from the community, and it is our social, moral, ethical, and regulatory responsibility to reinvest those deposits in the community.
- The best source of customers is our depository clients and their families and friends.

The RF credit analyst function is enhanced by employing some of the better educated people in the field of financial analysis, some of whom have MBA degrees; the department senior advisors and management hold business school degrees from some of the better business schools in the United

States. The goal of the RF credit analyst is to conduct a thorough analysis of the financing application at hand and to develop a number of scenarios and recommendations as to whether or not to finance the proposed project. The RF credit analysis staff is trained not only to protect bank interests, but also and primarily to make sure that the investment is in fact in the best interests of our customers. The RF bank staff must be trained to understand that the RF bank is not in the business of renting money; it is in the business of investing in and with the clients in order to cultivate an ever-larger family of successful and satisfied customers who have chosen to live riba/ribit-free, according to the values of the Judeo-Christian-Islamic system.

Recruiting and Interviewing RF Bankers

An important tradition that I learned during my career while interviewing candidates for Atlantic Richfield Oil Company (now owned by British Petroleum) at the University of Wisconsin and Massachusetts Institute of Technology (MIT) was the process of the interview. I wanted to make interviewing the candidate a real experience of adding a new member to our family and at the same time a memorable and useful experience for the candidate even if it was decided not to employ him/her. The process resembles the interview you hold when your son or your daughter brings home a candidate for a future serious relationship (i.e., marriage).

Candidate interviews are done in a unique way. The candidate is requested to be at the bank at 8:00 a.m. to see if he/she is an early morning person and if he/she will be on time that early in the morning. I start the interview by offering the candidate something to drink, to make him/her feel at ease, and I personally prepare and serve that drink.

I start by introducing the candidate to the interview process. I share with him/her my story, in order to structure his/her story in the same way. I also share with the candidate the goals of the organization and our dreams. I check whether the candidate did his/her homework on our organization by visiting the Web site and other sources on the Internet. The candidate is asked to tell us about his or her experiences in high school and what courses he/she liked and disliked, as manifested by the grades he/she achieved. We then proceed to the college years at length. In the course of the interview, I evaluate the candidate's character and the depth of his/her parent's efforts to bring him/her up with values and discipline, in order to gauge their character. I then proceed to tell the candidate that we at the bank commit to making him/her a very successful banker in two years, and that he/she does not have to have prior banking experience. I share with him/her that we can hire a well-dressed chimpanzee and teach it how to print charts and impressive reports. However, there are two traits that we cannot teach a chimpanzee: speaking the truth and not betraying the trust vested in him/ her. This segment takes approximately 90 minute to two hours.

Then the candidate interviews most of the staff members for 20 to 30 minutes each. This approach helps intensify the family feeling among the staff members and makes them feel that they are participating in the employment decision. It also enables the candidate to take a closer look at the family that he/she will join. After each of the interviews with the staff, I ask the staff member his or her opinion. At the end, I invite the candidate to come back to my office to debrief him/her and to listen to his/her feedback. A decision is then made, and the candidate is made an offer or declined.

When the candidate accepts the offer he/she is asked to complete an employment application, and the human resources department conducts a confidential background check to make sure that there are no prior derogatory or criminal records. The candidate is given two very important books. The first is the employee handbook, which details the policies, rights, and responsibilities of the employee. The other is a recording book. The candidate is requested to take clear and detailed notes during his/her training, communications, meetings and work. This book is one of the most important aspects of the employment.

Community Participation, Networking, and Customer Service

One of the challenges we faced was how to integrate with a new city and a new community. There are some who say that the easiest way is to call the Muslim community and try to solicit business from the masajid (mosques). That was a very easy task for me because of the credibility I have accumulated through serving the North American Muslim community in most cities in North America since 1968. However, I did not want to take the easy way out of a great challenge. Our goal was to sincerely offer the RF banking services we believe in to people of all faiths in our immediate neighborhood of a 50-mile radius. The other standard approach was to join the Chamber of Commerce organizations of the different cities. We found that such organizations are very difficult to integrate with because of the many old friendships and alliances developed over the years, which include other competing banks.

Two months before the new management took over the bank, we started an independent survey of the city of Whittier market. We identified businesses, colleges, and responsible officials in city government. We contacted Whittier College, California State Fullerton University, and California State Long Beach University so that we might get to know their professors and administrators, hoping to attract good candidates and interns from their business programs. These efforts yielded wonderful results. Our bank was introduced to the leaders of thought and the producers of talent in the immediate community. We understand that many of the professors spoke very highly of our team at the bank, and they also recommended their top students to interview with us. I was also honored to be invited to preside as the keynote speaker at commencement exercises at some of the colleges. A typical event is attended by at least 250 graduates and their families, totaling at least 1,500 guests. This presented a great opportunity and free advertising for the bank.

We decided to develop a strategy that helped us introduce what we do. The first step was to do business with the surrounding community. If we needed to print something, to replace the carpet, to make signs, to order food, or to fix the plumbing, we went to local providers, in order to give back to the community. In addition, the team decided to capitalize on my long-term experience in the interfaith movement. We looked for and located the interfaith groups in the city and started to participate first as individuals, then as a team from the bank. We participated in Christmas, Thanksgiving, Jewish festivities, Chinese New Year festivities, and Muslim festivities that the community sponsored,

This step proved to be one of the most important and significant contributors to bringing credibility to what we do and to sharing the Judeo-Christian-Islamic values of our new RF banking movement. I was asked to author a newspaper article on the economic meltdown of 2008, in which I discussed many of the Judeo-Christian-Islamic ideas of RF banking. The article was very well received in the community. I felt extremely fulfilled when one of the bank customers asked me, "Dr. Rahman, are you a Christian?" I asked him why he was asking. He said because of what you all do at the bank. I responded by saying that we are subscribers and believers in the Judeo-Christian-Islamic value system, and his feelings proved it. The bank has gained the accounts of most churches in town and many of their flocks. We also finance churches, schools, and places of worship for people of all faiths. We established contacts and met with the city manager and political and administrative leaders at city hall in order to introduce the new RF format of the bank and to share with them our vision and plans to make the bank an important institution in the city.

The new management team has made it a standard operating procedure to greet every customer who walks into the bank. I personally come out to introduce myself, learn their names and their businesses, introduce them to everyone in our family of employees, with a brief comment on their background, and invite them to my office. All of the tellers are trained to introduce themselves and share with customers the fact that they are aspiring bankers who will be graduating after so many semesters, and that they are here for hands-on training. The tellers are also trained to learn the name of the customer, how many children the customer has, and other details about the customer's business and family. We have trained the tellers and the operations personnel to be polite, courteous, and helpful when they receive a request on the phone; thanks to the use of the most up-to-date computer systems, the answers are usually readily available within a few seconds.

The operations staff checks every morning for NSF (non-sufficient fund) checks, and personally calls every NSF customer, asking them to come to the bank as soon as possible to cover their positions, so that we may avoid returning the check and creating unnecessary embarrassment for the customer. This practice is not done any more by most of the other banks, and it is highly appreciated by our customers. If the NSF behavior becomes chronic, we have a private meeting with the account owner and counsel him/her to either abide by the rules or leave the bank.

TRAINING PROGRAM AT THE BANK OF WHITTIER OPEN UNIVERSITY

One of the challenges we faced when we moved to run the Bank of Whittier as a successful RF bank was to find qualified staff. One option was to advertise for experienced bankers who had experience and a successful track record in the community banking business. We have attempted this option since 1998, without tangible success. Most of the experienced bankers we met and worked with are used to a standard operating procedure that made us wonder about their commitment to community service. The first thing they would ask for is a very high salary package. The package not only included a very high salary compared to the profit capability of the bank, it also included other perks—an expensive car allowance, a country club membership, or a generous expense account.

When we started planning the management changeover in July 2003, we decided to start with a core group of bankers from the community, consisting of a president, a chief financial officer, and a chief credit officer. They all accepted a very humble salary and benefits package, because they were committed to this new brand of banking. We also started interviewing fresh business school graduates. We were lucky, because the bank was located within a short driving distance from a number of high-quality business schools. We believe that if we employed superior graduates who had achieved a very high grade point average (3.75 out of 4 or higher), that would present us with serious hardworking young men and women who were fresh, smart, eager to learn, and excited about becoming the new RF bankers of the future. We also concluded that a well-designed training program should be designed and implemented to enhance the goal of producing a new generation of successful RF community bankers.

We pioneered the *Bank of Whittier RF Open University*. The university is convened twice a year. Each session lasts 45 days, meeting every weekday from 8:00 A.M. to 9:30 A.M. A rigorous curriculum was prepared, and the faculty consisted of upper management, invited guests, and experts in banking. The training program is enhanced by videos and hands-on training. In addition, we use outside auditors in all fields of banking operations to train our staff. The auditors were asked to engage the staff members in order to conduct their audits and to train the employees at the same time. This approach proved to be very successful. In a matter of 12 months, the employees started to operate efficiently and to be in full compliance with the auditors' findings. We also instructed the staff to consider the auditors their coaches, and not to argue or justify the errors they committed but rather listen and learn. In addition, management met with the auditors at least once each day to discuss any noncompliance issues and get the staff to fix them immediately. This policy has won us wonderful reviews from the outside auditors and the regulators.

In addition, we also recruited students at the business schools who aspired to become bankers to serve as tellers. This job gave them a chance to learn, to evaluate the bank staff "family," while at the same time enabling us to get to know them and to recruit from amongst them for future staff at the RF bank. It is important to note that management very closely reviewed the grades the candidates achieved in every course to identify where they would best fit. For example, if the candidate received an A or a minimum grade of B and mostly A's in the accounting courses, it would qualify the candidate to start in the treasury department. If the candidate received top grades in mathematics and financial analysis and had good verbal skills, she or he would qualify for the credit analysis department. In addition, superior staff members who provide outstanding performance in two years are sponsored by the bank to study in a three-year part-time banking MBA program in one of the superior-rated business schools that specialize in banking and finance. The program is held for two weeks every year; in the interim period, the candidate remains in touch with the faculty and is given assignments via the Internet. These reports and the results of the tests are reviewed by upper management.

The purpose of the Bank of Whittier RF Open University training program is to graduate qualified and high-caliber RF bankers within two years by familiarizing the employees with an overview of all U.S. banking regulations and other banking operating codes, as well as different U.S. banking acts. All new employees who join the bank are required to receive the same training within three months of their employment.

The following is a summary of the Open University curriculum. It is not exhaustive, but gives a quick review and highlights of the important segments of the training program.

Reading Discipline

The staff members are trained to read with their fingers. Each staff member is asked to touch every letter, in order to read carefully any document they are asked to review. Management watches the new candidate to make sure that finger reading is practiced as a unique and universal characteristic of the bank staff. If the new employee does not use this technique, she/he is considered to be not qualified to continue as a member of our family.

RF Banking Values and Social Responsibility

RF banking values are detailed, and our motto, *We Do Not Rent Money—We Invest in Our Customers*, is discussed and made clear. Contrasts between conventional riba-based banking and RF banking outlook and approach are made clear and discussed.

Social responsibility, as manifested by dedicated and humble service to the community, is drilled in all our presentations and training. In addition, we review the very popular movie *It's a Wonderful Life*. The movie depicts a savings and loan banker with his wife who have spent their savings and life developing the community by helping community members move from rundown apartments to beautiful homes financed by the savings and loan bank, which used its deposits to build homes, finance autos for taxi drivers, and meet other community needs. In fact, we tell the staff that the first RF banker in America was George Bailey (acted by Jimmy Stewart, the star of the movie).

Introduction to Banking

The training program also includes an introduction to banking, the creation of money, the Federal Reserve System, and interest rates. A brief review of economics and monetary theory are also discussed. The contents of this book are essentially summarized to the staff in the Open University. In addition, important banking concepts like the multiplier effect, the creation of credit, bank capital adequacy, and liquidity requirements are discussed. Finally, a brief review of important bank policies is introduced and discussed with the staff.

Character Building: Honesty and Integrity[2]

This part of the program focuses on character and discipline of RF bank employees as the trusted custodians and safekeepers of our customers' money and private information. We play out different scenarios in which that trust is compromised before the class, in order to make them aware of the severe punishment that awaits embezzlers and bank workers who steal.

Management stresses beyond any doubt or mercy that it will be uncompromising and very brutal should the slightest indication of such behavior be discovered.

Know Your Customers, Privacy, Customer Identification Policies, and Fraud Prevention

New Accounts Opening   After the crime of September 11, 2001 and the increased abuse of bank services in the United States by con artists, money launderers, and terrorists, strict regulations and security laws have been passed, making it difficult to open a new bank account for a new customer. This part of the program trains bank staff on the Customer Identification Program (CIP) at the bank and the required steps that must be taken to safely open a new account.

Staff is also made aware of and trained to follow the requirements and the guidelines of the USA PATRIOT Act.[3] This training program teaches the methods of *enhanced due diligence* and explains where to find documentation to assist in the verification of information.

Safeguarding Customer Information and Protecting Customer Privacy   The staff is trained to recognize the methods and techniques used by con artists, impersonators, and identity theft experts to achieve their goal of getting as much information about bank customers as possible. Privacy regulations are discussed as well. The program also uses a video that dramatizes the mistakes innocently made by bank employees that can compromise customer data safety.

The responsibility of keeping depositors' information confidential is one basic and required responsibility of banking and, in particular, RF banking. A video training program was developed in compliance with regulatory requirements and is designed in such a way that the staff will fully understand the responsibilities with which they are entrusted.

Discovering and Identifying Check Fraud   Bank staff—especially operations personnel, tellers, and the staff in bank treasury—are taught and trained on what to look for when a check is presented for processing, and procedures that should be followed to determine if the check is genuine or counterfeit.

Identifying and Preventing Fraud against the Elderly   Many elderly members of the community use banks to deposit their savings and to receive their Social Security monthly payments and pension monthly payments. Elderly citizens are frequently the victims of choice of con artists. We show and discuss a videotape that illustrates procedures that may allow bank employees to detect and ultimately prevent frauds committed against elderly customers of banks.

Bank Security The staff is trained in ways to enhance security at the bank, from bank opening and closing discipline to daily bank operating procedures, as well as the bank's program to defend against bank robbers.

Understanding Banking Regulations

All bank regulations are discussed in great detail, and a summary of each regulation is handed out to staff. In addition, the Open University program focuses on a number of important regulations that must be understood clearly and followed religiously by staff members to conduct a safe and reputable banking operation.

Prevention of Money Laundering and Complying with the Bank Secrecy Act

Bank Secrecy Act (BSA) and USA PATRIOT Act[4] Banks may be the most important starting point in identifying irregular and suspicious activities. Bank tellers, private bankers, and management are responsible for keeping the public trust by always staying alert to any abuse of that trust by people who try to circumvent the system and abuse it. This training program is designed to be hands-on training for the staff, teaching them to comply with the Bank Secrecy Act (BSA) requirements and the customer privacy acts such as the Gramm-Leach-Bliley Act (GLBA). The training includes information on programs used by the bank to open accounts and identify customers who deal with the bank, like the Customer Identification Program (CIP) and others. The staff is also made aware of the repercussions and the stiff penalties for violating the Act.

Additionally, the staff is trained on executing regulations issued by Fin-CEN,[5] which requires that special reports be filed with the government about those customers who try to, for example, structure deposits so that they might circumvent the laws. The staff is also trained on the details of checking information on customers using the data available from the Office of Foreign Assets Control (OFAC). Staff is made aware of the stiff penalties applied to institutions that do not comply with the OFAC requirements.

Risk Assessment for Noncompliance A major part of every financial institution examination by responsible government and state authorities is a close look at risk assessment and risk management. Financial institutions are used to doing in-depth evaluations in lending, data processing, and information technology (IT) areas, where a breach could cause serious damage. However, risk must also be addressed from every vulnerable location, whether in operations, administration, the back office, or in the branch.

This segment of the program focuses on training staff to identify and communicate the many types of risks that most often occur in the bank branch(es) and to handle those incidents in a safe and sure manner.

Special Courses for Credit Department Personnel

Fair Lending Act Fair lending is an important RF banking requirement as well as an important government regulation. It must be taken seriously by all, and it must be recognized and practiced by bank management and staff. The bank's staff members are trained that the principle of fair lending, dealing with all people graciously and respectfully regardless of their skin color, affluence, religion, national origin, gender, or language, is not only good service but demonstrates compliance with the laws of the land and with Shari'aa, which makes discrimination one of the most serious offenses against our Creator.

Staff is trained to understand that it is not enough to perform sophisticated credit analysis and generate glossy and detailed financial analysis reports. The credit analysis staff is trained to gauge the character of the customer, his/her background and training as depicted by their personal history (a resume of the applicant is required by the bank credit department as part of a credit application package), the nature of the business, how the business is managed, and the detailed background of the managers in charge. Another important aspect of the training sheds light on the importance of visiting the customer's place of business and facilities—including the questions they should ask and the clues they should look for. Officers of the credit department and staff are trained to identify credit risks in such important business activities as marketing, business planning, environmental protection, governmental regulatory compliance, competitive analysis, operations management, inventory controls, safety practices, employee relations, and sales management.

Predatory and Subprime Lending RF banking is a brand of banking that does not even consider being involved in the business of predatory[6] or subprime lending,[7] because these businesses are against the Judeo-Christian-Islamic moral and ethical values of the RF bank. The staff is trained that they are not in business to make money on commissions from selling loans to borrowers or to meet "loan production" quotas, particularly when it comes to customers who could not afford to pay the loans back. The fact that some loans may be, for example, guaranteed by the U.S. government's Small Business Administration (SBA) or that the mortgage will be assumed by one of the government-sponsored entities (GSEs, like Freddie Mac or Fannie Mae) does not justify being "flexible" in applying the strict requirements of RF financing. The staff is trained to understand that we—as a dedicated RF bank—are in business to help people succeed and to meet their commitments and obligations. We also teach staff that digging a deeper hole of debt for our trusted customers by giving them loans that they cannot service is not only improper or illegal, but against the values by which we, as RF bankers, exist.

THE BALANCE SHEET OF THE RF BANK

Before explaining how to run an RF bank in general, it is useful to familiarize the reader with some of the accounting concepts used in banking. Any company, and for that matter any bank, has to balance what it owns—its assets—with what it owes—its liabilities. The difference between the assets and liabilities is equal to the shareholders' equity. The following is a detailed description of the balance sheet of an RF bank, compared to that of a riba-based conventional bank. It is important to note here that an RF banker looks differently at various liabilities and deposit accounts and the classification of the types of liquidity available to him/her. For example, the shareholders' capital is looked upon by the RF banker as the highest risk capital, which should be—implicitly—used first in its financing operations. On the other extreme, an RF banker views the demand deposit accounts (DDAs) as those that must not be exposed to any risk, because they are considered a trust (*Amana*) to be kept as though it were in a safe deposit box.

General Concepts

Liabilities When a customer deposits money in the bank, this deposit is called a *liability*, because the bank owes the money to the depositor when he/she demands it. When a customer comes to a bank to invest in a time certificate of deposit (TCD), that means that the bank owes that customer this money and the profit (interest or the rent of money, in the case of riba-operated conventional banks, and rent income derived from the rent of facilities in the case of RF banks) distributed by the bank.

Assets The bank is expected to invest the money that its depositors have entrusted it with by, for example, financing the credit needs of customers who want to finance the purchase of a car, a home, a commercial building, or a business. The promise of these customers to pay back is formalized in an agreement between the bank and the customer and is called a promissory note. It is considered as one of the bank's assets. If the riba-based bank has excess cash waiting to be invested in financing facilities (loans), it prefers to invest this cash liquidity in short-term investment instruments to produce more income, in the form of interest income. The most secure investment is with the Federal Reserve (the central bank of the United States), and the bank receives the Federal Funds interest rate. The cash could also be invested in TCDs in other banks, in government-issued bonds, in mortgage-backed securities (MBSs), or in other short- and medium-term debt securities that pay an interest income. These are all called assets. In the case of RF banks, the investment activity is categorized in relation to the type of liability on the RF bank's book. Here is a detailed classification of these deposits:

- *Demand deposit accounts (DDAs).* As stated earlier, DDAs can only be invested in Fed Funds and receive Fed Funds interest, which, as was explained in Chapter 7, is different from the prohibited riba in the Judeo-Christian-Islamic value system.
- *Shareholders' equity and time certificate of deposits (TCDs).* These funds can be invested in the RF financing portfolio, based on the *mark-to-market* principle. The income is distributed to the TCD holders. To comply with the government banking regulations, TCDs must declare a specific rate when they are advertised. The first solution is to limit the maturity to one, three, six, or twelve months. The advertised rate is a portion of the rent return on the RF portfolio assembled by the RF bank in a finance portfolio/TCD maturity matching program. As the RF bank is established and is accepted by the public and the regulators, a variable TCD rate can be offered.

The Balance Sheet and the Shareholders' Equity   The responsibility of any accountant or bank chief financial officer (CFO) is to balance the assets with the liabilities and produce a balance sheet, which balances assets with liabilities. The balance (the difference between the assets and the liabilities) is the shareholder's equity. If the bank earns profit and, for example, its board of directors decides not to pay dividends to the shareholders, but to invest the profits back in the bank, the shareholders' equity increases. If the bank makes a loss, that loss has to be subtracted from the shareholders' equity, reducing it by the amount of that loss.

Comparison Between the Balance Sheet of an RF Bank and a Riba-Based Bank   Operating an RF bank in the United States requires using standard language and accounting principles and abiding by all U.S. accounting regulations, principles, and standards. However, that does not prevent the RF banker from thinking and constructing an (internal) RF bank balance sheet, based on the RF principles detailed in this book, without violating the Financial Accounting Standards Board (FASB) rules and regulations. RF banking and financing is about style, philosophy, mode of operation, character, and mindset. This prompts the RF management to look at different parts of the balance sheet with an RF perspective, upholding the laws of the land while also upholding Shari'aa. Exhibit 12.1 contains a table that attempts to contrast the RF bank's balance sheet with the conventional riba-based bank balance sheet.

EXHIBIT 12.1   RF bank balance sheet versus conventional riba-based bank balance sheet.

Riba-Based Conventional Bank	RF Bank
Assets	Assets
Investments:	Investments:
Federal funds sold	Federal funds sold
Interest-Bearing Deposits	Short-Term RF Credits
Loans	Asset/Service-Based Credits/Investments
Commercial	Commercial
Real Estate	Real Estate
Consumer	Consumer
Liabilities	Liabilities
Interest-Bearing Deposits:	Matched Rent/Income-Generating Deposits:
NOW, Money Market, Savings	RF NOW, RF Money Market, RF Savings
Time Certificates of Deposit	RF Certificates of Deposit
Shareholders' Equity	Shareholders' Equity

Please note that the income and expenses of the bank are handled in another financial statement, which accounts for all the income sources of the bank and its expenses.

Income   Ideally, the main income source of the riba-based conventional bank should come from the interest income earned on loans, because the interest rate charged is higher than all other sources of income, such as interest on TCDs with other banks, MBSs, or government bonds. In an RF bank, there is no interest income on loans, but there is rent income generated by the RF LARIBA model of financing.

There are other sources of income, such as the fees charged by a typical riba-based bank for its services. Example of these fees include *loan origination fees*, which cover the cost of time spent by bank employees (credit department and other administrative functions); *nonsufficient funds fees*, which penalizes those who write checks without having enough money in their accounts to cover the amount; *late payment fees*, which penalize those who are late in making the monthly payment on a loan; and *wire transfer fees*, which cover the expenses of wiring money from the bank or to the bank. Perhaps the largest of all fees and the highest of all interest income sources and fees is from the credit card business.

In an RF bank's case, all income generated from penalties charged for unjustified customer behavior is deposited in a special fund we call the M-Fund. (M is the first letter of the word *miskeen*, which means the needy. These are persons—in some cases employees with special circumstances, customers, or other individuals—who cannot make ends meet by relying only on their insufficient salary.) In addition, any unavoidable interest earned by the RF bank goes first to the M-fund and, if there are excess funds, then to registered and certified charities in the local communities, including faith-based organizations of all faiths.

Expenses   Regular bank expenses include salaries and benefits of the bank employees and the interest expenses paid to investors in TCDs or other money market instruments, in the form of interest paid on interest-bearing deposits of different types in the case of an RF bank and income generated from the RF portfolio in the case of an RF bank. Other expenses are the usual expenses necessary to keep a business going, such as rental of premises, depreciation of equipment and other facilities, computer data and item processing (e.g., handling and processing checks), and the computer accounting system itself, which is provided by an outside service company that services all bank check sorting and processing needs as well as banks' computer and accounting services needs. In the case of the RF bank, these expenses are the same, except for the fact that the RF bank does not pay interest, as in the case of interest-bearing deposits; instead, the RF bank holds rent-generating deposits and the depositors are paid a portion of the rent income of the bank's RF investment portfolio.

Another expense that the bank management always must estimate carefully and take into consideration is to allow for any loan (credit) losses. This expense is called the allowance for loan and lease losses (ALLL). The ALLL is planned for by allocating an expense to allow for these potential losses. This expense is like an emergency fund that can be tapped in case there is a nonperforming loan. The money charged to the profit of the bank is considered as an asset. If a loan fails and is considered a loss, that will produce a very serious expense item that can be detrimental to the bank. The first step is for management to try to pay for the loss from ALLL. However, if ALLL is not enough, then the amount is charged to the expenses, and if there is a loss, this loss is charged to reduce the bank's capital.

As an example, consider a situation in which the bank assets are $100 million, and out of these assets was a loan portfolio of $85 million. One of the loans, say in the amount of $5 million, does not perform as agreed, which means that the customer, for one reason or another, has not made payments, cannot honor the loan commitment anymore, and is bankrupt. The bank decides to expense this loan as a nonperforming loan. Suppose the ALLL was $2 million. The bank management may try to allocate it to ALLL and according to the rules they only can allocate $500,000. This reduces ALLL to $1.5 million. Assets would be reduced by $5 million—$500,000 from ALLL and $4.5 million is allocated to reduction in income. If net income was $4.5 million and the bank capital was $10 million, then the new reduced bank capital would be $5.5 million. This may result in a bank with inadequate capital ratios as required by the regulators. The bank is required by the regulators to raise more capital in order to continue its operations.

Another unfortunate situation may happen. If the economy goes bad, or if the loan department was sloppy and not careful about its credit analysis and financing discipline, the bank might have four loans (say, $5 million each) that are considered a loss. That would mean a loss of $20 million. The net result would be that the bank capital is wiped out. Of course, bank management can hide these losses in many ways. One of these ways is to keep renewing these loans and not recognizing the facts, but in the end such losses will have to be recognized. That is essentially what happened in 2008.

THE NEED FOR A GOOD DETAIL-ORIENTED MANAGEMENT TEAM AT THE RF BANK

The success of any bank depends mostly on its management. Some bankers may want you to believe that banking is a very sophisticated business. It really is not. It is a simple business, but it requires intensive and expert attention to the minute details. That is why the centralized model, in which mega-banks acquire smaller banks and centralize different bank functions (especially the lending activity) at the bank headquarters, has proven to be ineffective, as was proven by the 2008 bank crisis and by subsequent tests performed by regulators in the first quarter of 2009. The large size of the system reduces the human dimension of this personal business called banking. Banking is a business that handles peoples' needs and trust; it cannot be done by reducing the customer to an account or loan number, sent to a central location to be processed and evaluated. This approach has transformed the bank branches of many of the mega-banks and the investment banking institutions in small communities into "asset gathering" outlets, without paying attention to the most important asset for a bank: the customer and the community.

For example, at the Bank of Whittier, every morning at 9:00 A.M. the bank president (branch manager) convenes a 15- to 20-minute meeting. Meeting participants include the CFO, the chief credit officer, the head of private banking and operations, the head of the credit (loan) department, and the operations manager. The group goes through the bank ledger line-by-line to make sure that not a single penny or data entry is missed or recognized, and to decide what to do regarding the checks that were returned to the bank because of insufficient funds. The chairman of the bank starts early in the morning—around 6:30–7:00 A.M.—and pores over the ledger and sends his questions to the 9:00 A.M. meeting; in some cases, he attends the meeting.

In addition to the 9:00 A.M. meeting, the operations of the bank must be scrutinized in great detail. This is done in the 11:00 A.M. meeting. This meeting is convened by the senior vice president in charge of operations and is attended by the CFO, the operations manager, and the treasury department supervisors to ensure that all of the bank's financial activities have been accounted for, that all nonsufficient funds accounts have been called by their RF private bankers, and that the customers with NSF warnings came to cover the deficit (or, if not, it is decided that the NSF check must be returned).

RESTRUCTURING A RIBA-BASED BANK TO OPERATE AS AN RF BANK

As has been stressed throughout the book, RF banking is not about form; it is about substance and operations that fulfill the requirements of Shari'aa, which reflect the fundamental values of the Judeo-Christian-Islamic system. This makes the transformation of the bank to an RF operating bank much easier, without even the need for a regulatory change or transformation of the current laws of the land in the United States. We believe that RF banking and finance is all about training the management and staff and how they all handle the most important of all God's gifts—the trust given to us by our customers when they entrust us with their hard-earned money, savings, and retirement planning funds and their private personal information. It is also about how management looks at the balance sheet of the bank, how the RF credit (loan) portfolio is developed, and how the RF bank liquidity is invested.

The first step the new management took when it arrived at the bank with the new RF banking team was to assess what was going on at the bank, in order to progressively transform the bank into an RF operating bank. Here is what we did.

Evaluation and Review of Existing Services

Review Existing Loans and Add New Credit to the Portfolio Using the RF Finance Principle of Mark-to-Market
We were lucky to have a bank with a very small riba-based conventional loan portfolio that equaled about 20 percent of total deposits. That gave us a wonderful opportunity to start building an RF finance portfolio using the principles of marking-to-market and the RF finance model based on Shari'aa. The first step we wanted to take was to invest the large amount of cash we had on hand at the bank in different projects, such as commercial buildings, home mortgages, schools, faith-based worship centers, fast food franchises, medical doctors' clinics, and automobiles. We were lucky because we had accumulated extensive RF financing experience since 1987, when we started LARIBA.

The building of an RF finance portfolio needed time, and the bank had a very large cash position. In situations like this, a typical bank management contacts loan brokers to buy loans through them. This option was not available to us, because according to Shari'aa buying and selling of debt (*dayn*) is prohibited. In fact, this stipulation has been one of the most important factors that helped many Islamic banks fare better than conventional riba-based banks during the 2008 financial meltdown. In RF banking, the practice of investing the bank's money in different finance facilities must be conducted by the bank credit department, and it should be done with those customers who are known in person to the bank so that the money will be invested with them in the projects they need to finance. On the other hand, RF bankers are not allowed to sell their loans or sell the servicing of these facilities (servicing a loan means taking care of billing clients, collecting monthly payments, escrowing the funds needed to pay taxes and insurance, and responding to customers' needs), because selling debt and/or servicing is also not allowed.

I usually use a striking metaphor to make the concept clearer: "You cannot get married and turn around and sell your children." The finance facilities originated by the RF bank must be kept in the portfolio and serviced by the RF bank that originated them. It is much easier for the customer—who is looked on as a partner—to call us for assistance at any time. If the loans and their servicing were sold to an outside organization, as some banks do, the customer would end up calling a general number and speaking to a representative who has never met him/her and does not know anything about RF banking. At any rate, we were patient and built the RF financing portfolio at the bank in a prudent and meticulous way.

Investing the Bank's Cash   The RF bank management is trained to categorize the different types of cash that the bank has. It begins by investing the shareholders' capital, which is—by definition—supposed to be exposed to the highest risk in the risk profile defined and approved by the board of directors. Subsequently, the treasury, in its allocation of funds to RF financing, uses the investment deposits that are invested as time certificates of deposit (TCDs). The funds that are tagged as deposits in trust (DIT, or *Amana*), which are known as DDAs in riba-based banks, must not be invested because of the implied covenant made by the RF banker to the owners of these deposits to keep these funds safe. Because our DDAs, from experience, were approximately 20 to 25 percent of the total deposits, the ratio between finance facilities (loan) to deposits was kept by policy not to exceed that percent (75–80%). These funds can only be invested with the Fed.

Evaluating the Risk of Nonperforming Parts of the Financing Portfolio: Calculation of ALLL   To minimize the possibility of any unexpected variation in the portfolio performance, the Bank of Whittier's management pioneered a new risk-based system to evaluate the risk of nonperformance of one or more of the components of the financing portfolio. The following is a four-step summary of the procedure and methodology we developed.

1. The credit analysis team meets frequently to assess its credit facility portfolio in light of any significant changes in the economic, demographic, social, and political factors that have occurred in the quarter or are expected to occur in the short-term in the following quarter. These meetings are attended by the CEO, chief credit officer, credit analysts, treasury department, loan servicing manager, and private bankers. During the meeting, every credit facility on the bank's books is discussed by the credit analyst, the servicing department manager, and

the private banker in charge, as well as the rest of the participants including the servicing department manager. Based on the discussion, a vote is taken regarding the risk rating assigned to each credit facility and the need to keep it as-is, reduce it, or increase it.

2. The bank's CEO, chief credit officer, and deputy chief credit officer scan important financial, economic, monetary, and political news, analysis, research, and reports published by *The Wall Street Journal, The Financial Times* (London), *The Economist* (London), the Heritage Foundation, the University of Southern California (USC), the University of California at Los Angeles (UCLA), and various agencies of the federal, state (California), and local (southern California) governments. An integrated report on the state of the economy is published and distributed to the Strategic Credit Assessment Group (SCAG) to assist its members in formulating their opinions on risk factors affecting the allowance for loan and lease losses (ALLL) reserves.

3. Members of SCAG independently identify a matrix of the risk factors affecting ALLL reserves for the operating quarter to come. Based on this review, a probability-based qualitative/quantitative analysis is conducted by identifying in the matrix of variables the different economic, demographic, political, monetary, policy, labor and international factors. Each member of SCAG assigns factors to each of the variables, to include an estimate of how much each parameter will impact the different category the bank is active in financing. The result of the analysis produces a set of aggregated percent allocations for each credit facility that must be reserved in ALLL. This analysis is done independently by each member of SCAG.

4. The weighted average of the SCAG committee (usually six to seven members, with weights assigned based the member's experience and responsibility) is then applied, along with the historical credit facility loss factors, to calculate the required ALLL reserve.

Can the RF Bank Offer Unsecured Loans? What About Lines of Credit? Unsecured loans are loans granted by riba-based banks to individuals and institutions based only on the historic and projected cash flow. The riba-based bank does not take any asset as collateral for the loan. Because of the RF banking rules discussed in the book, unsecured loans are prohibited in an RF banking regime. As was detailed earlier, RF banking uses asset/service-based loans only, and the asset/service must be marked to the market.

If a customer is applying for an RF line of credit, the situation must be handled on a case-by-case basis. For example, if a medical doctor wants to finance the construction of his new home, an RF bank cannot simply offer a line of credit in the traditional riba-based conventional banking way. First of all, land is not accepted as an asset in most commercial banking regimes, because it is illiquid and nonproductive. The solution the RF bank management uses to serve situations like this is to evaluate the fair market value of the medical doctor's business, based on its financial statements and operating history. We then devise an implied joint venture between the bank and the doctor in which the medical doctor conceptually sells to the bank a share in his business in lieu of the cash that would be made available to him in a line-of-credit form. As discussed in Chapter 10, a lien is taken by the bank on the business. When the doctor withdraws money, the bank becomes an implied share owner of a percentage of the business, and participates in its profit in the percentage indicated. When the doctor pays the money back, the bank automatically (conceptually) sells the shares of the business back. This process is structured as a dynamic process using the LARIBA model and the mark-to-market principles discussed in Chapter 10.

Buying and Selling Loans   When the new management team took over the bank, we needed to aggressively add new loans to the bank's loan portfolio to increase income (as is done traditionally in riba-based conventional banks). Some of our management team recommended that we call loan brokers to buy loans from other banks and financial institutions. According to the Judeo-Christian-Islamic value system and Shari'aa, buying and selling paper debt and trading these "paper" instruments are not allowed for a number of reasons, as discussed in Chapter 10. The most important of these reasons is the fact that these loans were not constructed according to RF financing requirements. The idea was discarded. The other practical reason for management's decision not to buy loans from brokers is that the broker who will bring those loans (paper debt) will eventually try to "churn" them (offering them within a period of approximately two years to another bank), creating a speculative chain that does not create any benefit to the customer (whom the bank never meets, because it is a brokered loan) nor to the bank itself. The bank pays a commission to the broker who brings these loans and ends up losing that money within two years, along with the loans.

Our credit policy spelled out very clearly the condition of not buying debt, because of the RF bank's implicit function as an investor—in a riba-free way—with the customer, who should be known to the banker. Finally, it must be stated that the bank bought RF MBSs that were "manufactured" by LARIBA according to the Fannie Mae standards (RF MBSs). This was, in fact, not a purchase of debt but a practical and legal way, according to the laws of the United States and Shari'aa to invest, as the mortgages that constituted the RF-MBSs were produced by us at LARIBA, and every credit is known to us in full detail. The payment experience of each of the RF home mortgages in the RF/MBS was known to us in great detail because we were the ones who financed the underlying mortgages in an RF way. More details on RF MBSs will be included in the next chapter, which is devoted to RF financing case studies.

Selling the Servicing of the Finance Facility to Generate a Fee Income   After the financing facility has been booked by any bank, it must be serviced. This means that the servicing department must issue the monthly billing statements and mail them to the customers, receive payments, keep track of the accounting, keep track of the insurance validity on the property and whether insurance is current, and make sure that the customer is paying local, state, and federal taxes on time. In the United States, there are companies that are willing to "buy" the servicing of the loans and pay a generous fee to the bank or the finance company. As discussed in Chapter 10, it was decided not to follow this practice, because we felt that it did not fit with Shari'aa and Judeo-Christian-Islamic values. It would be unacceptable to invest in a customer and then sell the relationship so that when the customer calls, he/she is connected to a representative whom he/she has never met, who may not be familiar with the community and with RF banking and finance values.

Screening of the Existing Deposit and Investment Accounts   All of the existing accounts and the owners of these accounts were closely reviewed on a case-by-case basis and most of them were contacted and/or interviewed. We discovered that the bank had accounts for liquor stores, night clubs, bars, and check cashing companies. We proceeded to close the accounts of the liquor stores and the bars, for obvious reasons. We also concluded that the check-cashing companies were taking advantage of low-income citizens who did not have a bank account, and that the interest rates charged to these people were excessive. We decided to close those accounts, as well. It is important to indicate to the reader that while making the decision to close an account, we never gave weight to the size of the account. We focused on the requirements of the RF moral and ethical values, which manifest the values of Shari'aa and the Judeo-Christian-Islamic system.

Deciding on Types of Accounts Offered to Individuals, Families, and Businesses

Most banks in the United States offer a highly diversified array of services and types of accounts. One day, I asked myself about the motivation behind the different account types, names, and the conditions that have to be met, for example, for the customer to obtain a free business account service or low fees on income-generating accounts. It was clear that these many types of accounts were marketing techniques used by the new accounts departmentments of different banks to entice customers to open accounts and maintain their existing banking relationships.

In response, we convened a meeting of the concerned departments and after an in-depth discussion we agreed that the bank would offer simple and clearly defined account types and conditions, and that we would earn our income at the bank, mainly through reinvesting the funds in our customers by financing their needs. This practice brings our motto to life: *We Do Not Rent Money—We Invest in Our Customers*. The following is the list of account types that we decided to offer our clients. All these are offered at no fees.

Deposit-In-Trust Accounts (DIT)—Correspond to Demand Deposit Accounts (DDA) in Riba-Based Conventional Banks   These accounts comply with the U.S. federal banking Regulation Q, because they are looked on literally as money given by the customer for safekeeping at the bank. A DDA is a type of cash account that makes customer deposits available upon demand. Regulation Q disallows the payment of interest/profit on these deposits because they are not allowed to be invested or given as a loan—this money must be available any time the customer asks for it by writing a check or by ordering it to be transferred by any banking mechanism.

This type of account is exactly what is called in RF banking the *Amana* account, meaning a deposit-in-trust (DIT) account. In RF banking, the chief operating officer (COO) must pay close attention, with his CFO and the rest of the treasury supervisors, to make sure that the Amana/DIT accounts are not used for financing activities (lending) because that does not comply with our implied agreement with the clients who wanted to use the bank as a safe place to keep their money. DIT deposits can only be invested overnight in the Fed Funds to alleviate some of the fees charged by the bank. The RF bank may be allowed by Shari'aa to charge a service fee that pays for the cost of safekeeping and servicing these types of accounts, in case the income from the Fed Funds is not sufficient. As discussed in Chapter 5, the Fed Funds rate is the rate that reflects monetary policy regarding the printing of paper money (fiat money); it is different from the interest prohibited by Judeo-Christian-Islamic Law (Shari'aa).

Income-Generating Accounts for Individuals and Businesses: Regulation D Deposits   Investment banking firms (e.g., Merrill Lynch, Morgan Stanley, and Goldman Sachs) offer money market funds, denominated at $1 a share, which give a variable interest rate on the deposits. These money market funds are mutual funds that invest in short-term fixed-income interest-paying securities. In response, the federal banking regulators established

Regulation D, which allows the bank to open accounts as Negotiable Order of Withdrawal, or NOW, accounts for individuals, to allow depositors to earn income on their deposits. Later, businesses were allowed to open Money Market Accounts that also abide by Regulation D. One very important difference between the investment bankers' mutual funds' money market accounts and the depository institutions' bank money market funds is that the bank funds are FDIC-insured.

To limit sudden withdrawals of invested funds by the customers and to allow financial managers and bank treasuries to project their cash needs without compromising bank liquidity position, federal Regulation D places a monthly limit on the number of transfers the customer may make from his/her NOW or business Money Market Accounts (MMAs). Transfers affected by this regulation include:

- Automatic teller machine (ATM) transactions
- Transactions done in person at a branch
- Transactions sent in by mail, express drop, or night drop with an original signature
- Transfers made using the Internet
- Transfers made using the automatic telephone transfer system
- Overdraft transfers (made automatically to cover insufficient funds in other accounts)
- Transfers made by a bank service representative on customers' behalf
- Pre-authorized, automatic, scheduled, or recurring transfers

Regulation D allows customers six such transfers per month, per account, but only three of those may be made by check (a check counts against the month in which it clears, not the month in which it was written).

In an RF bank, the sources of income for these accounts are generated from the income the bank makes from the portion of the monthly rental payment that represents the bank's profit (return on capital invested, or RonC, as was described in Chapter 10). The money can be considered as a gift (*hebah*) to the depositors from the bank, in order to keep their short-term investments. In deciding on the level of hebah, it is obvious that the RF bank management takes into consideration what the competing Riba-based conventional banks are offering and tries to make the bank's hebah higher, to attract new customers and not lose existing customers to other banks.

Investment Accounts in Time Certificates of Deposit (TCDs) TCDs are the most important types of accounts for any bank. TCD money is invested in the portfolios constructed by the RF bank's credit department. This represents a very important challenge for the RF banker, because the RF bank management has to match the maturities of the TCD portfolio with the RF bank investment portfolio's (loan portfolio in riba-based banks) maturities. It is also important to know that the RF bank management, represented by the chief operating officer COO, the chief financial officer CFO, the bank treasurer, the chief credit officer, and the credit department, evaluates the expected return on a TCD investment that is matched to the credit (loan) portfolio in light of the bank's operating expenses, allowance for loan losses (ALLL), the average return on investment of the portfolio, the duration of the portfolio, and maturities, in addition to the rates offered by the competition.

This particular investment product is also very challenging because of two important limits and compliance requirements, which need to be met by any bank in the United States. These are the full disclosure of the (implied) interest paid to the TCD investor with different maturities and the penalty charged for early withdrawals.

The solution to this challenge depends on both sides of the financial ledger. On the assets side, the RF credit portfolio is constructed such that the implied interest rate (based on the actual market rental rate of the property or service, using the LARIBA RF Shari'aa-based model described earlier) is indexed to the rate by which the government declares the Fed Funds rate. That way, every time the Federal Reserve changes the rate, it reflects—in most cases, every quarter—the implied interest rate on the TCD is changed. On the RF TCD side, we offer our customers maturities that range from three to twelve months, and we discourage longer maturities so that we may comply with Shari'aa, which prohibits fixing returns in advance for a long time. In this case, the rates of return (the implied interest rate on the financing facilities) and the profit paid to the RF TCD holder (interest on CD in riba-based banks) are adjusted in sequence to avoid any violation of Shari'aa or of the strict U.S. banking regulations. As the RF banking industry matures and is accepted by both the regulators and the customers, a variable income TCD can be offered.

The rate of return on investment for RF TCD is calculated using two important guidelines:

1. *Competing rates offered in the market by all competing riba-based conventional banks:* The objective here is to make sure that the returns on investment/profit sharing given to the RF investor for investing in an RF TCD are at least the same return as (and hopefully more than) the riba-based returns paid by conventional banks.
2. *The profit distribution from the portfolio:* We ensure that the distribution is fair as disclosed to the customers.

Another important but challenging issue which needs a lot of future research is the ability of the investors in RF TCD to cash their deposits before maturity. In the United States, the regulation may require charging a stiff penalty. However, in case of an emergency such as a sudden illness, emergency funds needs, and the like, this penalty can be waived by bank management. Of course, clients cannot just unilaterally come to the bank to cash their investments before they mature, because they could cause a run on the bank that could have very negative repercussions on the bank's safety, soundness, and reputation. The difficulty here is in the ability of the RF bank to keep enough liquidity to pay the premature liquidation demands of the term depositors while most of the deposits are invested in medium- and long-term projects. In fact, if any bank fails to meet the demands of its depositors, the damage done will be serious and irreversible, and it could mean the closure of such bank. It is important for the RF bank management to take an active and very closely watched role in assessing liquidity needs based on experience, contact with the customers, and evaluation of the markets. In addition, it is recommended that the following steps should be taken in consideration:

1. Match the maturities of the RF TCD to the loan portfolio, and offer incentives to invest long term.
2. During the start-up of the RF bank (the first five years), consider financing projects with maturities ranging between three to twelve months in the first two years of operation, three months and three years in the following years, and then three months and five years in the following year. This way, cash will always be available for unexpected withdrawals and/or reinvestment.
3. The shareholders of the RF bank should stand ready to meet any run on the bank deposits by providing additional capital. The additional capital needs will be continually assessed by the RF bank's management and board of directors through continual contact with the shareholders to assess their ability, capacity, and willingness to meet additional capital needs. This in itself will make the shareholders, some of whom are also the managing directors and staff of the RF bank, careful about reviewing the assets/liabilities management and cash flow projections.
4. Commercial entities and individuals who seek financing from the RF bank should be required to bank with the RF bank and if possible to keep a balance on deposit as an investment with the RF bank.

The most important factor here is close and continual contact with every depositor, investor, and entrepreneur. If these contacts are developed to reach the level of a big family, then projections about the demands of the members of the family can be accurately assessed in advance, and liquidity can be planned without having to deal with any unpleasant surprises.

Credit Cards and Automatic Teller Machine (ATM) Debit Cards   An RF bank offers two types of card services. The first is a regular credit card, which is administered and the credit approved by an outside credit card company, to avoid participating in riba and to minimize credit risk at the bank. This service is offered as a convenience to some, but not many, of our customers, so that the bank can offer all services needed in the market. It is important to note that the management at the Bank of Whittier trains the RF private bankers to give customers who apply for and use credit cards a very clear warning (which is also prominently displayed on the bank's Web site):

> *Credit cards are offered for shopping convenience; each customer should spend within his/her means and pay the card charges within the month to avoid paying interest. Credit cards are not meant for borrowing with interest.*

One day, a member of bank management received a call from a banking regulator, commending us for our very unusual invitation to people not to use their credit cards as a means of very expensive borrowing and our encouraging customers to pay the charges off as soon as possible (preferably no longer than a month). It is well known in the riba-based banking industry that credit card interest charges and fees have grown recently to represent a significant source of income for most of these riba-based banks.

In addition, the RF Bank of Whittier offers a Visa-linked debit card that allows the customer to debit his/her account directly anywhere in the world. We did not call it *Islamic*, as some have done, because our disciplined policy requires that we call it what it really is.

Risk Management for an RF Bank

It should be stressed that the credibility and performance of a new RF bank are not only the professional duties of the RF bankers but also their responsibility before God. It is important to design RF bank operations, policies, and systems in a fashion that minimizes the RF bank's risk of failure, which would result in the loss of people's money and trust. If that were to happen, the dream of popularizing this new brand of banking would die for the next three to four generations, because humans tend to remember failures over an average of three to four generations. RF bankers simply cannot and should not allow this to happen.

The Source of Shari'aa and Edicts (Fatwa) Used by the RF Bank This is perhaps one of the most serious concerns for an RF bank, because it directly impacts its reputation and credibility. When the board of directors at LARIBA and at the Bank of Whittier discussed which model to use and which scholars to follow, we were extremely careful and deliberate. Many issues came up. The first was where the scholar was from. As it is known, opinions on Shari'aa—and, for that matter, general legal *Shari'aa*-based interpretations and opinions—vary from one country to another. In addition, some have a personal preference for a certain scholar while others do not. These concerns were especially serious when dealing with the first-generation immigrant communities. To avoid any conflicts or disputes, we decided to:

1. Focus on the sophisticated and educated Americans who prefer to read carefully what they'll commit to and who are Internet- and computer-savvy. This way they can read and understand clearly the foundations of our models.
2. Publish all the models used by all the scholars on our Web site and include a disclaimer that states that displaying these edicts (*fatwa*) and models does not mean that we claim that we have a fatwa from a certain scholar about what we do. We have presented the fatwa because we believe that the customer should decide based on carefully reading the foundation upon which the LARIBA model was developed. It is also believed that the eminent scholars' names should not be used along with the faith as a marketing tool to "sell" more loans.
3. Make our Shari'aa scholar and supervisors, who are well-versed in the application of Shari'aa, available to directly answer any inquiries about the model, the details of applying it, and the ways in which other models differ from the model we pioneered. In fact, the supervisors spend an average of 3,000 minutes on the cellular phone every month communicating directly with prospects and clients.
4. Document many of the questions asked and the answers given by the Shari'aa supervisor on our Web site.
5. Closely supervise company operations, including responses to incoming calls and inquiries to the RF finance officers (who are salaried employees and are not paid a commission based on the volume of loans they originate), the company telephone operator, the servicing department, and everyone else involved, to ensure they abide by Shari'aa. To do so means they must always state the truth and be cordial and helpful; they must never use clever and misleading sales techniques that claim lower rates to lure new customers; misstate

facts; nor put down or criticize the competition in order to "sell." This practice is enhanced by the Shari'aa supervisor and his staff scanning all incoming and outgoing e-mails and communications to ascertain compliance with the Law (Shari'aa).

Risk Management by Applying the Proper RF Financing Model   As indicated earlier in the book, cost-plus (murabaha) represents the least risky RF financing model. It is true that the profitability may be limited, and that the model itself is not accepted by many of the customers looking for RF financing because it is very close to and resembles conventional riba-based financing, but it offers a lowest-risk type of investment. The risk grows as we move from cost-plus (murabaha) to money management (mudaraba), joint ventures (musharaka), leasing (ijara), and RF financing of future production (ba'i ul salam).

It is recommended that for the first one to three years of operation, the RF bank should use the cost-plus (murabaha) approach, as we did in LARIBA for two years. Then you can slowly move into leasing and lease-to-own joint ventures using the RF LARIBA Shari'aa-based model as discussed in Chapter 10. To minimize risk during these first two to five years, the RF bank management should set aside sufficient reserves (ALLL) to allow it to meet any unexpected nonperformance of the financing activities in which it is participating.

Risk Management through Diversification of Clients   The RF bank management should do its best to spread its financing activity throughout the community without concentrating the financing into a small number of already successful businesspersons. This strategy will also result in more clients on the investment side and a bigger pool of referrals. Additionally, the probability of failure is distributed over a larger number of clients.

Risk Management through Diversification of Sectors of the Economy   It is advisable to recruit a viable board of directors for the RF bank. the members of which represent expertise in the business sectors to be financed by the bank. In addition, these directors must pledge not to finance their businesses with the bank to avoid the slightest concern of self-serving or violation of the U.S. banking Regulation O. It is also important that the RF bank, through its thorough analysis of economic activity as well as political, financial, and monetary developments, formulates an investment position on a quarterly basis, as discussed in assessing the level of ALLL. In this analysis, attractive sectors of the economy should be identified as well as unattractive sectors. In this way, the RF bank's credit policies committee devises an investment "pie" that allocates the investment of its funds in each sector. The allocation would be dynamic and would change as the economic projections change.

Risk Management through Diversification by Geographic Location   Close attention should be exercised by the RF bank regarding the locations it is interested in serving. For example, if one is in the United States, risk factors should be assessed for different markets in different towns, cities, and states to determine how much of the bank's money should be allocated in each location, based on that risk factor, without any discrimination or violation of the tenets of the Community Reinvestment Act (CRA). It is important to ensure that hidden discrimination is not practiced by denying lower income communities the services offered by the RF bank; all communities must be served in a fair and balanced way.

NOTES

1. Yahia Abdul-Rahman, *Strengthening Investor Confidence in Islamic Finance, Attracting Investors to Invest in Islamic Financial Institutions and Instruments in the US & Canada*, speech delivered at Monash University 5th Annual Islamic Banking Conference, Mandarin Oriental Hotel, Kuala Lumpur, Malaysia, September 3–4, 2007.
2. Many of the video training programs cited in the Bank Open University training program are designed and produced by Bankers' Hotline, www.bankersonline.com/bin/bhhome.html.
3. The USA PATRIOT Act, commonly known as the Patriot Act, is a controversial Act of Congress signed into law by former President George W. Bush on October 26, 2001. The contrived acronym stands for "Uniting and Strengthening America by Providing Appropriate Tools Required to Intercept and Obstruct Terrorism." For more details please visit the official U.S. government Web site: www.fincen.gov/pa_main.html.
4. Ibid.
5. FinCEN is The Financial Crimes Enforcement Network, which is one of the U.S. Department of Treasury's lead agencies in the fight against money laundering. It serves as a link between the law enforcement, financial, and regulatory communities. Please visit the Web site at www.fincen.gov.
6. The name "predatory lending" originates from the word *predators*, which refers to hunting animals. The implication is that these lenders take advantage of those who are in great need of a loan by charging them very high origination fees and by asking them to sign contracts that sometimes allow the lender to confiscate and foreclose on the property the first time the customers are delinquent in making a payment.
7. Subprime lending was invented by lenders and heavily promoted by the U.S. Department of Housing and Urban Development, as well as many GSEs. It

began as a financing approach for those who have low credit scores, but evolved to cover a much wider spectrum and was relaxed to allow every applicant to take loans that, in many cases, they could not repay because they did not have the income. Subprime lending was the straw that broke the camel's back and exposed many of the excesses that led to the 2008 financial meltdown in America and the world.

CHAPTER 13

Case Studies

Developing the RF Banking Investment Products

This chapter is designed to apply the riba-free (RF) banking principles discussed in the book to different financing situations. Portfolio managers are trained to diversify an investment portfolio between different asset classes to optimize the expected return in light of the risk level that fits the particular situation of each investor. The portfolio manager is trained to construct an *investment pyramid* (see Exhibit 13.1). Because the conventional riba-based banking system has been in existence for hundreds of years, serves some of the major world economies, and is standardized worldwide, the portfolio manager can tap many asset classes to build a certain portfolio. This is not the case in RF banking. This brand of banking has lagged behind the conventional system for about 600 years. The challenge ahead for RF bankers is to develop such products, with two important guidelines:

1. The product must comply with the Law (Shari'aa) and the laws of the land.
2. The product, at least in the beginning, must have the same feel and purpose as those offered by the conventional riba-based banks to enable the customer to conduct a fair and equitable comparison—and it must be at least of the same (or superior) quality.

In this chapter, the reader will be exposed to a number of real-life examples of financing conducted in an RF way. These cases are presented as an example of how to apply the RF principles to serve different financing needs and offer examples of the RF investment products that can be produced for the RF financial advisor. It is hoped that these "case studies" will make the RF financing and banking principles clearer and encourage the

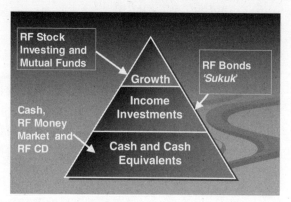

EXHIBIT 13.1   Riba-free investment tools.

readers to come up with new ideas, approaches, and products that are in compliance with the RF principles, offering new, less risky, and more rewarding services in the market.

THE INVESTMENT PYRAMID

When a financial advisor attempts to construct an investment portfolio for a customer, that portfolio is usually built using what is known as the *investment pyramid*. The pyramid consists of three layers, of which the foundation has the least risk and the top has the highest risk. Exhibit 13.1 displays the characteristics and nature of the products that fit each layer.

Cash and Cash Equivalents
At the bottom of the pyramid, the advisor allocates a certain percentage of the customer's wealth in the form of cash and other cash equivalents. The cash equivalents are instruments, such as money market funds. The challenge here is to develop an RF product that is equivalent to the money market fund, a short-term instrument that will offer RF customers an alternative to the riba-based money market instruments.

At an RF bank, this layer will include the demand deposit (deposit in trust, also known as DIT or *Amana*) accounts as well as other Fed Fund deposits with the Federal Reserve System.

Short-Term Investments
The next layer of investments is a longer-term investment that can mature in three months to three years. Riba-based conventional banks offer time certificates of deposit (TCDs) that mature in three months to three years or more.

This category includes short-term financing instruments structured using the RF finance principles discussed in Chapter 10, such as a one- to three-year RF financing of an automobile or a piece of equipment.

RF Bonds: Sukuk (RF Income Instruments that Replace Riba-Based Bonds)

The next layer is a higher risk investment category, which includes the investment in fixed-income securities (riba-bonds) in the case of riba-based conventional banks.

A new RF asset-based bond was developed to substitute for riba-based bonds. The RF bonds are called *sukuk*. (The word *sukuk* is the plural of the word *Sa'k*, which is the origin from which the word *check* was derived.) In this layer, the LARIBA model offers, as an example, two products, which were developed in the early 21st century and applied in Singapore.

Investment in Stocks

This layer represents the highest return, but also the highest risk. The RF guidelines for investing in the stock market will be summarized.

RF ASSET-BACKED BONDS (SUKUK)

RF Mortgage-Backed Sukuk Securities

A riba-free mortgage-backed security (RF MBS) uses the financing contracts developed to finance home mortgages according to the Shari'aa-based LARIBA model described in Chapter 10. The first RF MBS ever in the history of the United States was issued with Fannie Mae in 2002.

An MBS is an investment representing an individual interest in a pool of mortgages. Payments on the underlying pool of mortgages[1] that back an issue of MBS are *passed through* each month from the servicer of the mortgages to the security holder. A unique security identification number assigned by the Federal Reserve to each MBS is maintained and transferred on the Fed's book-entry system.

In these pools, the RF mortgages are assembled in $1 million packages, given a CUSIP number (CUSIP refers to both the Committee on Uniform Security Identification Procedures and the 9-character security identifiers that they distribute for all North American securities for the purposes of facilitating clearing and settlement of trades), and are bought by the bank, which uses them as a source of RF income for longer-term RF investors, who seek monthly or quarterly income. The income is generated from the rent stream of income paid—for example—by the house owner, as described earlier in the model.

The Development of MUIS[2] Waqf Sukuk:[3]RF Asset-Based Bonds Used to Unlock the Value of Trusts

This example is a product of a very interesting situation that helped the Singapore Muslim Community (MUIS[4]) unlock the tremendous value of the different trusts that were pledged to serve the interests of the Muslim community hundreds of years ago (these are called w*aqf*, which means pledged trusts that can only be used for the service of the faith). This example shows how MUIS was able to generate liquidity from the trust in an RF way using RF bonds (*sukuk*). These funds were used to develop old and undeveloped real estate properties into highly valued and market-rated properties.

The world is full of goodhearted people who want to leave a legacy by giving back to society in the form of donations or by pledging a productive asset that can produce enough income to help finance the operation of a place of worship, like a temple, a synagogue, a church, or a masjid (mosque). In the United States, donations of this sort are often motivated by reduction of taxes, retirement planning, and asset transfers to future generations to keep the family legacy alive. The foundations left behind by Ford, Carnegie, Rockefeller, and Kennedy are examples of such efforts.

In Islam, and for that matter the Judeo-Christian-Islamic value system, there is a similar system for giving that is motivated only by the interest of the donors to please God by donating assets that can be used as facilities for worship, education, health care, and administration of peoples' affairs, or that produce income to help the poor and the needy. Donations can also include income-producing assets. The income of these assets would be used to fund education, health care, research, and other public projects and needs. These trusts are called w*aqf*. The word w*aqf* literally means that the title of the asset has been "arrested." In today's lingo, a waqf is a *public charitable trust*, in which the assets are pledged to God. The title of the asset is treated as that of a ceased property that is pledged to God. This asset can be a prayers place (masjid), a hospital, a research center, a library, a school, or an income-producing asset, perhaps producing a stream of rent, crops, minerals, and oil and gas. These tangible productions can be sold to produce cash income that can benefit the beneficiaries and maintain the asset; if there is a surplus, it can be used to benefit other waqf assets. History shows that charitable waqf giving escalates with economic prosperity; the opposite is also true. Charitable waqf properties are usually not well maintained and are left to run down during times of economic and political decline. According to Shari'aa, assets that can be pledged as *waqf* can be classified in two types:

1. *Immovable:* Like real estate, including land, buildings, and other location-specific assets, such as fruit orchards, trees, water, and oil and gas wells.
2. *Movable:* Like cash and investments in stock portfolios.

An interesting situation came up during one of my visits to Singapore. The community had lost a prime multimillion dollar property in one of its most expensive areas in downtown Singapore because they did not have the money to develop it and they were not allowed to borrow money with riba. The big dilemma was that two more properties in prime downtown areas required renovatation and development by the municipality before a certain approaching deadline, otherwise those properties would be lost as well. I had a meeting with the leaders of the community and developed a riba-free approach to solving the problem. The approach involved the issuing of *RF sukuk* for the first time in the history of Singapore. The following is a summary of what was done, especially in this field of unlocking the vast economic and financial potential of the frozen assets of waqf, which had not been researched for a long time. This approach is now being implemented in many Muslim countries, and a special waqf bank is being sought to focus on this large market demand.

The Law (Shari'aa) states that, in general, the pledged assets of a waqf (public charitable trust) cannot be sold, granted to others, nor inherited by others. It must be used always for the purpose it was pledged to fill.[5] However, historians and scholars in Shari'aa have documented some exceptions, which were practiced under unusual circumstances that required modification of this rule.[6] For example, the second Khalifa (Omar Ibn Al Khattab) approved the change of use of a masjid (mosque) when he ordered that the old *Kufah* (in Iraq) masjid moved to a new location to improve the services. The old location was changed from a masjid to a market for date sellers. In addition, history records that both the second Khalifa (Omar Ibn Al Khattab) and the third Khalifa (Othman Ibn Affan) did approve the expansion of the original masjid of the Prophet Muhammad (pp) in Madinah. This opened to us some very interesting and creative ideas.

One of the two Singapore properties was a historic masjid in downtown proper. The problem was that the waqf consisted of a masjid in a prime area, and that it also had attached to it a prime piece of undeveloped real estate. The challenge was to see how it could be developed—as required by the local municipality—into a prime commercial building that could generate income for the waqf without violating Shari'aa conditions regarding the assets pledged as a waqf.

Naturally, the community would be up in arms if the leadership decided to demolish the historic masjid and build a modern and more efficient one.

along with a high-rise building that could produce enough income to enhance the fortunes of the community. After in-depth discussions with the architects and the developer, a plan was created to keep the masjid intact and to attach to it a long-term-stay hotel for professionals who come to work on special projects for periods ranging from one to twelve months. The problem was how to generate the money needed to finance this development. The solution offered was formulated by two Shari'aa advisors, Dr. Mohamad Daud Bakar (from Malaysia) and me. The solution involved using the LARIBA model of forming an entity that would raise the capital and appraise the value of the waqf asset. The combination would form a joint venture between waqf and the sukuk investors. The capital raised would be used to develop the property, lease it, and share the rental income while the waqf bought back the shares of the venture from the sukuk investors, using the LARIBA mark-to-market RF Shari'aa-based model in the same way as was described in Chapter 10. In this way, the waqf asset could be kept intact while its real value was unlocked to generate the capital needed to develop the property.

The Building of the MUIS Waqf Sukuk[7]   The effort involved the rescuing of two properties. The first was a high-rise building called *Fusion* that required S$25 million to renovate and to bring to required standards.[8] The property is located on the corner plot of the famous Raffles Hotel landmark and Shopping Arcade block. The other was a masjid property called *Bencoolen*, in a high-traffic market area close to the new business school. The property needed to be developed into a high-rise residence hotel and required an investment of S$35 million.

Charging, paying, receiving, and dealing in interest is clearly prohibited by Shari'aa. The sukuk (bond) issue is in fact a Musharakah (Joint Venture) agreement between MUIS and United Overseas Bank (UOB), which uses the LARIBA Shari'aa-based approach to formulate such a bond. Following is a description of the four steps we followed:

1. MUIS Waqf Fund (the owner of the property) and UOB entered into an agreement to jointly own the property. The property was appraised at S$34 million. UOB agreed to forward S$25 million to MUIS in order to own 73.52941 percent of the joint venture (obtained by dividing $25 million by $34 million). MUIS retained the balance, or 26.47059 percent, of equity in the property. The title of the property is held by MUIS, and a lien is placed on it for the benefit of the joint venture to utilize its usufruct as described in the LARIBA model in Chapter 10. This way the rule of not compromising or transferring the title of a waqf property is violated.

2. The Joint Venture participants (Musharakah partners) agree to sign a five-year lease of the property at a fair and mutually agreed-upon lease rate.

3. UOB agrees to sell its share back to MUIS at the same price, or $25 million, and to get paid after five years. The lease income, after expenses and applicable taxes, will be distributed between MUIS and UOB in the same proportion of ownership.

4. To abide by the laws and monetary regulations, and to benefit from the tax advantages of issuing a bond in the state of Singapore, the return on invested capital for the sukuk (bond) holder may be called *implied interest*.

The transaction is depicted in Exhibit 13.2.

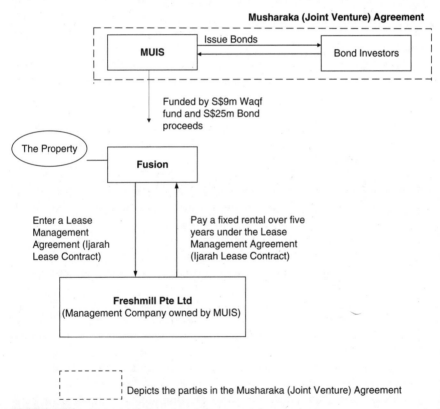

EXHIBIT 13.2 A pictorial diagram of the transaction structure.

RF STOCK MARKET INVESTMENTS

The next layer in the Investment Pyramid has to do with investing in the stock market. This section will detail how the RF parameters for investing in stocks were developed for the first time and which guidelines were used. In addition, many of the principles of RF financing and investing will be discussed in order to avoid participating in a bubble that would waste the hard-earned wealth of the customers involved.

The following are the guidelines that were developed for investing in the stock markets in an RF way.

Guidelines for RF Investing in the Stock Market

The spirit of investing according to Shari'aa is to participate in equity investing and not in debt-type investing. Equity investing means owning equity in the company (companies). Debt investing means lending money to the company using a riba-based instrument, such as a direct loan, an interest-based (renting money) promissory note, or a predefined interest-based bond.

Investing in equities is highly encouraged by Shari'aa. RF financing is all about equity participation in business activities that need financing. The author was part of a group of scholars and experts who started investing according to Shari'aa in 1988 in a $250 million portfolio. The portfolio performed better than the market averages. A number of guidelines were developed as early as 1988 to regulate investing in stocks based on Shari'aa. The following is a list of these guidelines:

1. It is preferred to invest in companies that operate in local communities to generate economic growth and prosperity that would create new job opportunities, peace, and harmony in the community.
2. Investing should be in socially responsible companies with a management dedicated to high ethical and moral standards.
3. Investing cannot be in companies which are involved directly or indirectly in divinely prohibited (*haram*) businesses, such as:
   a. Alcoholic beverages, intoxicants, bars, nightclubs and associated activities, casinos, hotels that operate bars and casinos, airlines that serve alcohol on their planes, or promiscuous activities. For example, Walt Disney Company provides family entertainment and theme parks, but it also owns movie divisions and trade names that may violate the promiscuous activities rule. Coca-Cola, in addition to its huge soft drinks business, has a thriving alcohol-related wine business. We could not invest in either of these companies.

   b. Pork and pork products industries,
   c. Tobacco products,
   d. Interest-charging and/or -paying entities, such as banks, finance companies, investment banks, insurance companies, and related businesses.
   e. Any other unethical activities and businesses that are not fair to their employees and customers or are environmentally irresponsible.
4. The company capital structure should have minimum debt. This has generated a lot of research and debate. The first issue was how to calculate the debt structure of the company. Should it be based on the company's book value or the company's market value? In the beginning, most scholars and Shari'aa committee members preferred using the book value as a basis for calculating the debt as a percentage of total company capitalization and preferred to keep debt as low as possible. Later on, as Islamic mutual funds started to grow in the market, the regulation was relaxed to replace book value with market value, which has allowed practitioners to expand the list of company stocks from which they can choose.
5. Equities in the U.S. market were screened as part of the research;[9] more than 10,000 companies were analyzed. The percentages of noncompliant stocks (in 2000) were:

   Prohibited business line: 22%

   Excessive borrowing: 62%

   Excessive interest income: 8%

   Other exclusions: 3%

   The total percentage of companies excluded was 95 percent. Out of 10,000 companies, only 500 were Shari'aa compliant.
6. The maximum debt allowed is 33 percent of the market capitalization, not the balance sheet capitalization (originally the ruling was to use the balance sheet capitalization).[10] However, in an RF regime using the mark-to-market approach along with the commodity indexation principles discussed in Chapter 5, a corrector should be used that reflects the overpriced assets in case a bubble is detected. For example, if oil price reaches $150 and, based on the commodity indexation principles, the oil price should be $50 – $70, that means the market valuation of that stock should be reduced to about one-third to one-half of its value, leading to a decision to sell out of the position to avoid participating in the bubble.
7. Company accounts receivables should remain at 45 percent of total company assets.

8. Interest income should be less than 5 percent of total revenue.
9. Investment should be in actual stocks backed by an operating company and not just a paper index. Indexes are only used for measuring performance results.

These foundations for stock market investing according to Shari'aa were adopted by the Dow Jones company to develop the Dow Jones Islamic Market Index (DJIMI).[11] Later, Standard & Poor's[12] introduced its own S&P Islamic index. These indexes formed the bases for many Islamic mutual funds available in the market today. Amana Funds,[13] one of the most successful funds, developed its own parameters and screens. Its two funds, the Amana Income Fund and the Amana Growth Fund, realized a five-star rating on the Morning Star rating system. The company was successful in getting some of the major brokering companies, like Charles Schwab and T. D. Waterhouse, to distribute its fund for retirement plan and general investors. This has increased the assets under management from approximately $65 million in the late 1990s to almost $1,000 million in 2006 and $1,800 million in 2009.

Normalization of Various Stock Market Indexes Using the Commodity Indexation

Perhaps one of the riskiest factors in the stock indexes, including the Islamic stock indexes, is that the market value of the stocks is included in the index without allowing investors to detect any bubble formation due to speculative market forces created by options and derivatives and excessive hedge funds market speculation techniques. In the case of the Islamic Shari'aa-compliant indexes, the use of market value to screen for the debt a company has on its balance sheet to be a maximum of one-third of total market capitalization can be particularly hazardous, because of the gyrations in the market value of stocks on the market, especially in the case of speculative market bubbles.

It is recommended that the index be normalized using a reference commodity like gold, silver, a staple commodity (as described in Chapter 5) or a combination thereof, depending on the market in question. In this approach, it is recommended that we relate the market index, say, to gold, and follow the gyrations in terms of gold to detect for bubbles and to reduce positions and exposure to the market accordingly. This approach is still in its infancy and requires more intensive research.

As an example, let us study the value of oil company stocks in the volatile period when oil prices skyrocketed to almost $150 per barrel in 2008. At the time, many analysts expected the price to reach $200 per barrel and recommended the purchase of more oil company stocks. However, based on the gold price and oil relationship and applying the commodity indexation rule described in Chapter 5, the data indicated to us that oil was extremely overpriced and suggested that oil prices were experiencing a serious bubble. This should have prompted the Shari'aa-based investors not to invest more in oil company stocks, but rather to liquidate their positions in oil company stocks, because the commodity price indexation principal suggested that the oil price must decline to around \$55 – \$75 per barrel. However, when oil prices reflect an extreme low in terms of gold, as happened in February 2009 when oil reached \$35 per barrel, Shari'aa-based investors should have accumulated more oil company stocks in their portfolios.

This approach can be generalized to the whole market by applying the commodity indexation principal to the index. The chart on the following page shows the relationship of the index in terms of gold price. The chart shows the relationship between the Dow Jones market index (DJIA), the NASDAQ market index, and the S&P 500 market index in terms of gold price.

Please note that these are not to be taken as predictive tools but rather as tools that would be used as a guide to directional movements into an overpriced—bubble—territories.

The charts indicate that:

- The DJIA value divided by the price of gold fluctuated in a channel in the range of 4 to 10 times the price of gold with a mean of seven. That means if gold price is \$950 the fair value of DJIA would be in the range of 3,800 and 9,500 with a mean fair value of 6,650. The important level beyond which the DJIA starts to be overpriced based on the commodity indexation rule is 9,500.
- The NASDAQ value divided by the gold price fluctuated in a channel ranging between one and four units of NASDAQ for each dollar of gold price with a mean value of 2.5. That implies that if gold price reaches \$950 per ounce that NASDAQ's fair value would fluctuate between 950 and 3,800 with a mean of 2,375. The important level beyond which NASDAQ starts to be overpriced based on the commodity indexation rule is 3,800.
- The S&P 5000 value divided by the gold price fluctuated in a channel ranging between one half and one unit of S&P 500 for each dollar of gold price with a mean value of 0.75. That implies that if gold price reaches \$950 per ounce that S&P 500's fair value would fluctuate between 475 and 950 with a mean of 712.5. The important level beyond which the S&P 500 starts to be overpriced based on the commodity indexation rule is 950.

The following table shows the "red flag" levels of the stock market indexes at different gold prices. Investors—especially those in the RF stock market portfolio and mutual funds investors—are advised to use these directional levels to exercise wisdom and prudence in their investment decisions.

| | Red Flag Levels of Market Indexes | | |
Gold Price $/Oz	DJIA	NASDAQ	S&P500
1000	10,000	4,000	1,000
950	9,500	3,725	950
900	9,000	3,600	900
800	8,000	3,200	800
700	7,000	2,800	700
600	6,000	2,400	600
500	5,000	2,000	500

It is clear that definite signals of a serious inflated market bubble have loomed since 2006. I would be the first to admit that this is an art—based on technical analysis—and not a science, but I call for more research and strategy development in this field. Many may argue that the approach may lead to premature selling, which happened to me personally when I got out of the market in 2006. However, it is better to err on the conservative side and miss 20–35 percent of the market's move to the up side than to sit in the market and lose 60 percent *of the entire value of the portfolio*. Many investors do not realize that if the market declines by 50 percent, that means that the market must appreciate by 100 percent in order to return to where it was before. This is a move that will require many years to achieve.

NOTES

1. A pool of mortgages is a loan or group of loans with similar characteristics. Minimum pool submission size in case of single pools is $1,000,000 for fixed-rate mortgages with monthly payments and $500,000 for fixed-rate mortgages with biweekly payments.
2. MUIS, also known as the Islamic Religious Council of Singapore, was established as a statutory body in 1968 under the Administration of Muslim Law

Act, Chapter 3 of Singapore (AMLA). Under the AMLA, MUIS is to advise the President of Singapore on all matters relating to Islam in Singapore.

3. Yahia Abdul-Rahman, research presentation at MUIS WAQF Conference, Singapore, March 6–7, 2007.

4. MUIS is the abbreviated name of the body that serves the needs of the Singapore Muslim community: "Majlis Ugama Islam Singapura."

5. Based on a saying—Hadeeth—of Prophet Muhammad (pp).

6. The two scholars, Abu Hanifa and Ibn Taymiya, allowed it with the condition that one must prove that there will be benefit to the public as a result of such modification. However, the scholar Imam Al Shafi disallowed it because it is the property of God.

7. Based on Yahia Abdul-Rahman, *A Memorandum of Understanding and Agreement, Musharaka Bond Issue by Majlis Ugama Islam Singapore (MUIS)*, which was authored in preparation of the first RF sukuk to be issued by MUIS in February 2001, to be arranged by United Overseas Bank, Asia.

8. MUIS—UOB Asia Ltd. Bond (sukuk) issue of S$25 Million in 2001, due in 2006.

9. Saleh Jameel Malikah, presentation at the LARIBA 2000 Seventh Annual Symposium on LARIBA (Islamic) Banking & Finance and Awards Dinner, April 29, 2000, Pasadena, California.

10. The original opinion was to minimize the debt so that it would be as close to zero as possible. With the resulting small number of companies in which one can invest, the scholars and financial experts agreed to use analogy, with the conclusions used to limit the change in inheritance distribution to be a maximum of one-third. The scholars used this as a foundation to limit the debt of a company that can be invested in to one-third of the capital at first, then relaxed the ruling to be the company's market value on the market. Another major issue erupted with the minimum debt. The issue had to do with the dot.com and technology companies that were sizzling in the market in the late 1990s and early 2000s. These companies had essentially no debt and were included in the Islamic indexes. With the bursting of the dot.com bubble in 2000, many of these indexes lost a major percentage of their value. Islamic mutual funds that started in the late 1990s ended up losing more than 50 percent of their value.

11. The Dow Jones Islamic Market Indexes (DJIMI) were introduced in 1999 as the first benchmarks to represent Islamic-compliant portfolios. Today, the series encompasses more than 70 indexes and remains the most comprehensive family of Islamic market measures. The indexes are maintained based on a stringent and published methodology. See the Web site for more information: www .djindexes.com/mdsidx/index.cfm?event=showIslamic.

12. The S&P Shariah index series is designed to offer investors a set of indices that are Shari'aa compliant. The S&P 500, the leading measure of the U.S. equity market, was one of the first S&P indices to offer a Shari'aa-compliant version. Modeled after its U.S. counterpart, the S&P Europe 350 and the S&P Japan 500 indices also offer their respective compliant versions. See the Web site

for more information: http://www2.standardandpoors.com/spf/pdf/index/
Shariah_factsheet.pdf?vregion=us&vlang=en.

13. Amana Mutual Funds Trust is designed to provide investment alternatives that
are consistent with Islamic principles. Generally, Islamic principles require that
investors share in profit and loss, that they receive no usury or interest, and that
they do not invest in a business that is not permitted by Islamic principles. Some
of the businesses not permitted are liquor, wine, casinos, pornography, insurance, gambling, pork processing, and interest-based banks or finance associations. The Funds do not make any investments that pay interest. In accordance
with Islamic principles, the Funds shall not purchase bonds, debentures, or
other interest paying obligations of indebtedness. See the Web site for further
information: www.amanafunds.com/amanx.html.

CHAPTER 14

Visions for the Future of RF Banking

THE 2008 GLOBAL ECONOMIC AND FINANCIAL MELTDOWN

As I started writing this book, the world was experiencing the deepest economic and financial meltdown since the Great Depression of 1929. This meltdown has touched every citizen in the world because of the efficient communication systems that have successfully interconnected the world's financial and banking systems. It is unfortunate and sad to experience the laying off of many employees who had nothing to do with what happened, the loss of their homes through foreclosures, the decline in living standards not only in the developed world but also in the developing countries, and the increase in poverty worldwide.

The core reason for what happened has been a culture of "making" money on money by renting it with interest (riba/ribit) and speculating with it instead of working hard to earn it. The financial and banking system in the United States is well-designed and regulated, but unfortunately it has been abused by some who claimed that they could create money by using hedge funds, financial speculation, and gambling. The unfortunate thing is that many pension funds joined the party, because they were impressed by the high returns realized by these funds. These pension fund managers should have known better; they were entrusted with the future retirement funds of millions of Americans. Many of those who speculated and gambled with peoples' money and life savings did not abide fully by the regulations. They had the wrong idea about money and what money is all about. They believed that if you have a lot of money, you can make a lot more—not necessarily by investing in productive activities, but by using options, derivatives, and financial gambling techniques that speculated on what the future holds. The 2008 meltdown proved that this was the wrong way to look at and invest money.

It is interesting to note that only 25 employees in the Financial Products division at AIG (AIGFP)—the huge international insurance company that employed 113,000 professionals worldwide—were responsible for bringing the whole company down. One of their tools was a product they designed to speculate on the movements in interest rates. For example, one of their bets would result in a profit or a loss of $500 billion if interest rates changed by a small percent in either direction. This loss, realized by the company, is equivalent to paying for the loss and damage caused by 62 California-size earthquakes.[1] Unfortunately, AIG grew so big that even with the most sophisticated management and supervisory tools and techniques, no one could regulate the activities of this small group of employees.

What is most sad and disappointing is the fact that we all were warned many times about the outcome of such speculative activities in the market. Those who were in charge used a bandage approach to fix these problems temporarily. No one took the time or spent the effort needed to meticulously and permanently fix the root causes of the problem. Here is a list of some of the small earthquakes that introduced us to what was waiting in 2008:

- The Savings & Loans junk bond crisis ($240 billion loss in 1989)
- The German commodity and metals company "Metallgesallschaft" ($1 billion loss in 1993)
- Barings Bank (speculation by one of its traders in Asia cost more than $ 410 million)
- Procter & Gamble Corp. (loss of $160 million in 1994)
- Orange County, California ($1.7 billion loss in 1995)
- Long-Term Capital Management Corporation ($4 billion loss in 1998)
- Global Crossing Corp. (billions lost in 2001)
- Enron Corporation (billions lost in 2001)
- WorldCom Corp. ($3 billion lost in 2002)
- Société General unauthorized trading ($7 billion lost in 2007)

Analysts in most of these cases concluded that the main reasons for not avoiding these losses were management's lack of clear and thorough understanding of the products and risks involved and the assumptions used in structuring these speculative financial products.

THE MEGA-BANKS AND FINANCIAL INSTITUTIONS

The primary reason for these mega-losses is believed to have been the lack of good and responsible judgment by those who were in charge. Many reasoned that what happened was due to the lack of suitable government regulations. That may be partially true, especially in the cases of hedge funds and derivatives and associated financial products. The real fact of the matter is that the prevailing culture of renting money prompted many money managers to believe that money can reproduce and become productive if it is placed in speculative and "smart" products. As we detailed in this book, money is a tool, and it does not reproduce unless it is invested in a productive activity that adds value to the economy of the community and the country. Theirs was an ill judgment, because speculation and its tools are a zero-sum game. Those who outsmarted other managers came away with huge profits at the expense of huge losses by others who made the opposite bet. As the hedge fund industry grew bigger, it dabbled in currency speculation, as happened in the 1997–1998 Asian Currency Crisis, which brought down the Asian economies. When the leaders of Asia complained bitterly about the need to stop these huge gambling activities and the way these activities were impoverishing their economies, they were lectured by the self-appointed and self-serving "free market" advocates and were marginalized. As the problem grew even bigger, these hedge funds did the unimaginable by bringing down the economies of the United States and the world in 2008.

No government can issue regulations that would guarantee good judgment. Good judgment has to do with a value system taught at home by the parents, by the values taught as families worship and become enriched spiritually, by the standards set by the school system, and by the university professors who teach finance. Judgment has to do with the prevailing culture, which is nurtured by the media that defines the norms of what is considered an acceptable behavior and lifestyle.

THE CULTURE OF RENTING MONEY WITH RIBIT/RIBA

As we sort out and sift through the events that led to the financial earthquake of 2008, we conclude that there must be an optimum size for a company or a bank, beyond which the company becomes inefficient and difficult to manage and may become a great liability to the economy as a whole (as in the cases of AIG and Citigroup). The towns and cities of the United States were built by community building and loan societies, which gathered the community's savings and invested them prudently back in these communities to finance the building of homes, cars, home mortgages, businesses, and other community needs. Many of these savings and loan local community banks were taken over by the big banks like Citibank. The progression of growth in the size of these banks tempted management to make more money by controlling more money. It was done first by becoming the large and certified banker of the government and then the preferred bank of the large corporations, because they offered larger loans at lower interest rates and costs through their vast networks worldwide. Instead of large corporations supporting the local communities by using the services of their local community banks, savings and loans associations, and credit unions, they all migrated to the big banks.

As these big banks ran into no other areas for growth, they started to focus on the local communities and the small investors by essentially gobbling up most of the small community banks and savings and loan branches. They lured the gullible and simple law-abiding citizens to do business with them through slick advertising. For example, credit cards, which were designed to facilitate the day-to-day buying needs of the consumer, were changed into instruments to encourage small-size consumers to borrow money and consume more—without being told the truth about the high costs of borrowing via credit cards. University and high school students were offered credit cards. Many of them did not qualify on their own merit; they were sent credit cards by mail, because the companies knew that their parents would foot the bill. Many parents were surprised to receive their children's large credit card bills, which had to be paid to save their sons' and daughters' financial reputation and future credit.

Credit cards were also used to lure consumers by offering zero interest for six months. However, the card issuers did not make it clear to the consumer that after six months the interest rate would go to, say, 8 percent, and that if there were a delinquency, the rate would reach as high as 28 percent. All of these "unimportant" details were printed in tiny letters that could hardly be read, to "comply" with strict consumer compliance regulations. The only reason a credit card company would change interest rates arbitrarily and charge a lot of fees is that the company is in the business of renting money that borders on defrauding people, by seducing them to spend more so that the companies can make more money. It is surprising to observe that an average citizen with humble income and assets is allowed to own ten credit cards and accumulate a debt of more than $100,000, as we experienced with the many decent fellow citizens who called us at LARIBA and the bank to help them sort out their personal financial problems.

Perhaps the saddest of all has been the way major banks handle overdrafts (non-sufficient funds checks written by customers who do not have enough money in their accounts). U.S. banks and credit unions are expected to make in 2009 an estimated $38.5 billion in overdraft fees, 90 percent of which will be paid by 10 percent of customers, according to a Moebs Services survey featured in the *Financial Times*.[2] The survey of more than 2,000 depository institutions found that the national median overdraft fee rose by one dollar to $26 in 2009, with larger institutions charging a median of $35 per overdraft. It also found that 44.5 percent of all institutions have overdraft income greater than net income. The highest overdraft fees were charged by the largest banks, said Mr Moebs. At banks with assets greater than $50 billion—a group including Citigroup, Bank of America, JPMorgan Chase, and Wells Fargo—the median overdraft fee is set at $33. At BofA, a customer overdrawn by as little as $6 could trigger a $35 penalty. If the customer does not realize they have a negative balance and continues spending, they could incur that fee as many as 10 times in a single day, for a total of $350. Failing to repay the overdraft within a few days results in an additional $35 penalty. Conceptually, banks can be looked upon to be officially in the business of renting money (riba/ribit) and not in the real business they were created to do: investing in local communities.

As if that were not enough, a wonderful government program designed to help students who are in dire need to finance their education at low interest rates was also abused by those who love to rent money. The student loan program became an easy outlet for students to live it up, to spend more, and in some cases use the money as a down payment for a car or a house by also using the subprime home mortgage facilities. The daughter of a friend of mine, who is only 26 years old, graduated with a law degree from a prime university that cost her $350,000. She financed this huge debt with a student loan. The sad part of the story is that she could not find a job. One can only wonder at how university graduates can start their careers and a family while owing these huge sums of money.

It must also be said that the student loan facility has helped inflate tuitions at universities and costs on campus. The culture of renting money and of spending today to pay later (with interest) has taken over American culture. The American lifestyle that once called for students to work hard while going to schools and colleges, taking part-time jobs as dishwashers, cleaning crews, waiters at restaurants, and tutors to help finance their education has largely gone by the wayside.

Perhaps the saddest part of this culture of renting money was accepting speculation and gambling techniques as a legitimate way of "making" money without having to work hard to "earn" it. These techniques were given fancy names and legitimate theories by distinguished professors at very prestigious universities. Investment bankers on Wall Street hired the brightest mathematicians from the best universities, such as, for example, CalTech (the California Institute of Technology, Pasadena, California, where Einstein was a visiting scientist), to work on these schemes and algorithms of gambling, using the same theories, algorithms, and solutions that are applied in the casino industry. These talented graduates were recruited to devise more sophisticated tools to outsmart others with money in order to win and "make" more money, instead of using their wonderful talents and education to design, for example, a better and more energy-efficient lifestyle and to teach the future generation.

The son of a friend of mine is a gifted mathematician. He was offered a multimillion dollar per year job at a major investment bank in New York to work on these mathematical models. As he explained it, one can only wonder at the way the stock market and the bond market were turned into a large gambling casino. It is puzzling that an investment bank could justify this large salary for a young university graduate who did not even have to assume any risk! This culture proliferated throughout the economy. Medical doctors have to charge their patients and insurance providers a lot of money, which they turn around and pay back to (possibly) the same insurance company, to protect them and their families against malpractice law suits.

Probably the saddest part of all is the mirage of wealth that many thought they had on paper for years, only to discover that it was just paper wealth. Unfortunately, that discovery came a bit late for the majority of the baby boomer investors, who were preparing to retire just as the bubble burst.

THE LIFESTYLE OF THE JUDEO-CHRISTIAN-ISLAMIC VALUE SYSTEM

As was stressed throughout this book, the Judeo-Christian-Islamic value system prohibits us from participating in the culture of renting money. Perhaps one of the most important prohibitions in the Jewish Bible (*Exodus: Chapter 22, verses 24–26*), the Christian Bible (*Exodus 22:25, Leviticus 25:35–37, Deuteronomy 23:19–20, Nehemiah 5:1–13, Psalm 15, Proverbs 28:8, Ezekiel 18:5–18, Habakkuk 2:6–7, Luke 6:27–36*) and the Qur'aan (*Chapter II—Al-Baqarah 275-278, Chapter III—Alee Imraan—The Family of Mary & Jesus (the family of Imraan):3:130, Chapter IV—An-Nissa'aa (Women):4:161, Chapter XXX—Ar-Rum (The Romans) 30:39*) is the prohibition of *Ribit* (Old Testament) or *Riba* (the Qur'aan).

As explained in Chapter 2, we know from the original Jewish teachings that a person of the Jewish faith who participates in ribit cannot stand as a witness in a Jewish court; the old Catholic teachings (before 1100 c.e.) hold that a person who deals in ribit is denied a Catholic burial. In the Qur'aan, charging of ribit/riba is one of the most severe offenses against God.

As discussed in great detail throughout the book, ribit/riba, according to Judaic, Christian, and Muslim teachings (which this book has pioneered calling Judeo-Christian-Islamic values) can be defined as the act of renting money at a price called *interest*. In the old days, the word *usury* was derived from the act of paying a price (interest) for the use of money. We also know that today's money is a thing, a manmade currency. It is fungible, just as an apple is. One cannot rent an apple from another, and the same applies to money. The minute money is handed over to another person, it becomes that person's responsibility to invest it prudently, and it is the responsibility of those who give it in trust (the bankers) to users (the borrowers) to handle it prudently.

That is why today's culture, which emphasizes spending as much as you can today by renting money with interest from banks, by using credit cards, and by using the family's home as a credit card (home equity line of credit and loans), is frowned upon and prohibited by all faiths, especially those in the Judeo-Christian-Islamic value system. Money is a measuring device that quantifies the success or failure of an investment. It is not for hire or rent to the highest bidder (at the highest interest rate). If we had evaluated the purchase of each item, based on its utility as measured by its actual market rent (rent of a car, a house, or a business, according to the *mark-to-market* and *commodity indexation* rules discussed in the book), we would have been saved from speculation and from the deep holes of debt many of our community members and our beloved country and the world are suffering from. That is why Jesus (pp) took it upon himself to drive the money-changers out of the temple.

It is believed that one of the important elements in solving the unfortunate financial meltdown is to simply reverse the trend of mergers and acquisitions that caused the financial institution to grow so large that it became difficult to manage and regulate. It is sincerely believed that it is the responsibility of the government regulators, through their periodic examinations, to decide whether an institution has outgrown its ability to manage risk. Time and again we were taught—by the hard school of loss of peoples' money and assets—that the investment banking culture is completely different from that of the commercial banker. Based on my own experience while working with Smith-Barney and Citigroup, it is evident that investment bankers and commercial bankers have two different temperaments, risk tolerances, and purposes. It was proven that the two cannot be merged or mixed. Bank of America tried it with Charles Schwab and failed; Citibank and Smith Barney tried and failed; and now Bank of America, after merging with Merrill Lynch, is once again finding out that what we learned in the late 1970s and early 1980s still holds true. Perhaps we should respect the experience that led to the *Glass-Steagall Act*, which installed a thick wall between the two activities after the Great Depression.

SOME ADVICE FOR THE NEWCOMERS TO THE RF LIFESTYLE

It would be useful to bring to the attention of all people who have decided to join the RF lifestyle a few recommendations as to what to do. We need not to overindulge. We need to live within our means, to stop overborrowing. We should not use credit cards as a means of borrowing, but should use credit cards judiciously and pay off credit card purchases within a month to avoid paying interest. We need to save (for a "rainy day") ten cents of every dollar we earn. We should not panic and sell stock portfolios "low" nor invest in the stock market once we are too old for the risk required. (The formula recommended is to subtract your age from your family's life expectancy—for example, if your family's life expectancy is 75 and you are 65 years old, the maximum exposure to investing in stocks should be 75 minus 65, or 10 percent of your total assets.) Furthermore, we should strictly advise our children to stop taking excessive student loans to live it up. It is better for a student to graduate in six years with a part-time job and no debt than in four years with $120,000 in student loans. We need to help each other, to buy within our communities, to reinvest in our communities, and to do business with our local community banks and credit unions. We need to help the elderly who were forced to take a 70-percent income cut because of the reduction of interest rates on CDs. It is sincerely hoped that the elderly Americans who live on Social Security and the few dollars they get from that reduced "interest" on their small savings will be helped and taken care of by the younger generations. After all, they are the ones who built the United States.

The RF bankers, bank branches, and Internet services should also become very active in the popularization of a new lifestyle—one that believes in minimum debt and in paying off that debt as soon as possible, in saving for the future, in living within our means, in offering a healing hand and resolution plan to those who need help, in encouraging students to do without student loans unless it is absolutely necessary. As RF bankers, we should lead a compassionate life that cares about others. This can most effectively be done in collaboration with local community and religious leaders in a wonderful interfaith cooperation that will lead to peace, prosperity, mutual respect, and a wonderful life for all.

NOTES

1. The highest insurance cost paid by AIG Insurance Company for a California earthquake was around $8 billion.
2. Saskia Scholtes and Francesco Guerrera, Banks make $38bn from overdraft fees, the *Financial Times*, August 10, 2009.

CHAPTER 15

A New Banking Vision for the 21st Century

As we journey into a new century, I dream of popularizing the RF banking brand and the RF financing methods using well-trained and dedicated RF bankers. Judgment of a person, a manager, an investor, a banker, a board of directors, a politician, or a community leader cannot be regulated by a government decree or a set of laws. Judgment is personal and depends on the prevailing culture. Making a judgment depends on the way people were raised by their parents, their value system, and their deep-seated belief that a higher authority—a much higher authority than government regulations and laws—is watching over them.

The RF banking brand has been tested in the United States since 1987 at American Finance House LARIBA, with great success and a proven track record. Later, we branched out to test it on community banking operations, to see first whether it could be implemented and second (and most importantly) whether the consumers in a small conservative city like Whittier, California would accept it. We are very pleased to report that the principles of RF banking and finance were accepted and proven to be successful not only by our auditors and examiners but also by many of our customers, who kept referring their neighbors, friends, and associates to do business with us. It was proven also that in 2008, in the midst of the worst banking and economic meltdown in America's history since World War II, RF banking and finance rescued both LARIBA and the Bank of Whittier from becoming a participant in that meltdown. The results show it.

Strategically, it is important to make sure that we learn from the mistakes and errors in judgment of the 20th century that led to the 2008 meltdown. The option of acquiring other banks has proven to be unsuccessful, especially in the area of creating a cohesive RF banking culture that trickles down even to the newest teller. RF bankers have to be trained from scratch, and these RF banking pioneers should be prepared to lead in the effort to produce more RF bankers who believe in the cause and the culture of RF banking. The other option of building a "brick and mortar" branch system has proven to be very expensive and difficult to manage, especially for a new banking brand that needs to be popularized with the lowest expenses.

To plan for the future, one must take a peek at and articulate a vision of that future. With the growth and sophistication of the Internet, it is a fact that most people do not go to their bank branches after opening the account. A new generation—not only in the United States, but all over the world—is now Internet bound. That is why the new RF banking system should benefit from the latest trends in Internet banking and Internet communications, without sacrificing security and privacy, by using the most up-to-date and sophisticated systems and techniques. We have attempted to do that at LARIBA and the Bank of Whittier, and we were very successful, not only in serving the city of Whittier and its surrounding neighborhoods in southern California, but also all 50 states.

One very serious hurdle would limit the expansion of our RF banking service to achieve our dream: the variation of banking laws from one state to another state in the United States. For example, a bank charter or license must be secured in almost every state to practice depository services in that state. It is true that a national bank can serve from one location, but there is another layer of regulation that limits the expansion outside that area—the Community Reinvestment Act (CRA). This is a very big challenge that has to be resolved.

As we proved that the pilot experiment worked, we have been contacted by many who believe in the RF banking and finance brand and its values and methods. They invite us to open branches in their communities. The standard response we give is "We would be happy to do so, if we can establish that there is real demand for our services." We usually propose the following steps, in order not to be hasty, not to waste money, and not to compromise our reputation:

1. Start a virtual branch in our computer system by creating a soft branch in the financial ledger. In the branch's ledger, we keep track of the new accounts and deposits made from that community, as well as the financing facilities (loans) invested in that community. When the level reaches a certain critical mass, we go to the next step.
2. Open a loan production office (LPO) that is responsible for promoting the financing of community needs; it is not allowed to take deposits, but can encourage the use of Internet banking.
3. Open a small branch and encourage Internet banking. If the branch is in the same state where the bank is chartered, local leaders of the community are invited to become shareholders. This adds local content and

contribution, in terms of money (capital), intellect, and reputation, to the effort. In addition, a small local executive board should be formed to give the effort a local feel and legitimacy. If the bank starts operations in a different state, shareholders from that state must be added as a prerequisite to opening that branch.

INDEX